Embodying **Relation**

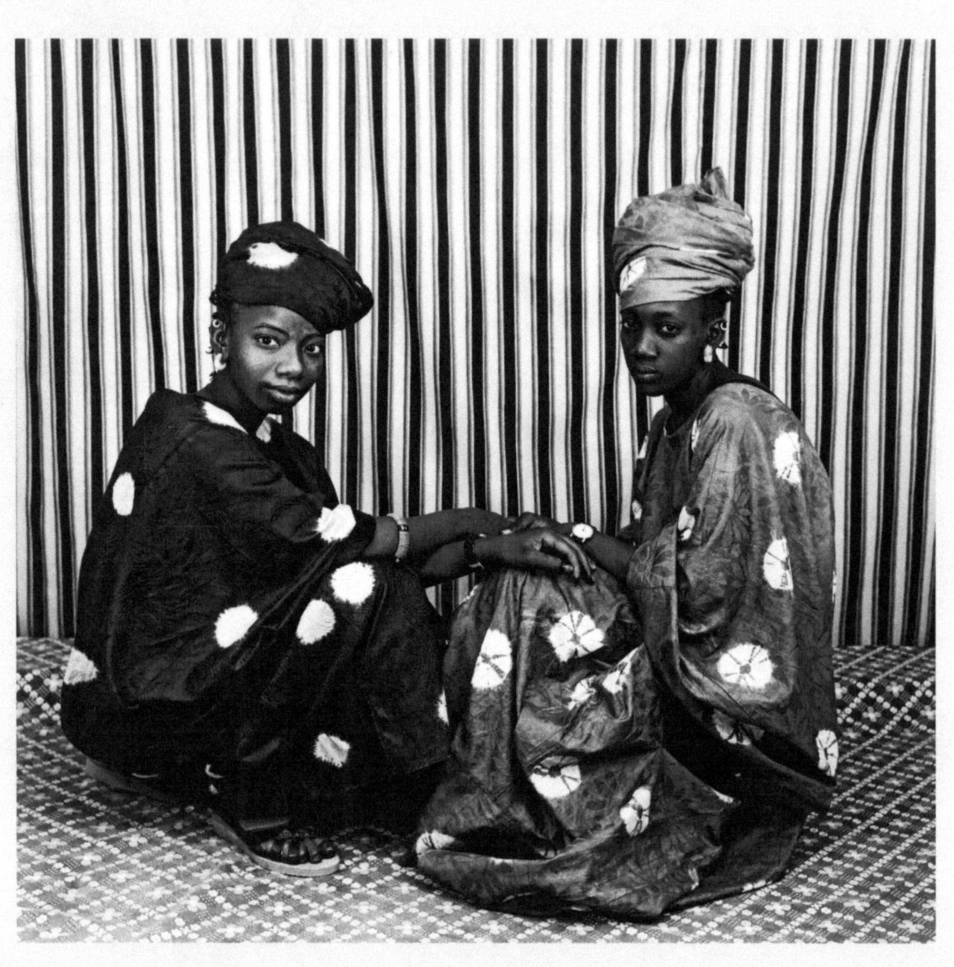

Embodying Relation

ART PHOTOGRAPHY IN MALI

Allison Moore

DUKE UNIVERSITY PRESS DURHAM AND LONDON 2020

Typeset in Portrait by BW&A Books. Designed by Amy Ruth Buchanan.

Cover art: Fatoumata Diabaté, *Sutigi, Bamako,* 2012. Courtesy of the artist and Patrice Loubon Gallery.

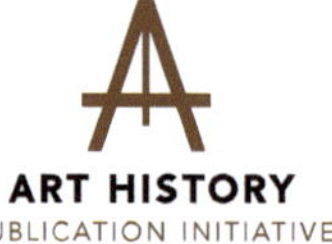

This book is made possible by a collaborative grant from the Andrew W. Mellon Foundation.

Duke University Press gratefully acknowledges the University of South Florida Publications Council Grant and School of Art and Art History, which provided funds toward the publication of this book.

Library of Congress
Cataloging-in-Publication Data
Names: Moore, Allison (Art historian), author.
Title: Embodying relation : art photography in Mali / Allison Moore.
Other titles: Art history publication initiative.
Description: Durham :
Duke University Press, 2020. | Series: Art history publication initiative | Includes bibliographical references and index.
Identifiers: LCCN 2019046724 (print)
LCCN 2019046725 (ebook)
ISBN 9781478005971 (hardcover)
ISBN 9781478006626 (paperback)
ISBN 9781478007340 (ebook)
Subjects: LCSH: Glissant, Édouard, 1928–2011—Philosophy. | Photography—Mali—20th century. | Art, Malian—Mali—Bamako. | Postcolonialism and the arts—Mali. | Photography—Political aspects—Mali. | Photography, Artistic.
Classification: LCC N7399.M3 M66 2020 (print) | LCC N7399.M3 (ebook) | DDC 770—dc23
LC record available at https://lccn.loc.gov/2019046724
LC ebook record available at https://lccn.loc.gov/2019046725

Contents

Acknowledgments

I would like to thank the inestimable efforts of Elizabeth Ault, Kate Herman, Ken Wissoker, and the Duke University Press publication team, including Maria Volpe, freelance editor Christi Stanforth, and Chris Crochetière of BW&A Books, as well as two anonymous reviewers who provided many important criticisms and suggestions; my PhD adviser at CUNY, Geoffrey Batchen; Okwui Enwezor, Candace Keller, Esra Akin-Kivanç, Rodney Mayton, Wallace Wilson, USF Publication Grant, Elisabeth Fraser, and Jeanie Ambrosio; the photographers whom I interviewed or studied and who provided essential information and images for my project, including Fatoumata Diabaté, Alioune Bâ, Seydou Keïta, Malick Sidibé, Mountaga Dembélé, Agence Nationale d'Information Malienne (ANIM), Hamidou Maïga, Adama Kouyaté, Soungalo Malé, El Hadj Tijani Àdìgún Sitou, Lennart Nilsson, Mayola Amici, Dawoud Bey, Lorna Simpson, Rotimi Fani-Kayode, Françoise Huguier, Felix Diallo, Mamadou Konaté, Emmanuel Daou, Sadio Diakité, Madame Coulibaly Diawara, Harandane Dicko, Abdoulaye Kanté, Moussa Konaté, Aboubacrine Diarra, Samuel Sidibé, Jude Thera, Shawn

Davis, Siriman Dembélé, Érika Nimis, Adama Bamba, Mamadou Konaté, Moussa Kalapo, Abdourahmane Sakaly, Sidiki Sidibé, François Deschamps, Adama Diakité, Joseye Tienro, Youssouf Sogodogo, Amadou Sow, Promo-femme, Madame Aminata Dembélé Bagayoko and Kadiatou Sangaré, Penda Diakité, Alimata dite Diop Traoré, Ouassa Pangassy Sangaré, Cinéma Numérique Ambulant (CNA), Stéphanie Dongmo, Tendance Floue, Meyer, Zanele Muholi, Mohamed Camara, Amadou Keïta, and Django Cissé, as well as essential help in communicating with the artists and many other matters from Yoby Guindo and Bakary Sidibé. Cherif Keïta, Laurel Bradley, and Doug Foxgrover were instrumental to our show at the Perlman Teaching Museum at Carleton College and to providing images for the book. I would like to thank Molleen Theodore, Amanda Preuss, Laura Colkitt, Marlena Antonucci, James Cartwright, Alexandria Salmieri, Vikki Mann, Nina Murayama, Karen Shelby, Nat Trotman, Beth Mangini, Megan Fort, Jill Lord, Yvette Lee, Clay Tarica, Kate Bussard, Dan Quiles, Kevin Mulhearn, Stéphanie Jeanjean, Elizabeth Watson, Laura Hengehold, Samara Sanders, Eric Lindberg, and their children Leif and Leila, Ryan Roberge, Joanna Lehan, Artur Walther, Sarah Brett-Smith, Susan Vogel, Kristina Van Dyke, Michelle Lamunière, Marta Weiss, and Nat Bletter. From CUNY Graduate Center, I would like to thank Patricia Mainardi, Rosemarie Haag Bletter, Romy Golan, and Francesca Canadé-Sautman. I also appreciate the Mario Capelloni Dissertation Fellowship, which helped me to finish my initial project, as well as many gallerists who provided crucial help in obtaining images and permissions, especially Jack Bell; Laneese Jaftha of Stevenson Gallery; Rebecca Mecklenborg and Evalina Sundbye of Jack Shainman Gallery; James Flach and Eva-Lotta Holm-Flach of Gallerie Flach, Stockholm; Elisabeth Whitelaw of the CAAC; and Thaïs Giordano of Gallerie Magnin-A in Paris.

Small sections of the introduction and of chapters 6 and 7 have been published in revised form as articles. A heavily reduced and revised version of chapter 6 was published as "Promo-femme: Promoting Women Photographers in Bamako, Mali," in *History of Photography* 34, no. 2 (2010). Parts of the introduction and chapter 7 were published as "A Lightness of Vision: The Poetics of Relation in Malian Art Photography" in *Social Dynamics: A Journal of African Studies* (September 2014) and reproduced in a book anthology, *Photography in and out of Africa: Iterations with Difference*, ed. Kylie Thomas and Louise Green (Routledge, 2017). Chapter 7 was inspired by an exhibition for Carleton College's Perlman Teaching Museum, *Photographing the Social Body: Malian Portraiture from the Studio to the Street*.

On a personal note, I thank my mother-in-law, Abby Wasserman, for her continual help, encouragement, and support, especially after the children were born. I thank my brother and sister-in-law, Eric Moore and Leeyanne Moore. I am so grateful to my parents, Zelda and David Moore, for their amazing love and support throughout my life, through many years of school and writing this book—they have always been there for me. A tremendous amount of gratitude is due to Joshua Rayman, without whom this book literally would not exist. Finally, I would like to thank my beautiful children, Isolde and Cormac, for their love and patience. This book is dedicated to my family.

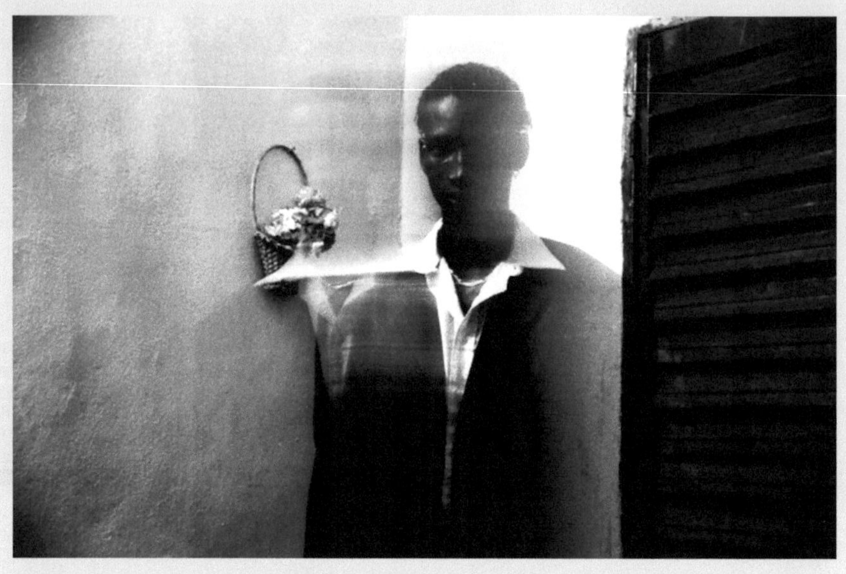

Figure Intro.1. Fatoumata Diabaté, *Sutigi, Bamako*, 2012.
Courtesy of the artist and Patrice Loubon Gallery.

Introduction

A Poetics of Relation

> But we need to figure out whether or not there are other succulencies of Relation in other parts of the world . . .
> —Édouard Glissant, *Poetics of Relation*

A young man stands in an entranceway. His look is wary, serious; indeterminate. Dressed for a night out in a dark jacket, he wears a neck chain that glitters between the wide white collars of his shirt. The silhouette of an earring encircles his left earlobe; sweat gleams on his forehead and highlights the bridge of his nose. His collar creates a sharp line leading to his double-exposed self, a barely registered simulacrum, faint imprint over a basket of flowers hanging behind him on a bare wall. The barred shutters indicate a Bamako doorway. His head is framed tightly within the hallway as his shoulders push outward, confusing the eye and imbuing his figure with power and presence. His left side is ghosted out, yet half of his face is obscured in darkness.

Sutigi, Bamako, by Malian photographer Fatoumata Diabaté, from her series *The Night Belongs to Us* (*Sutigi* in Bamanankan), shows West African youth enjoying the licit and illicit pleasures of nighttime escapades—"the beautiful age of youth characterized by insouciance and freedom," as the artist describes it (fig. Intro. 1).[1] The man pictured appears cosmopolitan, of the globalized world, yet the double exposure serves to emphasize not only shadowy presence, darkness, obscurity (*dìbi* in Bamanankan), and opacity, but also the tradition of doubling in West African portrait photography, a tradition borrowed from the influx of Yoruba studio photographers emigrating across West Africa in search of new business clientele in the 1950s, '60s, and '70s.[2] The contrast of darks and lights creates a sense of polyrhythmic Mande aesthetics, highlighting an asymmetry seen consistently in hundreds of studio portraits by famous Malian photographers Seydou Keïta and Malick Sidibé.[3]

This kind of poetic or philosophical photography—photography that asks the viewer to consider other meanings, other implications than what is immediately visible; what is called "art photography"—is a relatively recent phenomenon in Bamako, the capital of Mali. *Embodying Relation* describes how this art photography movement developed in Mali out of a lapsed black-and-white studio portrait tradition after a twenty-year lacuna. This book argues that Malian art photographs embody the concept of Relation propounded by Martinican philosopher, poet, and novelist Édouard Glissant (1928–2011). Unlike much contemporary photography now being produced in Africa, Malian art photographers tend to celebrate their culture, rather than focusing on social ills or the current exploitation of former colonial powers. Nor do most draw attention to the way that colonial rule violently and permanently changed the fabric of Malian society, or focus on the country's poverty; this art is not, in a word, overtly forming a postcolonial critique. Instead, Malian art photographs sidestep postcolonial considerations to potentially embody Glissant's exuberant notion of Relation, which embraces difference and diversity within wholeness or totality, encompassing both the recognition of others and their opacity, or unknowability. Photographs created by Malian artists, such as Diabaté's *Sutigi, Bamako,* speak to both local and foreign audiences, crossing cultural divides and allowing for interpretations on multiple levels, relative to one's knowledge and background. This is a manifestation of the Mande belief that knowledge is secret, precious, and never fully available; not everyone should or will have access to the same information.[4] In proffering newly configured images of contemporary Malian culture to non-Malian audiences, these photographs carry an optimistic potential to bring viewers into Relation, their imaginaries participating in an appreciation of Malian poetics that nevertheless does not straightforwardly offer Malian culture to the neocolonial consumerist gaze of the global art market.

Embodying Relation maps the genesis and dynamics of the Malian art photography movement. It shows how two Malian photographers' fame in New

York and Paris contributed to the founding of a photography biennial in their hometown of Bamako, which had dramatic effects both on local photographers and across Africa. Mali's new democracy, emerging three decades after independence from France in 1960, was the backdrop for the blossoming of this art photography movement. Democracy created the opportunity for international collaborative photography institutions and encouraged women's rights, and this study pays particular attention to the unprecedented debut of professional women photographers in this patriarchal nation. Through an understanding of these photographs as embodying Glissant's notion of Relation, I argue that Malian photographers contest globalization in the international interchange fostered by the biennale through a careful visual, cultural, and theoretical analysis of their works and the social and historical context of their production. Art photography in Mali is an example of a local aesthetics speaking both locally and globally, across different levels of cultural knowledge. This movement counters a homogenized contemporary art world through its difference and emphasis on Malian aesthetics.

The emergence of art photography began in the mid-1990s, when Bamako became famous as the home of renowned studio photographers Seydou Keïta (1921/3–2001) and Malick Sidibé (1936–2016). Exhibited anonymously in New York in 1991, Keïta was quickly "discovered" in Bamako by a French curator, leading to the subsequent "discovery" of his younger colleague, Malick Sidibé; their commercial portraits were soon shown abroad to great acclaim. Since that time, Keïta and Sidibé have become indispensable to an emergent canon of African artists.[5] The presence of Keïta and Sidibé in Bamako inspired the founding, in 1994, of the French-funded pan-African Rencontres Africaines de la Photographie (African Photography Encounters), or Bamako Photography Biennale, which has been celebrated ever since.[6] The biennale was instituted shortly after Mali's 1991–1992 transition from a socialist dictatorship to a Western-supported, multiparty democracy. Mali's relationship to France, its colonizer from the 1890s until 1960, improved greatly after this political shift, and France, in a neocolonial extension of its former role as cultural benefactor, joined Mali in supporting and financing the efforts of French photographers Françoise Huguier and Bernard Descamps and Malian photographers Alioune Bâ, Django Cissé, and Racine Keïta in creating and organizing the first biennale.[7]

This French-funded event gave Bamako a reputation as the "center of African photography." Yet the neocolonial power imbalance of the biennale enterprise, as well as the nature of the biennale itself as a pan-African venture, creates tensions between French influence and Malian endeavors. Still, the potentialities offered by the first biennale exhibition, and its subsequent, ever-larger iterations, ignited the imaginations of a small cohort of Malian photographers. The presence of the biennale as an ongoing institution also inspired foreigners and locals to collaborate in creating numerous photography institutions and exhibitions, thus contributing to the rise of a Relational art photography movement and sparking a revival of interest in black-and-white film photography, which had become commercially unviable by the 1970s.[8]

This blossoming art movement has given rise to a host of images that, like *Sutigi, Bamako,* creatively imagine older photographic traditions in the space of freedom enabled by the new notion that photographs can be art, rather than commercial portraits or journalism. Yet in contrast to African countries where art photography has gained a significant presence on the international market—South Africa, Nigeria, Egypt, Morocco, Senegal, Kenya, Ethiopia, Benin (the list is growing)—in Mali photographers have for the most part eschewed the reigning styles of global conceptual art or of critical documentary photojournalism.[9] Instead of following trends introduced by the examples of international art on offer at the biennales, the Bamakois art photographers have remained close to the values of Malian studio portraiture, balancing Mande aesthetics with imaginative approaches to contemporary concerns.

Mande is a linguistic and cultural complex that includes a wide-ranging group of ethnicities and language-speakers in West Africa, including Bamana and Malinke, and is said to comprise about half of the population of Mali. However, about 80 percent of Malians speak Bamanankan, and Mande is culturally dominant in southern Mali, especially in Bamako, the seat of the government. There has been a strong nationalist drive since independence to promote Bamana culture in particular (as Bamako was originally a Bamana village) and Mande culture more generally. Historically, Mande-speakers descend from the thirteenth-century Mali Empire, and one major noticeable aspect of Mande culture is a strong sense of pride and awareness of Mande history, which has been passed down through oral cultural traditions, such as the *Sunjata* epic. Another notable aspect of Mande society (which is also present in non-Mande Malian societies) is the social division among nobles, former slaves, and the caste groups of oral historians and singers, blacksmiths and potters, and other artistic professions. These divisions in some cases determine people's marriage options and professions, especially in rural areas, but in urban Bamako caste and ethnicity are becoming less important than class; ethnicity is itself an especially complicated and somewhat fluid matter.

Aspects of Mande social practices and values are intimately connected to aesthetics and can be seen as enabling Relation in their respect for the difference and humanity of others, in accepting another's opacity, or inability to be fully known, and in their communality. For example, *badenya* is a Mande social value of cooperation, derived from polygamous family structures in which children of the same mother and father are not in competition, in contrast to *fadenya*, which describes a sense of competition among half-siblings for the father's attention. Badenya is considered the primary force within Malian society, and can also be described as social capital, whereas extreme fadenya behavior is reserved only for unusual individuals (usually young men) who must strive to bring honor and success to their family's name; they are called heroes. These aspects of competition and cooperation can be seen in studio portraiture, along with other aesthetic aspects more specifically related to the medium of photography, such as polyrhythmic pattern, asymmetry, decoration, embellishment, clarity versus opacity or obscurity, and theme and variation, also understood as repetition with small and subtle differences. As we shall see, the complex meanings of dìbi (darkness, obscurity) in Mande society are similar in meaning to Glissant's use of the term *opacité* (French: opacity), in that both terms can refer to a sense of obscured knowledge, or of knowledge that cannot be known.[10]

Commercial portraiture always engaged the imaginary of its patrons and its viewers. The fact that Keïta lent his clients props, from eyeglasses to flowers, motor scooters to suit coats, meant that subjects could imagine themselves differently when pictured with signs of material success or cosmopolitan identity.[11] Moreover, portraiture always had communal reverberations—the earliest studio photographs were taken outdoors in courtyards, in front of the crowd of waiting potential clients. Photographs often commemorate family relations or friendships, shown not only in pairings and groupings, but also in the choice of wearing the same outfit to the photographer's studio, and in the way friends pose to mimic each other's movements. Studio portraits were aesthetic social documents, meant to be hung on the wall or kept in albums, or sent to family in rural areas to display the cosmopolitan sense of the urbanite away from home. Today's artists still tend to emphasize photography's social aspect by appreciating the beauty of the human body, which is understood as always already a communal body, while allowing individual creativity to flourish in ways previously unimaginable. Malian photography has thus retained a relatively autonomous local identity in creating art that stems from a history of portraiture that *itself* has been repositioned as art on the global stage.

Because of its cultural, political, and aesthetic circumstances, this art photography carries a powerful potential to embody Glissant's notion of Relation. A prominent Caribbean philosopher and writer, Glissant has become an essential figure in postcolonial studies, but his work moves beyond this school of thought. Glissant, who studied philosophy and history at the Sorbonne and ethnography at the Musée de l'Homme in Paris, was a contemporary of Frantz Fanon, Jacques Derrida, Gilles Deleuze, and feminist philosopher Luce Irigaray, as well as Malian photographers Keïta and Sidibé. Césaire's Négritude was influential on Glissant's thought, and he actively fought for Martinican independence. He shared intellectual circles and world experiences with these anticolonial philosophers and photographers.

The difference between Glissant and other postcolonial thinkers can be traced through a brief history of the field.[12] For many Anglophone scholars, postcolonial studies grew out of Edward Said's groundbreaking publication of *Orientalism* in 1978, which used a Foucauldian analysis to uncover and examine the prejudices inherent in the Euro-American study of North Africa and the Middle East. In turn, Said's work influenced other Anglophone writers from former British colonies, like Gayatri Spivak and Homi Bhabha.[13] Recently postcolonial studies has begun to acknowledge a longer Afro-Francophone lineage of thought, tracing itself back to Négritude, a philosophy and poetics that originated in Paris in the 1930s with Martinican writer Aimé Césaire, Senegalese poet and eventual president Léopold Sédar Senghor, French Guianese poet and politician Léon Damas, and others.[14] Césaire was a teacher and mentor to the doctor, psychoanalyst, and philosopher Frantz Fanon, whose revolutionary texts *Black Skin, White Masks* (1952) and *The Wretched of the Earth* (1961) offer analyses of the psychological effects of racism and colonial rule.[15] A more capacious understanding of postcolonial theory includes Algerian-born French philosopher Jacques Derrida's emphasis on *différance* and his questioning of European hegemonies of thought in relation to his experience as an Algerian Jew under Vichy's anti-Semitic rule.

While Glissant is often described as a postcolonial theorist, his philosophical notion of Relation exceeds the pessimism and the negative sense of "aftermath" effects often present in postcolonial theory, while posing a theoretical opposition to globalization in his concept of *mondialité*, often translated as "worldliness": an appreciation of respect for all people in their cultural and individual differences.[16]

If art historians have been slow to take up postcolonial theory, Glissant's work has proved an exception, at least among curators. In the past several decades his ideas have been actively discussed in contemporary art venues, including the platform "Creolité and Creolization," held in St. Lucia as part of Okwui Enwezor's Documenta 11.[17] In this exhibition, Enwezor drew on Glissant's notion of creolization for its Caribbean platform. The Swiss-born curator Hans Ulrich Obrist has been particularly important in bringing Glissant's ideas into the art world. Obrist recounts that Glissant's idea of Relation inspired his groundbreaking curatorial project "Utopia Station" in the 2003 Venice Biennale. Obrist later explained, in a small book he cowrote with Glissant for dOCUMENTA (13), which included several of Glissant's writing with drawings, "In his novel *Sartorius* (1999), Glissant described the utopian Batouto people, which derives its identity not from its own genealogy, but solely from being in constant exchange with others."[18] After Glissant's death Obrist curated an exhibition in Brussels dedicated to him, called *Mondialité*. Glissant himself was active in the art world. As a prize-winning novelist and poet, he was intimately aware of aesthetic concerns and the role of art in society; his friends included prominent modernist artists Wifredo Lam and Robert Matta, designer agnès b., and many others. Significantly, Glissant wrote an introduction to an exhibition catalog for agnès b.'s photography collection that includes prints by Seydou Keïta and Malick Sidibé, so it is certain that he knew their work.[19]

Glissant explains the concept of Relation in two key texts, *Poetics of Relation*, published in French in 1990 and in English in 1997, and *Philosophie de la Relation* (*The Philosophy of Relation*), in 2009. Relation developed out of Glissant's earlier theories of creolization and "Caribbeanness" (*Antillanité*), which was specific to Caribbean identity. As a Martinican, Glissant was at first influenced by, but later critical of, Césaire's theory of Négritude, with its emphasis on blackness and Africa as its origin.[20]

In contrast to Négritude, Glissant's conception of creolization emphasizes the distinctiveness of the Caribbean as an archipelago, a loose collection of islands connected to each other by history and geography, but separated by the sea; for each, the ocean's horizon is a constant reminder of the transatlantic slave trade as well as the colonizer's journey from Europe. Creolization acknowledges that each island is culturally distinct and specific, but shares some general characteristics with the others—each distinctiveness is created by a different mixture of specific African, European, and Asian cultures that replaced the wiped-out civilizations of indigenous people. Crucially, building on fellow Martinican philosopher Frantz Fanon, Glissant understands creolization rhizomatically, borrowing from French and Swiss philosophers Gilles Deleuze and Félix Guattari. The rhizome is a plant form with many roots that spreads horizontally, in contrast to the vertical hierarchy of a tree with a single root. Because of the variety of mixed cultures and ethnicities (*métissage*) which all came from elsewhere, the "rootlessness" or rhizomatic nature of Caribbean society contributes to the identity and process of creolization. As Caribbean author Maryse Condé explains, Glissant was the first philosopher to celebrate Caribbean identity *as such*, as a rootless or rhizomatic identity created and re-created in exchange with others, as in Glissant's famous maxim: "'I change, by exchanging with the other, without losing myself or distorting myself.'"[21]

While African identity is important in Caribbeanness, it is not the *only* identity—the multiplicity of cultural identities in the Caribbean is pointedly acknowledged.[22] Creolization becomes Relation when Glissant's theories open up from the Caribbean to address the world.[23] Yet Africa is still of primary importance as a facet of Relation—the first essay in *Poetics of Relation*, "The Open Boat," begins with the African slave trade.[24] For it is in the Middle Passage that Relation is born—in the communal experience of the existential and literal abyss: a past and present despair and a terrifying, unknown future. One's survival of the Middle Passage enables totality: "Not just a specific knowledge, appetite, suffering, and delight of one particular people, not only that, but knowledge of the Whole, greater from having been at the abyss and freeing knowledge of Relation within the Whole."[25] For Glissant, the experience of suffering brings a humility that enables empathy, and thus Relation. Both creolization and Relation offer alternative ways of confronting the violence and lingering effects of colonial oppression. Relation in particular offers an alternative method for opposing globalization and for understanding the world separate from the structures demanded and produced by capitalism. The concept of Relation, supported by corresponding neologisms and notions of creolization, opacity, errantry, chaos-world, echo-world, and *mondialité*, emphasizes process and exchange, going beyond postcolonial theories that reiterate static notions of mixed yet rooted cultural identities suggesting violence, negativity, and loss. Glissant's Relation posits identity as always in a communal (and thus unpredictable) process of becoming through exchange with other cultures and communities: a process in which everyone might potentially participate. But while a respect for fundamental difference is central to Relation, a local community must also be aware of the wider world; and, indeed, it is through interactions with others that one changes, without loss of self.[26] An inward-looking community, or one that holds itself separate from or superior to its neighbors, cannot participate in Relation. Nor can a culture heavily indebted to capitalist structures enable Relation to flourish.

In the epigraph to this introduction, Glissant suggests that Relation may exist in pockets throughout the world. But it is in the Caribbean's inheritance of Africa, through the centuries-long transatlantic slave trade, that Relation flourishes: according to Glissant, "Africa (for us a source and a mirage, retained in a simplified representation) has, therefore, its role to play."[27] The importance of conceiving of not just the Caribbean but the world as an archipelago, as Glissant explains in his essay "Archipelagic Thinking," is crucial to understanding Relation and to seeking its resonances in West African photography. For Glissant, the history of the Caribbean archipelago created societies of composite cultures with multiple origins in which tribalism is impossible. Understanding West Africa as an archipelago means understanding the Sahara desert, historically an important conduit of trade and other forms of exchange, as a kind of oceanic space linking Mali to North Africa. It means understanding how West African nations bear many similarities to the Caribbean islands where Glissant developed these theories, including effects of the transatlantic slave trade and their complicated postcolonial relationships to colonial powers.[28]

Thus, while Glissant's work drew on his Martinican heritage and theorized the Caribbean particularly, his work has also been influential on the African continent. Glissant's friendship with the Malian filmmaker, scholar, and writer Manthia Diawara especially speaks to the pertinence of his philosophy with regard to Malian photography. Diawara's 2009 documentary on Glissant, *Édouard Glissant: One World in Relation*, explains key aspects of Glissant's theories and has been widely screened at conferences and museums.[29] Noted Cameroonian philosopher Achille Mbembe dedicated an essay for the 2011 Bamako Biennale catalog to Glissant. In 2014, the Dak'Art Biennale of Contemporary African Art's theme was "Producing the Common," inspired by Glissant's notion of the *Tout-monde* ("Whole world," closely related to "worldliness"); and in 2015, the Pérez Art Museum in Miami hosted an exhibition curated by Tumelo Mosaka and Tobias Ostrander, titled *Poetics of Relation*, that directly engaged Glissant's philosophy.[30]

The acknowledgment of differences that cannot be grasped or reduced to particulars is crucial to Relation.[31] Celia Britton finds that Glissant's idea of Relation underlies all of his writing and can be found not only in his theoretical essays but also in his literary works.[32] She explains: "The starting point for this concept is the irreducible difference of the other; 'Relation' is in the first place a relation of equality with and respect for the Other as *different* from oneself. It applies to individuals but more especially to other cultures and other societies. It is nonhierarchical and nonreductive; that is, it does not try to impose a universal value system but respects the particular qualities of the community in question."[33]

Although Relation can potentially exist anywhere in the world, Glissant insists that it can be found only within cultures that acknowledge the importance of others as well as themselves. He notes, "Peoples who have been to the abyss do not brag of being chosen. They do not believe they are giving birth to any modern force. They live Relation and clear the way for it."[34] Glissant's use of "the abyss" here specifically references the horror of the transatlantic slave trade.[35] Yet the West African colonial experience may be understood as a different kind of abyssal experience—vicious, violent, and dehumanizing. In both instances, Relation emerges through a sense of chaos and fluidity, evading the violent constraints of slavery and colonialism to create a system of relations, what Britton calls "a fluid and unsystematic system whose elements are engaged in a radically nonhierarchical free play of interrelatedness."[36]

Glissant's idea of the nonhierarchical free play of relations is used here to consider the images and imaginaries of Malian art photographs, rather than as a description of real human relationships. Yet in many ways relation does apply to personal relationships, not least through its accounting for language.[37] *Poetics of Relation* is composed as a series of essays that were first presented as talks; a sense of orality is felt in the rhythms of speech used within the text, wherein Glissant addresses the reader as one might speak to a friend. Relation, however, not only exists among French-speakers but "is spoken multilingually. By going beyond the impositions of economic forces and cultural pressures, Relation rightfully opposes the totalitarianism of any monolingual intent."[38] The oppression of any single language is connected to the domination of a rooted culture for Glissant—consider the Roman imposition of Latin throughout Europe during the Roman Empire. By contrast, Relation evades this parochialism and evokes a multivocal difference. In this way, as in others, Relation differs from hybridity, in which elements of the colonized and the dominating cultures are identifiable and contribute to a synthesis of meaning.[39]

The tension between orality and writing that informs Creole as a vernacular language is part of creolization. Similar tensions exist in Mali, where an important fluctuation between oral and written cultures is noticeable, for literacy rates are low and oral traditions are still strong. Such differences inform how societies think about and imagine the world.[40] Art photographers tend to be highly literate and well-educated, sometimes speaking French at home, but they have also been surrounded by their country's rich oral culture and heritage; this familiarity with different forms of knowledge informs their photographs.

While Glissant was fascinated with language, his concept of Relation is also wholly physical and embodied in lived experience. Glissant criticizes the Sartrean existentialist idea of free will because of the historical experience of slavery and colonialism; instead, the mind is always rooted in the physicality of its body. J. Michael Dash, Glissant's biographer, writes: "The dismantling of the individual consciousness as free spirit has led Glissant inexorably toward the reinsertion of mind in body. Mind is always incomplete without body, and it is through the body that mind encounters outer reality. The body is then a vital zone of interaction between private and public, individual and collective."[41]

Glissant's emphasis on the relationship between mind and body comes from a distrust of the body's ability to escape the physical constraints it is subjected to. It also derives arguably from the body's inescapable *visibility*, and thus from racial identity, though this visibility is simultaneously the site of opacity and a racial imaginary. This connection of the body to visibility and racial identity links Glissant's ideas to those of Fanon, with whom Glissant's writings are in dialogue. Instead of conceiving of a bodiless mind knowing the world, the world and others are known through the inseparable experience of the body *and* mind, together.[42] The individual body is also important in its communal relation with others—as Dash notes, the communal identity is key to creolization, and thus to Relation.[43] Similarly, Malian art photographers emphasize the human body; their aesthetics and focus emerge from the history of studio portraiture to become a contemporary art that almost always takes the social body as a point of departure. The notion of the body as always already communal occurs in virtually all of the Malian photographers' work and is often emphasized.

Although Relation could potentially exist anywhere in the world, specific affinities with Bamako's history, cultural diversity, and geography set the stage for art photographs to embody Relation.[44] While of course Malian society has literally been postcolonial since 1960, when the country gained its independence from France, "postcolonial" is not merely a temporal demarcation. It also acknowledges how the cultures and ways of life that existed in precolonial societies were permanently affected by violent oppressions perpetrated by the culture of colonial domination. In Gyan Prakash's words,

"The postcolonial exists as an aftermath, as an after—after being worked over by colonialism."[45] Though Mali, unlike Martinique, is now an independent nation, it remains politically and economically yoked to France. The persistence of French governmental structures, including national borders, the educational system, the status of French as the official language, Mali's continuing economic dependence on France, and even to some extent culture and social attitudes: all attest to the continuing presence of colonialism in Mali. This dependency became particularly visible when France intervened to quell the 2012 coup and prevent civil war; the division between the North's desert nomadic lifestyle and the South's agricultural and urban cultures was created by French colonial boundaries. Mali's postcolonial situation created a culture of hybridity that places equality in doubt, demonstrating the legacy of one culture's domination over another's, and accordingly a sense of wreckage, destruction, and continuing *effects*.

Yet postcolonial theory does not account for the aesthetic approach and optimism of Malian photographs, conveyed through contemporary approaches to Mali's heritage and culture. As an impoverished West African nation with a remarkably rich culture and history, Mali is a logical place to begin seeking "other succulencies of Relation," especially as Glissant favored "small" (lightly populated) countries. Scholars ascribe a relationship of descent from Mali to Martinique, asserting that many enslaved people sold to Martinican plantations were of the Bamana ethnicity from the region that is now southern Mali.[46] In the film *One World in Relation*, Glissant remarks on this genealogy as a positive affiliation, although he also cautions that a focus on ethnicity leads to genocide and that the importance of the connection is not genetic but attitudinal: "Family is the same manners, the same way of responding to the world."[47]

This sentiment coheres with the Malian tendency to treat strangers like family, as seen in *cousinage* (*sanankuya* in Bamanankan), or joking cousin relationships. This practice is said to have been started by the Emperor Sundiata Keïta in the thirteenth century and is considered a remarkably successful way of encouraging peace and cooperation.[48] Different last names, of which there are a relatively small number, have associated joking cousins, so that anyone named Sidibé will be treated as a joking cousin by anyone named Kanté, for instance.[49] Joking cousins cannot be insulted by each other, must never harm each other, and must always do what a joking cousin asks. As Drisdelle and Pye-Smith note, "Cousinage exists not only between ethnic groups, but between different castes within each cultural grouping."[50] Thus in Mali strangers are already in relation to each other and can invoke such obligations as necessary, based on family names.

As a modern, urban capital, Bamako is a site of métissage—a mixing of castes, cultures, heritages, and diversity, which creates a cosmopolitan society. With Bamako as the seat of government and the political-cultural center of southern Mali (Mali south of Timbuktu), there has been a focus, especially politically since the 1990s, on the acceptance of difference, tolerance, and appreciation of other cultures, which helped it remain a peaceful democracy for two decades.[51] The Bamako art world is a Relational community that appreciates irreducible difference and interchanges with the global world through images and various foreign collaborations without losing itself. The Bamakois art world is also like an archipelago in that it consists of different institutions and associations in the city that have all sprung up without being rooted in past notions of art and that virtually all consist of Malian and Euro/American collaborations.

Relation enables an imaginary that contradicts and confounds globalization and its totalizing propensity through emphasis on the local in exchange with the global. The idea of art and literature as creating a potential imaginary for future possibility and change is something that Relation borrows from Négritude as well as the Harlem Renaissance; notably, both were literary and philosophical movements. This imaginary illuminates the peculiar circumstances of the Bamakois art photography movement, which was fanned into existence by the influence of the biennale. The arguably neocolonial entity of the biennale itself—a nexus of interchange between the global and the local—and the institutions it has encouraged have generated an imaginative space within which Bamako photographers are creating the new cultural form of art photography. And it is precisely this dialectic between local identity and global reception that gives photographs by contemporary Malian artists the potential to enact Relation through opacity as an aesthetic preoccupation. A "Glissantian strategy which highlights the relation to the global, while at the same time affirming the particularity of the local" is the notion of opacity, as H. Adlai Murdoch explains.[52] "Opacity" for Glissant is how a culture or an individual keeps its secrets to itself; it is in opposition to the required transparency and publicness of people's innermost selves (in this Glissant was prescient regarding social media). Most Malian art photographs incorporate opacity in some sense; their meanings and aesthetics are rarely, if ever, immediately clear to a non-Malian audience. Yet they are still appreciated for their seeming engagement with recognized, indeed, codified, tropes within global contemporary art; only on closer engagement with their aesthetics and meanings does their opacity become noticeable. The circulation of these opaque images in the context of the African Photography Encounters allows for Malians to actively contest the neocolonial agenda of its French directorship.

While Mali is one of the poorest nations in the world economically, it is culturally one of the richest, internationally famous for its sculpture, masks, and performances, as well as music, textiles and cloth, ceramics, and architecture. The biennale intercedes dramatically across this axis of poverty and culture, which is most blatantly visible when Western curators stay in luxury hotels and participants from neighboring Niger sleep on local roofs. Caught between French funding and the logistical difficulties of their nation's economic hardships, the Malian hosts, administrators, and photographers mediate between global wealth and local poverty. The art photographers in Bamako also mediate between older traditions and modernity, a tension that many countries and societies face in this rapidly accelerating age but that is especially key in Bamako, where traditional cultures are inseparably intertwined with the arts, and cultural mores and rituals are rapidly eroding. Art photography participates in international exhibitions and yet retains local meanings for a Malian audience, who may not always appreciate its aesthetic but who will certainly comprehend its content.

Photography in Mali has always embodied contradictions deriving from the colonial situation and its aftermath. With their conquest of the region in the 1880s, the French brought cameras, the devices of soldiers, colonial administrators, anthropologists, and Christian missionaries.[53] African photographers with close connections to the colonials opened Bamako's first studios in the 1930s, and portraits of the aspiring bourgeoisie became highly popular by the late 1940s. Since Mali's independence from France in 1960, studio portraits and press agency photographs have offered competing histories of how the citizens of Bamako envisioned themselves in opposition to how the socialist dictators allowed themselves and their citizens to be portrayed. Under the multiparty democracy that was shakily reinstated after the 2012 coup, hundreds of studios operate in the capital.

With the rise of digital technology, photography has become even more fluid. Images are sent around the world in milliseconds, leaving aside the need for expensive printing materials, framing, or paper. In Mali, where internet access is becoming more common, photographers are now learning digital technologies and beginning to exploit opportunities provided by the internet; as recently as the mid-2000s, by contrast, film photography and traditional black-and-white printing techniques were still primarily being taught and used. Indeed, film photography may have had its last hurrah in Bamako, as old materials and technologies in France were sent or donated to Bamako's photo institutions. This shift may contribute to the end of the movement or another beginning: the obsolescence of those techniques and the cheap, cast-off materials found a ready home in Bamako, but as supplies have petered out, so have opportunities. Two photography schools that opened in the 1990s in Bamako show such signs: a school for women called Promo-femme closed in 2009 for lack of funding, and the private school Cadre de Promotion pour la Formation en Photographie (CFP) has changed its focus from art to advertising photography. It remains to be seen whether the art photography movement, beset first by the expense of digital technologies and second by the political uncertainties of the coup, will survive, although the return of the Bamako Photography Encounters in 2015 and 2017, after a hiatus due to the coup, was an exciting start, especially as Bisi Silva, the 2015 curator, was the first African woman living on the continent to direct it.

Unlike the forms of long-practiced arts in Mali that have changed over time but continue richly into the present, like music, puppet theater, or dancing, sometimes absorbing non-Malian influences in their richness, art photography is itself a new art form emerging out of studio portrait photography. Commercial portrait photography was an art form of modernity that thrived during and after the colonial era and was introduced through colonial contact, although it quickly adopted Malian meanings and aesthetics. The art photography that has grown out of commercial studio photography's art world fame mixes global influences with local meanings, and for this reason, it moves beyond the ambivalence of postcoloniality to potentially embody Relation, engaging the imaginaries of viewers and carrying a sense of optimism and equality.

Photography—as a network or force of social and technological practices—is the medium par excellence for embodying Relation; for telling a visual history of Mali and for showing and producing Malian identity. In fact, photography can be understood through Glissant's notion of the *écho-monde* (echo-world) as showing the resonances and appearances of things in the world. Malian art photographs capture aspects of Malian culture in transition and transformation, with uniquely Mande or Malian aesthetic force. These photographs are irreducible to transparent aesthetics or conceptions, or to colonial or postcolonial thought; they are not "simplified representations," to refer back to Glissant's comment on how Africa figures in creolizing thought. Neither are they conceived through fidelity to a culture's rootedness or illustrations of an abstract rootlessness; their rhizomatic nature transforms Malian cultural scenarios through aesthetic or conceptual influences from international sources.

While Relation could potentially flourish anywhere, it is enabled here through the combined aspects of photography as a medium, Mande aesthetics, Malian cultural values, and the Bamakois art world that has emerged due to the biennale's existence. Valérie Loichot notes, "Glissant's aesthetic practice and philosophy consists in highlighting connections between artistic production in geographically discrete parts of the world."[54] The specific context of art photography's emergence in Bamako and Mali's history, cultures, diversity, and geography all contribute to art photography's potential to embody Relation. While Relation may be conveyed by art produced in other nations in Africa and elsewhere in the world, Malian art photography's embodiment of Relation emerges from the Relational attributes of Malian culture as conveyed through the aesthetics of art photography.

From the circumstances of this Bamakois art world, Malian photographers are forging new aesthetic approaches that can be perceived by the global art world, yet also remain resolutely attentive to a specific Malian particularity. The aesthetic qualities of Malian photographs, and the context of their production and exhibition, are what enable an affinity with Relation—indeed, that enable a poetics of Relation. Malian art photography is a new form, a poetics, that embodies an imaginary particular to Mali. As Betsy Wing explains, "For Glissant, the imaginary is all the ways a culture has of perceiving and conceiving of the world. Hence, every human culture will have its own particular imaginary."[55] Although Malian culture could be seen as rooted (although historical analysis shows it to be less "rooted" than often thought, considering the great waves of migration across the region after the end of slavery and during several jihads), art photography draws on contemporary culture. It is open to and embraces difference, yet speaks in its own cultural aesthetics. It conveys a sense of process and change, rather than stasis, and is optimistic and Relational.

For example, Alioune Bâ's photograph *Corps habitable* (*Livable Body*) resonates with different valences according to one's culture and knowledge. It shows a woman's body cropped from the waist down, her hand suggestively reaching to presumably untie her wrap of mud cloth (*bogolan*), with the words *CORPS HABITABLE* written in white capital letters on her bare bent leg, mimicking the white designs on the brown bogolan (fig. Intro. 2). The woman's midriff is in shadow, impeding visibility and making her ac-

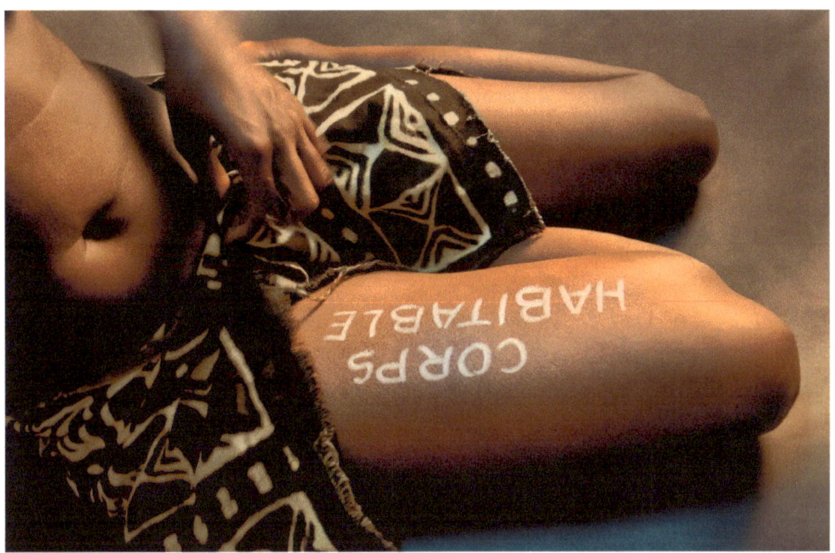

Figure Intro.2. Alioune Bâ, *Corps habitable* (*Livable Body*), from the *Body Writing* (*Corps écriture*) series, 2008. Courtesy of Madame Bâ Alima Togola and Perlman Teaching Museum, Carleton College.

tion opaque. A further visual difficulty or obscurity is caused by the upside-down writing; it is perhaps written for the woman rather than the viewer, or for someone (an absent presence, either person or culture) standing on her other side. There is an obvious sexual intimation with the gesture and pose, and a reference to pregnancy (fertility is an extremely desirable aspect of womanhood in Mali) but also more abstractly the idea of a woman's body as anyone's original home is also at play.

But the image also refers to bogolan's meaning—traditionally, and still in some Bamana villages, the dyed mud cloth holds important personal power, or *nyama*, for a woman who wears it in relation to her first menstrual blood or to a birth. This reading is tempered by the scandalous way the cloth is worn, revealing the woman's legs (for which she would be chastised on the street), and the fact that the cloth is not traditionally dyed mud cloth; its deep color and sharp white lines suggest it is quickly made for the tourist market. In the international world, where it became popular especially in high fashion through Malian designer Chris Seydou in the 1990s, bogolan has come to symbolize "Africanness," especially in the United States. The written French words (rather than in the Fulani or Bamankan language) are juxtaposed with the bogolan markings. In the traditional context, such designs compose a personal and private visual language of abstract symbols, Sarah Brett-Smith has argued. Yet just as the French language text might be incomprehensible for a rural woman in Mali, here the bogolan pattern meanings have been scrambled and made incomprehensible in a purely decorative cloth designed for tourists. Others might see the photograph as a man's view of a woman's sexual objectification, but I argue that its deliberate symbolism complicates that reading. The image might suggest a critique of the commodification of both the female body and the tourist cloth, but its emphasis on the woman's relationship to her own body, or on the idea of sexuality and love—for a livable body is presumably not just sexual, but involves a sense of living *with*—paradoxically conveys other meanings as well.

Thus, the photograph offers a range of interpretations, from the quick glance of a simplified celebration or objectification of an African woman's (hetero)sexuality, to a more complex and nuanced reading based on one's knowledge in relation to bogolan's meaning in Bamana culture, or to tourist bogolan's sale on the world market. Ultimately the work resists a cohesive, singular understanding: its very ambiguity and mystery, as well as its incorporation of a poetic fragment, thus potentially create Relation for the viewer.

In this book, my methodology takes account of the conflicting sociopolitical and historical forces operating on photographers, as well as individual personalities, bodies of work, and institutions. It includes visiting studios and conducting interviews, attending exhibitions, and incorporating research from a range of disciplines including art history, philosophy, sociology, anthropology, political science, postcolonial studies, and theories of photography. I also participated in this art world tangentially through co-curating an exhibition on Malian photography in 2012 at Carleton College in Northfield, Minnesota, that traveled back to Bamako in 2015.[56] While this book attempts to describe a photography art world in Bamako, surveying institutions and artists and paying attention to power dynamics, I am also interested in the photograph itself—in what an image *is* and *does*. I examine individuals' professions, their artworks and projects, and various confluences of events within the broader sociohistorical context of contemporary Mali. As a social history of art, this study includes a discussion of the broader institutional framework operative in Bamako, yet views that framework as constructed by individual personalities and ambitions acted on by historical and political forces. The text incorporates formal and contextual analyses of single photographs, yet its broader purview is informed by postcolonial theory and incorporates a feminist approach. Considerations of class, caste, ethnicity, and gender are included where relevant and possible. As art photography is a new cultural form in Mali, I situate the art photography movement within the broader context of photography in that country and trace its genealogy through traditional arts, modern art, and studio photography.

Because I wanted to examine how Malian photography has been influenced by international exchanges after the founding of the biennale, most of the photographs by Malians that I discuss were published or exhibited, almost always with French financial support in some form, either from the French Cultural Center and/or the French Cultural Embassy, to that branch of the French government that organizes the biennale (currently called CulturesFrance; formerly Association Française d'Action Artistique). I refer to photographs published in biennale catalogs and monographs coordinated by either Antonin Potoski, who was active in such publications from 1996 to 2002, or by Amadou Chab Touré for Galerie Chab.[57] This handful of books, and *carnets* published by the French press *Éditions l'Oeil,* were all supported by the French embassy, except in the case of Mohamed Camara, some of whose books were published in France with the support of his gallerist, Pierre Brullé. Two more recent books incorporated photographers and their works into larger cultural purview on Bamako or Mali.[58] Available for sale in Mali's National Museum bookstore and in several Parisian bookstores, in most cases these publications were made for a foreign audience, and they are written in French. Sometimes they are also translated into English, but none are in Bamanankan or any other Malian language, except for the title of the 1998 biennale, *Ja Taa! (Snap the Photo!)*.[59]

The absence of materials in local languages clearly shows that the publication or exhibition of these images was for a foreign audience, or a French-educated audience within Mali. Although I viewed hundreds of photographs in studios, this book mostly focuses on published or exhibited images because they have been brought into circulation and sent forth into the world to create effects and enact Relation with the multiple viewers who encounter them. The act of publishing or exhibiting these photographs rendered them visible to a larger audience, and activated their Relational potential, endowing them with meaning in a reciprocal aesthetic Relation between viewer and photograph and sharing their imaginaries with the world.

Thus the formal and/or conceptual qualities of these photographs appeal to an international audience, yet the images were made by Malian photographers in a context that was usually local. I examine their formal qualities from the perspective of someone trained in contemporary art history and photography history, as well as in African arts, in wanting to understand why these particular images were chosen. At the same time, through my interviews with photographers in Mali, I try to consider the *cultural* qualities of these forms—their localized meaning and interest—from what I understand of a Malian perspective.

While *Embodying Relation* focuses on photography in Mali, and specifically on developments in Bamako, the capital, whose urban culture differs quite strongly from that in other areas of the country, it is problematic to celebrate art within the context of nationalism or to make positive, uncritical claims for a "national" art. Wanda Corn notes, with regard to American art, that "exceptionalist studies today are considered forms of cultural aggression, compelling conformity of behavior and belief and asserting political claims for American national superiority."[60] Although I do not want to celebrate nationalist sentiments uncritically in the Malian context, national pride takes on a different meaning when operative in one of the poorest and least politically powerful countries in the world. Indeed, "Malian" identity is a concept that has only formally existed since independence in 1960, although notions of "nationalism" were operative in the struggle for independence. The forced institution of borders to create the French Sudan means that various ethnic polities' areas of habitation naturally spilled over the new national boundaries. But after a century that encompassed colonialism, the liberation struggle, independence, socialist dictatorships, democracy, and a recent coup that enhanced civil strife between the North and the South, nationalism has acquired an important resonance in contemporary Malian life, and culture in Mali has been a powerful means of reinforcing nationalist feelings.[61] Malians also look back to their history of great empires—in particular the thirteenth-century Mali Empire, for which today's nation is named—with great pride. In fact, Malians cite their cultural heritage, adherence to tradition, and pride in their past as reasons for becoming, until recently, one of the few peaceful democracies to survive the postindependence ethnic violence that suffuses most of West Africa.[62]

As nations are composed of many factions—ethnicity, class, profession, gender—it is inconceivable that a single photograph or body of work can articulate a definition of "identity" that will apply to the whole population. However, the "imagined community" of the nation is a strong force in people's views of their own self-constructions.[63] It is clear that among photographers working in Bamako—those who call themselves artists, those who exhibit internationally (or hope to), and those who work in the photographic institutions—that issues of cultural, political, historical, and national identity inform and often drive their production. As it is through Malian portraitists Seydou Keïta and Malick Sidibé that "African" photography has become popularly known, photographers working today may also be aware of the power of "Malian identity" as a promotional quality in the view of the international art world. However, most photographers whom I interviewed denied that a qualitative "Malian" photography exists, instead suggesting that each photographer works according to his or her own style. Paradoxically, this willingness to allow for difference is a highly *Malian* characteristic. This book, which necessarily unfolds under national parameters, thus takes account of the complexities of nationalism and urbanism, and their contributions to photographers' work.[64]

As a white, feminist North American researcher writing for an English-speaking audience about an African, Muslim, patriarchal culture in an economically disadvantaged country, I am deeply aware of and attentive to the necessity of self-reflexivity regarding my position in Western hegemony. This is an irresolvable contradiction, as any scholar who has managed to publish in the academic circles of the hegemonic West is obviously a beneficiary of the very structures of institutional and class power that the theory seeks to expose.[65] As part of my self-reflexive practice, I acknowledge the specific subject positions as well as what Glissant would call the opacity of the individuals discussed in this book. All of the artists and administrators whom I interviewed in Mali wield varying but definite amounts of cultural, social, economic, and, in some cases, political power, both in their local community, and in their ability to produce images that can "speak" to both local and international audiences while at the same time remaining opaque at different levels to these audiences. While this study focuses on photographers who work in and construct an imaginary of the liminal space between "the West" and "Mali," I acknowledge that my subject position inevitably influences my work.[66]

A few points about terminology must be explained. While I use the term "traditional" to refer to "precolonial" African arts, I use it with the understanding that traditions are transmogrified by social and local practices over time and are not fixed, static, and timeless entities. The use of the term "precolonial" can overemphasize the recent history of European conquest, as if thousands of years of struggles for conquest among various cultures and peoples within Africa itself were of lesser importance. I do not mean to make this presumption. But there is no term that easily designates "the area in West Africa that was to become the nation of Mali in 1960," since various empires had different boundaries. Therefore I sometimes use the word "precolonial" as a shorthand way to refer to the time before the French entered

Mali in the 1880s. As this book focuses specifically on the colonial and independence eras and on the technology of photography, introduced by Europeans who did not arrive in the French Sudan until the 1880s, infrequent usage of the term is acceptable in this context.

"Modern art" in this book refers to art made between roughly 1900 and 1950. It can be Malian or American or Japanese, but I would differentiate Bamana carvings for ritual use from modern art; the primary definition would be "art for art's sake"—or, in Adornian terms, the autonomous art object (usually but not always abstract). Modern art photography would include photographers like Aaron Siskind as well as earlier photographers like László Moholy-Nagy. While scholars like Okwui Enwezor argue that Keïta's photographs constitute modern art, I argue that they were vernacular portraits in the 1950s and became contemporary art (not modern art, although they shared some aspects of modernist photography aesthetics) in the 1990s. Similarly, I sometimes describe certain Malian photographers as utilizing a modern aesthetic—these are formal photographic aesthetic practices that contribute to abstraction, such as the close-up, stark contrasts, slantwise framing, or a bird's-eye perspective.

The term "contemporary" here refers to the chronological present and recent past. While I try to avoid making the distinctions of Western (usually French or American) versus Malian, sometimes such broad categorizations provide a useful shorthand. When I use them, I mean to refer to broad cultural attitudes or to people who may lack familiarity with art. Suffice it to say that Afro-pessimism as a visual economy is alive and well in the United States.

The first chapter, "Unknown Photographer (Bamako, Mali)," introduces the history of photography in the French Sudan (now Mali) and discusses its relationship to power as wielded first by the colonials and then by Africans. I follow this history through Mali's independence from France in 1960 until the transition to democracy in 1991–1992, showing how the history of photography is imbricated in the nation's political history, and making a case for understanding this history through postcolonial theory and Mande aesthetics.

The second chapter, "Malian Portraiture Glamorized and Globalized," examines the reception of Keïta's and Sidibé's works in the West (primarily focusing on the New York art world but briefly glossing Paris and London), arguing that the changed context of circulation and display of these reprints *constitutes* contemporary art in the New York art world, but can equally be understood as an emanation of Mande aesthetics. I also examine the effect of the globalization of Keïta's and Sidibé's works on their own practices, in fashion shoots and Sidibé's art project *Vues de dos*.

Chapter 3, "Biennale Effects: The African Photography Encounters," focuses on the institution that gave birth to the Bamakois art photography movement. I discuss the Rencontres Africaines de la Photographie from its founding to the present. Malian effort and effects are visible in various projects, images, and practices; I connect the Malian democratic state's emphasis on discussion, stemming from Bamana *ton* associations, to the biennale's emphasis on discourse and Relation.[67] I consider the importance of the biennale to photography throughout Africa, and the biennale's reception in the Malian, French, and American press.

In the fourth chapter, "Bamako Becoming Photographic: An Archipelagic Art World," the effects of the biennale are examined on the Bamako art world in terms of institutions, individuals, and photography education. Using a Foucauldian analysis as well as Bourdieu's description of an art world as a social field, this chapter examines the discursive practices and institutional histories that have surrounded the rise of art photography in Bamako in terms of Glissant's notion of an archipelago.

Chapter 5, "Creolizing the Archive: Photographers at the National Museum," explores bodies of work that stem from archival influences made by photographers who work or worked at Mali's National Museum, another important institution in the Bamako art world. The projects of Alioune Bâ, Youssouf Sogodogo, and Joseye Tienro tangentially apply the museum's mission to important aspects of contemporary culture. These projects *creolize* the archive, in Glissant's phrasing; their cultural relevance and aesthetics create imaginaries that enable Relation.

The sixth chapter, "Promoting Women Photographers," examines the issue of being a woman photographer in the Bamakois art photography world, considering feminist philosopher Luce Irigaray's theory of sexual difference as a way to account for Malian gender difference in connection with Glissant's notion of the irreducible difference of Relation. I discuss the work of five female photographers whose careers have been made possible by the biennale and its offshoots; in the career of rising star Fatoumata Diabaté, in particular, one can see the most benefits stemming from democracy, feminism, and the biennale.

The seventh and last chapter, "Errantry, the Social Body, and Photography as the Écho-monde," examines the diversity of ways in which Relation has been embodied in the practices of contemporary Malian art photographers. I show how the photographic practices of Mohamed Camara, Fatoumata Diabaté, Seydou Camara, Alioune Bâ, Bakary Emmanual Daou, Mamadou Konaté, Harandane Dicko, Amadou Keïta, and Django Cissé convey concepts of errantry, opacity, and the social body through reference to Malian culture and imaginative aesthetics. Finally, I suggest that photography in Mali can be seen as an écho-monde, a Relational medium par excellence.

Embodying Relation tells several stories. It documents how two African photographers' fame in the art centers of the US and Europe had unprecedented and widespread effects, in Bamako and across Africa. It shows how Mali's shift to democracy in 1991–1992 (threatened but not ended by the March 2012 coup) enabled an art photography scene to blossom in Bamako that continues today, despite political instability. This book also analyzes the unprecedented emergence of professional women photographers in a patriarchal nation. Most importantly, the book argues that Malian art photographs contest globalization. Art photography in Mali provides a fascinating instance of a local aesthetics speaking both locally and globally, across different levels of cultural knowledge, without losing its emphasis on Mande aesthetics and meaning: instead of emphasizing a process of globalization and the homogenization of cultural forms, Mande aesthetics and Malian cultural values incorporate modernist or postmodernist aesthetics, forging new cultural forms yet retaining their Malianness.

Glissant believed that, to change a mentality, it is first necessary to change an imaginary. The Bamako art movement's importance lies in the fact that it is a locality in dialogue with the world—it entices viewers to experience Mande aesthetics. In the vein of scholars arguing for a more complex understanding of contemporaneity and local aesthetic values, *Embodying Relation* offers an example of a different form of contemporary art practice that functions on the global scene, yet relies on indigenous social and cultural values.[68] This is, in a sense, shifting the terms of not just what is valued as contemporary art, but what is *meant* by contemporary art.[69] If scholars are to give credence to notions of contemporaneity, then they must also be willing to reexamine views of what contemporary art is. An art photography informed more by Mande aesthetic and social values—which are intertwined—will look different than avant-garde American art; but as is known now from decades-long experiments with abstraction and conceptualism, what an artwork means is as important as what it looks like. The point is to recognize and legitimize other forms of visual discourse that might be more relevant to local populations than the global discourse of contemporary art: these works hold local meaning and also carry significant meanings within the global art discourse, thereby embodying Relation.[70]

Glissant says that it is first in the efflorescence of art (poetry, literature, music, dance, photography) that irreducible difference can be acknowledged; in this poetic imaginary the way to equality can be discovered. I argue not for the direct political efficacy of this art, but rather for its possibilities in offering a vision that might not otherwise exist—and within this vision, circulating around and through it, touching its viewers and its makers, circulates Relation. This vision is not utopian; or if it is, it is not utopian in the conventional sense. For Glissant, utopia is change through exchange with others without losing one's self—it is not static but is "quivering" or "trembling," an ongoing process that is a "continuous dialogue."[71] Its imaginary plays on the surface of the photograph, which itself is contingently connected to reality, and is therefore irreducible. In bypassing the paradigm of the conceptual photography generally celebrated on the global circuit, Malian photography does not earn broad acclaim. Yet it is precisely in these modest overtures, quiet gestures, and specific Mande aesthetics that Relation beckons.

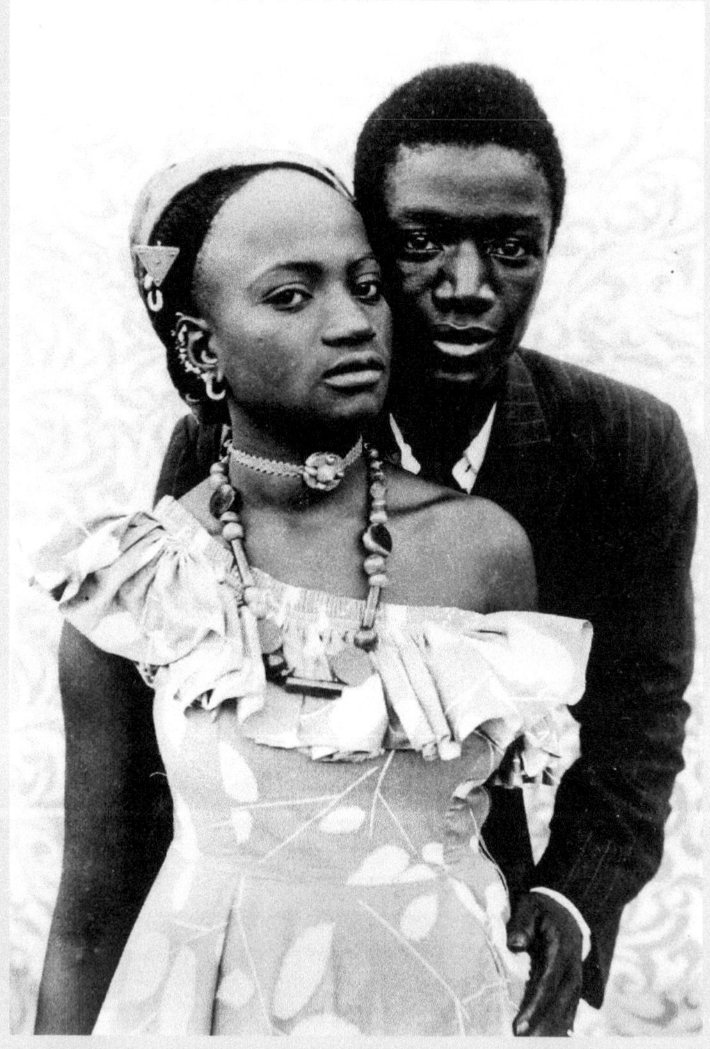

Figure 1.1. Seydou Keïta, Untitled ("Portrait of a Couple"). 1956/57, dated by arabesque backdrop. Printed in 1991 for *Africa Explores*.

Chapter 1

Unknown Photographer (Bamako, Mali)

We were already well known in Bamako but in the 1990s our work gradually became known internationally as well.
—Malick Sidibé

In 1991, black-and-white portrait photographs of anonymous West Africans, taken by unnamed studio photographers from Ivory Coast, Togo, Senegal, and Mali, were displayed in the groundbreaking exhibition *Africa Explores: 20th Century African Art*. The show, which opened in New York City simultaneously at the Center for African Art and the New Museum of Contemporary Art, argued for the importance of twentieth-century art produced by Africans, whose work had been dismissed by scholars as inauthentic or derivative because of its apparent assimilation of European styles or techniques. Now, portraits taken by African commercial studio photographers, commissioned by local clients to commemorate important moments in their lives, were being shown in the heart of the American art world.

Several striking photographs were included: the loveliest, of a couple (fig. 1.1). The woman wears a floral-patterned dress, its flouncy collar pulled down to bare her shoulder. She tilts her head to stand cheek to cheek with the man, drawing attention to her bejeweled ear and a brooch in her hair. She gazes inscrutably, almost challengingly, at the photographer. The man behind her stoops to fit his cheek next to hers, slivers of a white, open-collared shirt just visible under his dark pin-striped suit. He looks steadily at the camera with a hint of a smile curling his closed lips.

While she seems to resist the camera's—or history's—gaze, he bends forward eagerly. This tension, push-pull, is reiterated formally in the asymmetry of her bare right arm and bared left shoulder, the diagonal sweep of the flounced collar of her dress, the solid downward pull of the man's body framing her left side, his hand resting gently, demurely on her waist. The light gray of her dress fits her body like a second skin, and is framed by the darkness of her right arm and his possibly borrowed dark suit; his hand could at first glance be hers. His shoulders rise above each of hers, separated by a jog of the collar's flounce. The play of dark and light intertwines their bodies, and their limbs become interchangeable: one unit, a union. The pride of Négritude is in their eyes.[1]

If this is a wedding portrait, they are eyeing their future with equally passionate restraint and confidence. A backdrop's subtle gray-on-white pattern of curlicues flattens space behind them, removing the pair from the banality of the photographer's dusty courtyard to float against a decorative ambience. The caption reads simply: "Portrait of a Couple, 1950s, unknown photographer (Bamako, Mali), silver print, 1974, from original negative, 17 × 13 cm. Private collection." Today, the couple remains anonymous, but the photographer facing them at the moment their forms were seared onto a postcard-sized glass was Seydou Keïta—now considered one of the most famous African artists in the world.

How did this photographer from a desperately poor and marginalized nation come to be exhibited—anonymously—in the very center of the contemporary art world? In an ethical lapse, *Africa Explores* curator Susan Vogel exhibited Keïta's photographs without his express permission, reprinted from negatives she had collected while traveling in West Africa in the 1970s. History was in the making: Vogel's decision had dramatic ramifications, not just for Keïta but for many other African photographers as well.

Smitten by the photographs in *Africa Explores,* French curator and dealer André Magnin traveled to Bamako in 1992 or 1993 on behalf of the Italian French millionaire and art collector Jean Pigozzi to seek the photographer.[2] On arriving in Bamako, Magnin met Malick Sidibé, a former studio photographer who now ran a camera repair shop. Sidibé introduced or at least mentioned Keïta to Magnin; Keïta himself recounts that Magnin and "a guy" (who might have been Sidibé) showed up in the presence of French photographer Françoise Huguier. While Huguier had already organized a small exhibition of Keïta's work in Paris, with Magnin's and Pigozzi's patronage the two photographers were soon exhibited, often together, to great fanfare in the global art centers of New York and Paris, and widely across Europe. In 1993, Keïta's works were projected in the Arles Rencontres, and his photographs were shown in Rouen at the Troisièmes Rencontres Photographiques de Normandie and in Copenhagen at the festival titled *Images of Africa*. The following year, Keïta had solo shows at Shiseido in Tokyo and Fondation Cartier in Paris and was also shown in Paris at the Palais de l'UNESCO. The international success of Keïta's and Sidibé's exceptional portraits inspired Huguier to work with Bernard Descamps and Malian photographers Django Cissé and Alioune Bâ in Bamako to launch an African photography biennial in Mali's capital. The inaugural edition in 1994 was called the "Africaines Rencontres de la Photographie."

In the United States, Keïta, then seventy-some years old, had his first retrospective in 1996 at the Smithsonian National Museum of African Art, and both he and Sidibé were included in the groundbreaking exhibition at the Guggenheim Museum, *In/Sight: African Photographers, 1940 to the Present.*[3] Keïta's subsequent solo exhibitions at Gagosian Gallery, first in Los Angeles and then in New York in 1997, accompanied by a prominent review in the *New York Times*, familiarized his works to an American art public on both coasts.[4] Magnin also published monographs on each artist in 1997, further disseminating their works. Both Keïta and Sidibé also appeared in *You Look Beautiful Like That* at Harvard's Fogg Art Museum in 2001, and in Okwui Enwezor's exhibition *Short Century: Independence and Liberation Movements in Africa, 1945–1994* in 2001 in Chicago and New York. And in 2003 they appeared in Revue Noire's *L'Afrique par elle-même: Un siècle de photographie africaine* at the Musée Royal de l'Afrique Centrale de Tervuren in Belgium, completing a Europe-to-America-and-back-again circle of fame.

Enlarged in some cases to larger than life sizes and printed in high-contrast grayscale values, Keïta's photos showcased modern, fashionable West Africans, on Vespas or with radios, holding props or small children, against patterned backdrops. Sidibé's work featured lively shots of young people at parties or on the beach from the 1960s, carefully chosen by Magnin to contrast Keïta's solemn poses (fig. 1.2).[5] Eventually Sidibé's studio portraiture, from the 1970s as well as the '60s, became at least as popular as the early party shots (some of which were actually taken by his studio assistant and relative, Sidiki Sidibé), and, like Keïta's arabesque pattern, Sidibé's striped backdrop became his signature hallmark, as witnessed in his 2009 fashion shoot for the *New York Times*.[6]

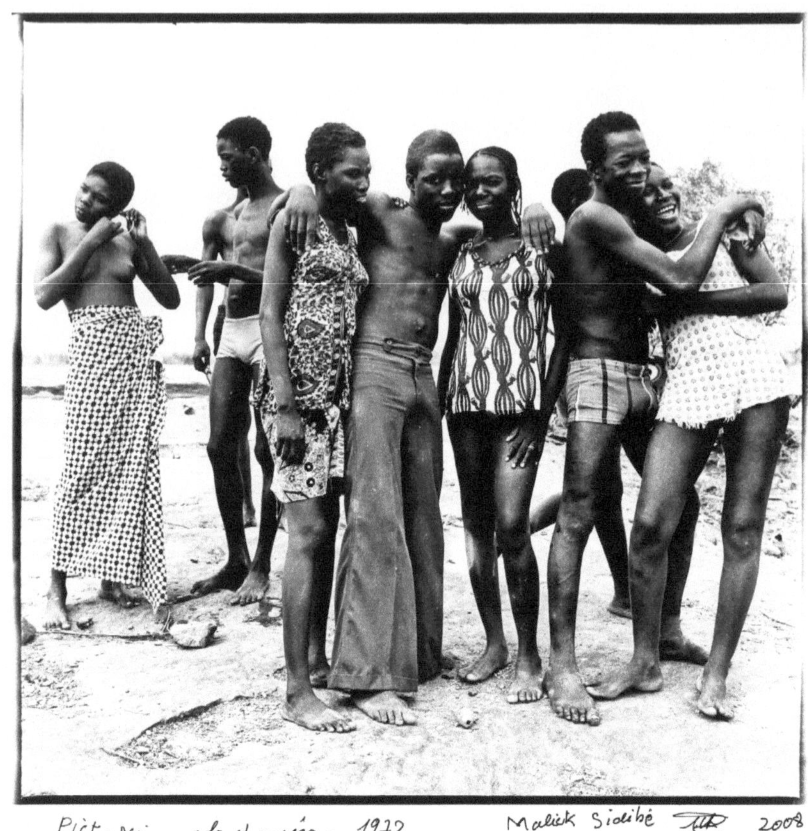

Figure 1.2. Malick Sidibé, *Pic-nique à la chaussée* (*Pic-nic on the Road*), 1972, 2008 print. Courtesy of the artist and Jack Shainman Gallery, New York.

Seydou Keïta's so-called discovery by the global art world set off an increased interest in all genres and forms of African photography, pursued in major exhibitions in Bamako and across Africa, in France, the United States, and eventually around the world.[7] This excitement was mirrored by the dramatic rise of contemporary art photography in South Africa after the end of apartheid, along with the Cape Town Month of Photography Festival, and paralleled a new turn toward self-reflexive anthropology, inspired by French postmodern philosophies, as scholars also began to interrogate and critique collections of old photographs of Africans taken by anthropologists, travelers, and missionaries.[8] A spate of publications and exhibitions raised awareness of photography and its historical relationship to Africa, creating a new field of scholarly interest fueled by the increasing interest in contemporary African photography being promoted in France and the US.

The Rencontres (or Bamako Biennale, or African Photography Encounters, as it came to be called) contributed to this artistic and historical fascination as the most important recurring photography event on the continent over the next two decades, giving rise to other photographic institutions within Mali and inspiring international photo exhibitions and biennials elsewhere in Africa. Together with the biennale, Keïta's and Sidibé's fame spurred an art movement among photographers in Mali where none had previously existed.

While Magnin contributed to the initial impact of Keïta and Sidibé in the art world, Keïta ended his relationship with Magnin, apparently because of disagreements about financial arrangements, and began working with Frenchman Jean-Marc Patras and the American dealer Sean Kelly. Keïta died in 2001 with 921 negatives said to be still in Magnin's hands; the ensuing debacle among the dealers and Keïta's heirs determined the limited recognition for Keïta's photographs in the coming decades. Keïta's reputation began to languish after the scandal and his death, because of the uncertain viability of his works and the question of whether they were authentically signed by the artist.

By contrast, Sidibé's activities and fame increased, eventually surpassing Keïta's—the preface to the 2007 Rencontres catalog mentions only Sidibé as an influence on African photography, surely because he had that very year received the Golden Lion Award at the Venice Biennale. Sidibé's work is represented by Jack Shainman Gallery in New York, which has reliably curated thought-provoking and historically accurate exhibitions, and La Galerie du Jour agnès b. in Paris. Sidibé was also very active as a mentor and photography educator in Bamako, and was generous with his wealth, supporting a large family, friends, and neighbors. He continued to live in Bamako until his death in April 2016, when he was universally mourned and globally memorialized, with obituaries in the *New York Times*, the *Guardian*, and *Le Monde*, among many other news outlets.

European and American dealers and African curators alike deliberately positioned the client-commissioned, commercial, vernacular portraits by Keïta and Sidibé, originally a collaboration between sitter and photographer intended for the sitter's private, personal use, *as* fine art in museums and galleries. Indeed, Vogel's original collaboration with the New Museum set the stage for their first appearance, so that the photographs awkwardly straddled the divide between Western and African contemporary art, which have historically different chronologies and reference points, and circulate in different forms of cultural production, with different valences, meanings, and audiences. Along with the photographs by Samuel Fosso of the Central African Republic and Nigerian photographer J. D. 'Okhai Ojeikere, both of whose works were also promoted by Magnin through Pigozzi's Contemporary African Art Collection (CAAC), these photographs became, for a time, *the* new canon of African photography.

But before delving into the global reception of Keïta's and Sidibé's portraits, it is important to understand the original context in which the studio portraits by Keïta, Sidibé, and in fact many others were produced, in order to realize how dramatic that intertextual shift from local to global reception, from vernacular to fine art, from personal to public, from sitter to author, has been. Despite all of the international focus on Keïta and Sidibé, they were just two of hundreds of studio portraitists working across all of Africa. However, the fact that both famous photographers worked in Bamako had significant ramifications for Mali. Portrait photography became a new form of cultural resistance that contested foreign domination, subtly but powerfully. In a polyrhythmic story full of spacings and time lags, it also gave birth to an art photography movement embodying Caribbean philosopher Édouard Glissant's notion of *Relation*.

> From 1840, daguerreotypists were . . . experimenting . . . all along the African coast: from the Somali coast to Capetown and Saint-Louis in Senegal.
> —Érika Nimis, *Photographes de Bamako de 1935 à nos jours [Photographers in Bamako from 1935 to the Present]*

While the recent fascination with African photography is a trend of the twenty-first century's global art world, photography's roots in Africa extend back to the medium's infancy in the nineteenth century, soon after the daguerreotype was patented by the French government in 1839. Photography reached Senegal and Egypt the following year, and Europeans opened studios in African port cities by 1845. Augustus Washington, an African American photographer considered the first "African" photographer in Central and West Africa, having repatriated to Liberia in 1854, opened his daguerreotype studio in Monrovia that year;[9] Africans John P. Decker of Gambia and Francis W. Joaque of Gabon were practicing commercial photography by the late 1860s.[10] But the new technology was slow to travel inland, taking forty years to reach the region that is now Mali.

As portraiture was becoming established for colonials and Africans, photography was also wielded by colonists to exert control over indigenous people in a variety of contexts.[11] The medium played an important role in military missions and enabled colonial administrators to survey the land and document new building projects. Photographs were used by missionaries to show evidence of their "beneficial" conversions. Anthropologists used photography to classify and compare cultural traits and physical features using the pseudoscience of physiognomy. Images circulated in the form of postcards, supplying the settlers and those "back home" with exoticizing shots of Africans and the African landscape, especially after 1908, when Bamako became the capital of the French Sudan (present-day Mali).[12] Postcards of nude and seminude women were circulated as thinly disguised pornography.

Colonialism exploited people by taking away their rights and their resources, destroying their cultural practices and their built environments, forcing them to adopt European ways of life, creating a cultural inferiority complex, and draining the continent of natural resources and its ability to support itself. As Aimé Césaire, one of the influential writers who created the philosophy and poetics of Négritude, explained:

> Between colonizer and colonized there is room only for forced labor, intimidation, pressure, the police, taxation, theft, rape, compulsory crops, contempt, mistrust, arrogance, self-complacency, swinishness, brainless élites, degraded masses.
>
> No human contact, but relations of domination and submission which turn the colonizing man into a classroom monitor, an army sergeant, a prison guard, a slave driver, and the indigenous man into an instrument of production.
>
> My turn to state an equation: colonization = thingification.[13]

As colonization treated human subjects as objects, photography reinscribed this relationship of power, reinforcing colonial dominance. While colonial photography varies in its subjects, approaches, contexts, practitioners, and intentions, photographs of Africans by Europeans were almost always dehumanizing and objectifying in some way, reflecting the denigrating power relationship that colonialism enforced. As Eleanor M. Hight and Gary D. Sampson write, "Overwhelming evidence . . . indicates that the images produced a dynamic rhetoric of racial and ethnographic difference between white Europeans and Americans and non-European 'races' and 'places.'"[14] Colonial photographs "most often envisioned their subjects as objects of both racial inferiority and fascination," visually re-creating the racist mindset and subjugating circumstances of the European-African encounter.[15] Indeed, these historical tropes of colonial photography, combined with more recent news photographs depicting Africa as a continent of disease, famine, and war, have created an "image world," in Christraud Geary's term, that is still the only "image world" of Africa for many in the West.[16]

In the African colonial context, as John Tagg admonishes, "photographs are never 'evidence' of history; they are themselves the historical."[17] The very form that these early photographs took—their ontological presence—was shaped by the forces of history that birthed them. Photography arrived in the French Sudan hand in hand with colonialism, as Europeans traveled along the Niger River toward the sub-Saharan interior.[18] France had the grand vision of expanding its empire from the Senegalese coast across to its central African colonies. The first documented photographs of Bamako and its denizens were taken on the Borgnis-Desbordes military expedition of 1883, which resulted in the capture of the city.[19]

Érika Nimis comments, "The most striking photographs are the portraits of the chiefs who compromised with the French."[20] Yet there were few options other than compromise for most Africans. Europeans had superior weaponry, and by the time of colonization, the great empires of the region had disintegrated.[21] Centuries of participation in the transatlantic slave trade had wreaked havoc in societies across West Africa, resulting in the destruction of communities and general insecurity, and warfare had destroyed these great empires by fueling inhumane practices and economies in human export. Villages and small groups incapable of banding together to defend themselves against the Europeans, with their superior weapons and their dishonest treatises, were defeated. In southern Mali, the French promised deliverance from Samory Touré, a jihadist warrior conquering thousands (fig. 1.3). Indeed, in the beginning, some African kings believed that the French would help in alliance against their enemies; they did not realize that the Europeans would bring only greater subjugation, the worse for its dramatic change in economy, culture, and governance systems. It is easy to see those pictured as compromised; but the real power lies beyond the frame with those taking photographs to document their victories.

Bamako, a small village, was captured and named the capital of the French Sudan in 1908, quickly growing in size and influence. The city's strategic location on the Niger River enabled Bamako to become an inter-

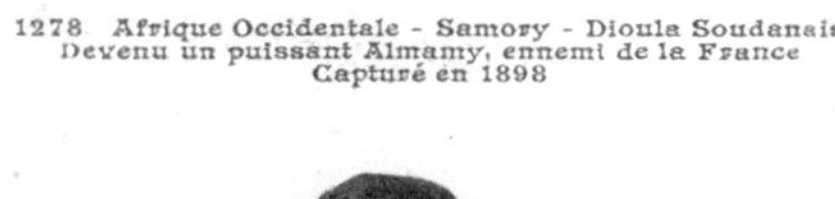

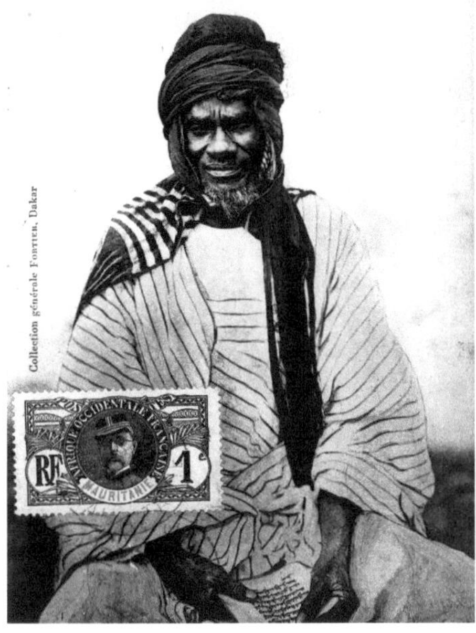

Figure 1.3. Samory Touré, postcard, 1898. Collection Générale Fortier.

mediary between the distant Atlantic and the "desert port" of Timbuktu in the east, and the city prospered from its location as a center of trade, especially once the railroad to Dakar, with its seaport, was begun in 1904—built, like most colonial endeavors, by forced labor, which ended in 1946. Because of the Great Depression, which affected the African colonies even more harshly than France—made worse by the fact that the French refused to acknowledge the effect of the failing world economy in their African colonies—the 1930s were years of poverty, and rapid urbanization and growth occurred in Bamako as the city attracted rural workers from surrounding areas. The first photography studios were opened in this decade when the city's population was booming. Photographer Seydou Keïta and scholar Manthia Diawara have both noted the opportune location of Keïta's studio near the railroad, a marker of modernity and urbanity that ushered in foreign travelers and new ideas, ensuring a continuous supply of clients in addition to local sitters.

As studio photography in the French Sudan was born under colonial rule, photographers necessarily had close relationships to the white colonists. Although itinerant portrait photography may have begun earlier, the Frenchman Pierre Garnier opened Bamako's first studio, Photo-Hall Soudanais, in

1935. Tanya Elder describes the business as a store that sold photographic materials and as a printing center for other photographers.[22] Garnier was just fifteen years old and fluent in Bamanankan, and after five years, he began to hire young African photographers to work for him. Photographers Youssouf Traoré, Mountaga Dembélé, and Seydou Keïta were among Garnier's employees.[23]

Dembélé began photographing in 1935, the same year that Garnier opened his studio, and eventually became the first African photographer to open a studio in Bamako.[24] Like many photographers of his generation, he performed military service during World War II, when the French conscripted Sudanese soldiers, called Tirailleurs Sénegalais, to fight in special battalions. Traveling overseas during the war gave many photographers the opportunity to learn new techniques in France and exposed them to new technologies. On a larger scale, Africa's participation in World War II also brought about the independence and liberation movements, as African soldiers threw off the mind-set of inferiority instilled by a colonial education as they noted that their fighting abilities equaled or excelled those of the Europeans. Africans also were bitterly aware of the contradiction in fighting to liberate France from the Nazis in order to return themselves to colonial servitude.

Dembélé returned to Bamako in 1945 and continued his profession as a teacher of primary school education. Unfortunately, most of his negatives are lost, but a surviving picture suggests that Dembélé likely pioneered in Bamako the patterned, fashionably modern type of backdrop for which Keïta became internationally famous (fig. 1.4).[25] As it was for Dembélé, photography was a sideline career for most of the first generation of African photographers in Bamako, including Keïta, who was also a furniture maker.

Like their clientele, the photographers themselves generally came from the newly elite classes. They had connections with either the colonial administration or the army and came from wealthy families. Elder notes, "In most cases they [photographers] were literate and incorporated into the colonial administrative structure, as teachers or functionaries."[26] Many had been educated by the "White Fathers," a sect of Catholic missionaries. A few Sudanese photographers even worked for the colonial police and thus were deeply implicated within the colonial system. (Keïta eventually worked for the police, but after Mali's independence.) The class system that developed under colonialism reversed former hierarchies—elite families sent slaves or outcast children to colonial schools out of distrust; but these boys became the men with the most education and thus the most power to advance in the colonial hierarchy. Education turned out to be the path to liberation.

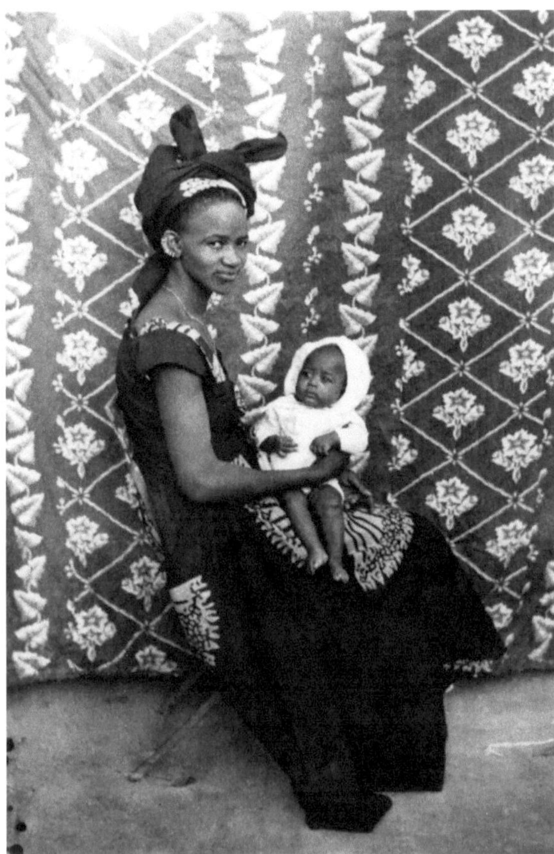

Figure 1.4. Mountaga Dembélé, Untitled, Bamako, ca. 1940. Courtesy of Érika Nimis.

Electricity was not common everywhere, so photographers had to come up with ingenious ways of printing and developing. Keïta said that when he went to take identity photos in the bush, he would rig up a system with a kerosene lamp to do his printing.[27] Photographers would often also use a printing frame, making use of Mali's strong and consistent sunlight to create contact prints directly from negatives, and Elder notes that photographers also used lamps and bicycle dynamos (generators) as light sources.[28]

According to Dembélé, Garnier worried about competition and would not allow his employees into the darkroom to observe his techniques.[29] This anecdote highlights the fraught nature of the relationship between colonizer and colonized—the colonizer is both dependent on but distrustful of those under his power, recognizing the imbalance that underlies every relationship. Keïta remarked in an interview with Lamunière that he learned some useful tips from Garnier, and in another interview with Magnin, credited Garnier with active interest in helping him learn certain techniques of photographing.[30] Dembélé created a darkroom for himself with equipment brought back from France, and several years later he taught Keïta how to print.[31] In 1948 Keïta began printing for them both at Dembélé's house.

To ensure enough light for a portrait, photographers posed their subjects outdoors, or in open-air courtyards. Backdrops were indispensable to create a "studio" setting, in the form of sheets of cloth held or tacked up against a wall. Keïta's "studio" was actually his courtyard, and his first backdrop was his bedspread. Indeed, his works can be dated by his backdrops, as he used only a single cloth for several years at a time. Until the mid-1950s, photographers used box cameras with glass negatives, from which they made direct one-to-one contact prints, resulting in small but detailed pictures. According to Elder, reflex cameras began to replace the box cameras in the early 1950s.

The first portrait photographs in Mali were exciting events, generating an audience who gathered around to watch the photographer at work, as in a photograph by Angolan-born Antoine Freitas in Belgian Congo (now Democratic Republic of Congo, or DRC), taken in 1939 (fig. 1.5).[32] While the viewer of the portrait sees in the final result only the subjects of the photograph, removed from the courtyard or village context through the use of the sheet backdrop, the invisible crowd outside the frame emphasizes the social nature of the occasion, as well as its importance. The act of having a portrait taken becomes a performance for an audience, highlighting the necessity of retaining one's dignity in front of a crowd of people. The process of having a photograph taken becomes as important as the final result and thus is somewhat akin to traditional arts, which usually operate in a performative context. Christraud Geary corrobates that in West Africa, "these outside settings were mostly public—the photographer and sitter surrounded by curious onlookers. . . . The sessions became performances for the camera *and* the onlookers. The photographic ritual would unfold under the close scrutiny of spectators, not as a solitary encounter between photographer and client."[33] This emphasis on the social and communal process of studio photography is one of the ways in which a Malian approach to photography differs from an American modernist approach, which focuses on the print as the "final product" and ultimate goal of the event.

Keïta, of Malinke ethnicity, was one of a handful of photographers working in Bamako when he opened his studio near the railroad in 1948. He was trained as a furniture-maker, but took up photography when an uncle brought a Kodak Brownie back from a trip to Senegal. It seems likely that his

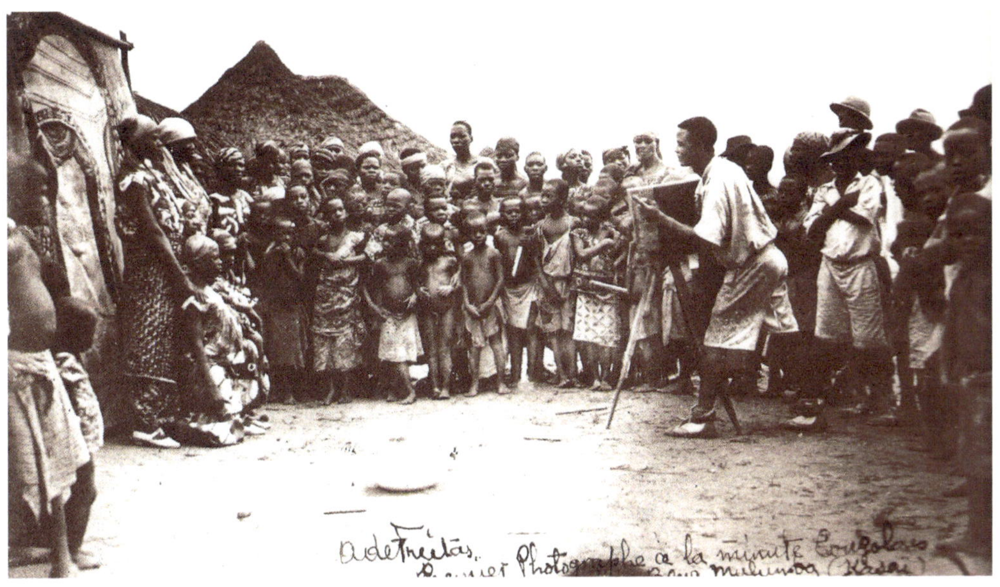

Figure 1.5. Antoine Freitas, *Untitled, Democratic Republic of Congo, Premiere Photographe à la minute Congolais, Bena Mulumba, Kasaï* (*First One Minute Congolese Photograph, Bena Mulumba, Kasaï Province*), 1939.

training in woodworking, which requires a creative, well-practiced eye, manual dexterity, and fine attention to detail, contributed to his skill as a photographer. Still, photography remained a sideline for another decade, as he continued to make furniture for ten years while working as a photographer.

Like Dembélé, Keïta served an African clientele, photographing the wealthy elite and those who worked in the colonial administration in the early 1950s. As photography became more popular and affordable, it spread to the bourgeoisie and to petty administrators, but "it still remained a luxury, primarily synonymous with social success."[34] The French colonial policy of "assimilation," Mahmood Mamdani notes, was only another form of coercion; while France did allow certain educated African men to become citizens, with equal rights to French men, rather than subjects or *paysans* (peasants politically at the mercy of colonial administrators' whims), the numbers were very few; becoming an *evolué* (literally, an "evolved" man) was an impossibility for the majority of the population of French Sudan until quite late in the 1950s.[35] By this time photography had become more affordable for the middle class; Keïta recalled that sometimes over a hundred people lined up to have their pictures taken on Saturdays, which shows the popularity of this new medium.

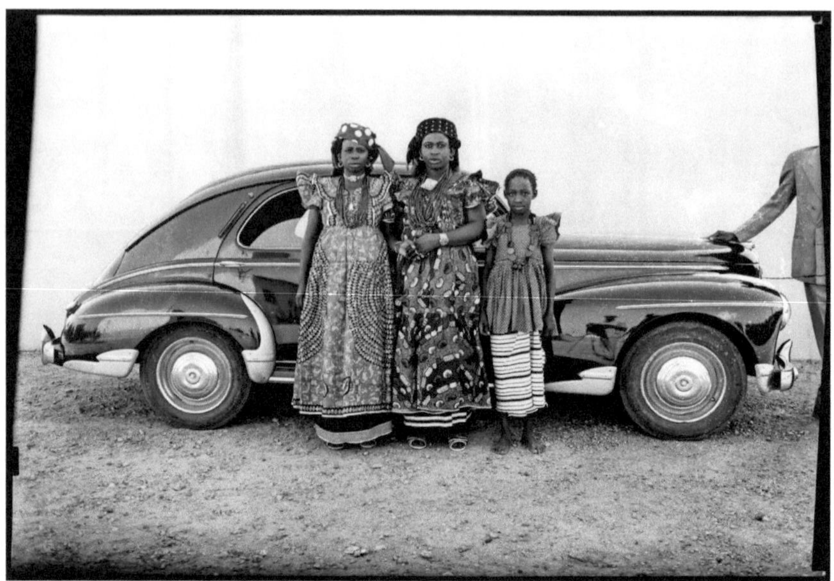

Figure 1.6. Seydou Keïta, Untitled. Modern gelatin silver print, May 21, 1954 (Previously credited 1949/51 by CAAC). Courtesy of CAAC—The Pigozzi Collection. © Seydou Keïta / SKPEAC.

By the mid-1950s, the colonial edifice was cracking. World War II had left France weakened; moreover, Africans' experience in the war belied the colonizers' assertion that they were unequal, and the irony of fighting against Germany for the freedom of French citizens was not lost upon them. In 1956, France gave the French Sudan and other colonies in West Africa limited self-governance. Most of Keïta's pictures were taken in the last decade of colonial rule and portrayed his subjects in dignified, often solemn poses, dressed up for the occasion, sometimes utilizing props owned by Keïta himself or bringing in their own sewing machines, bicycles, goats, or other valuable and prestigious items (fig. 1.6).

According to Manthia Diawara, Keïta's portraits visually reinforced the creation of a new and cosmopolitan identity: the Bamakois.[36] The various ethnic identities among the *métis* population in Bamako, composed of people who had come from all over the country for work, were fused into a new, urban, and modern identity. As much a bourgeois wish fulfillment created through props, pose, backdrop, and lighting as a reality, the Bamakois identity can be viewed as a kind of collective urban social imaginary, a simultaneous embrace of tradition and modernity performed by aspiring citizens in a dignified subversion of the colonial gaze (fig. 1.7).[37]

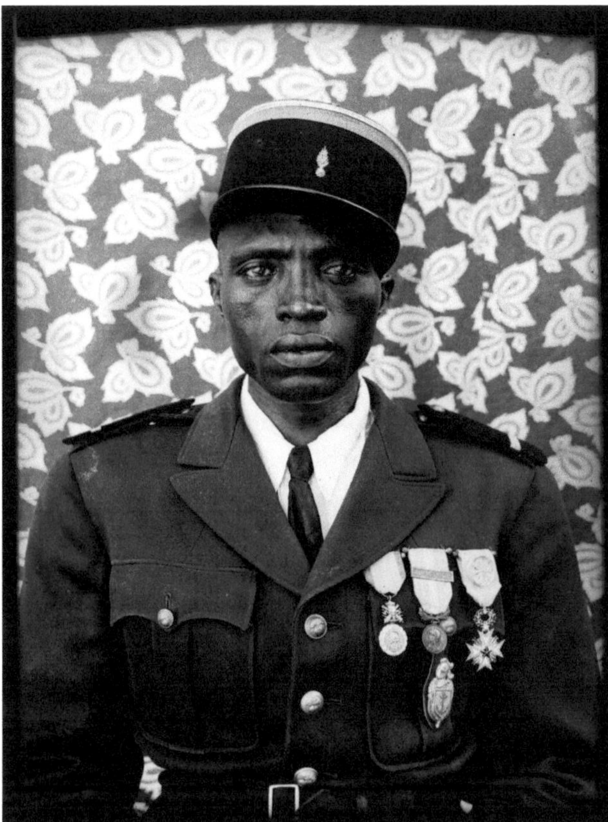

Figure 1.7. Seydou Keïta, Untitled (*Soldat avec ses medailles* [*Soldier with His Medals*]). Modern gelatin silver print, 1958. Courtesy of CAAC—The Pigozzi Collection. © Seydou Keïta / SKPEAC.

Yet Diawara's analysis does not explain the force of what Arjun Appadurai calls the "visual decolonization" of Seydou Keïta's and other studio photographers' portraits.[38] In the context of colonial-era French Sudan, Keïta's photographs constitute a form of visual resistance to colonialism. Amilcar Cabral writes: "For, with a strong indigenous cultural life, foreign domination cannot be sure of its perpetuation. At any moment, depending on internal and external factors determining the evolution of the society in question, cultural resistance (indestructible) may take on new forms (political, economic, armed) in order fully to contest foreign domination."[39]

As a new cultural form of resistance, Keïta's photographs marry Mande aesthetics with the modern technology of portrait photography to create images of people who visibly embody the decolonizing mentality that Malian activist Modibo Keïta, Mali's future president, called for through reference to the philosophy of Négritude.[40] It is not that every individual is thinking of liberation and posterity at the moment the photograph was taken.

It is that this practice *was creating a visual history of resistance*; history was being created, as well as recorded, every time a person had her photograph taken, because of the collaboration between the sitter and the photographer in the creation of pictures that followed the aesthetic principles of Mande arts. Especially because the portraits project into the near future as desired personas that don't yet exist, with props contributing to the fulfillment of a professional or personal embodiment within the image, studio portraits project a sense of liberation into the future that became an actual history of independence.

Keïta's portraits constitute a form of image resistance that circulated socially and in the visual imaginary. More than simply an urban Bamakois imaginary, this projection reached back to past traditions by incorporating a fully embodied connection to precolonial heritage, created by Keïta and his clients in collaboration through a layered inclusion of key tenets of Mande aesthetics. The habitus of Keïta's subjects shows the very pride in oneself, in one's beauty, and an optimism for the future that are integral to Mande notions of character and personhood.[41]

Rather than emphasizing modern art's strong distinction between original and copy, with its privileging of "originality" and its negative judgment of "copy" (although this distinction arguably has been eroded in postmodern art), Mande aesthetics can be understood as a dynamic interplay of form and embellishment, which essentially takes the form of a theme and its variation, an aesthetic form also seen in Mande music, which is polyrhythmic. In regard to oral storytelling traditions in Ghana, Jack Goody writes, "It is not simply that there is an absence of sanctions against deviation from the original, but rather that the whole concept of original is out of place."[42] In many cases aesthetic forms are passed down over generations, although they are also reinterpreted each time they are performed. Mary Jo Arnoldi explains that masquerade puppet theater, a rural form of secular entertainment, encompassing ritual agricultural celebrations, moral instruction, and social commentary, utilizes these ideas, both in the notions of *jayan* and *jako* (cultural form and embellishment) and in the similar aesthetic construct of *nyi* and *di* (goodness and tastiness), which apply to the basic form (good) and its embellishment (tasty).[43] Arnoldi supports and confirms the arguments of James Brink, who writes "that these two dimensions of form are complementary and that they establish through their reciprocal relations an aesthetic dynamic or dialectic, one whose circuitry is not unlike that which is implied in the relationship between a theme and its variation or a topic and its comment, for example."[44] Brink goes on to explain: "Managing the interplay between these two dimensions of form, that is, initiating and sustaining resonance between expression which is 'good' and expression which is 'tasty' is, for Bamana, what imbues form with transforming power, its capacity for creating valued existential states. The Bamana theory or ideology of aesthetic form, then, can be expressed as the managing of interplay between shape-defining features of 'goodness' and shape-exploiting features of 'tastiness' in an effort to create and control socially valued, efficacious power. More succinctly, art for Bamana is form managing power."[45]

If Bamana aesthetic theory is applied to studio photography, then the backdrop and the forward-facing client in a black-and-white film photograph would constitute the "theme" or the "goodness of the theme"—the static or constant form—whereas the individual's features and clothing, props and pose, the close-up or full-length view, as well as the overall look of the photograph when influenced by wind and lighting conditions, would provide the "tastiness" that embellishes the good form—its variation. But according to Candace Keller, based on interviews conducted in the 2000s, photographers do not utilize these aesthetic terms to discuss photographs.[46] The terms that Keller noticed in common usage are *jɛya* (clarity and lighting), *màsiri* (decoration), *nyègen* (pattern and adornment), and *dìbi* (darkness, obscurity).[47] Jɛya and dìbi—light and shadow—are integral concepts to black-and-white photography as a medium. Pattern and decoration conform more specifically to Mande interests in textiles, greatly admired for their patterns, while "decoration" seems close to "embellishment" in aesthetic judgment (fig. 1.8). The fact that jayan and jako are not used as *explicit* terms in discussion about photography does not mean that *form* and *embellishment* are not useful or operative concepts, however. The terms that Arnoldi, Brink, and McNaughton use are compatible in meaning with Keller's terms. Keller implies as much when she notes, "The aesthetic principles of *jɛya* and *dìbi* operate in and express tension, that is, the conceptual, physical, and visual tension between clarity and obscurity, stability and motion, *structure and embellishment*" (my emphasis).[48] Further following Arnoldi and colleagues, Keller explains, "Generally, a successful combination of these elements attains an aesthetic goal expressed as *nyi* (goodness), realized in the phrase *a ka nyi* ('It is good')."[49] Speaking more broadly, the aesthetic of repetition and variation, form and embellishment, is substantially documented in structuring music, poetry, and storytelling in Mande cultures. An appreciation of rich and complex patterns can be seen simply by looking at women's fashions. Complexity of meaning and the combination of long-held traditions with modern innovations are similarly legible in Mande cultural forms, as

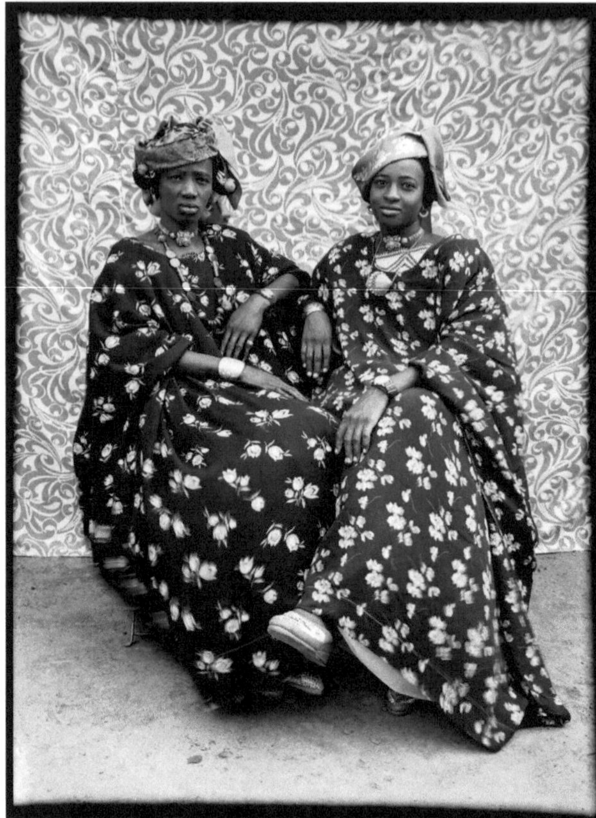

Figure 1.8. Seydou Keïta, Untitled. Modern gelatin silver print, 1956. Courtesy of CAAC—The Pigozzi Collection. © Seydou Keïta / SKPEAC.

can be seen in Tal Tamari's analysis of a 2002 urban praise song that combined aspects of modern innovation (French and English words, for example) with traditional forms.[50]

It is clear from looking at hundreds of photographs that such aesthetic interests are prevalent in Keïta's portraits. His use for several years of the same patterned backdrop, which contrasts with the individual patterns of a sitter's clothing, hairstyle, jewelry, and other accoutrements, can be seen as creating a highly desirable aesthetic, encompassing both continuity and variation (fig. 1.9). The backdrop removes the subject from banal reality and places him or her in a space connected to modern culture—namely, the constructed photograph—through one of its most distinctive visual effects: pattern. Sometimes wind creates a billow in the backdrop that shifts the effect of dark and light, adding a sense of movement, creating a flow of disrupted pattern and obscuring visual information.[51] The backdrop thus contrasts with the Western notion of photography's "truth function," what Chris-

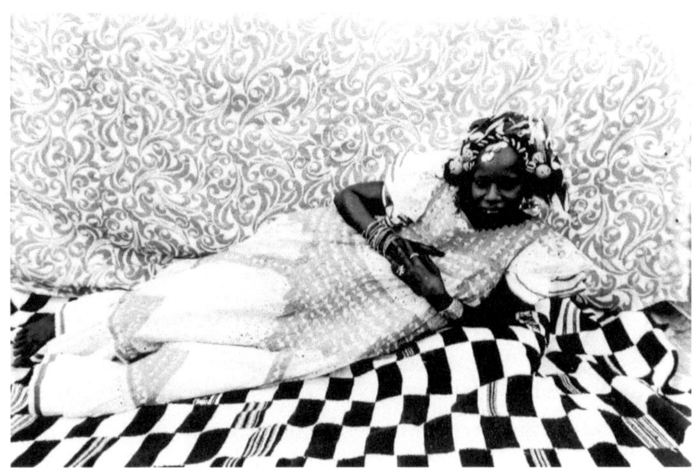

Figure 1.9. Seydou Keïta, Untitled. Modern gelatin silver print, 1956/57, dated by arabesque backdrop.

topher Pinney describes as colonialism's desire to create a fixed "truthful" certainty duly reported by the camera's lens.[52] This "truth function" is countered as well through the use of props and an emphasis on a future wish fulfillment in presenting the person's most beautiful self for the camera; all of this creates an anticolonial resistance of the imaginary.[53]

Keïta's photographs also exhibit Mande aesthetics in their fondness for visual asymmetry within a fairly harmonious or balanced formal composition. Monni Adams has commented on the West African preference for asymmetry in textile designs; likewise Keller has noted Keïta's and Sidibé's preference for asymmetry.[54] This asymmetry is not just inherent in the photographs but also energizes the fashions of the sitters themselves, particularly the women. Often one side of a woman's dress hangs or is pulled off of her shoulder; one side of her head wrap rises higher than the other (which is inevitable in the way that the cloth is wrapped), and jewelry is often worn asymmetrically in braided or styled hair. It is this Mande aesthetic of theme and variation, encompassing slight rhythmic changes, subtle differences, pattern, asymmetry, goodness and tastiness, clarity and darkness or obscurity, that gives these photographs their new cultural forms, to return to Cabral's argument.

It is through asymmetry and careful attention to decoration that women bring their Mande aesthetics to the portrait, in collaboration with the photographer. The fact that a large proportion of the clients are women makes a gendered reading of studio photography impossible to ignore.[55] When one considers both how these photographs were commissioned and collaborated on, as well as their impact on Malian social life and in the international art world decades later, the focus on an aesthetic of proud, beautiful women—be they young or old, married or single, cowives or sisters, mothers, grandmothers, or girls—made in collaboration with the photographer, underscores the importance of women in Malian society despite women's lack of legal or official power. As women, more than men, tend to carry the aesthetic burden of meaning-making in Mali, *what does it mean that women were collaborating with the photographer in the making of their own image?*[56] There is more power granted to *women* in these photographs than has been acknowleged; Teju Cole highlights this aspect in his review of the works of Keïta, Sidibé, and Ojeikere.[57]

In addition to Mande visual aesthetics, Keller has argued that the Mande social concepts of fadenya and badenya are aesthetically visible in Keïta's and Sidibé's portrait photographs.[58] Fadenya and badenya are concepts derived from the practice of polygamy and its effects on familial relations.[59] Badenya (translated as "mother-childness," derived from the relationship of one full sibling to another) embodies the social behaviors of cooperation, agreement, and stability. Fadenya ("father-childness," which connotes the spirit of competition between siblings with different mothers who must compete for their father's attention) connotes instability in society—the forces of competition, envy, and self-promotion. The tension between badenya and fadenya "should not be understood as a polar opposition, but rather as the intersection of two axes: the axis of individuality . . . and the axis of group affiliation."[60] According to Bird and Kendall, Mande society is relatively static and stable, as the forces of *baden* prevail and provide group cohesion. However, the community also relies on the actions of the "hero," an individual who breaks with traditional societal rules, to protect and save the society in times of trouble, and thus depends also on fostering fadenya among its young men.[61] The mixture of these contrasting ideas can be seen, for example, in a photograph by Keïta of two cowives shown sitting together with their presumably *faden* children, wearing matching dresses made from a Dutch-wax fabric print called "The Jealous Dark-Eyes of My Cowife"; the fabric's faden message belies the multiple effects of baden conveyed in the decision to have the same dress tailored in the same fabric and then to wear it together for the portrait (fig. 1.10).

If badenya, or the principle of mother-childness or social harmony, translates into social capital, as Stephen Wooten argues, Keïta's photographs served as conveyors of badenya when they circulated among friends and were shown and viewed in frames on the wall or stored in albums, to be appreciated by family and friends on special occasions.[62] Most commercial

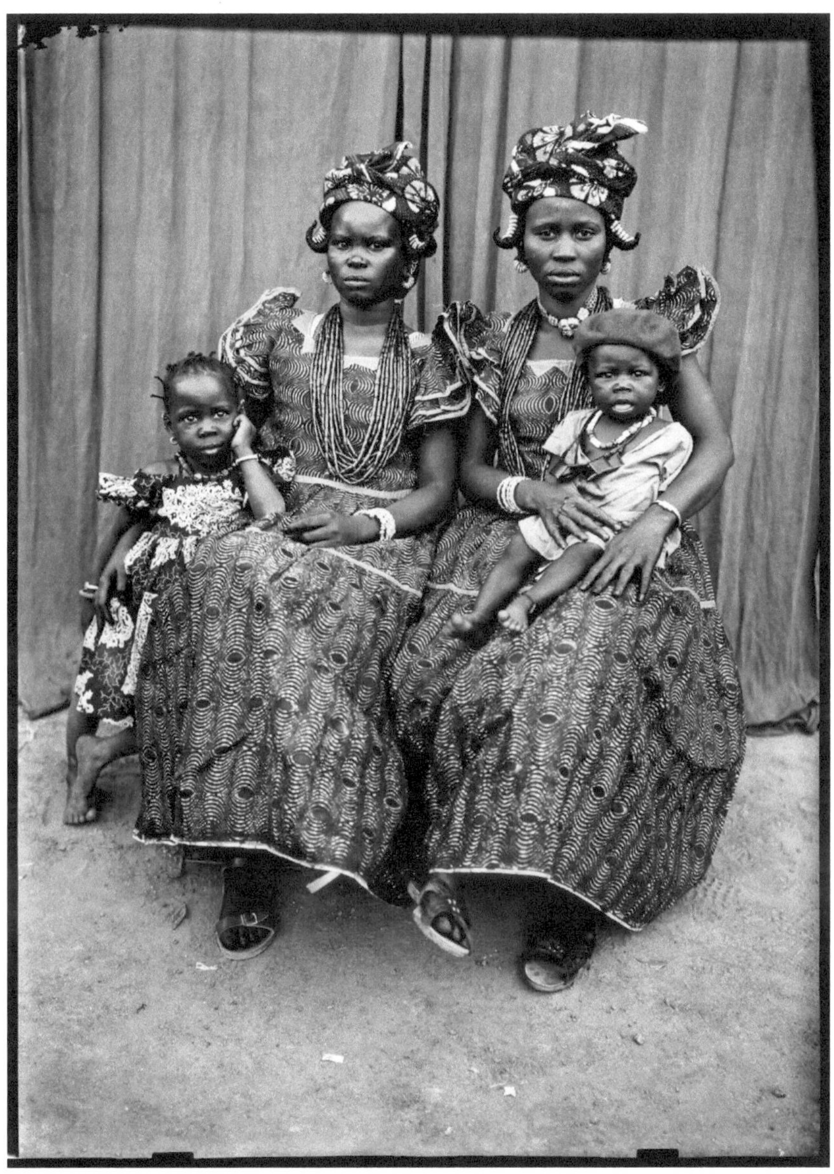

Figure 1.10. Seydou Keïta, Untitled (women wearing fabric pattern called "The Jealous Dark Eyes of My Cowife"), 1952/1955. Modern gelatin silver print. Courtesy of CAAC—The Pigozzi Collection. © Seydou Keïta / SKPEAC.

portrait photographs have always been first concerned with social connections and personal memory; Geoffrey Batchen notes that all vernacular photographs are "animated by a social dimension, a dynamic web of exchanges and functions."[63] In Mali, the social dimension of the photograph is particularly high, because Malian society operates with a very high quotient of what social scientists call "social capital."

According to David Halpern, social capital embodies "social networks and the norms and sanctions that govern their character. It is valued for its potential to facilitate individual and community action, especially through the solution of collective action problems."[64] Complex kinship ties (such as *cousinage*, the relationship between families that are considered "joking cousins," who are required to help each other in times of trouble and forbidden to do violence to each other), caste interdependencies, and a long history of interethnic interaction in a harsh geographic environment have created a culture where people depend on each other for help and support to a high degree.[65] In Mali there is a noted emphasis on talking and conversation as a way to solve problems, which stems from precolonial socially structured associations.

Studio photography can be understood as a way of reinforcing social capital, especially in considering the whole process, from the beginning of a picture's creation when clients engage the photographer, to the continued function of the photograph after it is taken. In fact, studio portrait photography is literally called "social photography" in Mali. Studio pictures commemorate religious occasions, celebrations, and outings, and document gatherings of family, friends, coworkers, and clubs. Women were a particularly enthusiastic clientele, often having portraits taken to record and display new hairstyles, outfits, and adornments. Social connections of all kinds were also useful to photographers in learning and keeping up their trade. Photographers had to use familial and personal contacts in order to acquire cameras, equipment, and information from travels abroad.[66]

The photograph's life after it was taken continued to further social capital. Photographs were usually printed as one-to-one contact prints, at small sizes, and were hung on walls, kept in albums at home, shown to guests, and sent back to families in faraway villages as tokens of familial connections and cosmopolitan aspirations. (The connections between urban and rural populations are often particularly strong in African cities like Bamako. In fact, people in Bamako who are from the same village often create clubs to help support the village.)[67] Sending photographs to those back home strengthens that relationship by sharing an urban experience with those in the village.

Through the exchange or shared viewing of such photographs, the relationships depicted are reinforced through shared memories.[68] Mutual emotional dependency is increased and familial or friendship ties are self-reflexively strengthened through the very act of depicting and memorializing the relationship. Thus, the process of having pictures taken and viewed results in an increase of social capital among the participants, and emphasizes the process-oriented nature of photography in Mali.

As a vernacular, common practice, Keïta's photographs arguably embody an "everyday" aesthetic, which McNaughton suggests is crucial to Malian social and artistic life; one that is reliant on people's dress and fashion, but one that also takes those fashionable elements and reinvents them through the medium of photography.[69] "Know yourself" is an important maxim in Mali: have moral and social dignity; know your limits and your strengths. One senses that the people in Keïta's photographs do know themselves; one senses it in their poses and gazes, in their choices of props, and their willingness to collaborate with the photographer. Especially with older people one can see this, and this is Keïta's aesthetic: he enables his clients to achieve that dignity through his pose and camera angle. While some scholars want to diminish the achievement of Keïta because so many other photographers were working at that time across Africa, it must be acknowledged that he was a brilliant, creative, and technically skilled photographer, who could not only capture Mali aesthetics and fashion but overlay his pictures with his own aesthetic eye, which resonates internationally.

What was life like for the couple in Keïta's portrait taken in Bamako in the 1950s and exhibited in 1991 in New York City? Independence was not a certainty, but was in the air, reaching from a group of university-trained elites in the 1930s to a much broader population in the 1950s, borne on the wings of Négritudinal aspirations but also associated with the French Communist Party. By 1956, forced labor had been banned and universal voting rights granted.[70] Frederick Cooper notes that a railway worker in the French Sudan might have the same workweek and benefits as one in France, although for peasants in Mali the situation was very different. The French policy of assimilation, nominal for so many for so long, was being put into practice, as French control over its African colonies declined. If the man in Keïta's portrait was a public worker or a wage worker, by now he would perhaps have a forty-hour workweek, complete with vacation pay and benefits. He might speak French, while the woman in the picture probably speaks a local language, perhaps Bamanankan. It is no wonder that many newly middle-class citizens flocked to Keïta's studio to have their portraits taken.

For the economic classes—workers and elites—who could afford to visit his studio, this was a time of relative affluence and optimism for independence at the end of colonial domination.

While photography spread more slowly to the rest of rural Mali, often arriving with missionaries, a number of photographers worked throughout Mali in the 1950s and '60s. The Bamako Biennale has been instrumental in attempting to oppose the perception of Seydou Keïta as the singular African studio photographer. Indeed, the second and third editions of the biennale, held in 1996 and 1998, respectively, showcased Malian studioists who had worked in the smaller cities of Mopti, Kayes, Kita, Sègou, Timbuktu, and Gao, including several Yoruba photographers from Nigeria who relocated to Mopti and opened studios in the 1960s and 1970s.[71] Félix Diallo (1931–1997), born in a mission in Kita, opened the town's first studio in 1955. According to him, this was a challenge; as "nobody knew what photography was in Kita in 1955, mothers did not want their children to be photographed."[72] In the same year, two brothers, Hassana Traoré (1930–1985) and Housseyni Traoré (1930–1996), began working as reporters in Mopti, Mali's second-largest city, and opened a studio in 1960. Elder lists four photographers working in Ségou alone. Their professions show their colonial, bureaucratic ties: Bogoba Coulibaly worked at the mayor's office; Amadou Toumani was employed at the post office; Gaoussou Sissoko worked in the Office du Niger (a colonial government office) as an accountant; and Mountaga Kouyaté was a teacher.[73]

Another photographer working in Bamako who has been exhibited and published posthumously was Abdourahmane Sakaly (1926–1988).[74] Sakaly was born in St. Louis, Senegal, of Moroccan parents, and he may have learned photography in the venerated studios of Meïssa Gaye and Amadou "Mix" Gueye.[75] Sakaly relocated to Bamako, opening his own studio there in 1956, and he continued to work until his death in 1988. Although Sakaly opened his studio during Keïta's time, his production span is more concurrent with that of Malick Sidibé, who opened a studio in 1962. Sakaly's North African lineage, and the fact that he was from St. Louis, where a racially stratified creole society had developed since the 1600s, may have given him a higher status than Keïta among the French colonials and the upper stratified society. Malick Sidibé has noted that Sakaly had "a certain class about him. He mainly photographed banquets in the big hotels, big receptions, and high-society parties and evenings."[76]

While France was so depleted by World War II that it granted *political* independence, it deliberately hoped to maintain its colonies' *economic depen-*

dence. Some scholars thus argue that imperialism ended with independence in name only: France's power simply became more diffuse, but just as pervasive. However, this view downplays the effect of independence on people's psyches; as Glissant notes, it is first the imagination that needs to be activated in order to produce change.[77] It was an exciting time, not least because the future seemed open to possibilities previously undreamed of except by a few. The freedom from colonial tyranny also carried very significant realities, even if those freedoms were soon quashed by Mali's communist dictatorship. Caught up in the decolonization movement sweeping West and North Africa, Mali won its political independence in 1960, joining neighboring Senegal in the Mali Federation, which ended within the year when relations between the two countries soured. Mali's new president, Modibo Keïta, had been a leader in the liberation movement. He turned away from Senegal's president, Leopold Sédar Senghor, with his philosophy of Négritude, because of Senghor's close ties to France.[78] Mali condemned France's Algerian War (1954–1962) and was unhappy with the fact that France still had 2,200 soldiers stationed in Mali, which shares a long desert border with Algeria.[79] President Keïta, long a member of the Communist Party, instead looked to socialism and the USSR and instituted a one-party Marxist state.

But the road to nation-building was rocky. African governments faced a paradoxical situation: on the one hand, their only experience as a nation was of a colonial government; on the other hand, that government had been designed to oppress and exploit. To find another form of government is the challenge of all new nations, and Davidson notes that for many it goes badly. One of President Keïta's early and unpopular moves, in order to become economically independent of France, was to localize the currency, inaugurating the Malian franc in place of the French-backed West African franc. This decision caused a great deal of economic hardship in Mali and immediately created protests from merchants involved in regional trade. Smuggling and trade on the black market ensued. President Keïta was a harsh leader and brooked no dissent. According to Pascal James Imperato, "When the people of the Bambara village of Sakoiba protested against his policies, its inhabitants were arrested, others invited to take their possessions, and the village physically leveled to the ground."[80] The Tuareg rebellion of 1961 was also dealt with in a brutal fashion, as the army subdued the Tuareg through aerial bombardments and by poisoning the desert wells.[81] Under his regime, rampant corruption flourished and there was starvation in the North.

In 1967 President Keïta turned back to France, signing monetary accords to bolster the Malian franc. Afraid that the liaison was hurting his socialist reputation, President Keïta revived the Popular Militia to root out government corruption; the militia was composed of thirty thousand young men who "manned roadblocks, conducted searches of home and person at will, detained many on the least pretext, and engaged in torture."[82] By 1968, discontent was widespread in Mali under Keïta's repressive dictatorship. The army removed President Keïta from office in a virtually bloodless coup and took control over the state and its apparatus, installing as leader a young lieutenant, Moussa Traoré, who ruled as dictator until the coup of 1991, which led to democratic rule.

After independence, photography blossomed in Mali as cameras became cheaper to acquire. A number of older photographers in Mali today, like many of the senior professors of arts at the National Institute of the Arts in Bamako, were trained in the USSR, or in Soviet-bloc countries like Poland or the German Democratic Republic.[83] According to Elder, returning Malian students brought back cameras from the USSR to sell for profit. Malick Sidibé often acted as a business intermediary, buying cameras from students and selling them to photographers. Mountaga Dembélé notes that such cameras were not expensive at that time, so that many more people could now afford the technology.[84] Studios became more plentiful, a photographic press developed—ANIM (Agence Nationale d'Information Malienne)—and pictures of President Modibo Keïta and other state officials were displayed everywhere, as were shots of state functions such as banquets, inaugurations, and dances (fig. 1.11).[85] Leaders in West Africa wanted to modernize their countries and hoped to project an image of modernization through photography. Elder writes, "It was important to make the State and its representatives 'visually' accessible to the populace."[86] She notes that cars, modern architecture, men in modern clothing, foreigners, and parades were all popular subjects. *L'Essor*, still a widely read paper today and now available online, was the state-run daily, the only newspaper until the uprising in 1991. The images that circulated were heavily censored and ideological, so that, although photojournalism flourished under the new government, the notion that photographs depicted "reality" was understood to be questionable.

In the 1960s, Seydou Keïta closed his studio at the behest of the government and began to take pictures for the police.[87] Malick Sidibé opened his studio in 1962. In contrast to Keïta and Sakaly, many of Sidibé's early postindependence pictures leave behind the formal constraints of the studio. Instead, the photographer or his apprentices traveled to parties and outdoor picnics to capture a youth culture influenced by the groove of James Brown and the political notion of pan-Africanism.[88] As Manthia Diawara attests,

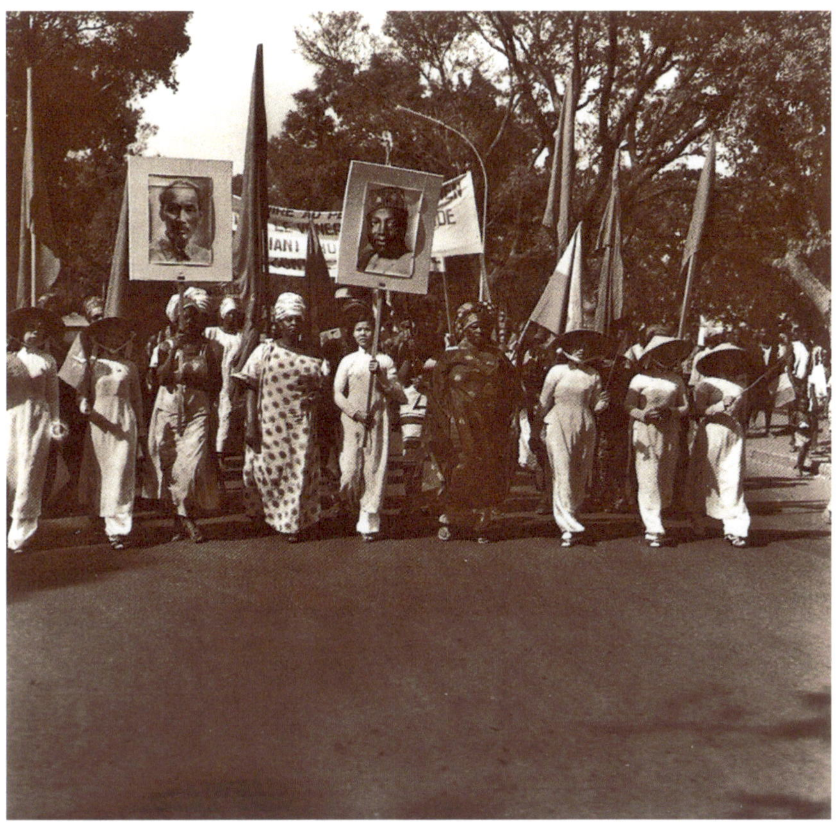

Figure 1.11. Agence Nationale d'Information Malienne (ANIM), *Malian and Vietnamese Women Parade in Bamako, ca. 1960, Holding Portraits of Modibo Keïta and Ho Chi Minh.*

the youth of Bamako downplayed ethnic affiliations, such as Bamana, Malinke, Hausa, or Fulani, in the spirit of a free and equal society united across Africa. Although young people in socialist Mali viewed American capitalism unfavorably, they identified with the American civil rights movement and the global youth culture of the late 1960s. Youths in Bamako mimicked the look and style of rock stars like James Brown, whose presence was spiritually invoked via his picture on record covers in Sidibé's photographs.[89] Keller has noted that the clothing styles and attitudes in Sidibé's pictures demonstrate a rebellion against the traditional aesthetics of older Bamakois, as well as the new curfews imposed by the socialist dictatorship.[90] Simon Njami writes that Malick Sidibé "does not simply express the joie de vivre and carefree attitude of this time, known as les années twist. His work is a

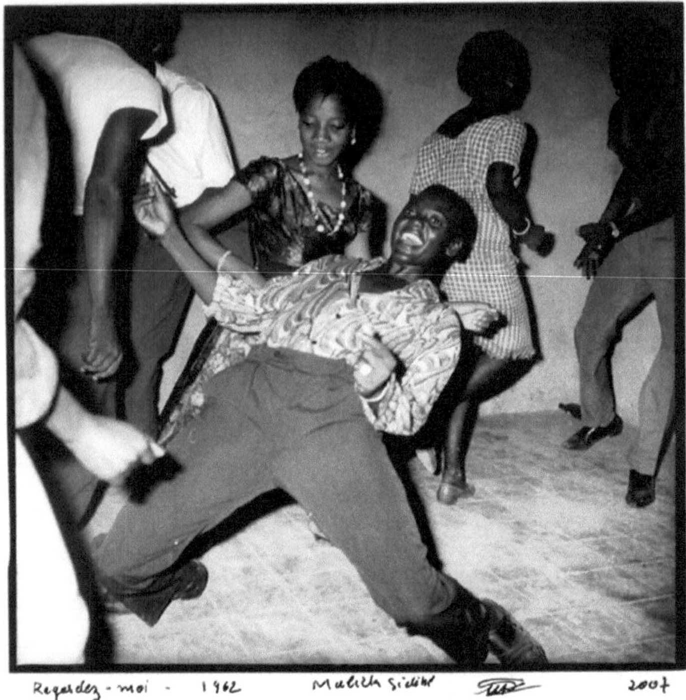

Figure 1.12. Malick Sidibé, *Regardez-moi (Look at Me)*, 1962.
Courtesy of the artist and Jack Shainman Gallery, New York.

living testimony to an epoch in which Africans believed that everything was possible."[91]

Regardez-moi (Look at Me!), a 1962 party shot by Sidibé or his studio, shows the energy and excitement that Diawara remembers (fig. 1.12). A man full of pizzazz in a deep backbend, feet wide and hands raised, grins in delight with the sheer physical audacity of his movement. A well-coiffed woman in a shiny, fitted bodice and long necklace turns smartly behind him, her bent elbow visually lining his outstretched arm, while other dancers are visible snapping fingers in encouragement. A couple in the back right of the frame create a complex set of interacting angles, their jewelry highlighted against their light wall in the background. The diagonal composition of the photograph creates dynamism and captures the essence of cool, while the title and figure display a bright fadenya aesthetic, emphasizing the central male figure as the center of the party. It's immediately clear why such photographs delighted admiring audiences in Paris and New York.

In-studio pictures by Sidibé also reveal the photographer's eye for energy

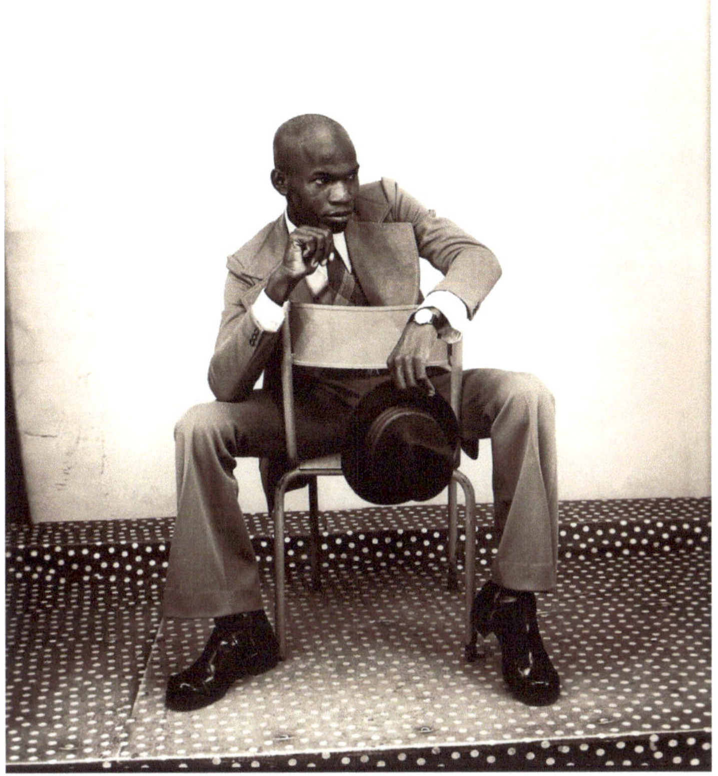

Figure 1.13. Malick Sidibé, *Amadou le tailleur modèle (Amadou the Tailor Model)*, 1981. © Malick Sidibé. Courtesy of Galerie MAGNIN-A, Paris.

and good humor (fig. 1.13). Sidibé's oft-used vertically striped backdrop gives a jazzy feel to his studio shots, and the young people who posed for him seem at ease, often grinning and proudly showing off their bell-bottoms, fancy hats, and scooters—the new styles and prestigious items of the 1960s and '70s. Their relaxed amusement and showy poses contrast sharply with Seydou Keïta's overtly formal, dignified portraits. As Diawara attests, Sidibé's aesthetic encompasses more of a diaspora aesthetic than Keïta's, because the fashions, album covers, and cinematic poses stem from the popular image culture of the international black diaspora. Sidibé's pictures also tend to emphasize more of a faden, or competitive, than a baden, or cooperative, aesthetic, because of the individualism inherent in this American-influenced diaspora aesthetic of youth, heralding the new world order after the end of colonial rule.

Although it was supposed to be transitional, the military rule of Moussa

Traoré lasted for eleven years, after which he engineered a transition to civilian rule with himself as president in 1979. Traoré retained socialism but relied even more heavily on France and the West for aid, badly needed when droughts in the 1970s and 1980s devastated crops and herds. The Tuareg especially suffered under the government's neglect, prompting an international outcry. The IMF and the World Bank became involved, requiring privatization and structural changes, and implementing financial policies that have since been shown to be disastrous. The US also donated a great deal of aid, and France eliminated some of Mali's debt. Student and teacher protests against the government began in 1979 and continued throughout the 1980s. In 1989, the fall of the Berlin Wall sent shudders across socialist Africa, and the student movement became more vociferous in its calls for change. In 1991 President Traoré was overthrown in a violent coup, and in 1992 Mali held free and open elections for a multiparty democracy. The lieutenant colonel who had led the coup, Amadou Toumani Touré (known as ATT), was the temporary president until the democratic elections of April 1992, and then he stepped down gracefully, ushering in a new era of democratic rule.

Major technological changes to photography occurred during Mali's socialist era, which contributed to the "deskilling" of photography. Studios began to work in color in the 1970s, which greatly diminished the quality of the pictures, as the color materials were of lesser quality. Photo-Kola was the first color lab to open in 1982, with Siriman Dembélé running the lab and keeping quality high. He soon left, however, to work in a lab in Burkina Faso, and Tokyo Color, which had opened in Bamako in 1983, quickly became the most prominent color lab.[92] The reliance on high-tech cameras and local color printing labs with poor facilities contributed to a lack of knowledge about lighting, proper composition, and the aesthetics of printing. While in the past, photographers like Keïta and Sidibé learned their craft working as printers or assistants to other photographers, the deskilling of photography has enabled photographers with no training to open up shop, working either in a studio or as itinerants, with a resulting decline of aesthetic specialization.

Today, digital is popular among younger photographers who can afford it. They use Photoshop-type programs to "fix" portraits by lightening skin and removing wrinkles, which used to be done by hand. Video is also popular, for weddings and other events. "Social" photography, or portrait photography and reportage, is still crucial to Bamako's culture, as the sheer number of photo studios dotting Bamako's streets attests.[93] But black-and-white photography is no longer practiced in most commercial studios, as customers desire color portraits and, increasingly, color videos of important events.

After the turn to democracy in 1991, opportunities for press photography expanded. The shift to democracy also created conditions that enabled Huguier, then working in Bamako, to conceive of an exhibition devoted to not only Malian, but African photography. With fellow French photojournalist Bernard Descamps and Malian photographers Alioune Bâ, Django Cissé, and Racine Keïta, Huguier organized the first biennale in 1994, two years after Alpha Oumar Konaré became Mali's second democratically elected president.[94] Konaré, a former president of the pan-African International Council of Museums (ICOM), held degrees in history and archaeology and was devoted to improving Mali's cultural institutions.[95] Konaré supported cultural developments and brought the problem of cultural preservation to international attention.[96] Culture, always important in Malian constructions of nationalist identity, became even more so after independence, and Konaré's projects reflected and contributed to this emphasis.[97] Konaré and his wife, Adame Ba Konaré, also placed great importance on national memory; such an interest would naturally include celebrating photography, with its close relationship to memory, through the advent of the biennales.[98] Unsurprisingly given the circumstances, the first Bamakois photographers to make "art photographs" were either portraitists or photojournalists, or they worked in photography in other professional capacities. For example, Cissé ran a photographic postcard business, Bâ worked as a photographer for the National Museum, and Racine Keïta worked for the television and film industry.

The first four biennales were held during Konaré's presidency, and with his support. Mali's political shift to democracy, and the stability and peace engendered by this transition, supported Bamako's development as a center for African photography. Western countries, particularly France and the United States, supported the transition to democracy and pressed for Mali's official abandonment of Soviet-bloc socialism. The US donated aid with strings attached, requiring that Mali continue to follow certain steps toward a functioning democracy and neoliberal economy. France, meanwhile, continued its neocolonial policy of cultural assimilation by financially supporting culture in Africa through its government office, Afrique en Créations, which funded the biennale. Democracy also provided greater opportunities for women, and thus for women photographers, especially once social worker Aminata Dembélé Bagayoko founded a photography school for women in 1996. The biennale survived the transition from Konaré's presidency to that of ATT, a former general, and has continued uninterrupted to the present,

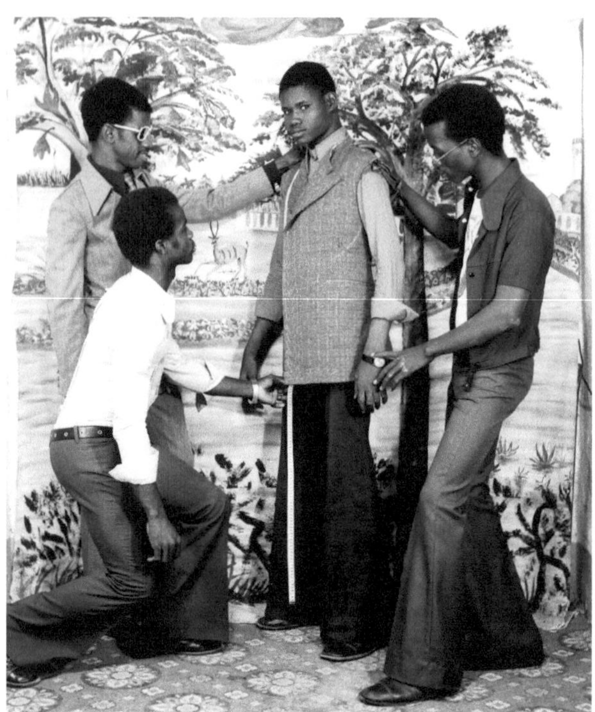

Figure 1.14. Hamidou Maïga, Untitled, 1973 (Tailoring, Studio Portrait, Bamako, 1970s). Gelatin silver print. Courtesy of the artist and Jack Bell Gallery, London.

Figure 1.15. Adama Kouyaté, *Ségou #19*, 1954. Gelatin silver print from negative, 2010. Courtesy of Galerie Jean Brolly, Paris.

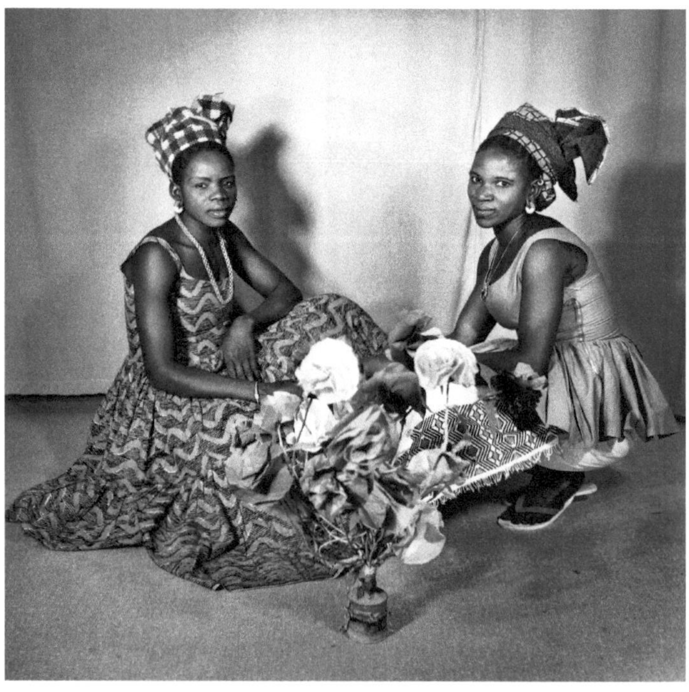

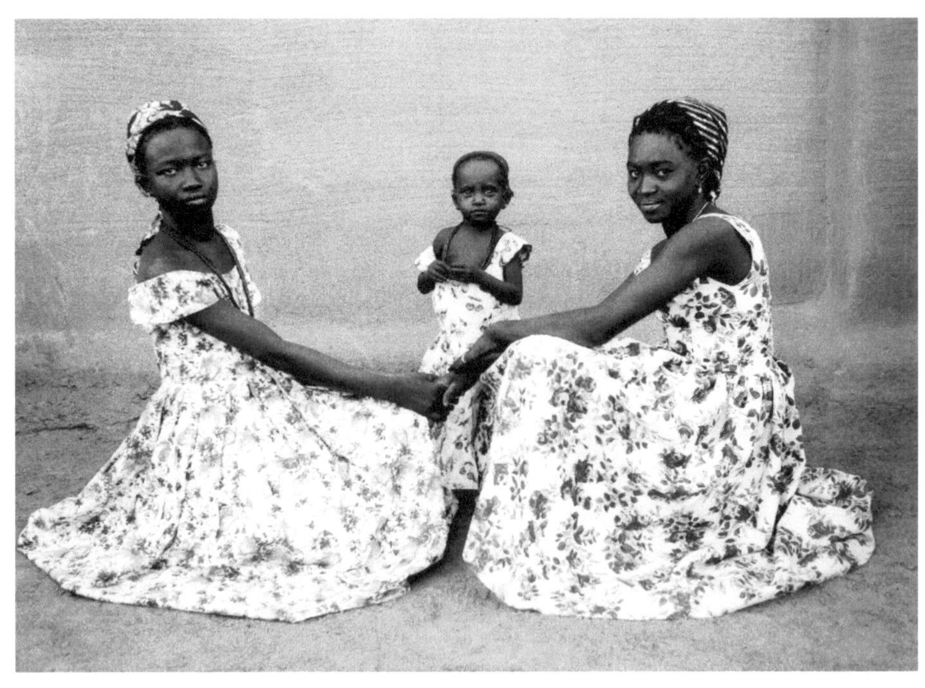

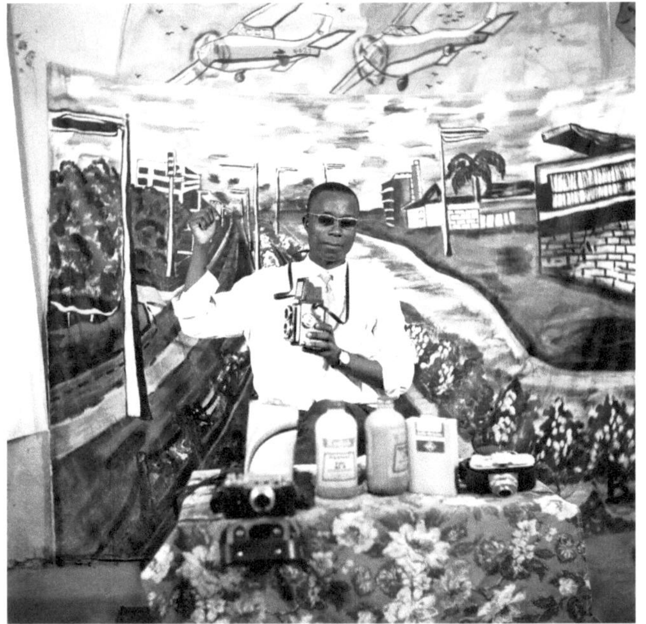

Figure 1.16. Soungalo Malé, Untitled. San, 1960. Courtesy of the artist and Emmanuel Daou.

Figure 1.17. El Hadj Tijani Àdìgún Sitou, *Self-Portrait*, 1971. © Tijani Sitou Estate. Courtesy of Candace Keller, Archive of Malian Photography (Matrix).

with the exception of the 2013 edition, which was suspended after the 2012 coup. The biennale's return in 2015 was considered highly successful, despite a terrorist attack on the Radisson Hotel in Bamako involving 170 hostages and 20 deaths, which occurred a week after the biennale opening.

Thus, the history of photography in Mali has always followed political, social, and economic changes. Photographers themselves have been caught at the apex of the clash between precolonial and colonial Mali, and continue to elucidate these tensions and contradictions in their postindependence practice. Despite the fact that recent decades have seen many studioists' images across Africa become available to the international public, Keïta's and Sidibé's portraits remain the most widely published and exhibited, and their images are the best-known.[99] Those of Keïta's pictures that have been chosen for international exhibition are technically superior and aesthetically stronger than those of many West African studio photographers.[100] That their work remains of prominent interest in the art world probably stems from many factors: they were first to be discovered; they conserved their archives (many photographers' archives were thrown out by relatives or by those who purchased the business); Keïta in particular was highly skilled, Sidibé had a creative and extremely modern eye; and Sidibé continued to work within and outside Bamako, carrying on his studio. The shift in aesthetics from Keïta to Sidibé not only shows the two different perspectives of the two photographers, but encompasses a cultural and temporal shift that exhibits society's changes in the decades pre- and postindependence.

However, in recent years, several other older studioists from Mali have been represented by reputable galleries or institutions. They include Abdourahmane Sakaly; Hamidou Maïga (Timbuktu and Bamako); Adama Kouyaté, who lived and worked in Kati and Ségou, with a five-year sojourn abroad; Soungalo Malé; and Tijani Sitou of Mopti (figs. 1.14–1.17). Indiana University Museum holds Sitou's works as a result of Candace Keller's initiative, and Jack Bell represents Kouyaté. Unfortunately, Hamidou Bocoum's work seems to have disappeared from the art world and market, as it is still represented only by the illegal holdings of Svend Erik Sokkelund.[101] The Archive of Malian Photography (AMP), a project created by Keller to save studio photographers' negatives from precisely this kind of situation, is operative now in collaboration with the African House of Photography.

While the history of photography in Mali is richer and more complex than a story of two studio photographers and their belated and sudden global stardom, Keïta's and Sidibé's fame dramatically and permanently changed both the world history of photography and had lasting and important ramifications on photography in Bamako. The shift from vernacular studio photography to fine art encompasses a broader significance than simply the material changes in form to the original, vintage prints. Malick Sidibé and Seydou Keïta, as a result of their international fame, also engaged in new but related projects, in fashion and fine art, stemming from their earlier portrait work. The anonymous maker of "Portrait of a Couple" has been named; what this naming entails is a complex shift in register of audience reception and intertextual meaning, bringing a Mande aesthetic to a broader audience, and thus into Relation. The ramifications of these shifts are contextualized and considered in the following chapter.

Chapter 2

Malian Portraiture Glamorized and Globalized

> But thought in reality spaces itself out into the world. It informs the imaginary of peoples, their varied poetics, which it then transforms, meaning, in them its risk becomes realized.
> —Édouard Glissant, *Poetics of Relation*

Glissant's *Poetics of Relation* was published in 1990 in French, the year before Seydou Keïta's debut in New York. The twenty-year lacuna for Malick Sidibé and the striking forty-year gap, in the case of Keïta, between the end of the two studio photographers' careers in Bamako and the beginning of their international art world fame gives the impression that these photographers entered the art world out of nowhere.[1] But it was no coincidence that Keïta and Sidibé rose to fame within the American art scene of the 1990s. The art world was primed to receive the novelty of their photographs' aesthetic and historical meaning positively. Numerous factors contributed to the openness of the art world—and particularly the New York art world—to these images in ways not previously possible. Keïta's and Sidibé's works enacted Relation as contemporary art in New York and Paris as Glissant's theory of Relation, which stemmed from creolization in the Caribbean, began to circulate among readers.

The decision to exhibit vernacular, commercial portraits, made in the 1950s–1970s in an entirely different social and historical context, *as art* in contemporary art museums, was obviously to some extent market-driven, as contemporary art had boomed in the 1980s, whereas the market for "authentic" African objects was petering out. But the market can only follow what is already occurring within the art world's parameters. The enlarged, high-contrast, meticulously printed photographs taken by Keïta and Sidibé but printed in high-tech professional labs in New York and Paris *are* contemporary art; exceeding the time and context of their original taking, they enter into a new visual discourse through their embodiment—indeed, their exacerbation—of numerous characteristics of contemporary art of the 1990s. Yet these photographs are still linked to their cultural context through certain Mande aesthetic concepts; while the jayan, or form—literally the glass or film negative—of the images taken by Keïta and Sidibé in the 1950s, '60s, and '70s remains the same, jako (embellishment) occurs in their changed size and printing contrasts.

Thus Keïta's and Sidibé's photographs are significant in terms of bringing Mande aesthetics to the diaspora and to the forefront of the global art world. Moreover, their presence actively highlights a number of primary concerns of the 1990s New York art world. While at the time they seemed marginal to an art discourse focused on American multiculturalism, queer identities, feminism, and postmodern abjection in the work of white artists, on looking back it becomes clear that Keïta's and Sidibé's presence in the art world expanded on and highlighted key aspects of major theoretical concerns and aesthetic historical shifts crucial to the 1990s art discourse. In fact, they were at the forefront of multiple valences: of blackness, of gender identity, of beauty, of postcolonial identity, of photography's shift from documentary to verité, of postmodernism, and of sexual identity.[2] Moreover, their entrance into the contemporary art world opened the way for contemporaneous artworks from Africa with more difficult subject matter or edgier aesthetic impact than studio portraiture.[3]

To understand how these photographs functioned within the 1990s art world, it is necessary to unravel various strands of seemingly unconnected histories whose convergence enabled the portraits to emerge as art. In fact, photographic portraiture from Africa had already circulated in the United States in a prominent print publication decades earlier, when Keïta's studio practice was in its early years: in 1949, a photographer named Mayola Amici was pictured working on the street in Stanleyville, Belgian Congo, in the August 8 issue of *Life* magazine—the same issue that included Hans Namuth's iconic photographs of Jackson Pollock painting in his Long Island studio (fig. 2.1).[4] Amici's photographs were taken under colonial rule, the

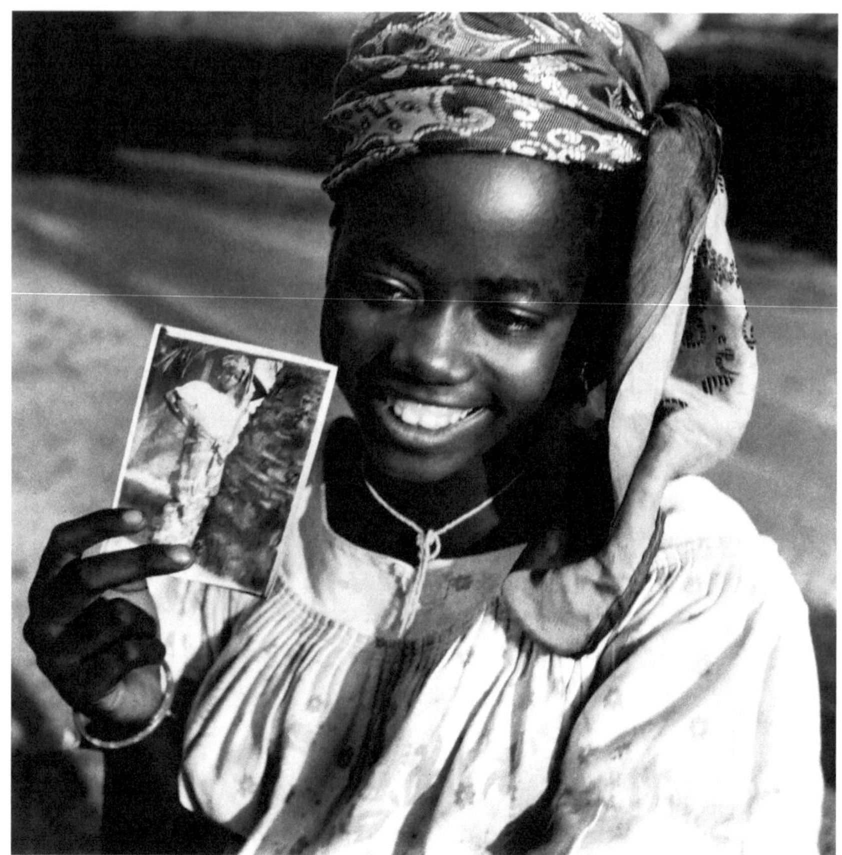

Figure 2.1. Lennart Nilsson, from *Mayola Amici, the Jungle Photographer,* Young woman with photo by Mayola Amici (originally appeared in *Life* magazine, August 8, 1949, p. 13). © Lennart Nilsson Photography.

invisible political backdrop for the American viewer, present only in the patronizing headline: "Congo Society Flocks to Jungle Photographer." Amici posed and photographed a young woman leaning against a palm tree under the caption "A Native Belle Gets Her Picture Taken." The portraits—seen in *Life* posted on a display board on a Stanleyville street—show the similar interest in certain poses seen in studio portraiture across West and Central Africa in the 1940s and '50s: a pair of seated women turned in to slightly face each other; the often-seen triad of two people standing behind and flanking a central, seated woman; three figures standing in a row. African art history was still being formulated as an academic discipline in the 1940s, resolutely focused on precolonial and nontechnology-based practices, which did not include photography. Although Amici's images presumably reached a wide swath of the American public, including those particularly interested in the arts, no one conceived of these photographs as art because the necessary apparatus did not yet exist, as art photography itself was a relatively new discipline pursued by the circle of artists around Alfred Stieglitz and, by the 1940s, the New York Photo League and offshoots of the Bauhaus in Chicago.

It wasn't until almost thirty years later, in 1978, that Stephen Sprague's groundbreaking article on Yoruba studio photographers was published in the art history journal *African Arts*.[5] Sprague's article revealed a breadth and depth of studio practices from Nigeria in photographs taken from 1975 to 1978, which included images of twin memorial portraits that replaced traditional *ibeji* sculptures. Two photographs show young girls in a so-called squatting pose before a variegated background of leafy greenery that effectively mimics the patterned backdrop of Keïta's bed-sheet backdrops. A rectangular patterned backdrop also can be seen on each side of the twin portrait. Another image from Oyus Photo Studio utilizes a painted backdrop, also popular in Mali.[6] Sprague himself was not an art historian but a professor of photography at Purdue University, although he was conducting research in Yorubaland with art historian Marilyn Houlberg. Yet because of the limited circulation of *African Arts* among scholars and the dearth of interest in colonial-era or postcolonial visual culture from Africa—and perhaps because of the imminent death of Sprague himself in 1979—these images and others like them languished in the archives at the Arizona Center of Creative Photography and were not resuscitated until the essay was republished in *In/Sight*'s exhibition catalog.

The fact that African portrait photographs had circulated broadly in 1949, and among specialists in the 1970s, without anyone claiming them as art, suggests that there was something specific about the 1990s confluence of historical factors that made possible this shift in register from vernacular portrait to fine art photograph. What were the conditions of the possibility of the reception of Keïta's and Sidibé's photographs in New York and, to a lesser extent, in Paris?

In the United States, the 1980s and '90s saw the rise of identity politics, or what was then called "multiculturalism," erupting across college campuses and sparking discussions in the sociopolitical sphere. Politics had remained on the edges of the mainstream art world through the civil rights, feminist, and gay rights movements of the 1960s and '70s, separated from minimalism and Fluxus alike except obliquely through careful and politicized aesthetic interpretations. Feminist art in the 1970s first began to address the aesthetic implications of gender identities. As identity struggles reemerged in the 1980s with the academic infusion of postmodernist philosophies (specifically Derrida's thinking *différance* and postcolonial theories formulated by Gayatri Spivak and Homi Bhabha), artists borrowed the '70s feminist slogan "The personal is political" and began to make personally inflected art directly addressing issues of identity and marginalized subject positions. Within this opening up of the white, male, heterosexual art world appeared images of African Americans in works by artists like Faith Ringgold, Dawoud Bey, Carrie Mae Weems, Lorna Simpson, Adrian Piper, and Glenn Ligon; for many of these artists, gender and sexual identity were also prominent concerns.

Until the 1980s, photographic images of African Americans in the art world were scarce. Gordon Parks and Roy de Carava were the most famous African American photographers, but they operated in the mainstream press and to a lesser extent in the separate world of fine art photography; Romare Bearden was the only prominent artist using photographic images of black people in his collages. The show *Harlem on My Mind: Cultural Capital of Black America, 1900–1968* at the Metropolitan Museum of Art in 1969 caused a furor of protest in black artistic circles due to its poor curation, but in 1979 Bey's *Harlem USA* (1975–1979), a riposte, was shown at the Studio Museum in Harlem (fig. 2.2) and less than a decade later, art historian Deborah Willis's book *Black Photographers 1940–1988: An Illustrated Bio-Bibliography* (Garland, 1988) offered the first historical survey of African American photographers. Also by the end of the 1980s, Simpson was showing male and especially female bodies in staged poses, their faces turned away from the viewer, with incorporated text (fig. 2.3), while Weems's *Kitchen Table Series* (1989–1990) featured a series of narratives around a woman sitting at her kitchen table with various family members and friends. By the early 1990s all of these artists were using photography's indexicality to stage black bodies within a predominantly white art world—white in terms of artists, viewers, subjects, concerns, and institutional affiliation—conceptually addressing issues related to race and sexuality.[7]

For the 1993 biennial at the Whitney Museum of American Art, subsequently dubbed the "Identity Biennial," Glenn Ligon rephotographed Robert Mapplethorpe's *Black Book*, which itself, as Kobena Mercer noted, was motivated in part by Mapplethorpe's observation that there were so few black people represented in the art world. But in Ligon's appropriation, *Notes on the Margin of the Black Book*, in which he paired the prints with texts by himself and others, including gay African American men like James

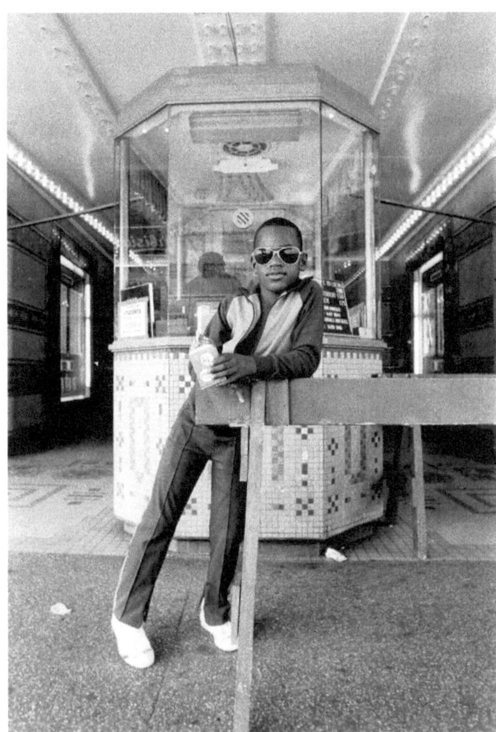

Figure 2.2. Dawoud Bey, *A Boy in Front of the Loews 125th St Movie Theater*, 1976. Courtesy of the artist and Stephen Daiter Gallery.

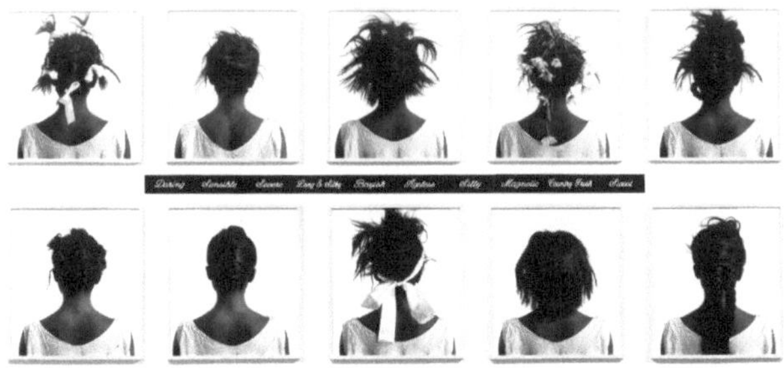

Figure 2.3. Lorna Simpson, *Stereo Styles*, 1988. Ten black-and-white dye diffusion Polaroid prints, ten frames total (one print in each), ten engraved plastic plaques. © Lorna Simpson. Courtesy of the artist and Hauser & Wirth.

Baldwin, the images are framed and problematized for their objectification of the black male body. Also shown at the Whitney were Daniel J. Martinez's museum tags that proclaimed, "I Can't Imagine Ever Wanting to Be White" (1993), which shocked and offended most of New York's white male art critics.[8] Coco Fusco and Guillermo Gomez-Peña showed *The Year of the White Bear* (1992), satirically reminding viewers of the colonialist fascination with people from Africa and South America in how they had been exhibited like animals. The video of Rodney King being beaten by the Los Angeles police was also shown, bringing media political culture directly into the art world through raw footage. Other artists included Simpson, Betye Saar, and Alison Saar; Homi Bhabha was quoted in the catalog, emphasizing the influence of postcolonial theories in the art world. Whitney curator Thelma Golden followed up the 1993 biennial, in which she had played an active role, with *Black Male: Representations of Masculinity in Contemporary American Art* the following year; this groundbreaking, controversial exhibition included works by Piper, David Hammons, Weems, Simpson, Andres Serrano, Fred Wilson, and Mapplethorpe.

While images of African Americans were becoming visible in New York museums and galleries, there was an exponential increase in worldwide biennials that coincided with the rise of multiculturalism in the US. Founded in 1994, the Bamako Biennale rode the crest of the wave of fascination with the biennial format, which scholars usually cite as beginning in 1984 with the first Havana Biennial. Havana opened the same year as MoMA's infamous *Primitivism* show, which incorporated decontextualized African and Oceanic work within modern art solely in terms of its influence on the art of modernists like Picasso; in 1989 the Centre Georges Pompidou's *Magiciens de la Terre* (*Magicians of the Earth*), or what Benjamin Buchloh called "the whole-earth show," was conceived as a response.[9] *Magiciens*, although controversial at the time, had a dramatic impact on African art. André Magnin, active in the African music scene, participated in the catalog and advised curator Jean Hubert-Martin on the selection of African artists like Chéri Samba and Kane Kwei, whose international careers took off after *Magiciens*. Magnin then went on to establish Jean Pigozzi's collection CAAC (Contemporary African Art Collection), soon to include Seydou Keïta.[10]

Held in 1991, *Africa Explores* hovered on the horizon of this explosion of multicultural art. It was a clear response to 1989's *Magiciens de la Terre*, but occupied a liminal position between contemporary art and historical African art, conveyed by its dual institutional homes. Interest in modern and contemporary African art in the US was expanding in the early 1990s: *Af-*

rica Explores responded to the Studio Museum's *Contemporary African Artists: Changing Tradition*, 1990, which included El Anatsui and Bruce Onobrakpeya, Henry Munyaradzi, and Souleymane Keïta. Jean Kennedy's *New Currents, Ancient Rivers* (1992) was the first major survey book of contemporary African art since the early 1970s, and in 1993 *Fusion: West African Artists at the Venice Biennale* was exhibited at the Museum for African Art, including painters and sculptors such as Moustapha Dimé, Mor Faye, and Ouattara. Seydou Keïta had a solo show in Washington, DC, at the Smithsonian Museum for African Art in 1996, the same year he appeared at the Guggenheim in New York as part of *In/Sight*. Moreover, contemporary African art was promoted by the founding of *Nka: Journal of Contemporary African Art* in 1994 by Okwui Enwezor, Salah Hassan, and Olu Oguibe; *Nka* has had a major impact as a long-term project of art criticism and historical writing devoted to the field.

In London in 1995, *Seven Stories about African Modern Art* was shown during the *africa95* exhibition season, which included South African photographer Zwelethu Mthethwa, whose color photographs of people in shanty-town rooms bore a striking and perhaps deliberate resemblance to West African studio portraiture. In Great Britain, the portraits by Keïta and Sidibé emerged after the British Black Arts Movement of the 1980s, with Rotimi Fani-Kayode as a prominent figure; his ecstatic homoerotic photographs were shown in the 1993 Arles Rencontres, where Seydou Keïta's works were first projected (fig. 2.4). Also, Yinka Shonibare and Chris Ofili, both of whom have strong familial ties to Nigeria, became prominent in the new global art scene of the late 1980s and early '90s through their association with Goldsmiths and the YBAs (Young British Artists), and their works included images of blackness: Shonibare's suite of photographs titled *Diary of a Victorian Dandy* (1998) included his own self-portraits, and Ofili painted a black Mary in *Holy Virgin Mary* (1996), which was included in the *Sensation* exhibition in London and traveled on the wings of controversy to the Brooklyn Museum in New York. In Great Britain, however, photography was less prominent than other mediums, and since Keïta and Sidibé were not from an Anglophone former colony, less attention was paid to their work. But across the channel in France, Keïta and Sidibé were positioned as artists, rather than commercial photographers, in a general gamut of genres published by Revue Noire that included press photography and contemporary art, as the founders of Revue Noire focused resolutely on a broad definition of art.

Behind this immediacy of imagery and exhibitions was the larger backdrop of historical decolonization from the 1960s through 1994, when apart-

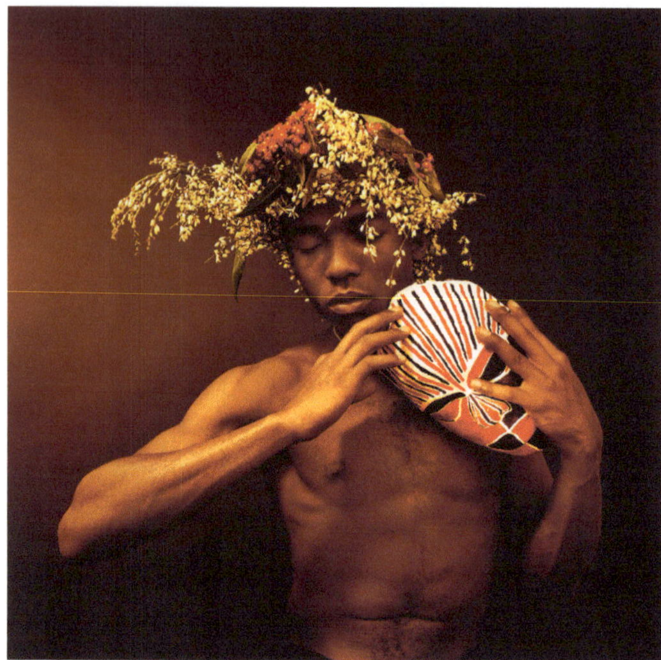

Figure 2.4. Rotimi Fani-Kayode, *Adebiyi*, 1989. Cibachrome print. Courtesy of Autograph London.

heid finally crumbled; moreover, the fall of the Berlin Wall in 1989 and the collapse of the Soviet Union in 1991 affected socialist dictatorships across Africa, including Mali, and, in the 1990s, a second, voluntary wave of Africans emigrated to the United States. These events resonated with the postcolonial theories coming out of postmodern philosophies, related to multiculturalism but occurring beyond the US's borders. Homi Bhabha and Gayatri Spivak drew on pioneering work by Edward Said and Frantz Fanon; the works of French philosophers Michel Foucault and Jacques Derrida, who had the greatest impact on American academia in the 1980s and '90s and who had lived in Tunisia and Algeria, respectively, were formative on their ideas.[11] Glissant himself lived in the United States from 1989 onward, first teaching at Louisiana State University, where he wrote on Toni Morrison's work and William Faulkner's novels about racial mixing, noting the importance of plantation histories across the Caribbean and the American South. In 1995 Glissant relocated to the Graduate Center, City University of New York in Manhattan, where he taught French and Francophone literature. Glissant's presence in New York speaks to American Francophone literature's embrace of postcolonial theory.

Concurrent with the rise of multiculturalism, the circulation of images of blackness, postcolonial theories, and the effects of decolonization was a seemingly separate but key factor to the positive reception of Keïta and Sidibé in the New York art world: namely, its dramatic embrace of photography. As the art market boomed in the 1980s, the once-separate field of fine art photography expanded into the realm of contemporary art. Photography had already entered the broader art world surreptitiously in its documentary relationship to conceptual art in the 1960s, and was important in its seemingly affectless and deadpan documentation of events, performances, and happenings; but those documents were not then considered artworks in and of themselves. The subjectivity of modern art photography—evidence of the artist's eye, hand, or mind in framing, composing, or printing the photograph—was abandoned in conceptual art.[12] As Abigail Solomon-Godeau, Rosalind Krauss, and Jeff Wall have noted, photography's rise to status in the art world and the art market, evidenced in particular by its size and cost, stemmed from the rise of conceptualism and the deskilling of photography in the 1960s, when artists without photographic training began using photography as a primary element in documentation of conceptual works.[13] Solomon-Godeau conflates these documentary images with the more conceptual modes utilized by such artists as Bernd and Hilla Becher, contending that the lack of authorial intention or sense of subjectivity obviated the sense of aesthetics of these works—the deadpan aesthetic of conceptual art coincided with the documentary aesthetic of earthworks and performances.

However, in the 1970s artists began using the photograph as reproduction, returning to ideas indirectly communicated by Warhol's series of photographic screen prints in the 1950s.[14] Victor Burgin had already begun using advertising photographs in conceptual works of the early 1970s, but in the late 1970s Cindy Sherman's *Untitled Film Stills*—film stills for which there is no film, starring the artist herself and seen as a feminist critique of Hollywood culture and popular imagery—set a precedent for a nonphotographer to make conceptual art using photography. The so-called Pictures Generation included Sherman as well as Richard Prince, Laurie Simmons, James Casebere, and Barbara Kruger.[15] This new, appropriated use of photography—a critique of the effects of living in an image-laden capitalist society—was theorized in art criticism with reference to postmodern philosophies. Douglas Crimp curated *Pictures* in 1977 at Artist's Space and penned "Photographic Activity of Postmodernism," while Craig Owens wrote about postmodernism and feminism with regard to the female artists in that exhibition.[16] Sherrie Levine's rephotographing of works by famous male artists from the past was an iconic reminder of postmodern's devotion to intertextuality as theorized by Julia Kristeva, and the reproductive nature of film photography, with its multiple copies made from a single negative, but lacking any one unique original print; they were also a feminist conceptual commentary on the largely masculine-oriented narrative of American photo history. Louise Lawlor also instantiated intertexuality by situating partial views of iconic masterworks from the recent past with interior design choices. By the mid-1980s and early '90s, when Simpson and Weems began using photography to make trenchant critiques of racism and sexism in American life, modernist photography was completely outré.

Solomon-Godeau describes the exhaustion of modernist photography, which, she says, reached a pinnacle at the exact time that the art world moved away from—or hollowed out—modernist strategies. She explains:

> To summarize briefly, one might say that the internal logic of the development of the *genus* art photography determined that its critical discourse would be premised on an aesthetic of the *photographic*, whether this aesthetic was thought to derive from the intrinsic beauties and qualities of the medium itself (the spectrum of tones from white to black, the clarity and precision of the camera image, the camera's ability to create spatial and formal abstraction from the random flux of the world, etc.) or, alternatively, as the deployment of the "artist's choices" inherent in John Szarkowski's ontology of the photographic image (the thing itself, the detail, the frame, time, and the vantage point).[17]

Though modernist photography was seemingly exhausted, its formal concerns return in Keïta's and Sidibé's works, although *as contemporary art*. The subjective eye and hand of the photographer and the formal play of contrast between black and white, resulting in a striking image, are modernist formal concerns. But their social and historical context, the client's collaboration, and an emphasis on the photograph as a document of an era complicate that modernist reading. These photographs speak to the New York art world by rejuvenating an aesthetic of modernist photography within a conceptual conflation of history, culture, document, portraiture, and authorship. They appear as verité because of the use of props and imaginative backdrops or poses; in fact, they were never meant to be "truth" with a capital "T," as photographers in West Africa always recognized that portraiture was not a direct reflection of a person's "self" but, rather, was its own mediating technology. Keïta's and Sidibé's portraits are aesthetic contributions to the present and function within the framework of the logic of conceptual art, while

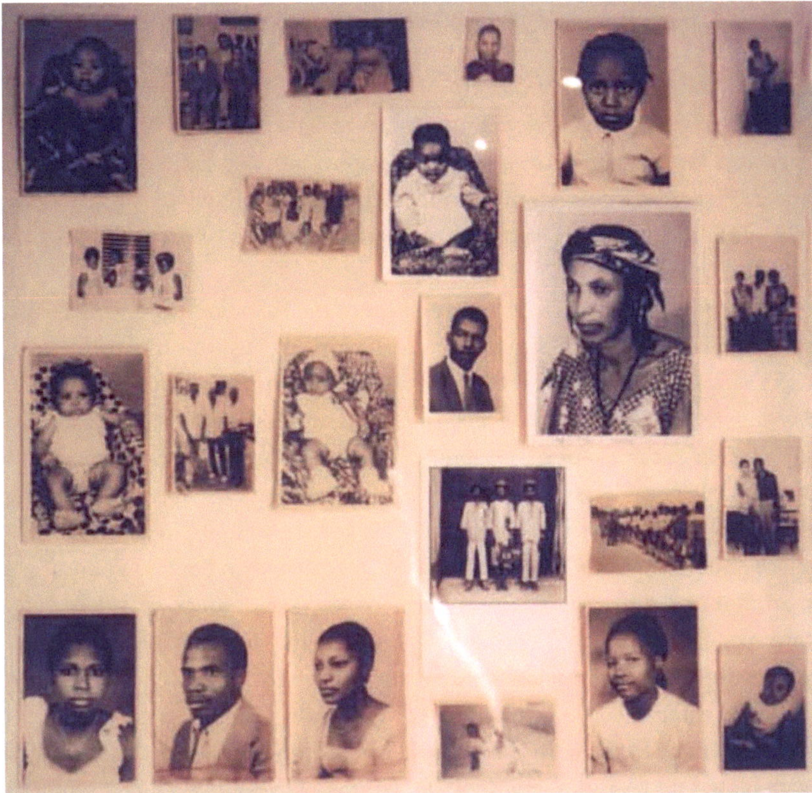

Figure 2.5. Malick Sidibé, vintage original-size prints shown at the 2005 Bamako Biennale in the National Museum. Installation shot by author.

also remaining autonomous works of art becoming ever more collectible on the fine art market.

In the similarity of backdrops used by each photographer, yet enlivened by the uniqueness of each individual client, the portraits presented a conflation of West African fashion, adornment, and props that was visible and exciting for an American audience. However, instead of describing Keïta's and Sidibé's aesthetics as modern or postmodern, they could equally be understood as jako, or embellishment, in terms of Mande aesthetics. Although printed from the same negatives as the 1950s or 1960s portraits, the images are not visually or formally quite the same as the vintage prints, because the *form* of the image, as well as the size and quality of the prints, has undergone a significant shift, affecting the tonal quality of the images themselves (fig. 2.5). Thus the art photographs by Keïta and Sidibé could be described as embellishments or variations of the original prints.

By the 1980s, Keïta's and Sidibe's production had ended in Bamako because of the rise of color labs: Keïta had retired and Sidibé was repairing cameras. The unearthing of a tin of negatives makes for a romantic story, but the idea of aesthetic riches unearthed in Africa stems from a slantwise look at a familiar practice—the photographs' removal from their familiar home and context is precisely what located them as foreign, unfamiliar. And that jump also required a certain aesthetic shift—the resizing and reprinting of these works.

In the 1990s, photography's entrance into the broader field of conceptual art was subtended by its competition with painting in terms of size.[18] Seydou Keïta's photographs were first shown as large-scale projections at the Arles Rencontres. (Projections had become popular since the 1980s, when Krzysztof Wodiczko projected onto monuments in Poland and New York, with a particularly notable projection as a famous protest against apartheid: in 1984 the artist beamed a swastika onto the South Africa House in London's Trafalgar Square.)[19] When displayed as artworks, Keïta's and Sidibé's photos are reprinted at art market sizes and with art market production values.[20] By contrast, the prints that Keïta actually sold on a day-to-day basis, which were one-to-one prints from glass negatives, were roughly the size of postcards, typically about seven by five inches (seventeen by thirteen centimeters). At Keïta's show at Sean Kelly Gallery in New York in 2006, some photographs were blown up to almost life size (sixty-three by forty-five inches, almost a hundred times larger than they would be printed in Bamako) and were exquisitely printed to highlight strong black-and-white contrasts.[21]

Charles Griffin, a professional printer who printed these Keïta works for Sean Kelly, deliberately emphasized grayscale values, while the Gagosian Gallery prints of 1997 had flashier, stronger contrasts. Yet Griffin had never seen a vintage print in which the contrasts are even less intense.[22] Describing an encounter with a vintage Keïta, Michael Rips notes: "The contrast and density of the blacks and whites were minimal, the light modest, and the patterns on the costumes barely visible."[23] When I saw what were claimed to be vintage prints in Bamako, the patterns were recognizable, but the grayscale was indeed low-contrast. There were also orange stains across some of them. According to Candace Keller, Keïta's vintage prints had less intense value contrasts because of the desire to create richly nuanced facial tones, allowing the sitter's individuality to shine forth.[24] In addition, there was a lack of quality materials available, and preservation of the negatives was not ideal.

Keïta's and Sidibé's photographs, which reveal details such as the edges of a backdrop that would have been cropped or covered by a frame in Bamako, fit into the New York art world's fascination with irony in their postmodern aesthetic of revealing the edges of the frame or seeming to deliberately mock the very backdrop they utilized.[25] Philip Kwame Apagya's photographs using painted color backdrops that seemed to stand in for a photograph, for "truth," were shown in New York, as were Kane Kwei's vegetable- or car-shaped coffins, which were seen as a pop response to the emergence of capitalism and consumerism in Africa. The use of borrowed props in Keïta's works, confounding the "truth" of who owns what suit coat or scooter, and the cinematic poses in Sidibé's, with a subject posed as an action film star—both of which contributed to near-future wish fulfillment in their original social contexts in Bamako—operated as and contributed to an overall interest in verité, in the lexicon of the global contemporary.

Keïta's and Sidibé's prints circulated within the same galleries and exhibition spaces as the conceptual photographic works by Weems and Simpson. Their conflation of modernist and postmodernist aesthetics with Mande aesthetics activated their Relational capabilities in the creation of images that both dramatically piqued viewers' interest and yet retained opacity, or a kind of inscrutability. These seeming "documents" of a colonial-era, little-known African world were presumably met by American viewers with some confusion, and they may have wondered when Mali gained independence, or where in Africa it was. Nowhere was the American predisposition to imagine a premodern Africa and to be surprised by urban imaginaries and modern technologies more upended than by these photographs. The photographs counter Afro-pessimism by revising American viewers' understanding of urban life in a West African nation and adding a frisson of historical, pan-African consciousness. Manthia Diawara describes Keïta's subjects as "us not-us," by which he means that Malians like himself are generationally removed from Keïta by the dramatic timeline of colonialism, while he and his teenage friends actually appear in Sidibé's postindependence portraits.[26] The people displayed in both portraitists' works are distinctly *not* American, by virtue of hairstyle, dress, clothing, and backdrop, and yet are not recognizably *Malian* to an American audience. They are reminders of a modern Africa, but one located in a little-known mid-twentieth-century past. Emphasizing the notion of a black Atlantic, Diawara calls Sidibé's portraits "Black photographs"; he says they partake in a "Diaspora" aesthetic, in that the youth borrow from album covers and film poses of Americans but also from the formal aesthetic of the African diaspora.[27] Indeed, album covers of Caribbean and American bands like Johnnie Pecheco, Tito Rodriguez, and

James Brown are shown in Sidibé's party photos—even the Beatles appear. When Sidibé's portraits were displayed in New York, they again partook in a "black" aesthetic, with their '70s bell-bottoms chronologically recognizable, their specific location in Bamako less so.

A more cynical observation is that the 1990s New York art world was already looking beyond its borders for inspiration, much as early twentieth-century European artists did in the early years of abstraction. After the fall of the 1980s art boom, fully immersed in a sense of postmodern failure of the possibility of originality in postcapitalist Western society, the art world welcomed multicultural approaches, especially when that art was less threatening than highly politicized works like Martinez's museum tags or Simpson's sharp critiques. Like James Van Der Zee's famous Harlem portraits of the 1930s, published in Willis's book in 1988, Keïta's and Sidibé's photographs presented a counterpoint to the critical art of Bey, Weems, and Simpson, which often offered bitterly ironic or satirical commentary on racial injustices through the juxtaposition of text and image. Keïta's and Sidibé's photographs seemed contemporary in being presented as contemporary art, in contemporary art spaces, yet were distant, removed in time, and "safe" for a white American audience to appreciate. As the United States was not directly a colonizer in Africa (and few white Americans know the history of Liberia), there is little "white guilt" associated with African colonialism, and the portraits offered pleasant viewing in contrast to news photographs reminiscent of the civil rights struggle or images of Black Panther militancy; similarly, they were not images of criminals or rappers or basketball stars, which were often the only images of black people circulating in popular culture—stereotypes that Bey, Simpson, and Weems sought to address critically.

In Keïta's portraits, figures are modestly dressed, showing little bare skin or cleavage, and they are not overtly sexualized; women appear stylish and beautiful, attractive but not sexy in an American sense. The play of pattern is stunning, as are the serious, proud expressions of the sitters. Sidibé's clients, by contrast, look *cool*, reminding viewers of 1960s and '70s styles and rock 'n' roll aesthetics. Sidibé's beach photos express a nonchalant attitude toward sexuality and even drinking, disallowed in Muslim Mali. After the AIDS crisis of the late 1980s, while contemporary art was embracing the return to the body through the theme of abjection, these West African bodies were beautiful and healthy; they actively participated in and arguably even instigated the return of beauty in contemporary art, although their contribution went unnoticed in critical reviews at the time.

While the changed context in which Keïta's portraits were shown in New

York, Paris, and elsewhere prompted various critiques from scholars, it is important to note that Keïta consented to this recontextualization, and indeed was proud to see his work printed so large and with such high contrasts. In an interview, scholar Michelle Lamunière asked him, "What are your thoughts about the enlargements that have been made from your negatives for recent exhibitions of your work in Europe and the United States?" Keïta replied, "You can't imagine what it was like for me the first time I saw prints of my negatives printed large-scale, no spots, clean and perfect. I knew then that my work was really, really good."[28] In this sense, Keïta's art prints, while dated to the 1950s, belong temporally to the 1990s. Thus in Keïta and Sidibé's case, their vernacular modernism reads simultaneously *as* contemporary art; this fluctuation of temporalities gave these works their aesthetic frisson and temporal ambiguity when seen in such exhibitions as *In/Sight* and *Short Century*. Although most art critics writing in the popular press have casually dismissed the import of this temporal lacuna with the use of the word "discovered," paralleling the Eurocentric trope often applied to the colonization of African lands, the Nigerian American critic Teju Cole, in his recent obituary of Malick Sidibé, importantly highlights that time gap, referring to Sidibé as the great photographer of "African modernity."[29]

At stake in this shift from vernacular, commercial, intimately sized portraiture to large-scale, high-contrast contemporary art is the globalization of Keïta's and Sidibé's images and the loss of "original" meaning. Globalization here refers to traversing the networks of capitalist arts institutions that enabled the circulation of their images on the art market and in contemporary art centers in New York and Paris; but paradoxically, in creating Relation their works contribute to other imaginaries than globalization—they contribute to mondialité, or worldliness, in a form of alter-globalization. The original context of their photographs' function in a familial Bamako community, which emphasized social cohesion, is lost in the transference to fine art; but there is the gain of new social functions within the museum context. For a small audience of diaspora West Africans, Sidibé's and Keïta's portraits offered the return of memories to viewers like Manthia Diawara, while for a more general museumgoing audience, these art photographs counter Afropessimism and celebrate beauty and cool in the context of blackness, countering an emphasis on whiteness in the New York art world.

Diawara explains that, in Bamako in the 1960s, the youth pictured in Sidibé's photographs appeared to be "mimicking the culture of the colonizer, which shut the door to authentic self-actualization. Looking at Sidibé's photographs today, it is possible to see what was not visible then on account of the rhetorical teachings of revolution."[30] As an adult who grew up in the youth culture of Sidibé's images, Diawara looks at these photos in his Paris apartment with a friend, and they remember their shared past in Bamako. All of the motivations and uses of photography are present and activated, including personal nostalgia, but also an *overall view of the time*. Diawara explains, "That the theory of decolonization could not recognize this at the time as anything but mimicry and assimilation is an indication of its failure to grasp the full complexity of the energies unleashed by independence."[31] This argument suggests that Sidibé's photographs enable Relation, allowing viewers to reevaluate their history and recognize the true import of the youth's engagement with '60s culture and the black diaspora.

Thus the shift from a local to a global audience is not a win-or-lose proposition. In a famous early essay on Keïta, Elizabeth Bigham warned that these images would be "permanently re-authored"; but every generation interprets images for its own needs.[32] With Keïta's recontextualization, or jako, the photographs reach a dramatically wider audience and have the potential to impact whole cultures. The enlargement, printing contrasts, changed context of reception, new audiences, and time lapses can be considered embellishments. If we understand that the aesthetics inherent in these photographs correspond to Mande aesthetics, then we see this cultural form as a variation—while individual images are variations on themes. Moreover, it then becomes clear why Keïta and Sidibé did not refuse their images' recirculation in a vastly different context (if such clarity is necessary and if acknowledgment, fame, prestige, and money were not universal enough reasons).[33]

What is most fascinating, with this changed form and changed audience, is how the meanings of the images and their circulation have shifted. The sitters' names are mostly forgotten at the expense of the artists'. The intimate, personal value of individual portraits belonging to the sitter or family members is replaced by the anonymous audience who values these portraits, not for the individual's personhood, but for their aesthetic value as a work of art, or a document of history. Whereas once these portraits contributed to social capital, or badenya, cementing familial and friendship bonds, reinforcing pride and feelings of Négritude in anticipating independence from colonialism, and contributing to consumer and education-oriented wish fulfillments, the photographs now inspire strangers to reconfigure their stereotypes and preconceptions about Africa's history: about colonialism, modernity, and postcolonial societies. The recontextualized portraits of Sidibé and Keïta enable viewers to participate in Relation, encouraging a spontaneous affinity for cultural contact and exchange through their globalized aesthetics.

While Keïta's individual clients' meanings have likely been lost—as they are lost in virtually all vernacular photography—it is worthwhile examining what meanings are *gained* by the recontextualization of Keïta's work as art. Most reviews have commented on how his work has been represented, so the interested viewer can easily learn basic information, such as the fact that the originals were one-to-one contact prints, the pictures use props owned by Keïta himself, and they were sent to relatives and kept in photo albums. The vintage prints I have seen by many photographers tend to be damaged and faded, the contrasts were bland, and the pictures were too small to convey much drama. Blown up, however, his pictures look magnificent. He portrayed his sitters as dignified and gorgeous. The enlarged prints demonstrate the incredible technical acumen and formal eye that Keïta employed, as well as the burgeoning import of the anticipatory moment in which he worked. They are documents of an exciting time in African history: the foment of independence froths on the surface of his pictures, reflected in the sitters' determined gazes, their confident juxtaposition of adornments and props signaling tradition and modernity held together through force of will.

The chronological vagaries of these images' trajectories—taken in the 1950s in Bamako, printed in the '70s for an art historian's private archive, shown and reprinted in the '90s in a New York art world on the downswing from the '80s art boom—speak to the particular social and political reception in the discursive spaces in which they circulated: a context that embraced the photographic and the influx of other cultures, sanctioned by postmodern philosophy and postcolonial theory. These reprints not only constitute contemporary art but also, in doing so, enact Relation. As Glissant explains, Relational identity

- is linked not to a creation of the world but to the conscious and contradictory experience of contact among cultures;
- is produced in the chaotic network of Relation and not in the hidden violence of filiation; and
- does not devise any legitimacy as its guarantee of entitlement, but circulates, newly extended.[34]

The prints by Keïta and Sidibé do not supply enough knowledge to create a whole world for their viewers, but they introduce an experience of contradictory and conscious contact among cultures. They circulate in the chaotic network of the global art world and of the imaginaries of their viewers; they are liberated from their rooted, historical past to circulate as contemporary art. Their circulation *as* photographs particularly enables them to participate in Relation. While some Africanist scholars are frustrated that Keïta and Sidibé have gained the lion's share of fame and thus seem to be *the only* African studio photographers visible in the art world, an increasing number of exhibitions has given attention to other studio photographers in recent years. As Mali gains more internet access, and as more of these photos are digitized, they will become available to Malians, and it is likely that Bamako families will find portraits of their relatives. But the recontextualized meanings given to Keïta's and Sidibé's artworks, this new story about preindependence subjectivity in Africa that Keïta's large prints tell with emotional immediacy, is important for the world to see. Here, in Bamako in the 1950s, Africans were modern, proud, wealthy, and about to take control of their own destiny. Just as importantly, in the postindependence, postcolonial era, the connection to global fashion and politics can be seen in Sidibé's prints.

While the American and to a lesser extent French and London art worlds were receptive to Keïta's and Sidibé's portrait photographs, their subsequent photographs, made after the pair became famous, are affected by their own works' globalization. Keïta's 1998 fashion shoots for *Harper's Bazaar* and Malick Sidibé's art photography series *Vues de dos* (*Views from the Back/Behind*), as well as his fashion photographs for magazines like *Elle* and *Vogue* and a 2009 spread in the *New York Times Magazine*, present examples of this phenomenon. For Keïta and Sidibé, fame had an impact on their lives, improving their finances; significantly, international fame also brought each one back to taking photographs, although Sidibé was much more active than Keïta, who was fifteen years older.

Like Samuel Fosso, whose self-portraits from the 1970s constitute an especially interesting case of metamorphosis from personal work to internationally recognized contemporary art, Sidibé's exposure to the contemporary art world influenced his subsequent photography. Sidibé's series *Vues de dos* continued a longtime interest in photographing clients looking over their shoulders—a pose borrowed from films—into a more conceptually oriented series of people posed with their backs to the viewer, in different scenarios, from the cinematic to the ordinary to the erotic.

As the change from commercial studio photography to art photography loses an important social dimension but gains in Relation, Malick Sidibé himself exemplified the community-oriented, socially involved values of the former. Although he was a world-famous photographer, Sidibé could often be found at his studio in the neighborhood of Bagadiji when he was home in Bamako. He welcomed anyone who visited, and greeted everyone who walked by. Family and friends would sit, talk, and drink tea outside the studio, as they do at most business establishments in the city. In an interview with Simon Njami in 2001, Sidibé spoke about his love for photographing people, and about the "new mentality" held by today's photographers. "Today . . . I often have the feeling that photographers think only of money. We were professionals and also had to earn our living, of course. But there is no passion today."[35] The shift to a capitalist money economy enforced by colonialism in Mali had ever-deepening ramifications for the communal nature of precolonial society. Sidibé, who worked in the postindependence era, comments on the gradual changes in society that occurred in the latter half of the twentieth century: "In our day, we lived in a community and were always together. The family was of great significance. Today, by contrast, the world has become much more individual. Music is a good example: at concerts the audience sit there passively, listen and applaud. But they should be taking part. In our days, we barely noticed the musicians; we listened to the music and danced until we were dripping with sweat. . . . Today the 'star' is separated from the audience. This is something I cannot understand."[36]

The tension between individual and community is particularly strong today in Mali (fig. 2.6).[37] Before colonialism, an individual's role, in terms of life choices such as whom to marry, where to live, and what to do, tended to be subsumed to the community under strongly delineated roles, designated by age, gender, and caste. Today, especially in urbanized Bamako, social hierarchies are breaking down and traditions are changing. The Western emphasis on individual freedom has instigated young people's rebellion against societal constraints. The shift to a capitalist economy and a high rate of unemployment for youth contribute to such tensions. Whereas in precolonial society these youth would have had a proper role and position in society (though subordinated to elders), now many lack an area into which they can fit as productive members of society. Such tensions are felt particularly in families, of immense importance to Malians, because of the "disrespect" shown to elders by youth.

Sidibé's analysis of the changes that music has undergone can equally be applied to photography, in that art photography lacks the social and communal value that studio portraits emphasized, and to which they contributed. Sidibé himself disliked abstract photography that does not show the viewer's face or body, and therefore cannot speak to a broad, popular audience. He said, "Art photography is not photography for me; the view of just a hand or foot, or a waist, is not photography. I want to be able to recognize the per-

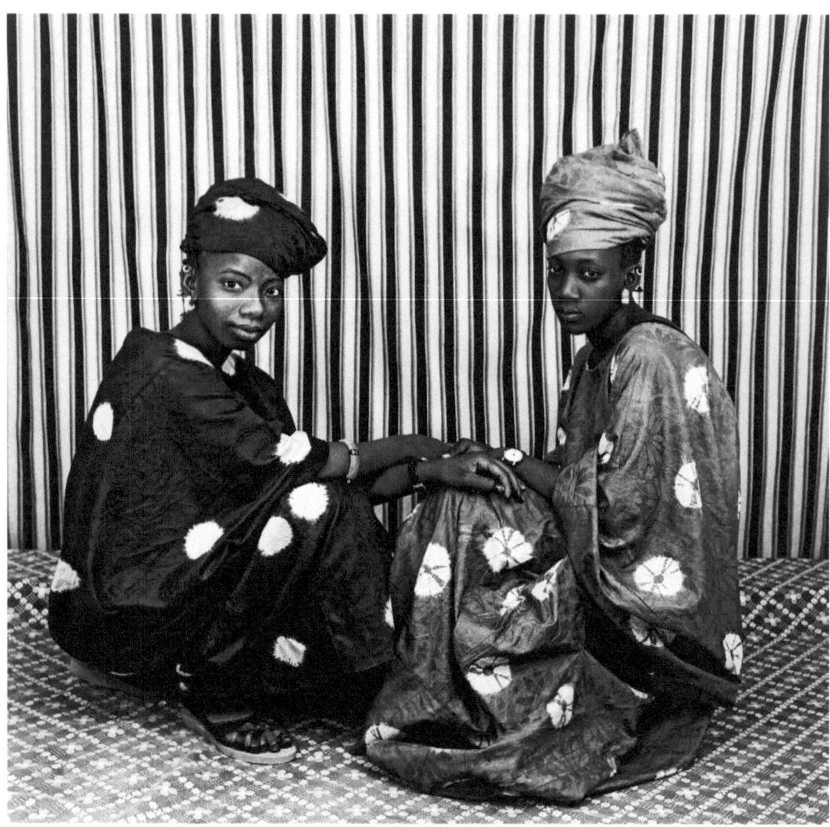

Figure 2.6. Malick Sidibé, *Deux amies peulh* (*Two Fulani Friends*). Printed 2001. Courtesy of the artist and Jack Shainman Gallery, New York.

son."[38] Interestingly, although his practice of "art photography" shifted in that the photographer began to pay models for their time, rather than being commissioned by clients, the social element remained strong. Sidibé hired women in the local community who might not have husbands to help them provide for themselves, while protecting their identities; in doing so, he kept the social contract between photographer and client invested, even while taking complete artistic control.[39] The *Vues de dos* series shows that he retained a strong social interest in photography even though he now commissioned models, rather than being commissioned by clients.

Sidibé began creating art photographs in his *Vues de dos* series in the early 2000s, which becomes particularly interesting in regard to the issues of legibility and communal values. While retaining the studio format, Sidibé took pictures of models with their backs turned, continuing his interest in pho-

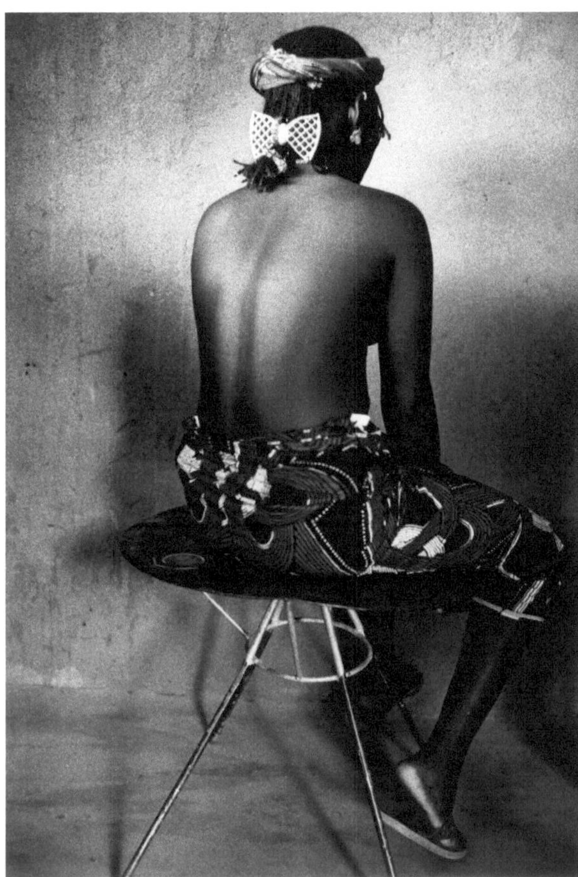

Figure 2.7. Françoise Huguier, *Young Somono Woman, Ségou, Mali*, 1995. Courtesy of Françoise Huguier / Agence VU / Redux.

tographing subjects from the back, which can be seen in numerous studio poses, but always with the client's head turned to show his or her face, as was appropriate for a portrait's commercial and memorial function.

This shift to art seems to have been inspired by Françoise Huguier's 1995 photograph *Young Somono Woman, Mali* (*Jeune fille somono*), which shows a young woman sitting on a stool, wearing only a wrap skirt, her body and face turned away from the viewer (fig. 2.7).[40] Huguier was in Bamako working on the biennale in the early to mid-1990s, and Sidibé owned a copy of her book with this photograph on the cover, titled *Secrètes*.[41] Sidibé may have been equally inspired by his colleague Youssouf Sogodogo, whose images of hairstyles, many photographed from the back, were published by Antonin Potoski and Chab Touré. It is also likely that he was influenced by Nigerian J. D. 'Okhai Ojeikere's photographs of women's hairstyles, which were widely shown by André Magnin at the same time as Sidibé's portraits, and in simi-

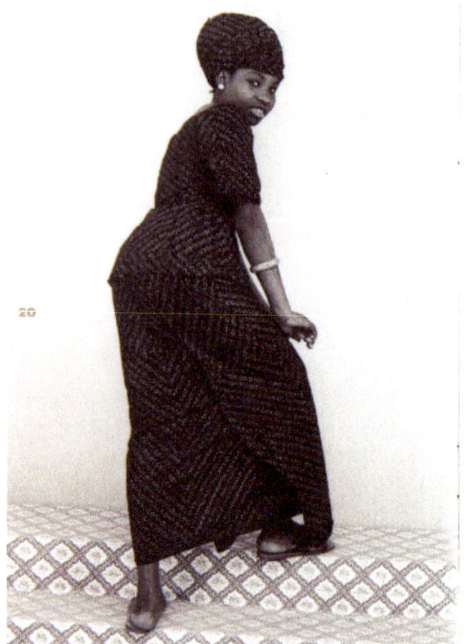
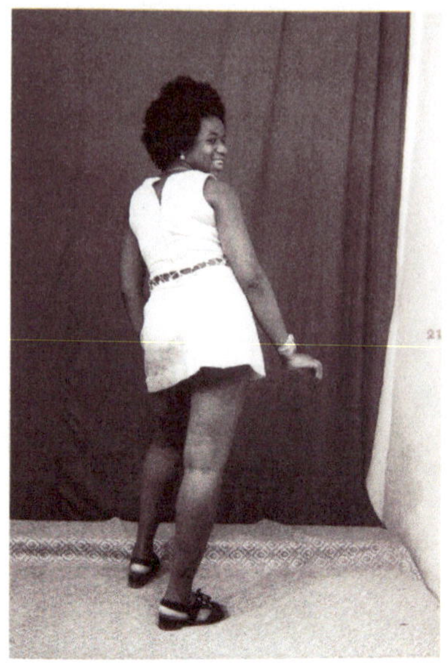

Figure 2.8. Malick Sidibé, Portraits from *Malick Sidibé: Photographe* (Éditions de l'Oeil, 2001). Text by Amadou Chab Touré.

lar worldwide exhibitions.[42] Sidibé knew all of these photographers personally and saw that their work was being shown as art in Bamako, Paris, New York, and elsewhere. He was also aware of the changing practices within Bamako toward making art, seen in Mamadou Konaté's abstractions and Alioune Bâ's series of hands and feet, and he taught workshops at the local photography schools.

The issue of influence in the *Vues de dos* series is avoided by scholars, presumably in the fear of removing the modernist value of originality from Sidibé's work. For example, Amadou Chab Touré makes a compelling case for continuity in Sidibé's work in *Malick Sidibé: Photographe,* published by Éditions de l'Oeil in 2001, a chapbook that encompasses both kinds of poses. While the title translates to *Malick Sidibé: Photographer,* the first page of the book announces that all of the images are "Views from behind: photographs, from 1977 to 2000" (fig. 2.8). To include all of these pictures as if in one series, from the studio portrait era to after the artist became internationally famous, shows a desire to emphasize continuity, present in Sidibé's ongoing interest in this pose. This emphasis on continuity is consistent with Mande aesthetics in highlighting a theme and variation. Focusing on the "Views from Behind" also emphasizes Sidibé's originality as an artist, his contribution in the sense of the modernist value of being the *first* to make an artistic breakthrough, which Touré surely recognizes, as he masterfully plays the space between the French market and local aesthetics. At the same time, Touré's approach contributes to the repression of Sidibé's studio portraits as commercial work, and not as "art" in the modern sense, and thereby downplays the remarkable creativity Sidibé displayed in taking on conceptual artistic modes late in his artistic life. As Touré points out, Sidibé's portraiture showed evidence of his interest in this particular pose since the 1970s, but Touré does not acknowledge the crucial break that occurs when Sidibé shifts to the head turned away from the viewer and uses models rather than paying clients. For Touré, this new approach constitutes a variation on a theme, or an interest that was long-standing for the artist, whereas from a French or American perspective, the approach of not showing the face constitutes an interesting conceptual rupture, while also referring back to the studio tradition in a critical fashion (fig. 2.9).

The concern for originality overlooks both Malian and postmodern approaches to photographic production. Sidibé's series involves precisely the Malian aesthetic embellishment or variation on and within the theme of

Figure 2.9. Malick Sidibé, *Vue de dos*, 2003–2004. Gelatin silver print, paint, glass, cardboard, tape, and string. © Malick Sidibé. Courtesy of the artist and Jack Shainman Gallery, New York.

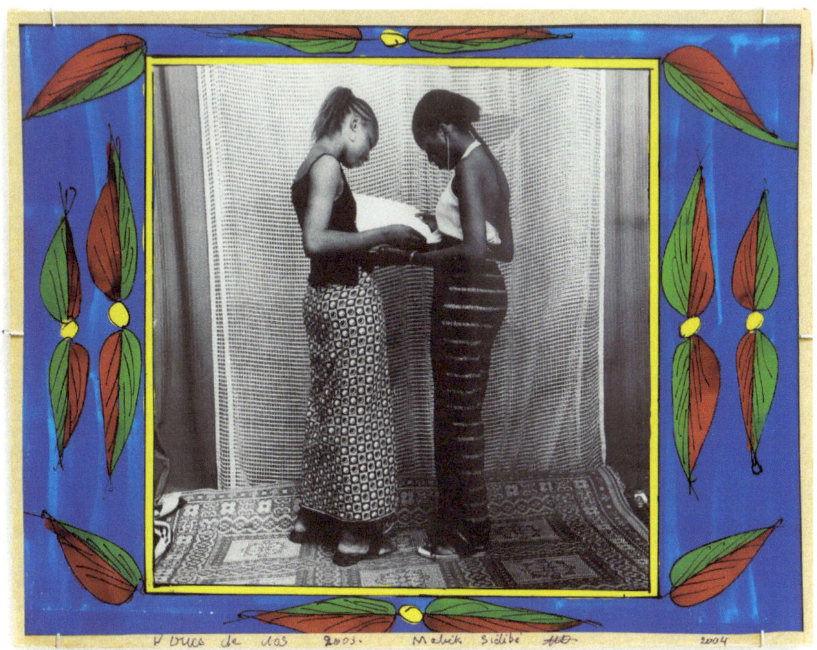

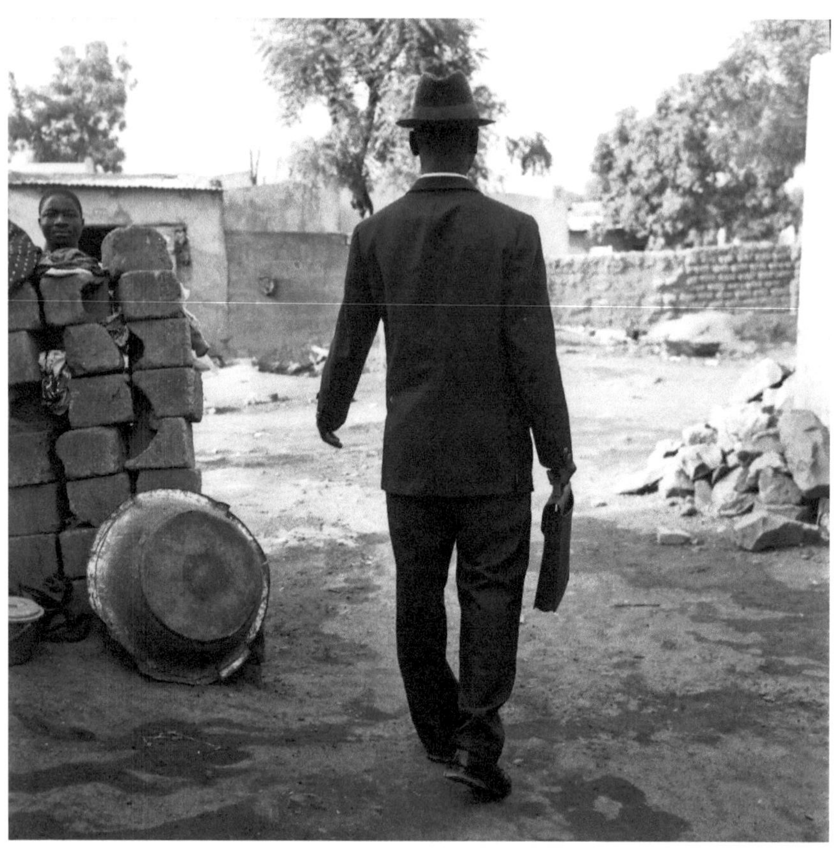

Figure 2.10. Malick Sidibé, *Vue de dos / Mon fils Siné sortant dans la cour* (*View from the Back / My Son Siné Sidibé Leaving the Yard*), 2001. Gelatin silver print. © Malick Sidibé. Courtesy of Galerie MAGNIN-A, Paris.

studio photography, in that it captures many views of people with their back turned, from mise-en-scènes to straightforward studio shots to intimate and erotic images. A postmodern approach to photography would similarly downplay the idea of originality, acknowledging intertextuality as operative in all artworks, and particularly emphasizing the idea of appropriation, which has become all but synonymous with contemporary art today.

The *Vues de dos* encompass figures in a range of contexts and poses. In one, *View from the Back / My Son Siné Sidibé Leaving the Yard* (2001), Sidibé's son Siné wears a sharp suit and a fedora and carries a slim briefcase, his foot cocked in the action of walking away (fig. 2.10). His dark silhouette presents a striking contrast to the light-filled dirt courtyard he is walking through, with its odd piles of rubble, a rusted metal bucket on its side, and a rickety cinder-block wall with a man's face peering enigmatically over the top. This cinematic picture plays on the juxtaposition of the wealthy-seeming, mysterious man with the everyday, impoverished background; there is an unknown narrative poised with significance. The suggestion is of an African man taking control of a situation despite difficult physical circumstances, or, perhaps, complicity: the rich men who succeed through corruption. One is reminded of films such as *Xala* or *Bamako*—the image of the African "big man" on his way to do business. The ambiguity produced by concealing the man's face sets this picture firmly in the realm of verité; yet this approach is belied by the literalness of the title, by which Sidibé seems to remove the concept of a cinematic narrative. By visually depicting such a narrative while overtly revoking that implication through his title, Sidibé highlights the infusion of Mande emphasis on family into his conceptual art. At the same time he refers back to the double play of his earlier studio photographs, in which a paying customer both remains himself or herself and poses as a cinematic figure.

Another photograph, *My Son, Amidou Sidibé, from the Back* (2001), shows Amidou standing casually in front of an open door covered by a lace curtain, positioned between a chair, cooking pots, and a wall, with a figure caught off-center in the background, and a small child entering on the right. Again the description belies the image, which is at once banal and significant. It seems again a film still or a filmic moment, caught as it is in the middle of a narrative and obviously in the middle of everyday life. The ambiguity of everyday life—the interest in the moment of narrative—is what these pictures seem to capture, especially for a viewer primed by Cindy Sherman's film stills to imbue them with meaning. Indeed, they seem to hover in between documentary and verité—to play with the very indexicality and banality set up by contemporary art photography—or by African portrait photography.

Some pictures *are* set in the studio and, if the subjects were facing forward, would constitute a typical studio portrait. These pictures clearly reverse the terms of the Western gaze, as Keller has suggested, since they were produced after, and obviously in response to, Sidibé's international exposure.[43] They explicitly confound the local logic of the studio portrait, which is above all to recognize the subject. Only one of these, *Large Family from the Back*, is printed in the monograph.

Another type of pictures shows women from behind, often with their shirt or blouse removed but wearing a bra (fig. 2.11). Several of these pictures were included in the 2003 Hasselblad Award book *Malick Sidibé: Photographs*.

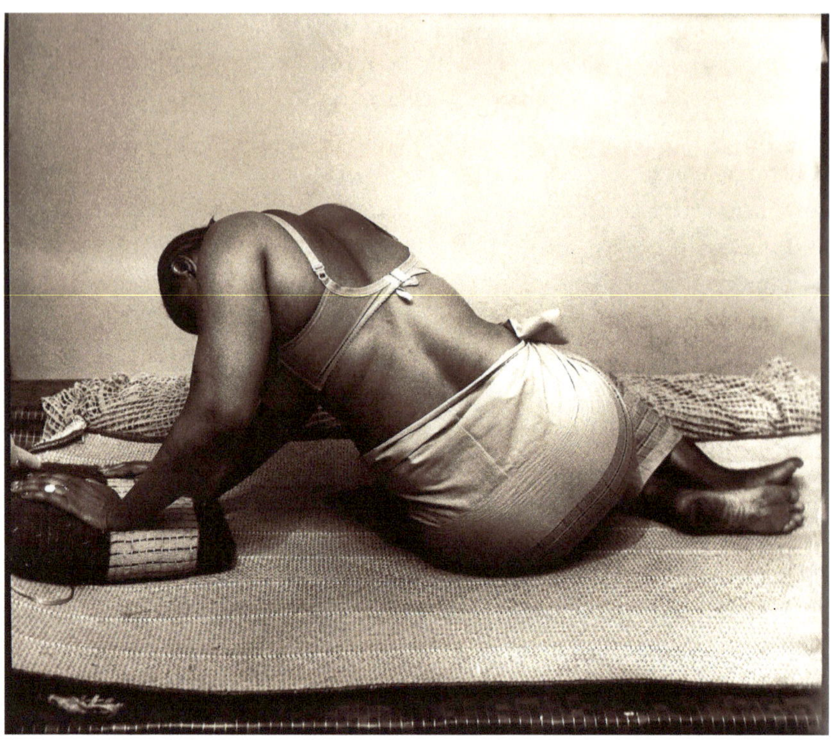

Figure 2.11. Malick Sidibé, *Vue de dos* (*View from the Back*). Gelatin silver print, 2001. © Malick Sidibé. Courtesy of Galerie MAGNIN-A, Paris.

In an interview, André Magnin asks Sidibé, "For the last two years you have taken photographs without being commissioned to, like your photographs from behind. How did you come upon this idea?" Magnin's question highlights the fact that Sidibé has taken up the mantle of "art photographer" by choosing to photograph without commission. Sidibé responds, "Like me you have undoubtedly noticed that, in the street, the men walk behind their women. They see them from the back, then they pass them and turn to look at them from in front. Only the photograph can tell you if you look nice from behind." Sidibé's last sentence disingenuously suggests that the women desire to have the portrait taken in order to see their own derrieres. But this contradicts the fact that Sidibé paid the models to take their pictures, and not vice versa.[44]

When I asked Sidibé about the series, he again explained that women look beautiful from behind—in other words, that sexual attraction was the impetus. The photographs of women from behind, particularly the ones wearing bras who are partially undressed, are meant to be beautiful and titillating. Sidibé's frank acknowledgment of his reasons for taking the "views from behind" complicates the notion that the pictures refuse the gaze, as they also celebrate feminine beauty as appreciated by male Malians, and in doing so potentially contribute to the objectification of women in deliberately mimicking an orientalist odalisque pose famous in the history of Western nudes for its objectification. Yet they refute this pose through their ordinary undergarments and turned-away faces, and in an American context through their body types. In this way they seem decidedly less objectifying than Huguier's "young Somono girl," whose skin is gleaming and who is slim and lit in the style of fashion photography. Sidibé's women look like real women, in their fleshy irreducible selves; these photographs are not falling into commercial stereotypes seen in *Vogue*. The pictures sexually objectify, or celebrate, their subjects, depending on one's point of view, taking art photography further toward the flirtation with the photographer and the titillation for male viewers that is already implicit in studio photography.

The power of Sidibé's *Vues de dos* turns on the knowledge of his earlier studio practice. Situated in the same studio space, wearing the same types of clothes, shot in black-and-white with the same lighting, but turned away, these subjects are portraits of anonymous women. Indeed, Keller notes that Sidibé "has further pushed the aesthetic element of *dìbi* in portraiture" in this series. "By withholding a great amount of expected information the viewer is drawn, in tantalizing and effective ways, to the individual and to the whole of the composition."[45] Sidibé did not like abstract art; he claimed that if one cannot recognize the person in a picture, the picture is no good.[46] Thus his subjects are recognizable, at least to the photographer, while they are mostly anonymous to the viewer. If his earlier commercial portraits capture an era in Bamako's history, what does it mean when today's pictures show people facing away? Does Sidibé's comment about the degeneration of society into individualism and material gain inform these pictures of Malians who turn away from the Western audience that celebrates those values, to become universal or communal types rather than individuals? Or do these portraits of opacity remind viewers of all that cannot be known—about individuals, but also about another culture? While the meanings of *Vues de dos* obviously fluctuate, among pictures and audiences, Sidibé's conceptual approach, generated from a longtime interest in posing his clients from the back, shows the photographer's creativity and ability to adapt to the changing times. His artworks circulate in Relation, using opacity as an aesthetic strategy, inspired by the interactions between the global art world

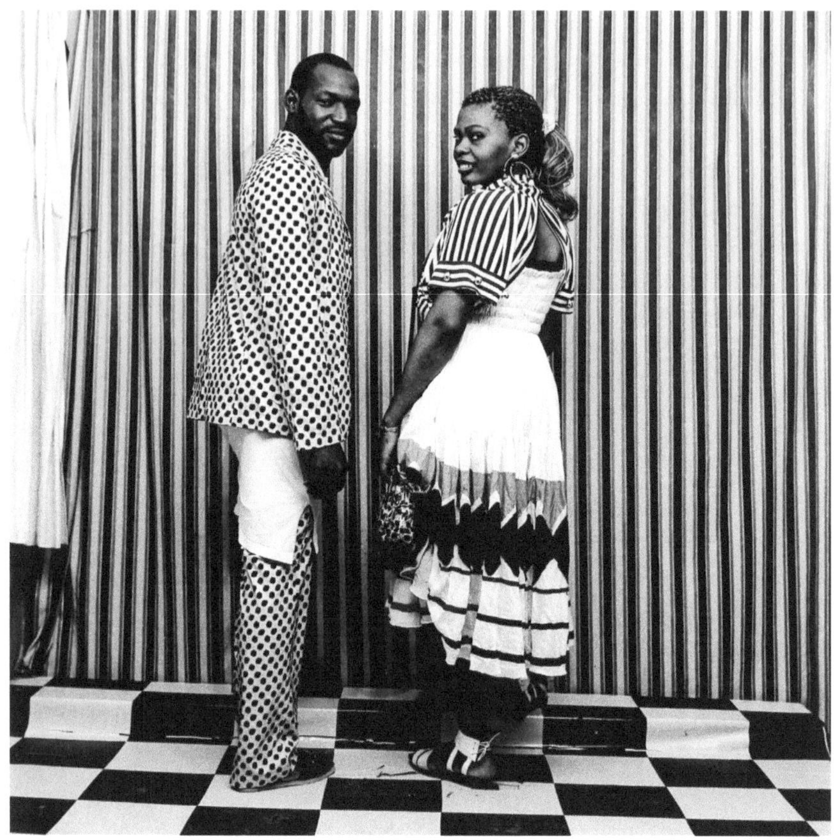

Figure 2.12. Malick Sidibé, *Prints and the Revolution*, as featured in the *New York Times Magazine*, April 1, 2009. As the *Times* noted, "Modibo Zounkara wears an Ann Demeulemeester cream-and-black polka-dot suit. Prada cream polo shirt. Dries Van Noten sandals. Kadia Coulibaly wears a Charles Anastase 1979 navy-red-and-cream dress. Tao Comme des Garçons navy-and-white jacket. Miu Miu bag. Chloé shoes. Louis Vuitton earrings." © Malick Sidibé.

and his own, earlier portraits, as well as by interactions among French and African photographers and curators.

Sidibé was commissioned to do fashion shoots for French magazines such as *Elle*, *Double*, and *Vogue*, and in 2009 he shot a series for the *New York Times Magazine*.[47] In this shoot, the striped backdrop became Sidibé's hallmark, similar to Keïta's arabesque pattern; this series essentially reified the striped backdrop as an unmoving, rigid shell or brand (fig. 2.12). Yet even so, the use of family members within the shoot is extremely Malian. Unlike Keïta's fashion shoot, which was discussed in one of the most commonly cited articles about Keïta by Bigham, Sidibé received bold praise from Nigerian critic and curator Bisi Silva, writing in *Artforum*.[48] Perhaps Silva's ambitions for contemporary African art and photography predisposed her to approve of these photos, or perhaps as a Nigerian curator she well understood the role of fashion in women's lives and in West African portraiture; in any event, there was not a hint of condemnation of Sidibé in her salutatory review. Because Sidibé continued his photographic practice, and enhanced his earlier portraiture with his *Vues de dos* series, these photographs do not create as glaring a contrast with his earlier work as Keïta's do; rather, they serve as a branding of Sidibé's signature style. But they also show Sidibé's interest in keeping up to date with global trends; while pictures of one man standing between two women (often cowives) is a common type in Malian studio portraiture, one woman standing between two men is a new take in reversing genders.

Like Sidibé's series, Seydou Keïta's fashion shoots for the May 1998 issue of *Harper's Bazaar* also reflect a conscious attention to an American audience, but in the context of a restricted collaboration with the editor of the magazine, Sarajane Hoare. Hoare chose the clothing designs (brought with her from New York fashion houses), the models (young women she and her assistant hired in Bamako), and the backdrops (bought at a market in Bamako).[49] Keïta's fashion photos, like Sidibé's, reproduce postcolonial capitalist relations, yet at the same time they herald a return to photography for an artist in his seventies who gave up working three decades earlier, in his first experiment with color photography.

It is uncertain to what extent Keïta was able to exert artistic control beyond these limitations.[50] The short text accompanying the photographs, written by Eve MacSweeney, refers to Keïta as "the surprise darling of the fashion world," because of his 1997 shows at Gagosian Gallery in New York and Los Angeles, and as a "local hero" in Bamako. Hoare is quoted on her reasons for flying to Mali to persuade Keïta to create the shoot. She describes Keïta's pictures as "classic portraiture at its best. It's amazingly sophisticated documentation, very beautifully done, and each photograph would be achieved with just one shot, which makes modern photographers look so wasteful." Hoare's appreciation of Keïta's thriftiness is the only reference to the economic disparity between Bamako and New York, although it is implied again when MacSweeney writes, "Instead of their own clothes, the models are wearing designs from the likes of Gaultier, Galliano, and Givenchy, paired with African-inspired turbans." Further on, captions to the photographs reveal that a scanty Lycra T-shirt costs $435.[51] Most clothing items pictured run between $1,000 and $2,000, while one gown from Chloé costs $3,050. In 1998, the estimated per capita income in Mali was $319.[52]

For what one might expect of such a fashion-world folly, the *Harper's* article is surprisingly accurate about Keïta's work and circumstances. The choice of the term "hero," for example, might seem inflated and corny, but in fact, according to Manthia Diawara, it is the correct local term for a man from Mali who has become rich and famous abroad.[53] The description of Keïta's portraits as "artwork . . . which grew from his years as a portrait photographer" is not inaccurate, although a reader might prefer a more nuanced analysis. As Keïta's commercial portraits for the international art world were printed by another person, and exhibited and sold as contemporary art in New York, technically the "art" did "grow out" of the studio work, as MacSweeney writes. Yet while the article contains no inaccuracies, the glib writing and lack of background context skim superficially over the historical circumstances of Keïta's studio practice and repress the economic inequity between New York and Mali.

These pictures may be Keïta's very first efforts in color. It is not known which pictures were *not* printed, nor how much control Keïta exerted over what he shot or what was printed, but it can be assumed that he was paid for the shoot. Keïta was returning, after a long absence, to a commercial practice, but for an American client, in a situation where the commissioner of the picture was different from the person portrayed, and where the point of the shoot was not to capture the sitter for posterity but to advertise the clothes the sitter wears.

Harper's re-creates the Keïta "look" as a simulacrum that lacks the local meaning of his original shots, but could also be understood as a variation on the theme of his 1950s portraits.[54] Although signature stylistic attributes signify "Keïta"—the use of black-and-white film, the models, and their fashionable clothes with strong patterns juxtaposed with backdrops bought in Mali—the pictures are missing the qualities that make his 1950s photographs so striking. The *reason* for being pictured is to advertise clothing, rather than to commemorate the clients, and the props and clothes do not look like those in the 1950s portraits, so the sum of the parts ends up as culturally "wrong"—that is, they do not match up visually with one of Keïta's 1950s portraits.

For example, one color photo in *Harper's* shows a woman reclining on her elbow on a pile of folded blankets, wearing Isaac Mizrahi's "ethnic ball-gown" (fig. 2.13). The woman seems to be wearing a European milkmaid-style corset, which barely contains her cleavage, and a wide, puffy skirt. These styles are not historically Malian. In a 1950s studio portrait, the model would have removed her decorative Manolo Blahnik shoes and set them neatly on the ground next to her or in front of her, as women do in many Keïta portraits. People in Mali, like people in the US, do not wear shoes when they are lying in bed, which is always the mise-en-scène when a client lies down for a portrait. The model also grins toothily—an expression rarely, if ever seen, in Keïta's formal pictures.

In another *Harper's* frame, the models are shot from a low angle, which further elongates the already tall, slim women.[55] Such an aesthetic of women's bodies belongs to American fashion, not Malian fashion, which traditionally has admired strong women who can work hard in the fields, and voluptuous women who appear fertile. It is unlikely that if Keïta wanted to make the women "look beautiful like that" (the famous phrase he used with his clients), he would emphasize their height and thinness to such a degree. In fact, almost all the models, with their self-conscious grins, look more like they are posing for Malick Sidibé than for Keïta. Only the unreadable expression on the model in the middle of the three women reaches beyond the contrived setting of the picture. While the clothing patterns clash with the chosen backdrops, the designs are not of the same flora or fauna designs so common to Keïta's clientele. (One can often see the repetition of fabrics among different clients, sewn in different styles, which must have been fashionable at the time.) The *Harper's* models wear almost no jewelry—most women who posed for Keïta showed off their jewelry if they had it—and if the folded cloths in the *Harper's* shot are meant to signify prestige items, as in one 1950s portrait where a woman lies on five layers of blankets, it is unusual to see a woman resting on *folded* blankets—they are always spread out on the bed (figs. 2.14 and 2.15).

Keïta's *Harper's* pictures utilize textile backdrops, but, although genuinely "Malian" (they were bought in Bamako, as the article points out), these backdrops are a different type of textile than what Keïta typically used, and they create a different visual effect. Keïta's backdrops were of cloth fashionable in the 1950s, "wax print" fabric based on Indonesian designs, made in Dutch factories and shipped to Africa.[56] While this is still often the case today, tastes and styles have changed. In the *Harper's* pictures, the signifiers do not make sense—at least, in terms of the 1950s portraits. They have been thrown together from a purely visual interest in Keïta's works; they do not cohere into the readable whole that one at first expects. Thus the fashion shoot is like bogolan cloth made for tourists. Bogolan's abstract symbols, when created for local use, embody powerful meanings to the women who

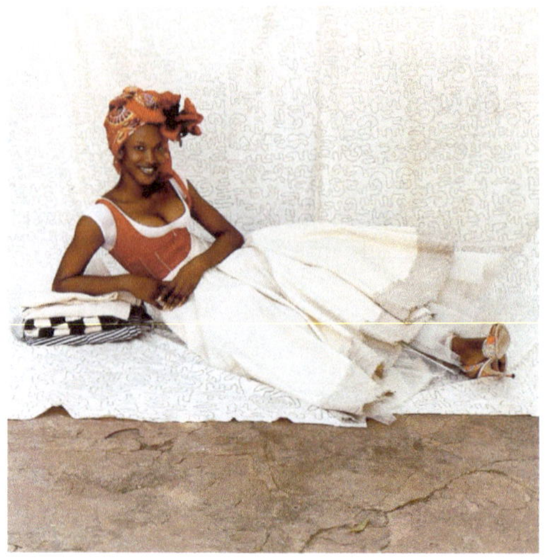

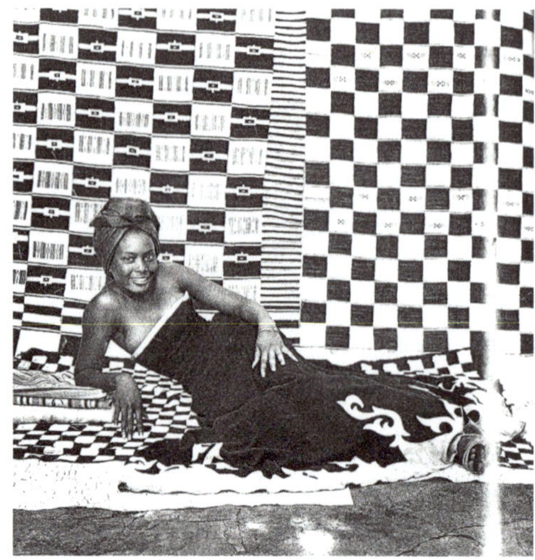

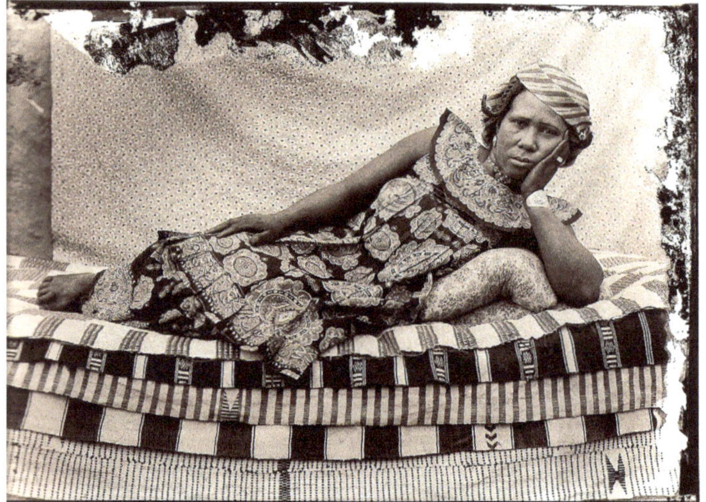

Figure 2.13. Seydou Keïta, *Sunday Best*, *Harper's Bazaar*, May 1998.

Figure 2.14. Seydou Keïta, *Sunday Best*, *Harper's Bazaar*, shot in black-and-white, May 1998.

Figure 2.15. Seydou Keïta, Untitled, gelatin silver print. Courtesy of CAAC—The Pigozzi Collection. © Seydou Keïta / SKPEAC.

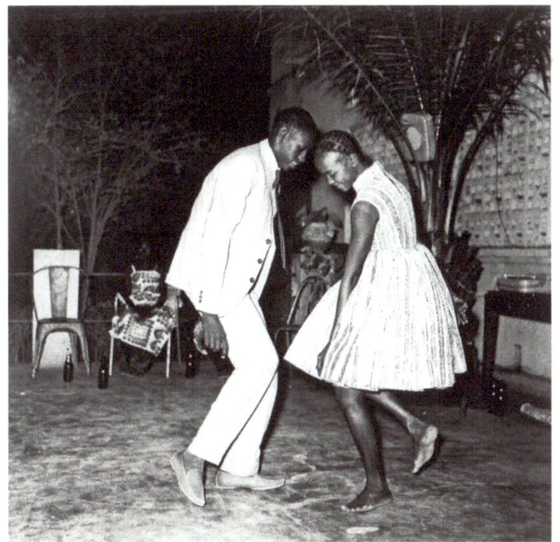

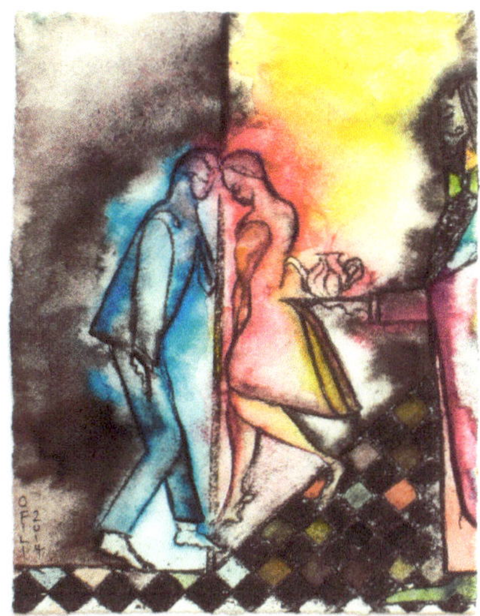

Figure 2.16. Malick Sidibé, *Nuit de Noël* (*Christmas Eve*). Gelatin silver print, 1963. Courtesy of the artist and Jack Shainman Gallery, New York.

Figure 2.17. Chris Ofili, *Mali Memory* (*Tea Dance*). Archival pigment print on Arches Aquarelles cotton rag paper, 2014.

made them; but when bogolan is made for the tourist market, the symbols are thrown together purely for the sake of visual effect and *mean* nothing, except that they are made for outsiders.[57] These pictures are, essentially, Seydou Keïta's tourist art, created for a commercial market. The jumbled signs here create a story, not only about Mali but also about the relationship *between* Bamako and New York, a relationship that emphasizes Bamako's effort to please and New York's frivolous use of money.

Yet none of what occurs in the *Harper's* scenario seems vastly different from Bamakois culture, aside from the amount of money involved. Women in Bamako will spend a good deal of their own, or their husband's, income to dress up.[58] Hoare was savvy in noticing the affinity between Malian studio portraits and fashion photography. It is safe to say that, in the *Harper's* fashion shoot, the collaboration is between Hoare and Keïta, or between *Harper's Bazaar* and Keïta. If any person is qualified to be a fashion photographer, it is Keïta, who knew how to help a woman show off her most beautiful attributes and stylish adornments. The history of photography, like the history of art, is rife with after-the-fact "artists" who also worked commercially. Scholar Elizabeth Bigham wants to "emphasize the collaborative authoring of Keïta's

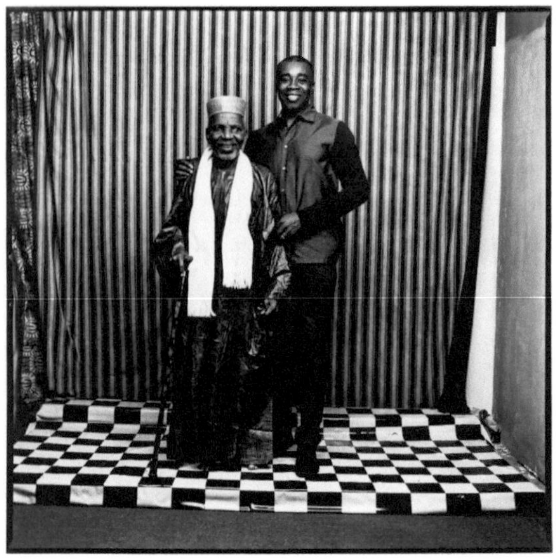

Figure 2.18. Malick Sidibé, Untitled (*Chris Ofili with Sidibé in Studio Malick*), 2014. © Malick Sidibé. Courtesy of the artist and Jack Shainman Gallery, New York.

portraits precisely because this quality may so easily be obscured given the remarkable renown . . . that he has achieved in the international art world."[59] Years after Bigham's article we can only bemoan the loss of context of all of these images, yet at the same time can appreciate their availability.

But, philosophically speaking, an interest in returning past meanings to Keïta's photographs, as to artifacts, has a pitfall, in believing that such meaning *can* be retrieved and that his pictures in the present do not contain value without that meaning. Scholar Geoffrey Batchen writes, "Any study of vernacular photographies must of course trace the presence of the past, but as an erasure (an absent presence fissured through and through by differences and contradictions) motivating the object in the present."[60] This theory frees the viewer to read meanings applicable to his or her own time and frame of reference. An emphasis on an impossible return to the past denies the very important impact that these visual, aesthetic artifacts—the wall-sized Keïta prints shown at Gagosian and Sean Kelly—have in a society that so rarely recognizes Africans as anything other than poor and diseased.

The globalization and glamorization of Keïta's and Sidibé's works, as well as African photographers like Samuel Fosso and J. D. 'Okhai Ojeikere, dramatically influenced numerous artists in Africa and the United States. Allan deSouza created a series of scanned prints from a family album from his childhood in Kenya, with his mother standing in front of blooms that create a patterned backdrop, heightened by the artist's digital drawings on the photograph. Kehinde Wiley and Mickalene Thomas have utilized the trope of figures against a floral or patterned backdrop in their paintings; Wiley actually borrowed from a famous Malian Dogon sculpture of the original man and woman for a painting of two men sitting next to each other. Kenyan British artist Grace Ndiritu made a video using colorful Dutch-wax cloths, lying in an odalisque pose with her head covered by cloth, while Benin artist Leonce Raphael Agbodjelou took photographs of male bodybuilders holding flowers in front of colorful backdrops in his series *Citizens of Porto-Novo.* Famed artist Chris Ofili made a print from one of Sidibé's photographs, and in turn was photographed at Studio Malick (figs. 2.16–2.18). The legacy of Keïta's and Sidibé's impact on the American and African art worlds continues to be felt—to return to the epigraph at the beginning of this chapter, Keïta's and Sidibé's Bamako prints become a spacing out of thought into the world, informing the imaginaries not only of global art audiences but especially of African and diaspora artists, whose poetics they dramatically influenced and transformed: in them the risk of Relation is realized.

Chapter 3

Biennale Effects

THE AFRICAN PHOTOGRAPHY ENCOUNTERS

A cultural presence can be active and ignored, whereas an intervention can be, on the contrary, spectacular and neutral.
—Édouard Glissant, *Poetics of Relation*

The Bamako Biennale—often translated as the Meetings or Encounters of African Photography—is the most concentrated site of resistance for the assertion of Malian culture in the world of art photography. Founded in 1994 by several French and Malian photographers and funded by the French Ministry of Culture, the biennale is where the forces of art world globalization and paternalistic French neocolonialism converge with the bureaucratic Malian state and the local aesthetics and power dynamics of Bamako's photography scene. Harboring intensely ambivalent tendencies, the biennale is nevertheless the most powerful force in the flowering of art photography, not only in Bamako but across the continent. The biennale is paradoxical, much as Glissant's thought is paradoxical. According to Michael Wiedorn, paradox "allows Glissant to pursue his—arguably quite political—goal of using art to breathe new life into thought."[1] Glissant's philosophical approach "undoes" Western philosophical tradition while relying on it to formulate his ideas against it. Just as Martinique, as a department, is governed by France and yet is distinguishable from France, the biennale as an institution is French-controlled and yet decidedly not French. The biennale is in one sense an instantiated, neocolonial dissemination of French cultural thought; at the same time, it is remarkably African in showcasing photographers across the continent and in spurring the growth of African photography.

The biennale was founded when French photographers Françoise Huguier and Bernard Descamps, working in West Africa for Agence VU, noticed a dearth of African photojournalists and organized the first exhibition in 1994 to support African photography with the active participation of Malian photographers Alioune Bâ, Django Cissé, and Harouna Racine Keïta.[2] Bâ was the official photographer for the National Museum, and Cissé was locally famous as the city's commercial postcard photographer.[3] The two French photographers traveled with Bâ and Cissé, in pairs, and from that collaboration grew the idea of the biennale. In an interview, Alioune Bâ noted that the biennale began in dialogue with Malian photographers.[4] Marie Lortie asserts that the biennale was rooted in the exchange between Seydou Keïta and Huguier. Huguier had met Keïta and organized a small exhibition for him in Paris, although Magnin is credited with giving Keïta his wide exposure. Amadou Chab Touré also gives credit to Huguier for the biennale's founding.[5] The international exhibitions of Keïta and Sidibé, occurring in the early 1990s, certainly increased the impetus to fund and support the biennale.[6] As this discussion makes clear, the narrative of the biennale's founding has changed over time, as more influence with regard to Malian photographers is acknowledged. However, Huguier's importance as the impetus for the biennale is undeniable.

Huguier, a photojournalist, had traveled across Africa in the late 1980s, deliberately photographing in the path of the famed surrealist ethnographer Michel Leiris. Leiris's participation as archivist and secretary in the 1931–1933 ethnographic expedition from Dakar to Djibouti, directed by Marcel Griaule, resulted in his book *L'Afrique fantôme*. Huguier exhibited photographs in Bamako's National Museum from her project, *Sur les traces de l'Afrique fantôme*.[7] The subsequently published book shows Huguier's fidelity to Leiris's method in particular, in inserting diary entries to accompany her photographs; both projects seem exoticizing to contemporary sensibilities.

Interestingly, Glissant, who studied at the Musée de l'Homme, discusses Michel Leiris at length and finds that his life's project was not exoticizing in a negative sense. He notes that Leiris was involved in a search for himself. In *Poetic Intention*, Glissant writes, "We hate ethnography: whenever, executing itself elsewhere, it does not fertilize the dramatic vow of relation."[8] He explains how Leiris struggled with his attempt to be objective, eventually recognizing its impossibility; his book, with diaristic notes and recordings of dreams, was as much about his own experiences as those of the people he was supposed to observe. "'The attentive observer' that is (or was) the ethnographer must *inscribe himself in the drama of the world*: beyond his analysis—in principle, 'solitary'—he must live a poetics (sharing). Thus Leiris."[9] For Glissant, Leiris could redeem his ethnographic project through openness to others and changing from his experience, even while participating in the Dakar-Djibouti project under colonial auspices.[10] In this sense, Huguier, in following in Leiris's footsteps, also participated in Relation when she actively involved herself in the lives of Bamakois photographers and collaborated with them to create the biennale. Thus the biennale began in a Relational impulse, but the need for financial support from the French government perpetuated a neocolonial relationship.

To examine the importance of the biennale as an institution is to acknowledge the multiple and contradictory nature of its effects.[11] The Bamako Biennale provides a range of opportunities and sometimes conflicting agendas that offer different valences to different actors. It is a complex bureaucracy and configuration of events with far-reaching effects that can be neither dismissed out of hand as absolutely neocolonial, despite strong tendencies in the biennale organization based in Paris, nor uncritically celebrated as purely positive for the development of photography in Africa in general, or for Mali in particular. This chapter teases out the nuances of the biennale's varied effects with particular emphasis on the way in which Malian artists and administrators exert their influence, both in creating photographs that convey Glissant's Relation to an international audience, and in providing moments of antihegemonic articulation of Mande aesthetics or Malian culture that counter the dominant French neocolonial hegemonic organization of the biennale.[12]

The biennale has been influential and indeed instrumental in its encouragement of a Malian art photography movement, and all of the photographers interviewed in Bamako were grateful for its presence, even if some were critical of its approach. The event's biannual calls for proposals have provided motivation for Bamakois photographers, offering a theme to work toward and feedback in the basic sense of inclusion or lack thereof in the biennale's exhibitions. The biennale also provides workshops and usually includes at least one exhibition devoted to photography by Malians. Local photographers can also participate in or organize the "Offs" exhibitions shown at the same time, or take part in some of the activities that are outreaches of the biennale, such as panel discussions. However, photographers must be already active within local circles in order to have access to the biennale, as historically participants have been required to register and pay fees for a biennale pass.[13]

Most importantly, the event has lent the city's photographers a needed raison d'être for their creative work, which is generally unrewarded financially or by an audience, and helped to create a close-knit, badenya-oriented community of arts photographers, institutions, and administrators. The biennale legitimates the artists' striving for poetic or creative approaches to photography and brings them into visual and conversational contact with photographs and photographers from elsewhere in Africa, providing much-needed support from artists facing similar practical and infrastructural challenges in the making of their work. At the same time, the biennale brings a particular set of aesthetic standards to bear upon local photographers, a standard that lines up with a prevailing emphasis on a global conceptualist approach to contemporary photography. In contrast to more conceptual approaches concerned with the overabundance of photography in the digital age, its fraught physical past, outmoded materials, or its uses in terms of surveillance, art photography in Mali does not currently question its existence as photography.[14] The only artist who takes a somewhat conceptualist approach—but one still strongly connected to Malian photo history—is Moussa Kalapo, with his series of people holding their own old family portraits, called *The Metaphor of Time* (2015), shown in the 2015 Bamako Biennale.[15]

With curators mostly educated and based in Europe, despite close ties to Africa, the biennale selection committees have, at least until the 2015 edition, typically reproduced this global conceptual aesthetic standard, or focused on more documentary modes involving postcolonial critique, and thus delimited the opportunity to make or show works with other aesthetic or conceptual values than those celebrated in the global canons and trends of contemporary photography, at least in the International Exhibition.

Furthermore, a distinctly neocolonial attitude and set of power relations permeates most aspects of the French organization of the biennale. French power is implicit in the financial structure, as the biennale was created and is paid for by the French government, with French officials making key funding decisions, which affect such decisions relating to curatorship, artist selection, prizes, and who is funded to attend. This French infrastructure has been historically ambivalent about Malian collaboration. For all but one of the editions, the curation has come from outside Mali, and Malians have mostly facilitated organization and coordination rather than taking leadership roles in the artistic vision of the exhibitions. The office through which the biennale is organized remains in Paris, with shaky communication to Bamako and no funding support available in between biennales.

Meanwhile, the notably corrupt Malian government, which fell prey to the 2012 coup, provides daunting bureaucratic challenges for a Malian administrator trying to work on the biennale during its off seasons. It is clearly upsetting to the Malian organizers that the government does not want to fund the biennale. The African House of Photography, Maison Africaine de la Photographie (MAP), founded in 2004 and presumably named after the Maison Européene de la Photographie in Paris, never housed the archives or photographs for which it was originally created.[16] This lack of state support, which forces administrators to rely on France and the EU for funding, certainly suggests a postcolonial stagnation. During the decade-long presidency of Amadou Toumani Touré (ATT) in particular (2002–2012), support of the biennale declined from President Alpha Oumar Konaré's (1992–2002) active encouragement.

The political circumstances of the African Photography Encounters are relevant to its existence as a biennale: as Caroline Jones bluntly puts it, "Biennials are an excellent way to pursue 'politics by other means.'"[17] In Bamako, the interface of the two governments, Mali and France, is mediated by the artistic director. The production of a set of durational exhibitions and performative events, workshops, panels, a catalog, and a web presence—in short, the production of the entire biennial—not only becomes the cultural event in and of itself, but its every structural decision is a negotiation of wills among the three powerful decision-making entities, even though Lucie Touya of CulturesFrance has insisted that all decisions are made jointly between Paris and Bamako.[18]

Bamako is one of over a hundred photography festivals that have proliferated with increasing speed since the 1970 founding of the Arles Photography Biennale, on which Bamako was modeled. The rise of art biennales in "exotic," sometimes impoverished locales is a defining feature of the global art world. While these biennales are often decried as examples of art world excess and spectacle, many of these exhibitions are in fact decentering the art world, allowing artists from the "periphery" to show in global events and receive significant exposure to a wide international audience. This was American critic Richard Vine's assessment of the 2003 Bamako Biennale, which he praised in *Art in America* as the most exciting photography biennale, in terms of quality, in the world. For him, it was a "salutary shock to realize that, for a decade now, one of the world's best gatherings of fine-art photography has occurred biannually in one of the earth's poorest countries—a nation with an average income of less than $300 per capita. Moreover, the event's participants are drawn almost exclusively from a continent whose resources have long been expropriated by foreign powers or squandered by homegrown tyrants."[19]

While scholars assert that the biennale was based on Arles, the 1996 catalog refers to the first edition as the "Fespaco de la Photo," quoting "Malian friends' expression who hope that the Bamako Biennial will have the same success, without a doubt, as the famous Ouagadougou film festival has."[20] While French photographers used their personal familiarity with Arles to structure their imaginary of Bamako, Malian photographers turned to FESPACO in Burkina Faso in a similar imaginary, connecting to a festival on the continent and emphasizing a closer connection between photography and film than the French photographers perceived.[21]

This connection to FESPACO (Festival Panafricain du Cinéma et de la Télévision de Ouagadougou) was surely noted by Harouna Racine Keïta, in particular, one of the Malian cofounders of the biennale who worked for the Centre National de Production Cinématographique in the capital, where he was the director of photo-cinematography and the head of the Montage Section.[22]

Founded in Ouagadougou in 1969 as the Pan-African Film and Television Festival, FESPACO included Mali in its second edition.[23] Like the older generations of photographers in Mali who studied in the Eastern Bloc, the well-known Malian film directors Souleymane Cissé and Abderrahmane Sissako were trained in cinema in the USSR. Given the close relationship between Burkina Faso and Mali, as well as the interest in photography's relationship to film and video, FESPACO's importance is underacknowledged as an influence on the Bamako Biennale. In the 2001 catalog, Amadou Chab Touré also refers to FESPACO, showing it was an active model in the Malian photographers' imaginaries, as film is simply fast-moving photographs. Film also connects to art photography's roots in the popular form of studio portraiture, as films are more relatable than contemporary art.[24]

Because of the rise of biennials and their dramatic impact on the reconfiguration of the art world in global terms, studies on the subject of "biennial culture" are increasing. Critical scholars seem to assume that biennials are all similarly structured and that they are dominated by a small set of reigning global artists, who alone benefit from their globalized exposure. However, as Simon Sheikh notes, many biennials are actually deliberately regional in scope, including major exhibitions like Manifesta, the Havana

Biennial, and the Whitney Biennial.[25] Criticisms are also leveled against corporatization and nationalism, as a biennial's function is expected to enhance the tourist industry of its location, rendering the biennial a spectacle of trendy new styles rather than a place to engage with "serious" art. While this may be true in some cases, the biennial as a cultural institution embodies a more flexible and complex format than often recognized and provides "peripheral" areas with an interface with the global art world, offering opportunities to those limited in finances and the ability to travel.

Moreover, biennial effects are complex and unpredictable, not unlike Relation. A biennial embodies a more flexible structure than a museum because the gaps caused by its temporal repetition are tied to post-Fordist labor practices.[26] In a biennial, the emphasis is on the present (the new exhibition) more than the past, but the past remains present within the formal structure of the biennial. What is notable about the biennial as a form is the recurrence of the new within a temporally repetitious format, not unlike a form and its varied embellishments. Thus, the structure of the biennial as an institution can be seen as similar to Mande aesthetics in their emphasis on repetition and variation. Biennials are also where important new work is shown, long before museums—even contemporary art museums—can discover the newest movements. And the market connection is not far beyond the curatorial logic; artworks shown in the Venice Biennial are often claimed beforehand and paid for soon afterward, when they appear at post-biennial fairs like Art Basel.

Whatever its benefits or detriments, Nikos Papastergiadis and Meredith Martin argue that the "biennale is increasingly taking form as one of the most powerful vehicles for articulating the palpable tensions and latent possibilities in contemporary aesthetics and politics."[27] These scholars elaborate three models of biennales that have developed since the founding of Venice in 1895.[28] The first is the Venice Biennial itself, with its traditional (meaning conservative) format of one international pavilion in which European and American art continues to predominate, and smaller national pavilions; the second is Havana, which is "horizontal," emphasizing regionality and anti-Western capitalism; and the third is Documenta 11, curated by Okwui Enwezor, the Nigerian-born curator who implemented a "discursive" model with conversations and platforms in locations beyond Documenta's usual home in Kassel, Germany, including Vienna and Berlin, New Delhi, St. Lucia, and Lagos. In other scholars' less differentiated formulations, Documenta 11 and Havana are usually grouped together as examples of the political and global possibilities of biennials, again in contrast to Venice, whose Euro-American hierarchy is dominant.[29]

But separating Havana and Documenta as models acknowledges the importance of regionality and discursivity as two distinct agendas. Both of these agendas are operative in the Bamako Biennale, even as it maintains a very traditional or conservative focus on the prestigious "International Pavilion." Yet Bamako fits neatly into none of these categories, showing how variable the categorical type of institution a "biennial" can be. Because the French tend to perpetuate a top-down hierarchical model in terms of decision-making, the Bamako Biennale is in many ways a neocolonial biennale. This is surely why it has not generated significant study among neo-Marxist art historians, yet it nevertheless contributes to a critical visual discourse and to a dehierarchization of East and West, South and North through the images and exhibitions themselves as well as a regional horizontality fostered by informal conversations, workshops, and discursive platforms.

While Papastergiadis and Martin argue that it is difficult to qualitatively examine the effects of biennales in general, the impact of Bamako has been obvious and measurable, because of the almost complete lack of art infrastructure on the African continent before it. Bamako's specific regional focus on the African continent also allows the biennale more focus than more inclusive biennials, enabling an emphasis on local aesthetics and concerns specific to African countries.

Indeed, the Bamako Biennale's scope and specific focus on the African continent gives it a special importance within broader "biennial culture," similar to the Asia Pacific Triennial or Dak'art in its attention to regional dynamics. Dak'art, the contemporary art biennial in Dakar, Senegal, is especially important to consider because of Senegal's proximity to Mali, and because Dak'art's eleventh edition in 2014, called "Producing the Common," was inspired by Glissant's notion of the *Tout-Monde* (All-World), by which he means a world that is composed of "the ex-colonized, the ex-colonizers, the ex-masters, the ex-slaves, the ex-aristocrats, the ex-workers, etc., we are all in the All-World now. Not one of us can pretend to be shielded from that. So let's try to see—this is our utopia—how we are going to get by in this *Tout-Monde*."[30] Dak'art, as a state-funded biennial of contemporary art, rather than a French-funded biennial of photography, seems much more Relational as an institution than the Bamako Biennale, whose *effects* can be Relational but whose structure is in many ways neocolonial.

Dak'art's first two editions occurred in 1990 and 1992, surely influencing Huguier's decision to create a photo biennial in Mali, although the Malian cofounders were more influenced by the Ouagadougou Film Festival in Burkina Faso.[31] Dakar, as the colonial capital of French West Africa, and thus as the center from which colonial enterprises and ideas radiated, exerted an important influence on colonial-era Mali. After both nations gained independence in 1960, they briefly joined political forces for several months, until a rift between Senegal's president, Léopold Sédar Senghor, one of the philosophical founders of Négritude, and Mali's president, Modibo Keïta, caused a severe break. Senghor governed a democracy from 1960 to 1980 that richly supported artists, setting the stage for Dakar's current contemporary art scene, and maintained close ties with France. By contrast, Keïta disowned France and turned to the USSR and communism, ruining Mali's economy and apportioning minimal funding toward the arts.

Dak'Art was launched in 1990 as the Dakar Biennial of Arts and Letters. It was created as a follow-up to the 1966 Festival des Arts Nègres, which occurred during the first decade of Senghor's presidency. While both Bamako and Dak'art are pan-African biennales that owe their existence to the expansion of contemporary art in Africa and to the worldwide explosion of biennales, there are crucial differences between the two related to government support and medium that make them in actuality less comparable than they seem.

One extremely important difference is funding: Dak'art is funded by the Senegalese state, whereas Bamako is funded, and thus largely controlled, by France, which gives a very different valence to the event (notwithstanding Senegal's long and close ties to its former colonizer). According to Joanna Grabski, Dak'art's presence has fueled the city's artistic economy and vice versa, with an "Offs" exhibition of local venues that rivals Dak'art's official expos. Tensions between the Senegalese government and the city's artists, as well as between the international expos and local artists, drive discursive debates about Dak'art, rather than the struggles over decision-making that implicate France in Bamako's neocolonial funding status.[32]

Another crucial difference is medium, and the history of each biennale's medium within its own nation. From 1960 to 1980, President Senghor provided government patronage in support of a particular "Négritude" aesthetic, which resulted in state-supported institutions and distinct schools of aesthetics in Senegal. This twenty-year support of modern artists working in an "art for art's sake" mode created a substantive art world, so that today's artists operate within a rich environment of artistic traditions and institutions, where the profession of artist is admired and acknowledged.[33]

Painting, sculpture, and installation were the dominant mediums at Dak'art through the 1990s and into the 2000s, when film, video, and photography became prominent as well.

By contrast, the Bamako Biennale's founding was an anomalous and surprising development in relation to the city's commercial photographic history. The Bamako Biennale was created to specifically celebrate commercial photography in the form of African reportage and studio portraiture, rather than to promote a solely "art for art's sake" approach. Bamako's festival is medium-specific, highlighting not only the artistic but also more practical or commercial forms of photography, and, more recently, videography. The Bamako Biennale still includes a wide variety of approaches toward photography. Art photography did not exist in Mali, nor in most places in Africa, until after the biennale was founded. Moreover, the biennale was founded because of Keïta's and Sidibé's fame in the international art world, a context that differed significantly from the photographers' earlier roles and practices in the city; and their fame occurred decades after they had stopped taking portraits. Photography's form of circulation, indexicality, and its own paradoxical nature, insofar as the viewer is unable to separate the photograph from its subject, also connects that medium to Relational effects.

In contrast to Mali, Senegal has a long and intimate relationship to France, which began in the mid-1300s, and this makes strong distinctions between "French" and "Senegalese" culture dubious, at least in the coastal cities of Dakar and St. Louis, where there is a history of cultural métissage. For example, studio portraiture from St. Louis is famous for portraying intermixed families of wealthy signare women who married French colonial men. By contrast, the French conquered the interior region that became Mali late in the nineteenth century, and with fewer personnel and less assimilation in terms of cultural mixing as a result. In other words, the postcolonial situation is negotiated differently in Senegal than in Mali: Malians' pride in their heritage, the remnants of Mali's great empire, is still powerful in southern Mali. While young men desire to go abroad for economic reasons, they desire to return because of this powerful attachment to their heritage. Thus the Bamako Biennale's peculiar fascination lies in the paradox of how its neocolonial structure contrasts with its Relational effects, found in an art photography movement that embraces international ideas without giving up indigenous Mande aesthetics, epitomizing Glissant's notion of changing through exchange with the other without losing oneself.

To some extent, the problematics of the Bamako Biennale reiterate the same tension between the international and the local faced by most bien-

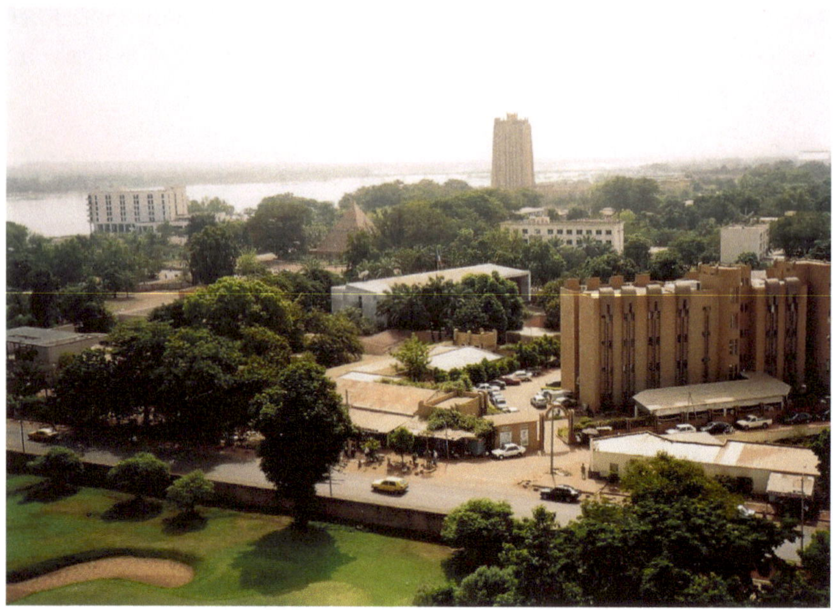

Figure 3.1. View of Bamako looking toward the Niger River from the Sofitel Hotel, 2005. Photograph by author.

nials' host countries, especially in nations with smaller local art scenes and therefore fewer places for local artists to show. However, in certain major respects Bamako is unique. Unlike many biennials, the major impetus of Bamako was not to bring tourism to the city, but instead to encourage the work of local photographers, especially in the realm of photojournalism, and to expose their services and talents to a wider world. Cofounder Françoise Huguier, herself a photojournalist for VU, wanted to enable news agencies to hire African photographers for reportage on the continent.[34] Although the biennale undoubtedly has been welcomed by several hotels, tourism has not happened on any scale—the few hundred visitors who descend on Bamako every two years are barely noticeable in an uptick of taxicab services and the few restaurants and hotels catering to wealthy visitors (usually Europeans, Americans, and some Chinese). Tensions between the artist community of the host country or city naturally occur because of the internationalism of the biennial as an institutional genre (fig. 3.1).

While acknowledging the Bamako Biennale's relevance and relation to the art world, it is equally important to situate the biennale within the scope and history of festivals in Mali, thereby articulating the biennale's difference from precolonial and socialist-era festivals, which sought to create community through commemorating mythic or religious histories in towns and villages, or foster national pride during the postcolonial socialist era. By contrast, the biennale's communal effects have been limited but potent: it has encouraged a small community of photographers to consider themselves artists, engaging a cosmopolitan imaginary and interacting with a transnational community. Despite the neocolonial structure of the biennial, at its best it works—if only for a limited number of Malian photographers and culture workers—to tie together the traditional and the modern, which are lived simultaneously, and to provide a new public space for discussion in modernized urban locations, which can be understood symbolically as part of the function of democracy in Mali, given its sociohistorical context.

During Mali's socialist period, between 1960 and the coup d'état of 1991, the government supported youth festivals to encourage nationalist and socialist sentiments.[35] Under Mali's first president, Modibo Keïta, a state-sponsored arts and sports festival—La Semaine de Jeunesse (The Week of Youth)—was held annually until 1968, when Keïta was replaced in a coup. Under the subsequent president, Moussa Traoré, The Week of Youth was suspended, but then reinvented as the Artistic, Cultural and Sport Biennale (La Biennale Artistique, Culturelle et Sportive), which lasted for two decades, from 1970 to 1990. Traoré tried to rid the festivals of their associations with the former president and dictator Modibo Keïta, and popular and praise songs mentioning his name were forbidden.

But essentially the same rhetoric of nationalism continued, with the stated goal of bringing together diverse groups of young people to celebrate national heritage and socialist values. In the 1990s, after the shift to democracy, the state-run festivals became less popular. Mary Jo Arnoldi suggests it was because of the privatization of the performances under capitalism—people could now see popular musicians perform more often throughout the year.[36] But by moving the youth festival away from Bamako to regional cities such as Segou in 2003, the event was rejuvenated. Just a few years earlier, in 2001, the annual Taureg Festival of the Desert, a festival of music and art, was created to soothe political tensions between the alienated and nomadic northern Tuareg peoples and the southern-based Malian government, in hopes of encouraging national unity through a celebration of world music and specifically of bands like Tartit.

In contrast to these festivals, which were specifically inaugurated to encourage a sense of national community, and which were clearly and successfully (at least in terms of their popularity) instrumentalizing culture for political ends, in line with the government's socialist agenda, the Bamako

Biennale was formally conceived of as an *international* exhibition, organized to celebrate and encourage photographers across Africa. French domination in the form of financing and impetus was present from the beginning. While Malian photographer Alioune Bâ recounts that the biennale emerged from a collaboration among himself, Huguier, Bernard Descamps, Django Cissé, and Racine Keïta, the biennale would not have occurred without the inspiration of Huguier in particular, who was working and exhibiting in Bamako with the Arles Photography Rencontres on her mind. Given the new form of a photography biennial, based on the Venice Biennale model (which Arles is also based on), in contrast to the Malian youth and performance festivals, which drew on precolonial traditions already much valued by Malians, French influence clearly also marked the biennale's exhibition format. At the same time, the Malian government, under President Konaré, welcomed the Encounters, while the French government had to be persuaded; this imbalance subsequently shifted in later years after Konaré left office. In other words, the biennale did not grow out of an existing cultural form; it was more like, in Njami's words, a UFO landing in the city: unsettling, but also creating excitement and opportunity.[37]

As of 2018, the biennale is funded by the Institut Français under the office Afrique et Caraïbes en Créations, which began in 1990 as an independent colloquium of African and French professionals working in the field of culture. At the end of the colloquium, the organization was endowed with funding in order to promote contemporary African culture in Europe. The office responsible for the biennale has changed names numerous times since the biennale's founding in 1994, when the office was Afrique en Créations, supported dually by the French Ministry of Culture and the Ministry of Cooperation.[38] The two goals of Afrique en Créations were to support African cultural development and to provide African artists with access to the global market, and these services were considered a form of developmental aid by France.[39] In 2000, Afrique en Créations was subsumed under AFAA (Association Française d'Action Artistique), which supported artistic projects in France and around the world. In 2006 AFAA, under which Afrique en Créations still existed as a department, was reorganized and renamed CulturesFrance. In 2007, CulturesFrance provided assistance to thousands of projects in over one hundred countries across the globe in a seemingly benign, but obviously ideological, form of cultural colonization. Four years later, in 2011, under French president Nicolas Sarkozy, CulturesFrance was again reshuffled and retitled, becoming today's (2011–2020) Institut Français.[40]

AFAA is an outgrowth of the French colonial policy of assimilation, which was a belief in the supremacy of French culture, with the goal of enforcing French culture on Africans and others in France's wide-ranging colonies. The original government office that eventually became AFAA was founded in 1922, under the name Association Française d'Expansion et d'Échanges Artistiques (French Association of Expansion and Artistic Exchange), and in 1934 changed its name to AFAA. In 1946 the Association pour la Diffusion de la Pensée Française (ADPF—Association for the Diffusion of French Thought) was founded, which eventually merged with AFAA. The organization began as a scholarly community, which became a state agency. Perhaps not surprisingly, given the French government's reluctance to acknowledge its colonial history, no mention of colonialism appears in the AFAA literature and websites; yet the organization was founded during the height of France's colonial rule, when France controlled large regions in West and Central Africa.

The 2016 website of the Institut Français shows the tone adopted in relation to its history of empire and colonialism. The section under "Our History" (written in English) refers to those fraught enterprises with the euphemism of "diplomacy through culture": "France has a long tradition of pursuing diplomacy through culture going back to the Ancien Regime. This was a time when culture and diplomacy were closely interlinked, and when the French language and culture permeated the world."[41] Here there is no mention of colonialism or of Francophonie—only a confident assertion of the need for French culture throughout the world. This self-confident tone is visible in AFAA's dealings with biennale organizers and artists alike and appears to be rampant across the organization.[42]

But in 1994, when the first biennale was ushered in on the heels of Mali's democracy, under the guardianship of Mali's first democratically elected president, Alpha Oumar Konaré, the French government was reluctant to participate.[43] Presumably the French government could not acknowledge the importance of vernacular African studio photography or African reportage; namely, the African implementation of the perceived Western technology of photography did not seem viable to France. It took the female French photographer Françoise Huguier to press the point, and the art world to validate it.

The first biennale celebrated Seydou Keïta and Malick Sidibé, whose international fame contributed to the impetus for holding the biennale, and included studio photographers, art, and photojournalism from other West African countries and South Africa. Subsequent editions, held every two years except for a skipped year between 1998 and 2001, and a four-year suspension (from 2011 to 2015) because of the 2012 coup, have vastly expanded the number of photographers and types of genres included, and the festival has taken on a truly pan-African dimension.

Yet the biennale remains a somewhat contested event within Bamako's community of photographers, in part because of its nature *as* a biennale, and in part because it is largely controlled by the French government. It is useful to delineate the ways in which the biennale exhibitions have acknowledged and contributed to a Malian approach to photography, because only through this careful analysis can the full nature of its effects be understood. While the most Malian-centered biennales were arguably the third, in 1998, and the tenth, in 2015, most iterations have at least nodded toward the biennale's host country in some way. If the biennale is understood as a hegemony, as described by Chantal Mouffe, then the disarticulation of certain features of the biennales, and their rearticulation within a Malian approach to photography, contribute to a counterhegemonic practice.[44] By "a Malian approach" I mean not simply the inclusion of photographs by Malians, but the overall way that aspects of the biennales express Mande aesthetics and culture, requiring non-Malian visitors to become aware of Malian culture and its difference from their own.

One of these dis- and rearticulations is experienced in the seemingly simple but powerful fact that the biennale is held in Bamako. From an African perspective, the location of the biennale on the continent is its most important aspect in enabling photographers to meet, see work, and make connections.[45] While visiting Bamako may be a new experience for some African participants, the construction of the notion of "Africa" as a place of home, community, and relatedness seems to create a sense of immediate belonging and pride in an African biennial, although in talking with visiting artists such pride was not arrogant or vain, and was usually tempered with thoughtful criticality. African photographers are well aware of the lack of venues and opportunities on the continent, so they continue to attend despite the biennale's contested reputation. The biennale also entices curators, critics, and audiences from the US and Europe who might otherwise never travel to see art in Africa; in 2006, for example, AFAA paid to bring in a curator to visit from New York's International Center of Photography.

The biennale has changed and grown dramatically over the quarter of a century since it was founded in 1994.[46] The first edition of the Bamako Biennale included studio portraits, some archival images from various governmental press agencies, and art photographs. Photographers mostly hailed from West Africa, although South Africans also participated, with the notable inclusion of two women, Jenny Gordon and Ingrid Hudson. Presumably Huguier, as a female photojournalist, was well aware of the challenges facing women in that field and desired to afford African women such opportunities. Now-illustrious photographers like Santu Mofokeng of South Africa, Samuel Fosso of Democratic Republic of Congo, Boubacar Touré Mandémory of Senegal, and Rotimi Fani-Kayode, of Nigerian British origin, were among the handful of artists exhibited in the first edition. Fani-Kayode's Yoruba-inspired homoerotic art, shown in an exhibition organized by the French press Revue Noire, was especially noteworthy, as the explicitly sexual pictures would be considered shocking in Bamako and in most of Africa. At the same time, what gave the biennale its impetus was the presence of the world's most famous African photographers at that time, Malick Sidibé and Seydou Keïta, hailing from their hometown of Bamako, so a certain national pride was at work.

Malian photographers Alioune Bâ, Harouna Racine Keïta, and Django Cissé participated in the first biennale, along with Seydou Keïta and Sidibé. Archival press photographs from government agencies in Guinea and Mali were also included. Although illustrated pamphlets describing the proceedings were printed, the first two editions were not accompanied by published catalogs, as the later editions were. The biennale thus demonstrated to local photographers that studio photography could be considered worthy of exhibition, and also provided examples of art photography by other Africans to its viewers, most of whom were photographers themselves. This exposure was especially valuable before the internet became widespread in Africa.

Bernard Descamps organized the second edition two years later, with a French writer and photography critic, Louis Mesplé, who had been the director of the Rencontres d'Arles from 1991 to 1994 and had contributed to the founding of Bamako's biennale. The 1996 exhibition was broader in geographical scope, including photographers from East and southern African countries, such as Ethiopia, Kenya, Mozambique, Namibia, and Djibouti. A number of Malian studio photographers' archives had been recovered since the first biennale, such as those of Adama Kouyaté (b. 1927 in Ségou), whose work was recently exhibited internationally with Gallery 51 in Antwerp, Belgium, and Kélétigui Touré (b. 1922 in Kayes). Three other studioists—Abdourahmane Sakaly (1926–1988), Hamadou Bocoum (1930–1992), and El Hadj Tijani Àdìgún Sitou (1932–1999)—were shown by a Danish man, Svend Erik Sokkelund, who took the photographers' negatives and kept them illegally.[47]

By contrast, the Oscura pinhole workshops, a pan-European collective with a whimsical, activist bent, coordinated by Elisabeth Towns, taught children to create pinhole cameras. This was a creative and educational endeavor that prefigured contemporary art photography's current fascination with outmoded DIY technologies and obsolescent effects. (For example, in the 2017 Whitney Biennial, the Puerto Rican artist Chemi Rosado-Seijo organized a working classroom for children from the Lower Manhattan Arts Academy.) The collective also curated an exhibition of portraits by Kélétigni Touré. In addition, there was reportage, and curators included Guy Hersant, Yves Pitchen, Bernard Descamps, Jean-François Werner, and Svend Erik Sokkelund.[48] There was also an "Off," called "Les Cocotiers," at the Palais de la Culture.

For the third biennale, in 1998, Descamps handed over the artistic direction to Malian artist Abdoulaye Konaté, who now heads the Balla Fasséké Conservatory of Arts and Multimedia in Bamako.[49] Mesplé remained involved as the financial director. Amadou Chab Touré was appointed adjunct curator to the chief curator. The lack of trust involved in withholding financial direction from a Malian is obvious, although the funding was provided by France via Afrique en Créations, which has been true for all of the biennales. The third edition published the first officially printed and bound catalog, called *Ja Taa! Prendre l'image*, which translates as "Snap the picture!" in Bamanankan and French. The use of Bamanankan, the lingua franca of Mali, symbolizes the fact that, of all the editions, the third biennale incorporated the most Malian input.[50] The publication of the catalog was financed by the Prince Claus Fund, a Dutch nonprofit organization that funds African endeavors.

The 1998 biennale "professionalized" the program, according to Jeanne Mercier, by inviting debates about technology, ethics, and the roles of photography in African cultures.[51] Another new aspect was sponsorship by Kodak and other photography companies, and financial support from the European Union. The show was also the first to include photographers from North Africa—an area typically not associated with "Africa" in the French mind-set. As Mali shares a border with Algeria and has a long history of interaction across the desert with North Africa, this inclusion signals a Malian perspective instead of the typical French division between "Afrique Noire"—that is, sub-Saharan Africa—and the Maghreb. The third edition also popularized and increased the "Contours," or "Off" projects, a series of events designed to popularize the biennale locally.[52]

While the "focus" of the third biennale was Ghanaian photographic practices, the show continued the ongoing search for newly rediscovered

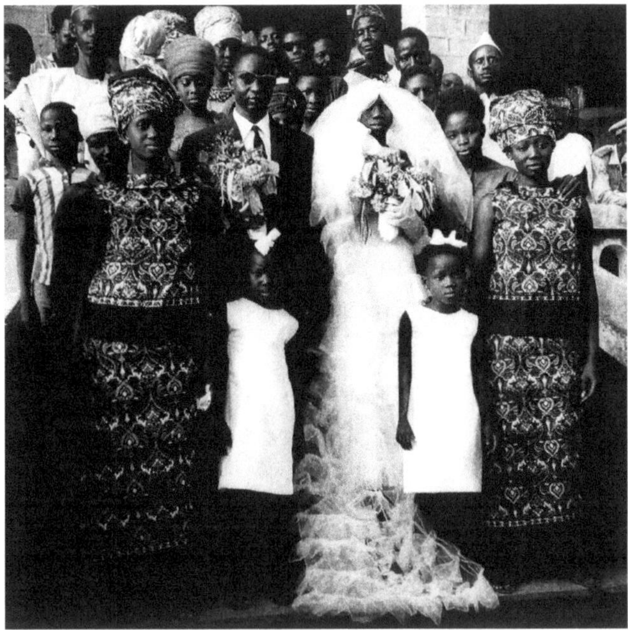

Figure 3.2. Felix Diallo, *Wedding Portrait*, 1960s–1970s, restored in Photoshop in 1998 for Bamako Encounters (original negative was damaged). Courtesy of Paul Diallo, Érika Nimis, and Candace Keller, Archive of Malian Photography (Matrix).

Malian studio photographers, exhibiting a tribute to Félix Diallo (b. 1931–1997) from Kita (fig. 3.2), the Traoré brothers from Mopti (b. 1930), and Touré M'Barakou (1922–1992) of the Gao region.

The show also included two artistic projects by Malian photographers: Emmanuel Daou's *Masks and Symbols* and Mamadou Konaté's series of abstractions, titled *Everyday Finery* (fig. 3.3). Konaté's abstract close-ups are unusual, as abstraction and experimentation are not popular ideals among Malian photographers.[53] Daou's series, which was reviewed in the local paper, *L'Essor*, addressed genital circumcision (fig. 3.4). The review and the series do not appear to pass judgment on the practice, except insofar as the review notes that the Dafing people combine Islam with animism in this practice. This even look at a practice that many Americans criticize, and that is being fought against in Africa by prominent African feminists, suggests a Malian perspective to which European or American viewers may very well not relate. The inclusion of Daou's series in the 1998 biennale is another moment when the impetus of the biennale—which seems to be often oriented toward a European audience—is disarticulated and then rearticulated

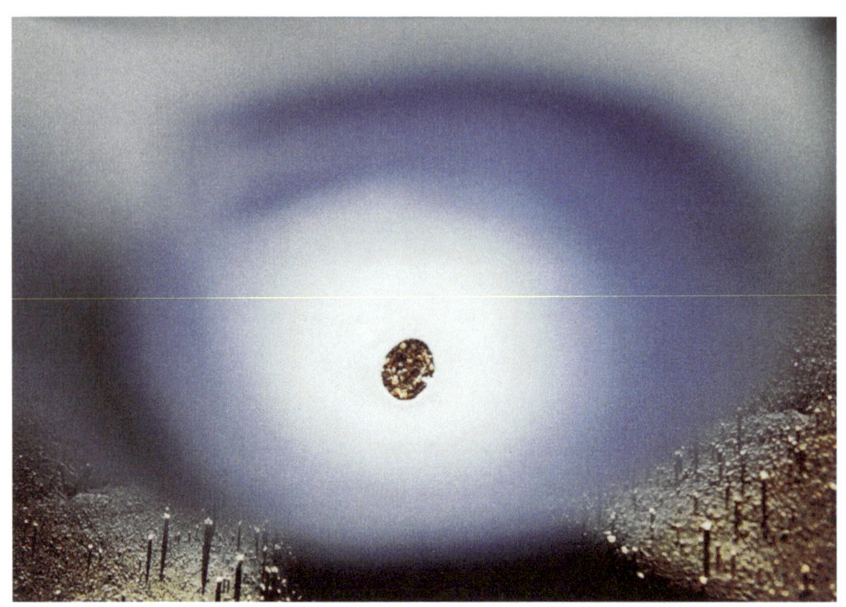

Figure 3.3. Mamadou Konaté, *Les parures du quotidien* (*Everyday Finery*), 1998. Courtesy of the artist.

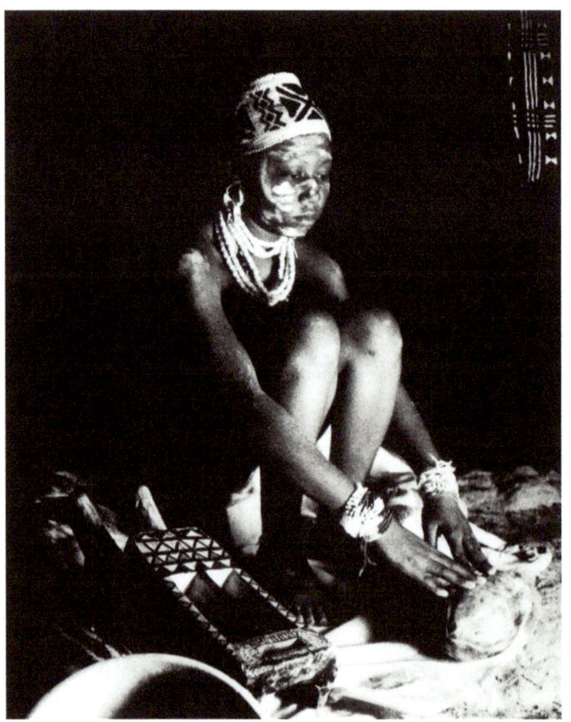

Figure 3.4. Emmanuel Daou, *Une jeune femme—masques et symboles* (*A Young Woman—Masks and Symbols*), 1997–1998. Courtesy of the artist.

from a Malian perspective, which offers the subject to knowledgeable viewers without overt criticism, allowing the audience to consider their own ideas about it.

When Afrique en Créations was subsumed under AFAA in 2000, important changes in the aims and operations of the Bamako Biennale occurred, which seemed to delimit Malian authority in some areas and to promote it in others. The priorities of the biennale changed, and the European Union required AFAA and the biennale organizers to make stronger and more successful attempts to include the local population as an audience.[54]

Simon Njami created striking changes when he became the chief curator in 2001. His appointment—a role he kept for the following three editions—marked a noticeable shift in the substance, shape, and reach of the biennale. Paul O'Neill argues, "In the absence of any alternative narrative or substantial opposition, the curator becomes the subject most conspicuously responsible for the production and mediation of biennials."[55] While a variety of forces, particularly institutional ones, affected the biennale, Njami's curatorship was crucial because of his lengthy involvement and his ethical commitment to the biennale and to Africa, coupled with a creative approach to widening the biennale's scope and including Malian interests.

Njami was born in Switzerland of Cameroonian descent and is now based in Paris. He cofounded the Parisian press Revue Noire, which published the first major survey of African photo history, *Anthology of African and Indian Ocean Photography* (1998), an extension of the exhibition *Afrique par Elle-Même* in the 1998 biennale. He was involved in the biennale through Revue Noire press from the beginning. Although Njami thought the choice of setting the biennale in Bamako was originally unwise, due to government bureaucracy and the city's poverty and lack of infrastructure, he resisted French efforts to relocate it to another country. Njami had an ambitious and unusually thoughtful vision for the Encounters: he hoped to build up its reputation so that it would remain as a permanent contribution to Bamako and to African photography. This is why he remained as curator for so long, leaving only when its foundation was secure. To promote curatorial opportunities on the continent, he always worked with a team of eight to ten young curators from Africa; among these were later biennale directors Michket Krifa and Bisi Silva.

Njami brought money, resources (especially in contacts with other photographers and curators), prestige, and visitors to the biennale, and the first one that he directed, in 2001, augmented the format of the exhibition dramatically. The 2001 biennale included more than 2,500 images—three times the number of images shown in any previous edition.[56] After Njami took the reins, the duration of the event extended to a month instead of a week; six hundred visitors attended; the biennale was organized under a theme, "Intimate Memories of a New Millenium" ("Mémoires intîmes du nouveau millenaire"); and artists from the diaspora were included as a major presence for the first time.[57] This last innovation is conceptually appropriate, as Njami himself belongs to the transnational cadre of curators and artists working on the international level.

Njami describes himself as a maverick curator who refuses to work on any project without the freedom to do it his way.[58] He was on a freelance contract with AFAA/CulturesFrance and so was beholden neither to the French government nor the Malian government, whose bureaucracy slowed down the biennale's organization. His independence gave him the ability to evade bureaucratic quagmires to get things done. As Njami explained, to get nails to hang the photographs, someone had to sign a piece of paper and get the president's signature. Also, Njami did not want to include the minister of culture's writings in his catalogs. It is clear that, from Njami's perspective, governmental interference from both Mali and France was problematic.

Abdoulaye Konaté, the Malian artistic director of the 1998 biennale, partnered with Njami for the 2001 edition. Presumably because of Konaté's efforts, Malians again showed a strong presence, with three artists (out of thirty-two total) shown in the International Exhibition. Alioune Bâ's architectural series included photographs of the city's relatively new Modibo Keïta memorial building and its matching landscaping, emphasizing the geometric abstraction of that building's neo-Sudanic style. Abstraction connected the three Malian artists, seen also in new works from Mamadou Konaté's color series of close-ups, *Les parures du quotidien* (*Everyday Finery*), shown in 1998, and Youssouf Sogodogo's black-and-white series taken on a farm and of a highway. The biennale also incorporated the "disclosure" (rather than "discovery"—a sensitive distinction accorded by essayists Njami and Amadou Chab Touré, who credit Abdoulaye Konaté with bringing the work to light) of a studio photographer from Kayes, Sadio Diakité (b. 1929), in a monographic exhibition, corresponding to similar newly exhibited portraiture by Doudou Diop from Senegal and Gabriel Fasunon of Nigeria (fig. 3.5).[59]

A more Malian aesthetic can be seen in the smaller, national exhibitions. A show in the 2001 Encounters titled *Mali: Striking Out in Creation,* curated by Amadou Chab Touré, included color photographs of Baye Fall worshippers by Abdoulaye Baby. Baye Fall is a Sufi sect who dress distinctively, work

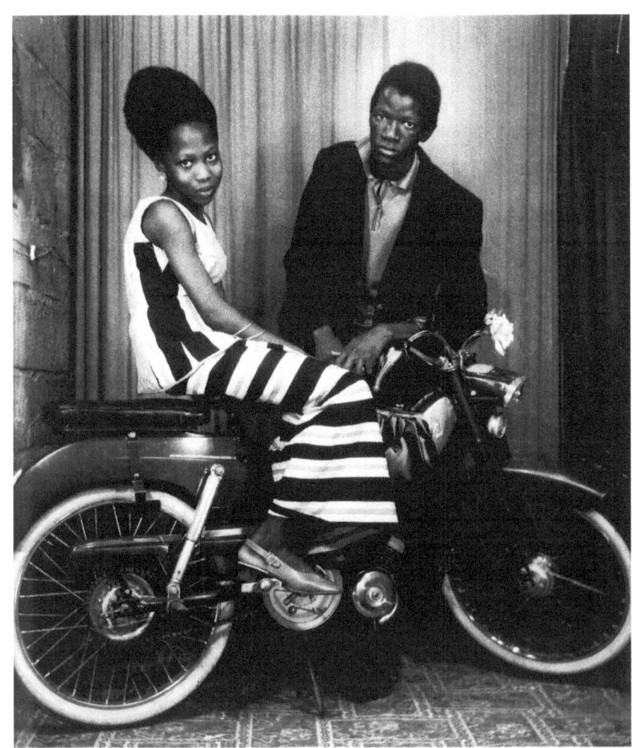

Figure 3.5. Sadio Diakité, *L'homme et femme avec une moto* (*Man and Woman with a Motorcycle*), ca. 1960s, printed in 2001 for *IVes Rencontres* Bamako. Courtesy of the artist's estate.

hard in lieu of praying, and live on alms. Baye Fall is more famous in Senegal, home of Touba, the Baye Fall mecca, but there are also Malian followers. In addition, the show included black-and-white reportage of hunters at a festival by Yacouba Dembélé and Abdoulaye Kanté (fig. 3.6), a black-and-white diptych of hands in a corrugated barrel by Aboubacrine Diarra (fig. 3.7), and images of a makeshift shade shelter and a photo of voluminous fishing nets over a mat or blanket with a small pile of clothing and beads, by Joseye Tienro (fig. 3.8), as well as Emmanuel Daou's almost visually opaque photograph of an older man at the hunters' festival sitting among other hunters and their guns and holding a silvery gleaming water bag, misting from its chill condensation (fig. 3.9). Hunters are considered of high status in Mande culture, dating back to at least the Mali Empire. Daou also exhibited a striking photo of a locked window with geometric patterned bars obscuring the face of a well-dressed man wearing a silver bracelet, sleeping inside (fig. 3.10). Tienro's photographs show tent structures for shade that can be seen in photographs taken by colonial officers in the late 1800s. Most of these locally inflected photographs are visually difficult to read, confusing the eye with shade and light, texture and pattern. They refuse clarity, emphasizing dìbi or opacité because of the pattern created on their surface. They are visually complex, polyrhythmic, and specific to key aspects of Malian culture: thus they entice viewers into Relation. Touré's essay on the history of studio photography's transition into art in Mali refers to scholar Érika Nimis's recent book *Bamako de nos jours*, published by Revue Noire just a few years prior, and lionizes Alioune Bâ, Amadou Traoré (AT), Mamadou Konaté, and Youssouf Sogodogo as "the new classics," showing his awareness of this history in the making.[60]

Njami subsequently directed the fifth, sixth, and seventh editions in 2003, 2005, and 2007, respectively, and his rambling, inclusive, poetic, and allusive style and stamp can be seen throughout the biennale, particularly in the introductory catalog essays. In the 2003 biennale, "Sacred Rites, Profane Rites," Seydou Keïta was given an homage, along with two other non-Malian photographers (Mohammed Dib and Van Leo).[61] Mohamed Camara's *Chambres maliennes* (*Malian Rooms*) were included in the International Exhibition. In the preface to the exhibition catalog, Moussa Konaté, the director of MAP, emphasizes the importance of the biennale in fostering debate and discussion, noting:

> We are aware that the role of an event like the Bamako Encounters cannot be limited to simply putting images on display. The African biennial cannot afford to be merely a gigantic exhibition and a gathering place for

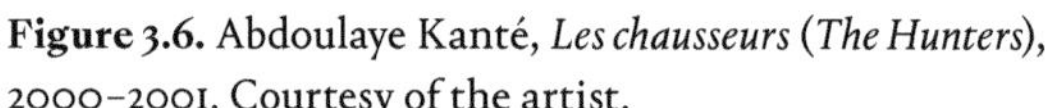

Figure 3.6. Abdoulaye Kanté, *Les chausseurs* (*The Hunters*), 2000–2001. Courtesy of the artist.

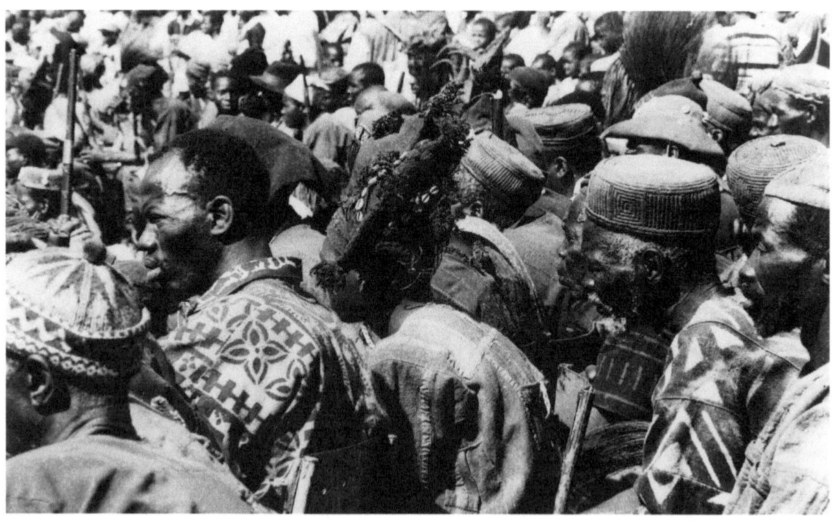

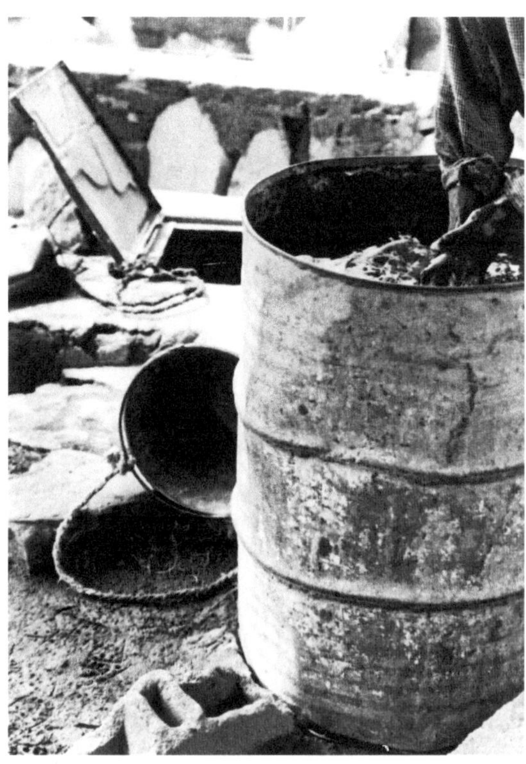

Figure 3.7. Aboubacrine Diarra, *Poubelle* (*Garbage Can*), ca. 2000–2001. Courtesy of the artist and Kani Sissoko.

Figure 3.8. Joseye Tienro, *Les filets* (*Fishing Nets*), 2000–2001. Courtesy of the artist.

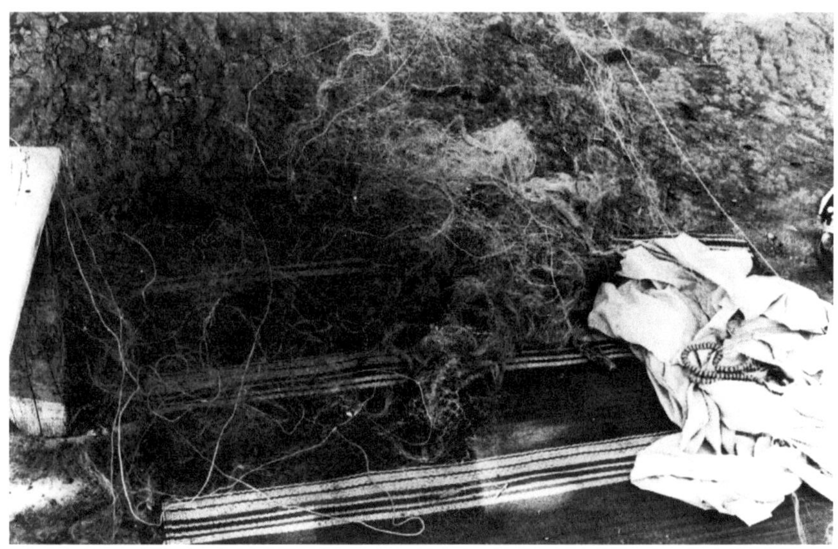

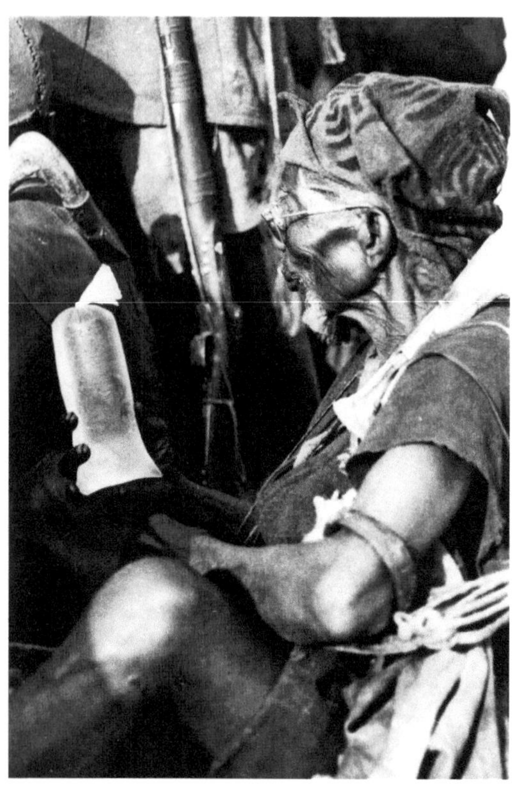

Figure 3.9. Emmanuel Daou, *Chausseur avec de l'eau* (*Hunter with Water*), 2000–2001. Courtesy of the artist.

Figure 3.10. Emmanuel Daou, *L'homme dans la fenêtre* (*Man in the Window*), 2000–2001. Courtesy of the artist.

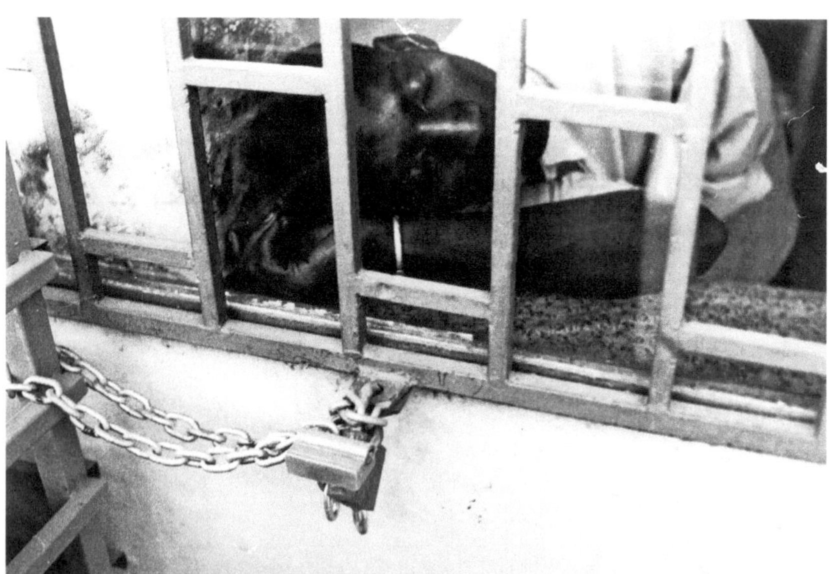

> photographers and professionals. It must be a place of debates and innovation, a place of *encounters* [his italics] and confrontation. Africa must move ahead into the third millennium with efficient arts, proven skills and awareness of its role in the dissemination of its culture. This is why the Office of the Encounters now has a physical space and, starting in the autumn, will become the prefiguration of the future Maison de la Photographie Africaine, whose role will be to ensure the permanent presence of photography on Malian soil. This Maison de la Photographie, *which will eventually take over the organization of the biennial* [my italics], aims to become the resource centre of African photography and a place for dissemination, distribution and reflection.[62]

Unfortunately, this concrete outline of MAP's future remained unrealized. The reference to debates and confrontation parallels Mali's burgeoning democratic state in its efforts to foster a national political discussion, specifically in its historic 1991 National Conference and the 1994 forum of the Éspace d'Interpellation Démocratique (EID, or Question and Answer Assembly).[63] The National Conference allowed voices to be heard from different classes and sectors of society, in direct contrast to Mali's colonial history and thirty years of postindependence dictatorship. As political scientist Susanna D. Wing argues, "The National Conference helped to embed the democratic ideals of dialogue and debate in contemporary Malian political culture."[64] She explains:

> While anyone could speak, you had to be persuasive in order to convince others to adopt your point of view. People spoke in Bambara or in French, whichever language they preferred. Indeed, other languages were also used and translators were provided for them. . . . For the first time, the voices of farmers, students, and representatives from the North were being heard in the political realm in Bamako. Although women were vastly outnumbered, their voices were also heard.[65]

While the National Conference was a one-time occurrence, the EID, instituted in 1994 by Konaré's government, was a groundbreaking and singular effort in West Africa to constitute an ongoing space of debate and discussion that attempted to involve the whole populace. Citizens could publicly ask questions of the government: submitted questions were given to a jury and then read on radio and television, to be publicly answered by state officials.[66] The EID's attention to justice and democracy essentially founded Mali's nascent democracy on populist participation, contributing to the legacy of Konaré's regime.[67] By 2002, the year before Moussa Konaté penned his preface, the EID needed revitalization, because it could not accommodate the vast numbers of questions and participants. It seems highly likely, however, that Konaté, as a government official, was expressing a similar impulse to discuss, debate, and carefully examine the institution of the biennale even as Mali's populace was invited to debate and discuss its democratic ideals and practical solutions.

But the emphasis on debate in Malian society reaches further back than the 1990s, for it had roots in the precolonial *ton* association of the Bamana people. Democracy in Mali emerges from a long discursive tradition. Wing writes,

> Among the Bambara . . . *tonw* (associations) are used as community organizational tools. *Ton-sigiw* (formal meetings of associations) are carefully structured so that any individual is given the opportunity to speak in turn. This historical method of policy-making and governance within Bambara communities has been re-created at the national level. Although this is a distinctive Bambara tradition, members of other cultures within Mali have welcomed this method of governance. Its success in transforming a precolonial model of governance to the postcolonial nation-state and across cultures is a positive sign for the adaptability of the model to other states.[68]

Thus, Moussa Konaté's emphasis on debate in the preface to the 2003 biennale catalog draws not only on Mali's emerging democratic process but also on precolonial traditions from a cultural group with widespread influence and power in postindependence Mali. This postcolonial Malian contestation of the "top-down" hierarchy of the French organization of the biennale can be seen as a counterhegemonic resistance emphasizing Malian politics, culture, and history, which resonates with the kinds of horizontally structured biennials in which discursivity plays a prominent role, such as Enwezor's Documenta 11.[69]

The 2005 biennale, "Another World Is Possible" ("Un autre monde est possible"), marked Njami's third edition as director. In an attempt to reach the Malian public, Njami created the exhibition *People of Bamako* (*Gens de Bamako*), held at the Museum of the District of Bamako. Despite AFAA's injunction to prioritize a local audience in 2001, Mercier notes that the Malian public "was never touched."[70] But in 2005, with the assistance of the Malian photographer Amadou Sow, who worked at the African House of Photography, Njami invited dozens of local households to lend family portraits

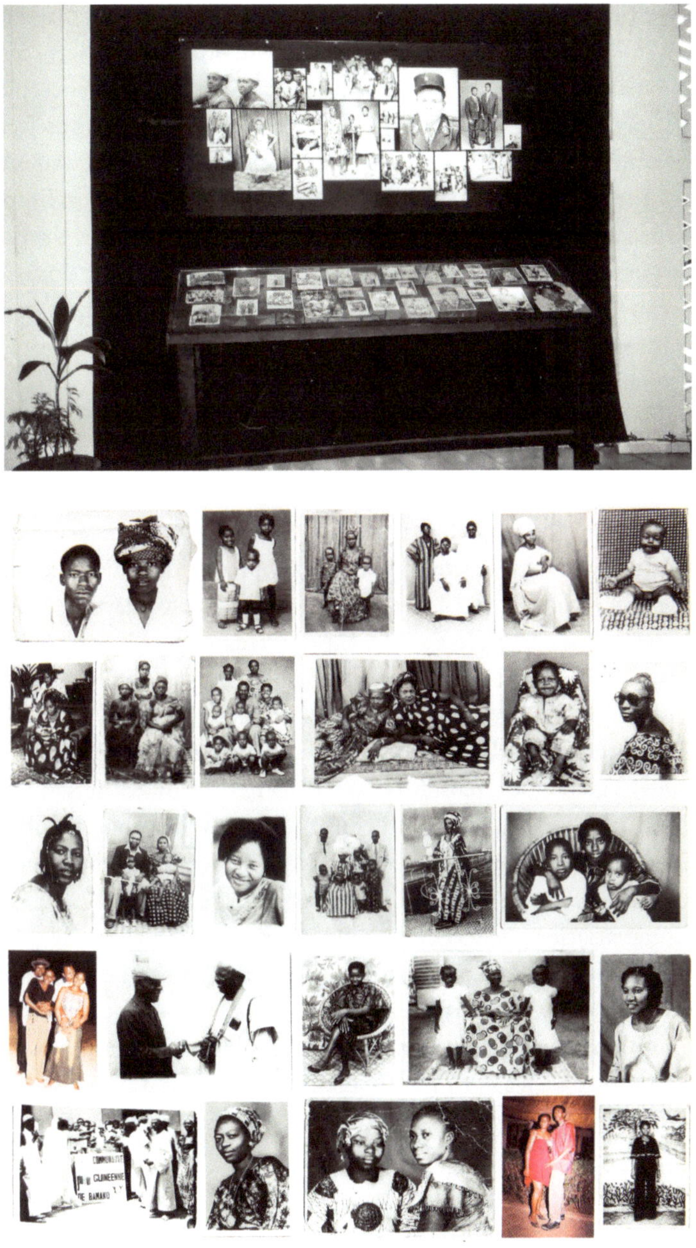

Figure 3.11. *Gens de Bamako* (*People of Bamako*), 2005, installation view at the Museum of the District of Bamako, with vintage prints below and scans above. Photo by author.

Figure 3.12. *Gens de Bamako* (*People of Bamako*), 2005.

taken by studio photographers (figs. 3.11 and 3.12). These small, weathered originals, taken over seven decades by Malian photographers, were displayed anonymously in long glass cases. In Mali, it is considered unacceptable to display a person's portrait publicly without the subject's permission; thus, Sow explained that the reason for the anonymous display was that often the lender of the photo did not have or could not obtain permission from everyone in the picture.[71] The pictures were also digitally scanned for preservation purposes, and the digital prints were included in the catalog. Collages of the scans were hung above the cases exhibiting the originals in the Bamako Museum, creating a more dramatic effect and allowing easy viewing from a greater distance.

Although the exhibition hall was empty when I visited several days after the biennale's opening, Sow assured me that a number of lenders had come to the opening festivities. Considering that few local Malians attended or seemed to know about the biennale's existence, *People of Bamako* was an important attempt to bridge the wide gap between the biennale's international audience and its host city.[72] The project revealed the formatting changes, in size and print quality, undergone by the enlargements of Keïta's and Sidibé's works, by showing vintage "vernacular" photographs. Yet *People of Bamako* did not shy away from highlighting the reproductive nature of photography, and its most cutting-edge technology, by exhibiting the digitally scanned prints *along with* the originals. It is surprising to find an exhibition that both celebrates the singular, original print and highlights photography's multiplicity. This formal approach could be considered another example of Mande aesthetics, in its allowance of varying formats for the same images—theme and variations, with the embellishment in this case being the digital scanning and collage, to provide a counterpoint to the glass-encased vintage prints. Usually, emphasizing unique prints seems to necessitate the repression of reproductions in pandering to the market for "original" prints, but this approach speaks to the different use value and material nature of the two types of photographs in what could be seen as photography's jako, or embellishment.[73] Thus, the exhibition demonstrated the complexities of Malian studio photography as well as of photography in general, and in doing so it enabled Relation for Malians and non-Malians alike.

The anonymity of the clients was also in this case matched by the anonymity of the photographers, in contrast to exhibitions that emphasize the photographer's production by only using his name.[74] By showing portraits from a client-based, rather than photographer-produced, perspective, the exhibition reminded viewers of the social nature and commissioned status of these images, while opening the biennale to personal interest from the city's denizens.

In another instance of Malian influence, the 2005 biennale shared certain forms of decision-making power by allotting the printing of all of the black-and-white prints at the CFP, Bamako's private photography school, to director Youssouf Sogodogo and his students, although this innovation unfortunately did not continue.[75] Also noteworthy in 2005 was the fact that the female Malian artist Fatoumata Diabaté won the AFAA prize, created for young, aspiring artists. Diabaté had graduated from Promo-femme, the photography school for women, and the CFP. In an interview, Njami noted that he had particularly wanted to promote a woman in order to further the cause of feminism among African photographers. Diabaté is an ambitious and serious photographer who has continued to be a productive and successful artist, encouraging other women as a role model.

The theme in 2007, the last edition curated by Simon Njami, was "In the City and Beyond" ("Dans la ville et au-dela"). The catalog format differed from Njami's other three editions, as it was printed in a smaller and blockier shape, breaking up a sense of continuity from the past three similar-looking books. Moussa Konaté wrote the introduction to *In the City* and notes that it was the first time that video installations were included, as they were becoming increasingly popular among photographers: "The city, a place that concentrates the consumer goods, appears as an area of meetings and sharing, but also appropriation and exclusion, a space of expression of powers and counterbalance, creations and recreations."[76]

Konaté's description of the city as "a place that concentrates the consumer goods" highlights the urban/rural divide in Africa, where rural towns and villages tend to have minimal opportunities for consumption, in contrast to the gleaming supermarkets and pervasive box stores available to many American rural communities. He also notes how economic discrepancies create flows in power, noting both the positive and negative connotations of the African city. Malian photographers included in the 2007 International Exhibition were Adama Bamba, with a striking black-and-white series called *L'infini, l'inachevé, l'imparfait* (*Infinite, Unfinished, Imperfect*) of stark rebar grids emerging from unfinished concrete structures against a white sky and a tunnel vision reminiscent of modernist photography but lacking its finished beauty; the beginning constructions suggest the Cité Administrative, Bamako's new government complex, which Muammar Qaddafi showily financed in Bamako from 2003 to 2010 (fig. 3.13). This is a rare instance of architectural photography.

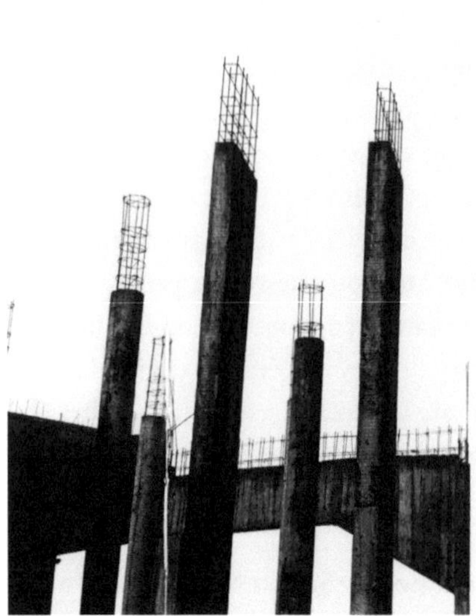
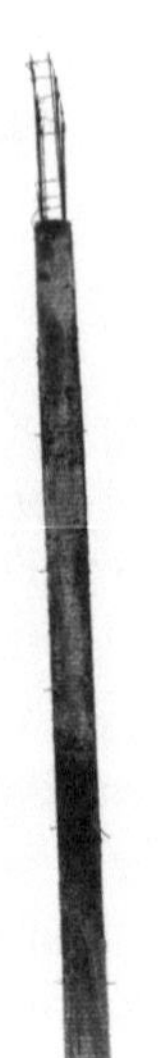
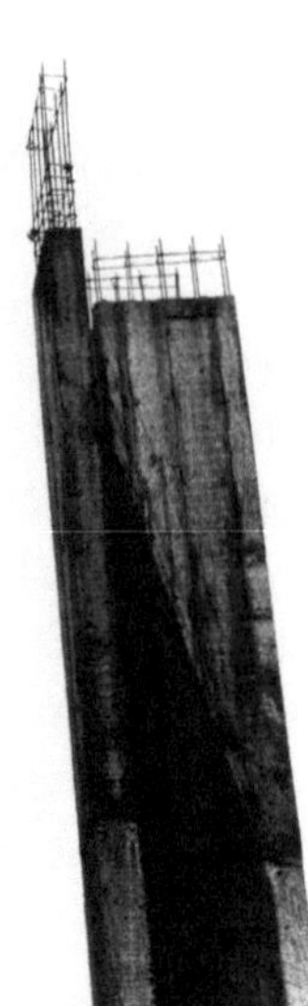

Figure 3.13. Adama Bamba, Untitled (*L'infini, l'inachevé, l'imparfait* [*Infinite, Unfinished, Imperfect*]), 2007. Courtesy of the artist and Amadou Keïta.

The other three Malians in the International Exhibition worked in color. Mohamed Camara returned with images from a new series, *Certains matins* (*Some Mornings*), and Emmanuel Bakary Daou and Harandane Dicko were included. Despite Njami's assertion that the biennale is supposed to show new photographers, the Malian selection clearly favored repeating artists. In his essay "Contours" (Outlines, or "Offs"), Samuel Sidibé notes, "The concern to make the Encounters become a popular event has, since the fourth edition [2001], been at the origin of Outlines."[77] The three-week-long Cinéma Numérique Ambulant (CNA) incorporated local audiences by sending two professional European photographers into city neighborhoods with two female Malian photographers to take portraits during the day and project them on local buildings at night, complete with music and festivities. "Photo ambience," run by Balani, a nonprofit music and culture organization founded in 2002, included music, games, and interviews.

Contours also introduced the praise song, Njami's innovative idea to use a popular Mande genre, normally sung by casted, trained griots, or praise singers, for disseminating interest and information with a "hymn to Photography, which will be continuously broadcast on radios."[78] This was a particularly innovative way to reach a broader public, as music and praise songs are extremely popular; this idea appealed to the oral culture of the nation, and shows the most perceptive and Relational attempt of the biennale to incorporate Malian influence. Another traditional approach was reinvented in the "New Images, New Supports" project by Cultur'elles, which included the intersection of photography and textiles in creative juxtapositions.

Video workshops in Mali and Provence presented by the French Cultural Center and Balla Fasséké Conservatory (CAMM) were organized by Jean-Paul Blachère and included Mohamed Camara. Since 2005, CAMM and ENSAD (École National Supérieure des Arts Décoratifs) in Paris have had an institutional partnership. For this year, students collaborated in photo and video reportage on health and lifestyle in Mopti, Mali, supported by the Ministry of Health.[79] The 2007 edition traveled extensively around the globe: to France, Spain, Sweden, and Germany, but also to Argentina, India, Israel, and Japan, and throughout Francophone West Africa.[80] The introduction by Olivier Poivre d'Arvor and Sophie Renaud of CulturesFrance names only Malick Sidibé as an influence on African photography, highlighting his Venice Biennale Golden Lion Award, and eclipsing, at least temporarily, all mention of Seydou Keïta.

In 2009, Simon Njami, who had brought the Bamako Biennale to a vast scale and global notice, stepped aside. Njami's hopes of being replaced by a continent-based curator were not realized immediately, as the next two editions—2009 and 2011—were cocurated by two Paris-based curators, Michket Krifa (of Tunisian descent) and Laura Serani (of Italian descent), neither of whom is black. As the first women to head the directorship, their efforts were notable: their individual interests were visible in the increased emphasis on Maghrebian and Egyptian photography. But since Serani's claim to the position rested on her previous work as a curator in Paris's photography museum Maison de la Photographie Europèene, the pairing seemed off-kilter. Krifa's cultural expertise was presumably meant to balance Serani's more European-oriented "artistic" eye (a problematic assumption), but the pairing of two women, neither with a strong connection to sub-Saharan Africa, after the singular leadership of male curators, seemed curious, as neither had a prior deep or broad knowledge of photography across sub-Saharan Africa.

Notably, the shift in artistic directorship, from Njami to Krifa and Serani, coincided with a shift in the Malian collaboration. Samuel Sidibé, the director of Mali's National Museum, who holds a PhD in African history from the Sorbonne and an MA in art history and archaeology, took over the communication lines and managing directorship between Bamako and Paris from Moussa Konaté, who remains the director of the African House of Photography (MAP).

As Samuel Sidibé notes in his catalog introduction, the title of the biennale again changed, this time to reflect the importance of Bamako as the host city. It was now called *Encounters of Bamako 09: African Photography Biennial: "Borders."* (Samuel Sidibé notes that the exhibition is already called that by professionals and photographers.)[81] In the CulturesFrance preface, Olivier Poivre d'Arvor, Sophie Renaud, and Paul de Sinety note the new team in Mali and say with regard to the "duo of women": "Poised between the Rencontres d'Arles, a partner of this year's Biennial and Paris Photo, they contribute to the emergence and the participation of contemporary African photography and its Diasporas on the art market."[82]

The 2009 biennale showcased Malian photographers quite prominently. In the International Exhibition, six Malian artists (out of fifty-three total) were included: Seydou Camara showed a series on albinos ("Bibiana"), as did French photographer Alain Turpault; Aboubacar Traoré showed a series titled *The Illegal Side of the Border* (on the Sotramo drivers); Mohamed Camara returned for his third biennale with the series *Malians in Paris*; and Salif Traoré's *Unachieved Dreams* focused on an association called ICOMA (Ivorian Congolese Malian) trying to work in Mali and achieve success without leaving for Europe. Two Malians showed videos rather than photographs: Tiécoura N'Daou showed a color video titled *Inside and Outside*, and Mohamed Konaté showed a black-and-white one called *Eldorado*.

The 2009 biennale included a *Focus on Mali* exhibition whose tripartite format was divided into contemporary art, archive photographs from AMAP (Agence Malienne de Presse et de Publicité, the colonial government press agency), and Malick Sidibé's recent fashion series for the *New York Times Magazine*. "Contemporary Malian Photographers" was curated by Samuel Sidibé and showed Emmanuel Daou (his pictograph series), Amadou Keïta, Adama Bamba, Alimata Diop dite Traoré, Mamadou Konaté, Harandane Dicko, and Fatoumata Diabaté in a mix of black-and-white and color. Notably, this show also featured a marriage video, which Sidibé notes is more vernacular and commercial than the other work, but he explains that he included it because it is a necessity of professional bread and butter and thus representative of Malian photography today.

Krifa curated a small but powerful collection of anonymous images from the AMAP, noting their colonial titles: of Mopti's mosque from above with a '50s-style car pulling up, *Peul Women*, *Young Girl from Bamako*, *Gundam Nomads* (riding off into the desert on camels, with the scratches on the negative most striking on the darkening sky), and *Bustar*, of a man in a raggedy suit and fedora holding an enormous game bird upside-down, apparently in the middle of the bush. The selection of Malick Sidibé's fashion photography for the *New York Times Magazine* was curated by Laura Serani.[83] This exhibition strategically used Sidibé's new fashion work, which shares the same overall aesthetic of his earlier studio portraits, to stand in for the whole genre of studio portraiture, for a biennale public which had presumably had its fill of traditional studio portraiture, on view in some form or other since the 1994 biennale.

The 2009 biennale's subject of borders is of utmost importance in Africa —the drowning of migrants trying to cross the Mediterranean from Libya to Italy, or from Morocco to Spain, has finally become an issue for the European Union to address. Interestingly, in the catalog, which includes a brief anecdotal essay by Manthia Diawara illustrating the difficulty of traveling between national borders in West Africa, and an essay by the writer Nuruddin Farah, there is also a remarkable short essay by Michel Foucher—a geographer, geopolitician, diplomat, and member of Foreign Affairs Council—that notes former Malian president Alpha Oumar Konaré's strategy "to lend support to the dynamics of 'grassroots' integration, which link and articulate lands, people and activity beyond the limits of borders." "Once he became Chairperson of the African Union Commission, A. O. Konaré was able to convince his peers to adopt an ambitious 'border programme' starting in 2004. The aim of the programme is to reaffirm and encourage locally instigated acts of cross-border cooperation, while promoting their transparency. . . . The wager is that African unity is forged primarily in those cross-border regions. And there, as anywhere else, culture is first and foremost a question of exchange and recognition."[84] The wording of "exchange and recognition" sounds remarkably like Glissant's famous quote "I change through exchange with the other." Thus Foucher's essay shows the farsightedness and broad-mindedness of Mali's extraordinary first president.

The 2011 biennale, "For a Sustainable World," also curated by Krifa and Serani, addressed the environment; for Africa, sustainability is a dual-edged sword. Parts of Africa are being ecologically damaged, such as the desertification occurring along the edges of the Sahara, or the rampant destruction caused by mining for coltan, the key mineral of the digital age, or technological waste dumped by Western nations. At the same time, the struggle for basic economic survival renders African nations at a disadvantage as they modernize more slowly. While sustainability is the concern of wealthy nations who can afford to consider long-term effects, it is hard not to appreciate the need to bring such a concern to all parts of the world. But the artists mostly highlighted dire consequences rather than offering solutions.

In fact, there are local approaches to combatting desertification in the Sahel by farmers who plant particular kinds of trees that engender fertile soil and shade, but such kinds of productive initiatives were mostly absent in the biennale, except in Malian photographer Mamadou Konaté's series of children planting seedlings.[85]

The 2011 catalog is especially significant because it contains an essay by philosopher Achille Mbembe dedicated to Glissant, who had recently died, in February 2011.[86] Titled "The Seed and the Silt," the essay considers Glissant's ideas in relation to the environment, particularly Glissant's emphasis on silt rather than the proverbial seed considered so important in many African philosophies. Silt is sand or dirt carried by rivers, which contributes to fertile agriculture when the river overflows its banks. The Nile and Mississippi River deltas are examples of the importance of silt, and Glissant's interest in it relates to its movement as well as its environmental benefits. Mbembe writes,

> For Édouard Glissant, silt played the same role as did seed in African myths of the perdurance of the world. Silt, for Glissant, was not simply sloughed material—a substance apparently dead, a part apparently lost, torn from its source, tossed by the waters.
>
> He saw it also as a residue settling on the banks of rivers, in the midst of archipelagos, at the bottom of oceans, along valleys or at the foot of cliffs—everywhere, and above all in those arid and deserted places where, by an unexpected reversal, there emerge from refuse new forms of life, work, and language.
>
> For him, the perdurance of our world should in fact be conceived starting from its obverse, the cannibal structure of our modernity, whose origin was coeval with the African slave trade.

Mbembe explains that Glissant's emphasis on silt provides a way to rethink both the environment and the future by looking toward what can be created out of the devastation, both of the earth and of the slave trade, in bringing together disparate parts (the rootlessness of the Caribbean, the rich soil displaced). "Perdurance" is a philosophical understanding of objects and people extending through time and space; Mbembe uses the term to show Glissant's emphasis on the African slave trade that caused the creolizing societies of the Caribbean and thus how Relation is born through terrible violence and the abyss. This essay emphasizes the importance of Glissant's thinking to contemporary African philosophy and creates a direct relation to the Bamako photography biennale.

In 2011, the "International Exhibition" was renamed the "Pan-African Exhibition," which it always had been, but the title celebrated the specificity of the biennale's continentwide focus, imbuing it with a sense of political unity. Also new in the catalog was the approach to national identity—in the table of contents, only the names of artists are printed, in contrast to the standard inclusion of their nation, although the artist's country of origin is included underneath their name within the catalog text.

Samuel Sidibé's preface, "For a Sustainable Biennial," clearly states his concerns: in the essay he entreats Mali's government to support the year-round work on the exhibition, which he states is too "ad-hoc."[87] He mentions the Sindika Dokola Collection exhibition curated by Njami, which is an anomaly because Dokola is a private collector, although African private collections are growing. Sidibé discusses "conserving our photographic heritage," as the National Museum is involved in conservation projects of archiving studio photographers' negatives.[88]

Malian artists included Drissa Coulibaly, whose color photographs of small-scale gold mines show their negative effects on the landscape through mounds of dirt. Bakary Emmanuel Daou's black-and-white photographs utilize an aesthetic of darkness, opacité, or dìbi in their emphasis on the deleterious effects of plastic bags—in one night scene, children crouch or sit inside abandoned open refrigerators. An enormous plastic bag obscures the child in the middle, and there is an off-kilter symmetricality that suggests an altar (fig. 3.14). Fatoumata Diabaté's *L'homme en animal* (2011) shows a series of children from Sikasso "playing roles from traditional tales" with animal masks (fig. 3.15). She notes, "I feel that life can only be sustainable if it is based on non-superficial values and customs. These customs are crucial—the traditional tales told to children educate them, encouraging them to reflect on humans and animals, on their environment, and on the future."[89] Diabaté's series thus emphasizes a Relational approach to the subject of sustainability. Mamadou Konaté, like Diabaté, took a positive approach toward the theme of sustainability, showing "children being taught how to plant trees" (fig. 3.16). The image of two girls' arms, holding a seedling between them, harkens back to studio portraits in which two women hold hands before a vase of flowers, as in Adama Kouyaté's work (see fig. 1.15). Both Diabaté and Konaté created series that celebrated positive steps toward sustainability in aesthetically striking ways that retained cultural significance to Mali, thus enabling Relation, and Daou's series was paradoxically beautiful and frightening. In contrast to the biennale's focus on the negative effects of pollution, the Malian artists' works emphasized children as the next generation

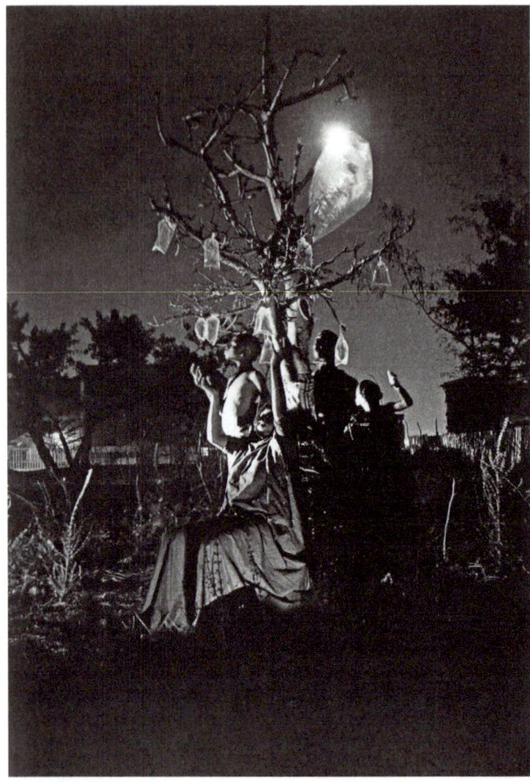

Figure 3.14 (*left*). Emmanuel Daou, *Baobab symbole de longévité* (*Baobab, Symbol of Longevity*), 2010. Courtesy of the artist.

Figure 3.15 (*below left*). Fatoumata Diabaté, *L'homme en animal, Sikasso* (*Man in Animal, Sikasso*), 2011. Courtesy of the artist and Patrice Loubon Gallery.

Figure 3.16 (*below right*). Mamadou Konaté, *Preparing the Future of Our Children*, 2011. Courtesy of the artist.

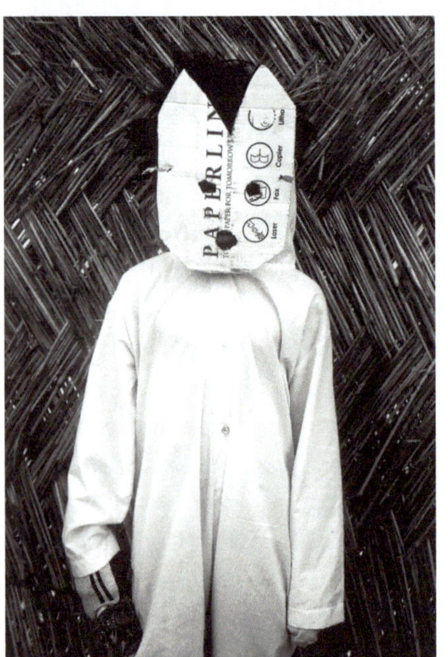

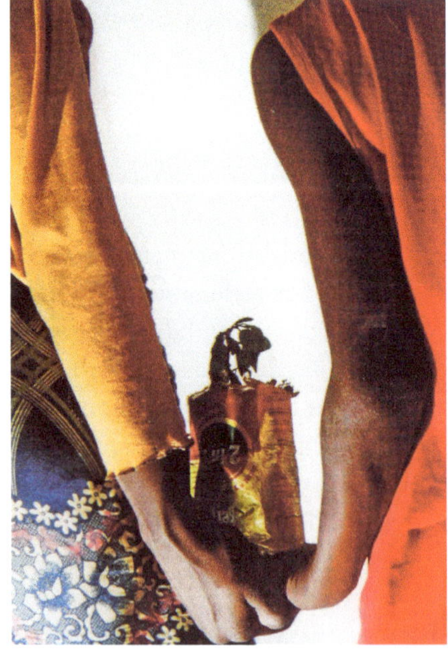

to inherit the earth and offered promising solutions or curious and symbolic images to encourage reflection, rather than knee-jerk critique.

In 2011, a workshop and exhibition called *Bamako: The Mali Version*, directed by Ananias Leki Dago, featured Malian artists including Daou, Bamba, Salif Traoré, Konaté, and Amadou Keïta,[90] whose works were heavily symbolic and didactic, similar to the lyrics of much Malian music. Complementing the emphasis on the present, the archives of Soungalo Malé were shown with Abderrahmoune Sakaly and Malick Sidibé; five hundred works from each artist were to be conserved by the National Museum's Archives of Malian Photography project founded by Candace Keller. The Association for Women Photographers (Association des Femmes Photographes du Mali) also had a photo tent set up in the park outside the National Museum, offering to take pictures of visitors. At the time the group had approximately fifteen members, some of whom had been educated at Promo-femme and some at the CFP. The president, Amsatou Diallo, had worked with students for UNICEF, who gave cameras to at-risk teens in Niger and Mali and brought those with the "best" photographs to the biennale opening, where their works were displayed.[91] Projects with children have often been shown at the Encounters in hopes of helping raise the children's self-confidence and awareness of art.

Since its inception, and increasingly as it has expanded, the Bamako Biennale has been remarkable for its diversity of work, of genres, and of approaches, with attention paid to art, conceptual photography, photo essays, photojournalism, and commercial studio work across Africa, revealing socially important and visually exciting practices in Sudan, Egypt, Ghana, Burkina Faso, Senegal, and Brazzaville, Congo, to name a few. It is not merely seen as a contemporary art festival, allowing for innovations in photo journalism, discovering new studio photographers, celebrating archives, and so on. Installations have also been included, along with a smattering of film, video and performances, and projects with children in the "Offs." Workshops and master classes have been held, sometimes for a week or a month in France or in Bamako, and are exhibited during the show; others are held during the actual biennale, along with debates and dialogues. In 2003, the budget for the biennale was $1 million, of which more than three-quarters came from the French government and the EU.[92]

As the biennale has grown in scope and stature, its reception in the African, French, and American press has increased. Vine's surprise about the biennale underscores the fact that the reception of the Rencontres has been limited, both locally and internationally. The lack of local press caused the biennale to generate its own "newspaper" celebrating all of the biennale events every day during the *semaines professionals* ("professional week," i.e., the first week of the biennale, the one all of the international visitors attend). This self-generated hype did little to include a local audience, although the reporting does perhaps spur the growth of local art criticism (of which there is almost none, because there is no culture of exhibition viewing in the city; Candace Keller implies that the profession of "art critic" would be culturally foreign in her discussion of photography aesthetics). In any event, the self-generated paper and the video may have served to reinforce community among the biennale participants. And certain journalists who seem to consistently cover the arts wrote several reviews of the 2005 biennale for local Bamakois periodicals, including *L'Essor*, the oldest and most influential newspaper.[93] The reviews are not critical but celebratory, and they emphasize Malian participants.

In terms of international reception, by far the most press reviews have been published in French magazines and newspapers: the Rencontres earned reviews and mentions in *Le Monde, Le Figaro, Le Phare, La Tribune,* and *Libération.* In 2003, *Le Monde* ran a positive review that covered two-thirds of the page, mentioning photographers Van Leo, Santu Mofokeng, Ricardo Rangel, and Mohamed Camara, while *Libération* gave the 2003 biennale two descriptive pages and three images.[94] The biennale was also mentioned in *Elle* and in *Jeune Afrique*; the latter published a variety of reviews, including a short piece on wrestling images from Senegal and two longer, more comprehensive reviews.[95] That year *Photo Nouvelles* and *Paris Photo Magazine* also took note. While *Elle* and *Vogue* choose an exotic image to accompany a brief and superficial text, most reviews engage with the premises of the exhibition and the intellectual position of the curator. In general, the biennale receives more attention in France in part because sections of the exhibition have regularly traveled to participate in the Arles Rencontres, but as later editions of the biennale have traveled extensively, notice of Bamako abroad has increased.

The biennale's reception has been decidedly more limited in the Anglophone world, although with the 2015 edition that circumstance has changed. Historically, only a few journals have run reviews, with Vine's four-page article in *Art in America* in 2004 one of the most comprehensive and informative.[96] Joshua Cohen's review of the 2007 biennale in *African Arts*, which didn't appear until summer 2009, showed that finally Africanist scholars were taking interest in the biennale and in African art photography; previously most scholars interested in the biennale hailed from photography or photo history backgrounds. In 2010 Bisi Silva wrote a review in *Artforum* on the 2009 biennale. I wrote a review for *Artforum* in 2005, but when I pitched it for the 2011 edition, *Artforum*'s new international editor showed no interest. The essay that was most important in terms of publicizing the biennale in the US was surely Holland Cotter's review in the *New York Times*, run as part of a larger series on arts in Africa (Senegal, Ivory Coast, and Ethiopia) April 15, 2012. Cotter wrote about the ninth biennale, held in 2011. An image of a man in Bamako riding his motorbike past a biennale billboard even graced the cover of the Arts Section of the Sunday *New York Times*.[97] Unfortunately, the billboard picture was by a French photographer, one of the few Europeans in the whole show; apparently the irony was lost on the newspaper.[98]

By 2015, Anglophone reception changed, surely in part because of Silva's reputation and connections; she invited Teju Cole, photography writer for the *New York Times*, to contribute an essay to the catalog. Because Mali had been in the news with the coup and its violent aftermath, and because of Cotter's review a few years prior, not to mention the broader interest of news sources in the internet age, notices of the biennale's return after the 2012 coup, along with substantive reviews, were run in the largest daily newspapers of England and the US: the *Guardian* and the *New York Times*.

According to the *Guardian*, with the 2015 edition Silva hoped to address the local public more effectively than in the past. "We have to situate it within the context. For me an important direction was making this international event more local."[99] She explains, "The result was the Focus Mali project, which included an exhibition of new Malian photography; a collaboration with more than 15 photo studios across Bamako; and an ambitious educational programme working with pupils from 100 schools."[100]

In the exhibition catalog, Bisi Silva noted, "The initiative will work with 30 professional Malian photographers who will host workshops and educate students on the significance of visual representation through photography."[101] It was also notable that the main International Exhibition, located at the National Museum, was made free to the public. Silva's curatorship clearly marked a new turn for the biennale in terms of African, and to some extent Malian, emphasis. Arguably, the 2015 biennial enters into Relation, with its theme ("Telling Time"), and its focus on Mali's recent coup, and also in encouraging new forms of portraiture.

The Malian contributions in 2015 were spectacular, including Seydou Camara's *Manuscrits de Tombouctou* (2009–2013) and Daou's *Le temps Ebola* (*The Time of Ebola*; 2014) (fig. 3.17). Aboubacar Traoré's *Inchallah* (2015), which shows people with round black helmets on their heads, making them look like motorcyclists, extraterrestrials, or enormous ants, was featured on the

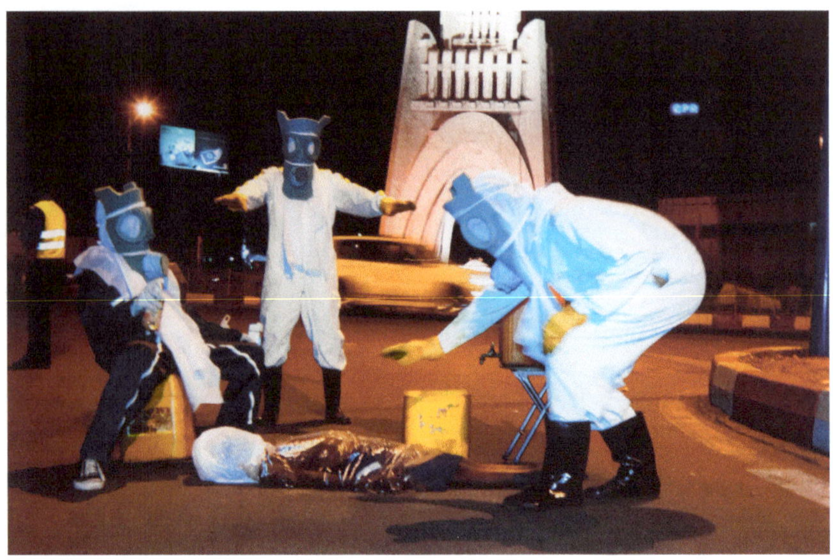

Figure 3.17. Emmanuel Daou, *Le temps Ebola* (*The Time of Ebola*), 2014. Courtesy of the artist.

website and described as having to do with "religious fanaticism."[102] Salif Traoré made a reappearance with *Introspection* (2012), which depicts the walls of building, and Moussa Kalapo's *La métaphore du temps* (2015) showed people holding up older studio portraits from family albums (fig. 3.18). "This collection of photographs represents an important commitment for Moussa Kalapo who, since 2014, has been an active participant in a program to conserve and preserve Malian photography and to affirm the potential of its history."[103]

In addition there was a "Focus Mali" section, which had *[Re]Generations*—a retrospective history of the biennale itself, and Mali Jaw, in which studios from various Bamako neighborhoods were invited to display archived photographs, with a nice photo by Alioune Bâ of a man with a hot pink shirt walking by Studio Malick Sidibé.[104] *En connexion . . .* involved the younger generation with a "militant artistic discourse," including a photograph by a young woman named Fatoumata Diallo of girls in shiny checked cloth, one looking up and one down, with a man in background, called *Maaloud a Dilli Dina I* (2015). The similarity to portraiture was strong, but slight differences—such as the young woman looking down, or the man awkwardly positioned behind the two women—suggest a subtle critique of that genre. The first Bamako Encounters pamphlet was also reprinted within the *Telling Time* exhibition catalog, which was important for scholars and artists as few people

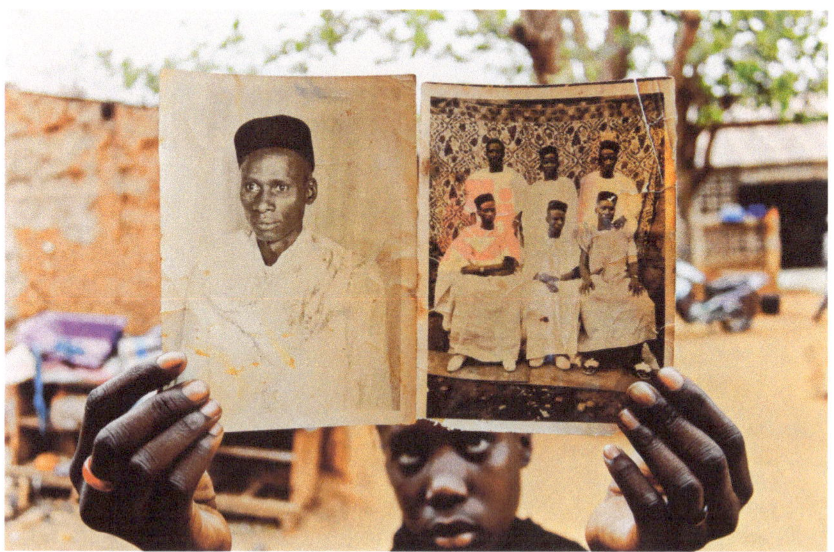

Figure 3.18. Moussa Kalapo, *La métaphore du temps* (*The Metaphor of Time*), 2015. Courtesy of the artist.

have access to the first three exhibition catalogs. Also important to Silva was *Scénographie*—exhibition spaces designed by Ivoirian architect Issa Diabaté with Dramane Cherif Aidara, providing, in the words of the catalog, "intimate viewing experiences"—"a minimal design aesthetic that allows the projects to breathe, while also highlighting the original architectural forms of many of the biennale's historic venues."[105]

The 2015 biennale clearly had the most emphasis on Malian activities since the 1998 exhibition. Also, it is clear that Silva's approach was meant to approach the issue of the public from a variety of angles—the long-term approach of educating students, the immediate approach of having studios display their archives in their own neighborhood, and an emphasis on aesthetics among a younger generation of artists. It was also exciting to see a mixture of projects by photographers of different generations and educational backgrounds: some, like Daou, who have exhibited since the very first biennale; others, like Seydou Camara and Salif Traoré, who are educated in the new institutions of CFP; and Moussa Kalapo, who, like Youssouf Sogodogo and Joseye Tienro, has been directly influenced by his work for the National Museum.

While Bamako has been growing internationally in terms of reputation based on reviews and art world attention, it has also had dramatic effects on artists' careers and has inspired new photographic exhibition venues and institutions on the continent. Ananís Léki Dago founded the Rencontres du Sud (Encounters of the South) in Abidjan, Ivory Coast, in 2000, as a direct result of participating in the Bamako Biennale. He saw both the opportunities and the failings of the biennale and acted accordingly in creating a biennial with a national, rather than international, focus.[106] In 2001, Fotofesta Maputo began in Mozambique.[107] The relatively well-known Lagos-based photography collective Depth of Field got their start when a number of its members met at the 2001 Bamako Biennale.[108] Depth of Field was subsequently included in London exhibitions in 2005, and in *Snap Judgments: New Positions in Contemporary African Photography* at the International Center of Photography in New York City in 2006.[109] Photographer and curator Akinbode Akinbiyi, a mentor to Depth of Field, curated a section of the 2007 Bamako Biennale and later was instrumental in founding the collective Black Box in Lagos, Nigeria. Bisi Silva, who had cocurated the Finnish (Invited Guest Country) exhibition for the 2007 Bamako Biennale, founded the Center of Contemporary Arts in Lagos in 2007, and also created an International Residency Art Photography program in 2010 to focus on art photography.

Two new biennials in Africa that debuted in 2010—LagosPhoto in Nigeria and Addis Foto Fest in Ethiopia—were directly inspired by the Bamako Biennale. Ethiopian photographer Aida Muluneh, who earned a BA in film, radio, and television at Howard University in 2001, won a prize in the 2007 Bamako Biennale. She credits the biennale for her decision to found Addis Foto Fest three years later, noting: "I exhibited at the Bamako Biennale in 2007 and when I went back to Addis it became critical to have a festival with all of these components in a week-long event. All over Africa there really aren't a lot of photography festivals. As a photographer it was really important to not just give opportunities to photographers on the continent but also to induce photographers abroad to come to Ethiopia and really see the activities in our country."[110] LagosPhoto, launched by Azu Nwagbogu, is sponsored by the telecommunications company Etisalat and coordinated and founded by African Artists' Foundation, a nonprofit Nigerian group. As its founder, Nwagbogu, noted, photography is relatively inexpensive, and everyone can do it.

Because exhibitions of African photography have largely been held in New York, Paris, London, and Germany, it is important that these large-scale festivals exist on the continent, and in this way Bamako has been significant in contributing to the creation and continuation of an art world in Africa. As this list shows, photographic institutions largely are generated within the cities and capitals, and few of Africa's fifty-four nations have formal photographic institutions, such as schools, museums, galleries, workshops, or magazines. The relative sparseness of such institutions across Africa underlines the importance of the Bamako Biennale in creating a meeting space and exhibition opportunities for the continent's and diaspora's curators, critics, and artists, and makes the growth of Bamako's institutions that much more remarkable.

Selections of works from different biennales have traveled to other international institutions, such as the Arles Photography Festival, Paris Photo, the Museum of the African Diaspora in San Francisco, and the Calouste Gulbenkian Museum in Lisbon, Portugal. Bamako has also launched the careers of numerous now well-known artists, from Santu Mofokeng and Samuel Fosso from the first Rencontres, to more recent successes like Sammy Baloji, Edson Chagas, and Lolo Veleko.[111] Naturally, the biennale has been important for the international exposure of several Malian artists, including Mohamed Camara, Fatoumata Diabaté, and Harandane Dicko, who collaborated with the British Museum on an exhibition titled *Money in London and Bamako*. Erin Haney and Jennifer Bajorek have also noted the importance of Bamako on collectives and on artists working beyond photography into other mediums, such as Bartheleny Toguo's Bandjoun State, an art space in Cameroon; Sammy Baloji's participation in art collectives in DRC; and Baudouin Mouanda and Armel Louzala, members of the Congo-Brazzaville collective Ge.ne.ration Elili, who were both included in the 2009 biennale.[112]

The Bamako Encounters are most important in their offer of professional, social interaction—the exchange of ideas, the opportunities for artists to meet and show portfolios to curators, the chance to see what else is succeeding in terms of viewing exhibitions, the workshops; and the debates and discussion: the biennale offers educational skills and experiences. It has also developed an important platform for marketability. In the fact of its existence, the biennale gives creative photographers across the continent a sense of meaningfulness, ambition, and hope, as well as ideas to consider. The effects of the biennale are multiple and sometimes contradictory, involving French power through the neocolonial apparatus in the diffusion not only of French thought and culture but also of Malian politics and cultural values. However, with changing political leadership the politics of the biennial has changed. For most of its history its political efficacy has been far less useful than its artistic importance, especially for the African continent, although after the coup the biennale took on new importance in terms of showing the continuance of Mali's ability to support contemporary culture and an international entourage.

As Carol Magee noted, photographers, administrators, and attendees were excited that the biennale continued in 2015, despite the warnings of attacks due to political instability.[113] The continuance of Dak'art the following summer, in 2016, with its support from New York–based art magazines like *Even* and *Artforum*, helped to keep interest alive in the continent's art worlds.

According to Simon Njami, Bamako *could* afford to fund the biennale, as photography is relatively inexpensive and much of it can be handled digitally, except the final printing and hanging of works. Aida Muluneh answered Marian Nur Goni in an interview about the funding and printing and framing of the Addis Foto in 2012, showing a much different attitude than the one underpinning the Bamako Biennale—one she surely adopted in awareness of Bamako's flaws. Muluneh explains: "The festival was produced with 25,000 euros. All the production was completed here in Addis Ababa. I am a believer in establishing and developing the photography industry locally, hence the intention is to produce all the works locally. Yes, of course, sometimes the quality isn't 100%, but at least over the years we can establish Addis Ababa as a central place in Africa for producing quality images."[114]

Admittedly, Muluneh did not have to pay for international flights for visiting artists. But it is more indicative of Mali's situation that the government has little interest in supporting the African Photography Encounters. This is perhaps understandable, in that the biennale is not a "festival" except in the loose sense of the word. It is neither indigenous nor culturally supported—it does not even involve very many people of Malian nationality. At the same time, it heralds a new internationalism and allows visitors and locals the chance to network. Bamako has been a *crucial center* of African photography and for the art world, even if it has not lived up to people's dreams. As a Malian festival it attracts no local audience. Yet the Encounters keep art photography in Mali alive, enabling aspects of Malian culture to circulate in the world and to enter into Relation as visual culture. That is perhaps the best that it can do, given the current political stagnation in Mali.

In considering the balance of global and local forces on the biennale, it is crucial to see both that the biennale's structure is political—it is a government institution, although ostensibly a "collaboration," one in which the power is economically and technologically weighted toward France—and that politics in Mali, as in many African countries, is often informal—it permeates everyday life and can be found in unexpected places.[115] Although photographic arts are economically and politically supported by the French and Malian governments, in a clear example of Marx's model of a cultural superstructure founded on an economic base, it is critical to note which aspects of the Bamako Encounters or its structure are dearticulated by Malian or African cultural forms, because those are moments of local influence. It is also provocative to consider the biennale as operating within a Mande aesthetic framework, in which the form or structure of the biennial repeats, while the images themselves, which change individually from edition to edition, theme to theme, are the embellishment. When the biennale, with its foreign structure, becomes accessible to the Malian public, that is also a political act—an act of reciprocity and exchange—and thus the biennale shows Relation by bringing Malian public into a cosmopolitan sphere that creates a feeling of belonging. In this way it is a form of badenya.

Historically, in African studio photography, images are often more than just indexical documents: they create mythologies; they embody spectacles and performances, wish fulfillments; they are visions of the future, memories of the past, celebrations and critiques of the moment; and they circulate as social relations or badenya. That is where the political may lie hidden in the aesthetic: in the reinforcement of badenya relationships, for example, and in the CNA, and also in the education of children—in teaching them how to see photographs and thus see ideologies and their own surroundings more clearly.[116]

Njami talked about various hard-to-attain interventions for a public that lacked interest in art photography. This lack of interest was reiterated by Antawan Byrd, an associate curator of the 2015 biennial. He noted that Malians were willing to pay to attend concerts and sports events, but wouldn't attend the biennale even though it was free. Yet history shows that Malians were avid consumers of portrait photography (like the rest of the world), so the interest in fostering art photography connects to already present interests. While it is often assumed that biennials *should* address local publics, Simon Sheikh questions this notion.[117] For him, "it is, rather, a question of how a biennial produces, or attempts to produce, its publics that must be analysed and criticized. One must ask what assumptions of place and participation are at work, what notions of subjectivity, territoriality and citizenship are invoked. And one must ask in what way participation is valued in terms of cultural consumption and legitimation."[118]

Sheikh argues that it is important to be aware of what is at stake in claiming that a local public is desirable, especially when the public rituals of attending the biennale—viewing static photographs alone in a clean, well-lighted space, the subjects of which often have little to do with one's daily life or immediate surroundings—register as decidedly alien in Bamako. Attempts to reach the Malian public that seemed most successful were *Gens de Bamako* and the CNA, where people see photographs of themselves and families. Fatoumata Diabaté's *Studio de la rue (Studio on the Street)* also performed a form of Relation by turning the biennale public into the self-conscious customers of the 1950s, '60s, and '70s. (An American scholar noted that it was thrilling to be photographed in this way, though it also felt slightly embarrassing.) This engagement seems to capture precisely what Glissant meant by Relation—an earnest yet ludic engagement with others. As Diabaté was already famous within the biennale cohort, she was able to photograph other prominent participants such as Simon Njami and Abdoulaye Konaté, adding a twist of consciously celebratory history, if also irony, to the work.

Despite its neocolonial qualities, the biennale is crucial for its sheer existence in Bamako as a major event that enables works to be shown, photographers to meet and talk, and ideas to be exchanged. The biennale has also been hugely influential on the burgeoning field of African photography. Since there are few major photography events in Africa, the biennale has been the widest reaching, the most consistent, and the longest running. It has provided a much-needed exhibition venue and meeting ground for photographers, curators, and collectors across the continent. For visitors, the tempo of experience slows to a Malian pace, and aspects of Malian life infiltrate all spaces. This antihegemonic articulation—the importance of Bamako to the biennale—was especially highlighted in the 2015 edition, when curator Bisi Silva's and writer Teju Cole's introductory catalog essays elaborated on aspects of daily life in Mali's capital.

It seems clear that the only way art photography in Mali will be of interest to the general population is if it is either sociable and festive or financially rewarding. For now, the Cinéma Numérique Ambulant seems the closest to sharing the communal values of traditional social portrait photography in a contemporary spirit. The emphasis on repetition or embellishment on a basic theme keeps artists connected to the original form, which, writ broadly, encompasses all recognizable visual aspects of Mali—its views, countryside, cityscape, social interactions, cultural values—its tangible and intangible heritage. This connection to Malian culture keeps the past within the present, to be enacted performatively and socially.

Chapter 4

Bamako Becoming Photographic

AN ARCHIPELAGIC ART WORLD

This flood of convergences, publishing itself in the guise of the commonplace. No longer is the latter an accepted generality, suitable and dull—no longer is it deceptively obvious, exploiting common sense—it is, rather, all that is relentlessly and endlessly reiterated by these encounters. On every side the idea is being relayed. When you awaken an observation, a certainty, a hope, they are already struggling somewhere, elsewhere, in another form.
—Édouard Glissant, *Poetics of Relation*

The inauguration of the Bamako Biennale triggered an excitement about photography in Bamako that spurred the founding and proliferation of new photographic institutions and programs, as well as increased exhibition and workshop opportunities for photographers at existing art centers. Several photo schools and workshops sprang up, and other, already-established institutions began to promote photography in their programming. Photographers have created collaborative associations with dues-paying members, and nongovernmental organizations (NGOs) and individuals have created photographic projects to encourage children's imaginaries.

These new ventures have distinguished Bamako as a relatively singular city in Africa; few cities outside South Africa have schools and galleries devoted to photography. Thus the beginnings of a local photographic art world could be said to have developed. Most of these institutions and projects are supported through European or American funding or individuals; while some have flourished, others have faltered. The dynamics of this art world fluctuate with political decisions by the Malian government and funding opportunities, but all are influenced by the founding and biannual recurrence of the African Photography Encounters.

This art world is like an archipelago in Glissantian terms because the institutions, projects, and associations exist individually, as intermixtures of Malian and European or American funding and influence; yet they are all similarly inspired by and interact with the biennale. Photography was born under colonial rule in the 1930s and thus as a new medium and image-making technology it is not rooted in precolonial social or artistic traditions. Its genealogy can be traced as a creolizing technology in an urban context that also is entirely postcolonial. Thus Relation may emerge from this archipelagic art world through interactions, publications, exhibitions, and images.

While this notion stretches Glissant's metaphor of an archipelago, the point is to conceive of these hybrid, Malian-Euro/American institutions as creolizing and potentially furthering Relation, rather than to view them as mere repetitions of postcolonial effects.[1] Relation pertains to equality, whereas postcolonial implies inequality; the hegemonic force of funding or publishing from French or other sources might seem overpowering in contrast to Malian efforts, but this perception does not acknowledge the strength of Malian photographers' influence in collaboration and pride in their cultural heritage, it similarly diminishes their photographs and the fact that their works can function in multiple ways, as Mande aesthetics and as contemporary art, for different audiences. Glissant himself was educated at the Sorbonne, and he acknowledged the positive aspects of all cultures that contributed to his own creolizing identity; his introduction to agnès b.'s exhibition catalog, which includes photographs by Seydou Keïta and Malick Sidibé, suggests that he would support the circulation of Malian images into the world.

Bamako sprawls on the banks of the Niger River and is bordered by the Manding Mountains. Approximately 14 percent of the country's population lives in the capital; an increasing number of people come in search of job opportunities. In the 1990s and 2000s, Bamako was much more modernized than the rest of the country, with paved main highways and roads traversed by a multitude of scooters, cars, and *sotramas* (vans that serve as a privatized transportation system), and several tall buildings that lend the city a distinctive horizon along the river's north bank. The city has electricity that usually works, chlorinated drinking water, many open markets, a handful of Lebanese grocery stores and internet cafes catering to foreign aid workers, and a photo studio on almost every corner. The downtown is taken over by a huge open-air market, the vast Grand Marché, and in some parts of the city herds of goats and sheep stand across from vibrant nightclubs. Like many capitals, Bamako attracts citizens from across its nation, and from neighboring countries. The social mélange of ethnicities and castes, together with modern amenities, colonial architecture, and postcolonial sprawl, have produced its own unique, urban culture.[2] As the seat of government, Bamako has been said to centralize Bamana culture.

A small market town ruled by the Bamana Niaré clan before colonialism, Bamako became the capital of the French Sudan and was retained as the capital after the country's transition to independence. In his characterization of six general types of postindependence African cities, Anthony O'Connor refers to Bamako as a "colonial" city.[3] Its government, infrastructure, socialization, community organization, population, social imaginary, and physical spaces were reorganized and transformed by the French to become economically, as opposed to spiritually, functional.[4] Thus Bamako could be considered the *most postcolonial* of Mali's cities, in contrast to Djenne or Timbuktu, for example, which have been important trading centers since medieval times and today are UNESCO world heritage sites.

It is precisely Bamako's "colonial" past extending into its highly postcolonial present that makes the city conducive to the growth of an art photography movement. Because Bamako has an airport and is a hub of transportation, it is today a way station for tourists and scholars en route to the more art historically famous regions of Djenne and Dogon country; Vogel bought Keïta's negatives in the 1970s on her way through Bamako, since her original research was conducted in Ivory Coast. In other words, the characteristics that made Bamako an important city in Mali and in West Africa contributed to the eventual internationalization of Keïta—his pictures documented a wide variety of people because of his location, and that same location encouraged his eventual discovery, no doubt through his local reputation. Similarly, the influx of modern imagery in Bamako—visible in newspapers, cinema, and a few billboards—would also have presumably created a public that was more visually oriented toward the two-dimensional form of photography than people in villages who did not have access to modern imagery. Thus, studio photography participated in the modern visual culture of the city. In 2011, only a few billboards used photographic images; for the most part billboards were painted, and the kind of constant photo-image advertising seen in American cities on the outside of buses, on the inside of subways, and along the street was mostly absent. Many people had televisions, however, which affects visual culture, and weddings and funerals are now often videotaped instead of photographed.[5] Cell phone internet usage seems likely to have changed Malians' visual experiences, like it has in the rest of the world.

Because there was no tradition of "art photography" in Bamako until the founding of the biennale, the question of who became art photographers, and to which traditions they look back to or emerged from, is important for considering the movement's presence and concerns today. French philosopher Michel Foucault's concept of genealogy allows an understanding of photography as a *discursive practice*, one which constitutes subjects in different roles—as photographers, as culture workers or brokers (arts administrators), and as viewers or viewing publics. French sociologist Pierre Bourdieu defines the art world as a *social field*: an arena, composed of professions, that reproduces a hierarchical domination of power but allows for contestation of its domination and, crucially, can potentially contest its own subordinate position in the state.[6]

While Foucault and Bourdieu differed in theorizing the nature of how power works in society, their theories offer useful approaches to understanding the nascent art world in Bamako, primarily because, in my view, no one schema can adequately explain society or power, especially when those models are taken from a French context and applied to another (even a French-influenced) cultural situation. In Bourdieu's terms, the institutions that teach and exhibit photography constitute a social field. While this field may be locally powerful, it is *subordinate* both in the larger field of power of the state and in the larger field of power that constitutes the global art world. In Foucault's terms, the *discourse* produced by photographers and institutions combines aspects of international influence and local aesthetics, which play out in varying relations among institutions and individuals and which are visible in the resultant images and practices. If, in examining these institutions, Bourdieu's and Foucault's ideas can be conceived of together, they allow a glimpse of the workings of Bamako's art world relations.[7]

American philosopher Arthur Danto's famous notion of the art world—as a community of arts professionals who give value and parameters to the meaning of contemporary art—adds crucially to Bourdieu's institutional approach here. In the American context, Danto was responding to Andy Warhol's challenge to the traditional notion of art. Warhol's exact replicas of commercial Brillo boxes that could be bought in a grocery store are handcrafted opposites of the readymade, seeming to lack any aesthetic purpose other than to exactly reiterate a factory-made consumer aesthetic. Warhol's Brillo boxes threw the very notion of art into crisis, requiring an art world—

a community of professions and individuals—to assert the value of such conceptual artworks. The Brillo boxes are one of the earliest examples of the conceptual drive in today's contemporary art world, which problematizes the very grounds of modernist ideas of art making rooted in the autonomous art object and the idea of "art for art's sake."

For Malian photographers, the new concept of "art photography" requires Danto's community of interpreters to recognize art photography's new aesthetic and exhibition value. Although introduced and in part reproduced by French and American aesthetic ideals of modernist photography, art photography in Bamako also emanates Mande aesthetics; the "code" of understanding photography as art is locally and internationally legible for a small group of administrators and photographers working in Bamako. The discourses of photography in Mali allow for an aesthetic mode of interactions of power, as Mande aesthetics permeates the various aspects of interactions and institutions.

A genealogy of the new field of art photography indicates how Danto's theory helps to understand the Bamakois art world. Just as Keïta's and Sidibé's photographs were legitimized *as art* in New York's art world through the embellishment of printing contrasts and enlargements, so were art photographs such as Rotimi Fani-Kayode's homoerotic nudes legitimized *as art* by the first Encounters in Bamako. Along with Fani-Kayode's images, press photography and portraiture were equally celebrated in the biennale, and those photographic approaches also equally constitute "art photography" in Bamako. The movement encompasses a wider range of photographic genres than the New York art world, incorporating reportage, ethnographic photographs, and portraiture, because of the flexibility of Mande aesthetics within the Bamako art world.

Categorizing African contemporary visual production is a vexed issue, but it continues to be of art historical interest—not for the purpose of creating rigidly defined categories, but in order to differentiate specific histories and circumstances that pertain to an artwork's meaning and value.[8] In *Africa Explores*, Vogel and Mudimbe differentiate traditional, performative types of art that create or are imbued with a sacred power from works made by artists trained at a Western or Western-influenced academy and from art that would in the US be called "material visual culture"—that is, popular, local, without sacred or metaphysical power, and not taught at an academy but instead passed down through familial introduction or apprenticeships. Studio photography, as a new technology introduced by the French for the purposes of commercial portraiture, developed under a different route than that of traditional arts *or* modern arts in Mali. Thus portrait photography would fall into the "popular" category, but *art* photography would fall into the category of artists trained at Western or Western-influenced academies. The first-generation photographers were trained as apprentices, which follows both African and European arts systems (in Mali, a common path is traditional smithing or woodcarving, similar to routes taken by European studio photographers). This is a rough categorization; some "art" photographers were first and foremost studio photographers—that is, they come to art photography from a "popular" background. However, many studio owners, like Malick Sidibé, as well as photographers who never worked in a studio, were originally trained as artists in other fields, such as drawing, painting, or jewelry-making, at the National Institute of the Arts in Bamako.

Although some prominent older photographers were trained abroad as photographers in Communist-bloc countries during Mali's socialist era, from 1960 to 1991, today virtually all of the younger generation of art photographers (born in the 1970s and after), including all of the women, were trained in the new photography schools in Bamako. These photographers also often undertake apprenticeships at studios, or internships with press agencies; many of them supplement their education with workshops sponsored by the Jean-Paul Blachère Foundation or the biennale, or various residencies in France. Remarkably, Mali's most successful photographer in terms of global art world recognition, Mohamed Camara, received no *craft-based* training at all before his international breakthrough exhibitions at Paris Photo and the Tate Modern; but he is the exception that proves the rule, as it were. So it can be seen that most photographers who practice art photography cross over between the two strains or currents of "popular" and "academically trained artist," but that all are responding to the development of the biennale as a showcase for art photography.

As in most African countries, "art" as it was understood in Europe did not exist before European infiltration and colonialism. Mudimbe explains, "What is called African art covers a wide range of objects introduced into a historicizing perspective of European values since the eighteenth century."[9] Sculptures, masks, and costumes were used in conjunction with rituals, music, and dancing, on religious, political, and social occasions, and acquired meaning in specific contexts. Mande societies comprised three castes, one of which was the *nyamakala*, or "people who handle nyama." This includes the male smith-sculptors and female cloth-dyers, who handle healing arts and circumcision for their respective genders. Smithing or making Bamana mud cloth, called bogolan, requires handling nyama, power or energy that permeates living beings and that can be harmful or healing depending on the situation in which it is released.[10] The material arts of smithing and cloth-dying involve a lifetime of inculcation in Bamana spirituality, taught by an older, more experienced person. The objects are commissioned for a particular person or social group (i.e., a masking society) and carry a spiritual potency. Sarah Brett-Smith writes, "The primary purpose of Bamana ritual objects is almost never aesthetic pleasure. . . . In fact, sculpture does not exist as a term."[11] Instead, the word *mako* is translated as "need," "necessity," or "lack" and is included in the names of sculptures, as in the phrase she quotes, "'wood carvings that fix needs.'"[12] Thus, according to Brett-Smith, the Bamana "view carved objects primarily as solutions for urgent and inescapable needs."[13]

Bogolan cloth, as shown by Victoria Rovine, has undergone a shift from traditional meanings and forms to become a medium of contemporary art in the hands of the Groupe Bogolan Kasobane, a collective of mostly male artists working in Bamako. But while bogolan's trajectory into fine art makes an interesting comparison to photography, bogolan differs significantly in that it existed as a centuries-long precolonial medium whose functions and uses changed in an urban context; traditional bogolan-making is still practiced by women in rural Mali.[14] Moreover, the cloth has come to symbolize Mali (and more generally, West Africa or Africa) throughout the world due to its interaction with the international fashion world, and the cloth's historical aesthetic remains crucial to the content of the resulting contemporary work. In contrast, photography has no aesthetic other than itself—photography's nature is such that it takes on the form of the world around it, making it especially mercurial, difficult to pin down, fluid, and potentially Relational because of its accessibility and seeming legibility. Whether printed at any size or glowing on a screen, a photograph is merely a two-dimensional surface that opens out into infinitely variable imagery.

Photography is also unlike such traditional arts as bogolan in that, as a modern medium developed under colonialism, it includes practitioners from all castes, ethnicities, and economic classes, although many of the "art" photographers mentioned in this book tend to be elite in education and class. In contrast to the traditional arts of Mali, whose creation and use are inseparable from cultural and religious uses, various photographers told me that their medium possesses no nyama, or magical or religious power, although *gris-gris*, or negative magic, can exist in photography as in all areas of life.

One similarity that photography generally shares with Mali's precolonial sculptural traditions is the transformation it has undergone, both locally when the medium received attention from an international audience, and internationally, when the work is exhibited outside its original social context. The objects take on different meanings, from functioning in a social context to functioning as "fine art." Unlike studio photography, the shift toward creating art photography effectively limits its viewers to an international audience, rupturing the social and communal ties to a local economy of exchange that studio photography still perpetuates. Similarly, nineteenth-century American geologic survey photographs, such as those by Timothy O'Sullivan, also underwent a transformation in meaning when they were incorporated into the New York art world as "fine art" photographs, to serve an ahistorical market explosion.[15] It seems that eventually all photographs, and perhaps all objects of visual culture, if far enough removed in time or space, can be seen as "art," especially when they are rare or serve a politically dominant canonical narrative.

While many Malian sculptural arts are associated with nyama and ritual performances, African entrepreneurs who discovered the burgeoning European interest in African "curios" began selling off powerful masks and sculptures in the late 1800s. Soon African carvers began creating objects for the European and American trade, resulting in what is sometimes called tourist or "airport art," although this work has become economically viable and artistically interesting in its own right.[16] Such work is now practiced by hosts of carvers in the long stalls of the Artisanat across the street from the state art school, the National Institute of the Arts (INA).

INA was founded by the French colonial government in 1932 as the Maison des Artisans Soudanais, to keep alive precolonial arts, specifically sculptural and carving traditions, in a modern context.[17] French teachers introduced the modern art form of painting at INA.[18] After independence, INA's role was to teach traditional as well as modern arts forms, so that students on graduation could relocate to rural towns and villages to teach traditional arts in a nationalist revival. Many professors at INA studied in the USSR or Soviet-bloc countries, when socialist realism was predominant. While there is a tangential connection between some art photographers who were trained at INA (Malick Sidibé studied there as a jewelry-maker, for example), it is important to note that photography was not taught at INA and was not considered a fine art; it was a commercial, vernacular practice. Photography did not enter the curriculum at INA until recently, when Keïta's and Sidibé's fame revolutionized the field.[19] However, the focus on aesthetics and design from INA likely contributed to the aesthetic eye of Sidibé, Sogodogo, and others.

In Bamako a graduate school of the arts, called the Balla Fasséké Kouyaté Conservatory of Arts and Multimedia (Balla Fasséké Kouyaté Conservatoire des Arts et Métiers Multimédia, or CAMM) was founded by President Alpha Oumar Konaré and opened in 2004.[20] The conservatory has a photography program but apparently no photo printers, at least in 2010. The government also supports the African House of Photography (Maison Africaine de la Photographie, or MAP), which was the home office of the biennale in Mali until it moved to the National Museum. Private ventures include the Association Seydou Keïta and two private photography schools: Promo-femme (a school specifically for women that is now defunct) and the CFP. There is also the arts collective Centre Soleil, which hosts the occasional photography workshop.[21] Although Bamako does not have a comprehensive fine art gallery system, Galerie Chab was run from 2000 to 2010 by Amadou Chab Touré.[22] AMAP (Agence Malienne de Presse et de Publicité), the Malian press agency, hires photographers and provides an important internship for Alima Diop, while Emmanuel Daou also works as a photojournalist. Finally, there are numerous photographers' associations that do not necessarily occupy a fixed physical structure or building but that involve a structured set of official professional relations, membership dues, and community.

The blossoming of these new institutions has contributed significantly to Bamako's burgeoning art photography movement. The discourse of *art* photography—how it is practiced, taught, learned, shown, written, talked, and thought about—is constructed by these institutions and the people who work and study within. This discourse is multivocal and multivalent. It privileges certain aspects of photography making, such as personally interacting with subjects on the part of photographers, interviewing sitters, traveling to photography festivals and other cultural events, learning from mentors and teachers, and collaborating with fellow students, and diminishes other aspects, such as experimentation, conceptualism, criticality, and ruthless individualism and ambition.

But this discourse is animated, even in off years, by the imaginary of the biennale, and its potential, which exerts a symbolic force even when it isn't actually taking place. The biennale usually intervenes locally, with such "Offs" projects as the Cinéma Numérique Ambulant (CNA) and others, like those supported by the Jean-Paul Blachère Foundation; others are created by Malian associations. Overall, however, the art photography discourse incorporates, and indeed is shaped by, key elements of Mande culture, which are sometimes specifically invoked and at other times reproduced not by any emphasis on photography per se, but by operating alongside photography, at times contradictorily, with an emphasis on process, honor, privacy, and secrecy, causing friction with the very ambitions of the capitalist art world it attempts to inhabit.

The art photographers welcomed the creative opportunities afforded them by the biennale, which opened up traditional notions of photography.[23] As many art photographers hail from either studio or fine art backgrounds—or, like Malick Sidibé, both—the opportunities that the biennale afforded in terms of conceptualizing the function of photography were, in a word, exciting. Working in black-and-white was, in the first decades of the 2000s, for many the surest sign of the *artist* as photographer, although now with digital technologies many also work in color. The success of Camara, the young artist given a solo exhibition at the Tate Modern in London, who had worked with a color digital camera, may have increased photographers' appetite for color. Complete abstraction is not appreciated; I saw only a few truly abstract images—in the style of Rodchenko or Moholy-Nagy, for example—by a couple of photographers. Similarly, in 2006 I rarely saw pictures that were composed of unusual viewing angles, extreme contrasts, unrealistic color choices, or unexpected subjects. While *formal* innovation was not the main concern of most of the photographers with whom I spoke, the excitement about pursuing subjects other than portraits for photographers was palpable.

Yet for a city with so many photo studios and such a rich history of and connection to portrait photography, the biannual occurrence of the Bamako Biennale seems to go virtually unnoticed in daily life. The event is only visible in particular venues, such as the National Museum, which itself stands a bit apart from the city behind high walls. Closer to the downtown, biennale-related exhibitions are usually found in the French Cultural Center and more recently at the Institut National des Arts. Discussions and symposia sometimes take place at the Conservatoire des Arts, a drive up into the hills surrounding the city; MAP is far from the city center and from other photographic institutions, located near the former airport; sometimes bars like Bla Bla, a hip bar oriented toward international NGO workers, are included, and the city's Bamako Museum is incorporated, as well as sometimes the train station. In other words, a cursory spatial locating of the biennale's venues and offices establishes its deep connections to the city's colonial past and its postcolonial present.

The National Museum, discussed in chapter 5, houses an important collection of precolonial objects and archival material and is considered one of the finest in West Africa. It supports the art photography movement because four prominent art photographers work or used to work at the National Museum; furthermore, the director of the museum now runs the Malian part of the biennale organization. The museum has also exhibited photography in its programming, and its temporary exhibition gallery usually showcases the International Exhibition during the Encounters.[24] The city museum, called the Museum of the District of Bamako, is also usually an exhibition space during the biennale and sometimes holds photography exhibitions at other times of the year; local shows were often put on by the two photography schools, CFP and Promo-femme.

The French Cultural Center (CCF) has been another important institution with regard to the art photography movement. The CCF has international cultural offerings, such as films and performances, in its vestigial continuation of the French colonial policy of cultural assimilation. The building contains exhibition spaces, a library, and an outdoor café. The CCF often displays local contemporary photography exhibits and is one of the official venues of the biennale. The café provides the opportunity for informal gatherings of internationals and expatriates, especially during the opening week of the biennale.

The French-Polish writer and photographer Antonin Potoski worked at the CCF from 1996 to 1998 and continued to publish photographers' works until 2002. His activities and collaborations with local photographers had a dramatic impact on the Bamakois photography movement and introduced me to the art photography movement. Potoski's publications on photographers Youssouf Sogodogo, Mamadou Konaté, "AT" (Amadou Traoré), and Mohamed Camara have contributed both to the photographers' sense of themselves as artists and to the perception of Bamako as a city of published and exhibited artists. These publications were available at the National Museum bookstore and were shown to me by the artists in 2006, fueling my sense that an art world was actively in the making.

Association Seydou Keïta (ASK) was founded by French dealer Jean-Marc Patras and the Malian photographer Alioune Bâ in 2001, shortly before Keïta's death. Patras is the secretary, and Bâ was the president until 2011. Bâ is also one of the National Museum's official photographers and an art photographer in his own right, which is how he came to know Seydou Keïta. Patras has offices in Paris and coordinated gallery shows with Sean Kelly in New York. In 2005, thousands of Keïta's negatives languished in a metal trunk in the office of ASK, in ninety-degree temperatures, due to the florid controversy between the Pigozzi and Magnin team and Patras, which has made Keïta's prints virtually untouchable by the art world because of their hazy legal status.

Although ASK has a gallery space, it is located in a rather inaccessible neighborhood where the old airport used to be, although it is possible to walk there from the African House of Photography. Across the street from ASK, a decidedly different collective arts venture, titled Centre Soleil, has hosted photographic and digital workshops, although its focus is on drawing, painting, bogolan (mud cloth painting), and sculpture.

The African House of Photography, home to the biennale's organizational center, has two air-conditioned offices in a building with a lovely open-air gallery in which photographs are shown during the biennale. Unfortunately, the offices do not contain archives or an indoor, protected gallery space, which has been a constant complaint of MAP's director, Moussa Konaté. Despite these problematic issues, MAP has hosted various exhibitions and projects.[25] Konaté related that MAP holds exhibitions from organizations in France, particularly if they send laminated materials, because of the outdoor space and because MAP lacks much of a budget to hold its own exhibitions.[26] Recently, MAP has been collaborating with American scholar Candace Keller's project Archives of Malian Photography, funded by grants from the British Library and the National Endowment for the Humanities, along with Matrix: The Center for Digital Humanities and Social Sciences, and Michigan State University, where Keller is a professor, to digitize and catalog 100,000 negatives from studio photographers Mamadou Cissé (1930–2003), Adama Kouyaté (1927–2020), Abdourahmane Sakaly (1926–1988), Malick Sidibé (1936–2016), and Tijani Sitou (1932–1999).

Two private photography schools and photography programs at both the college and graduate government schools have prominently contributed to the burgeoning art movement. Both schools have been quite influential on younger photographers. One, the Cadre de Promotion pour la Formation en Photographie (CFP), was founded as Helvetas in 1998 by the Swiss NGO of the same name.[27] However, in 2004 and 2005 leadership and financing was shifted to Malian hands, along with the name change. The president of the CFP, Aboubacrine Diarra, also works at the National Museum as a photographer, and the director, Youssouf Sogodogo, used to work there but now is occupied full-time at CFP. The CFP offers a two-year course of study, where students learn about technological and aesthetic aspects of photography. An exchange with the Swiss school in Lausanne continues, so that a few of the students each year are Swiss. A representative project in 2005, called "Bio-Coton," documents an organic cotton farm in a village as part of an initiative toward sustainable agriculture, which relates to Helvetas's work in Mali.[28]

In 2006, Sogodogo of the CFP stated in numerous interviews that the school encouraged women to become photographers by ensuring that each incoming class had an equal number of women and men. A representative photography project on the school's website celebrated thirty years of Helvetas in Mali; the photographs were all taken by a woman, Fatoumata Kanté dite Batoma.[29] However, a November 2020 scan of CFP's website suggests that this no longer is the case, although there are several women attending. In 2005 and 2006, Sogodogo was very supportive of several students, including Fatoumata Diabaté, Harandane Dicko, Seydou Camara, and Salif Traoré. These four have gone on to be exhibited and published in the Bamako Biennale and other international venues. However, according to informants in 2011, the school subsequently became more focused on commercial or advertising photography, and less focused on fine arts, presumably for financial reasons. There were also breaks with students. The school's policy was to keep the negatives of its students as its own property, which made it particularly vulnerable to distrust. The CFP's role changed because of economic reasons; namely, the lack of viability of supporting an art photography school in Bamako, as François Deschamps noted.[30] The other private school, Promo-femme: Center of Audio Visual Education for Young Women, was founded in 1996 and closed in 2009.[31] While open, this school had an enormous impact on the gender demographic of young photographers, producing graduates who were notably among the few female photographers in the city.

The state-run art schools have had considerably less of an impact on the movement, although exhibitions during the biennale are held at the National Institute of the Arts. (Photography education at INA is covered in more detail later in this chapter.) The public graduate school of the arts, the Balla Fasséké Conservatory of Arts and Multimedia (CAMM), includes a photography program, although it is hampered by a lack of equipment. The school's director is Abdoulaye Konaté, the most famous contemporary Malian artist (other than Sidibé and Keïta); he makes conceptual textile-based hanging works and installations.[32]

The conservatory's approach to teaching photography and aesthetics is supplemented by local as well as international artists and scholars. In 2006, Amadou Chab Touré, a philosopher who owned the only photography gallery in Bamako, taught aesthetics at the conservatory. Touré had formerly taught at CFP, and then opened a photography gallery called Galerie Chab in 2000, which he ran in Bamako for ten years. Touré sometimes organized or participated in the Contours (the "Off" exhibitions) of the biennale, and exhibited many Bamakois art photographers in solo or group shows.[33] He eventually closed the gallery and left the city in 2010. In a 2006 interview, he expressed concern that the market for such work is not strong and that it is mostly composed of Western expatriates in Mali. He also exhibits European photographers and now shows Senegalese and other West African artists, representing Carpe Diem in 1:54 in London, from a gallery in Ségou, Mali. Touré's criticisms of the photographers in Bamako echo those of internationally renowned curators like Okwui Enwezor, who emphasize a globalized conceptual approach because African artists now operate in the global art world. Enwezor and Okeke-Agulu explain their view that "to be contemporary . . . means having the conceptual capacity to deploy a response to the present through self-reflexive reanimations of methods of creative inquiry."[34] For the most part, while Malian photographers are decidedly contemporary in that they are making art that responds to their present circumstances in a contemporary medium, they are not operating in an art world that engages those particular debates. They are instead deploying Mande idioms and local aesthetics in a communal context that is less concerned with postcolonial critique, conceptual originality, and self-reflexivity in regard to Western art history, broadly conceived. They are more concerned with questions of the continuation of the tradition of Mande values and the history of Malian photography through variations of form and embellishment. While this is generally unrecognized by critics unaware of Mande culture and not attuned to aesthetic subtleties, this approach is what makes these Malian photographs truly Relational.

Although Malick Sidibé was nominally the photography professor at CAMM, his own work was actually printed at the CFP because he no longer ran a darkroom and there were no printing facilities and few cameras available at the conservatory in 2010 and 2011.[35] Candace Keller was invited to teach a history of photography class at CAMM. Also, the American photographer François Deschamps, a professor of photography at SUNY New Paltz, spent a Fulbright year at the conservatory (2010–2011). In his role as photography professor, Deschamps noted the lack of printers at CAMM and arranged for students to use the high-quality laser printers at the House of African Photography through his contact with Moussa Konaté. Deschamps arranged for three of his best students to learn how to use the high-quality

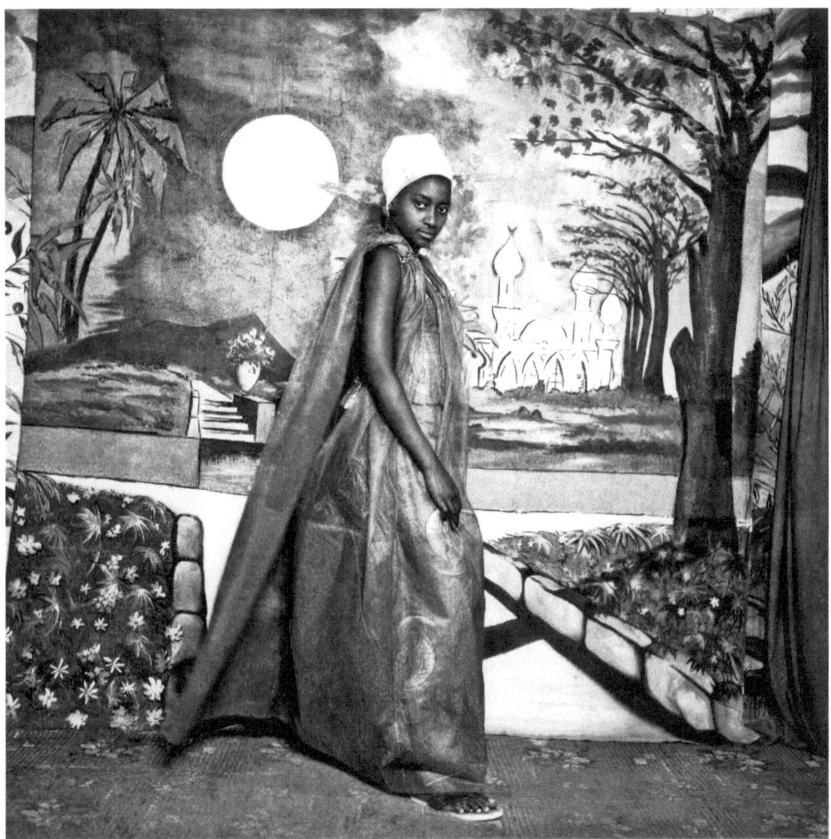

Figure 4.1. Abdourahmane Sakaly, studio portrait, 1960s. Courtesy of the artist's estate and Perlman Teaching Museum, Carleton College.

laser printers at the MAP in exchange for helping Moussa Konaté print local studio photographer Abdourahmane Sakaly's images from scanned negatives for an exhibition at MAP (fig. 4.1).[36] This exchange, which was mutually beneficial to the African House of Photography and to the CAMM, resulted from a social rather than a purely utilitarian relationship, thus illustrating the ineffable benefits of social capital.

Deschamps's subsequent art project, *Photo-Rapide* (2010–2011), in which the artist photographed people on the street in Bamako, was inspired by Keller's scholarship on Malian studio photography. Deschamps wanted to reverse the process of photography in creating a more equal power dynamic with his subjects. After taking the photograph, he gave it back to the person he had photographed in a frame (it was immediately printed with digital technology). The subjects could choose from a series of frames that Deschamps had made whose patterns represented local visual imagery. Then Deschamps gave the subjects a framed photograph of themselves, and rephotographed them holding the original picture (fig. 4.2). This project invited a sense of Relation between the people that Deschamps photographed and himself. In his subsequent project, *Malimerica* (2011), he photographed Americans before various studio backdrops painted by a Malian friend, Jo Koné, whom he commissioned for the project. Deschamps thus incorporated a spirit of Relation into his artistic and teaching projects, as an American artist working in Mali; he delved into research in order to try out Malian aesthetic and social approaches and ideas and bring them into his work, and he brought this aesthetic to the US in the form of studio portraiture.[37]

While all of the new photographic institutions promised increased opportunity for a developing photo community, few of them have been solely Malian enterprises. Almost all of them involve an exchange with a Canadian, European, or American institution entailing financial backing. The CFP was originally founded by the Swiss NGO Helvetas and retains its link with a Swiss art school, although it is solely Malian-funded and -run. ASK appears only nominally Malian; although headed for a decade by Bâ, who showed new exhibitions in the gallery, the actual handling and printing of Keïta's negatives occur in the Paris office run by Patras. These projects are decisive contributors to the development of new forms of photography in Africa, and they offer opportunities both for the reinforcement of a new understanding of African modernity and creativity and for increased financial opportunities within Bamako itself.

All of these institutions have undergone changes since 2006, in most cases limiting opportunities within the Bamakois art world. Promo-femme closed in 2009. CFP changed its mission, focusing more on commercial advertising photography than art. The closing of Promo-femme due to lack of funding was detrimental for female photographers, as was the turning away from art to commercial photography at CFP, suggesting that the biennale and its possibilities did not provide enough support for Malian photographers to constitute a sufficient economic return. Gallerist Chab Touré left Bamako for Ségou, where he opened the art space Carpe Diem. He has continued to showcase Malian artists, including photographer Harandane Dicko, at the London African art fair 1:54. The Malian participation of the MAP was shifted out of the hands of Moussa Konaté into the control of Samuel Sidibé at the National Museum, and Alioune Bâ left ASK after a decade, after realizing the position was too political.[38]

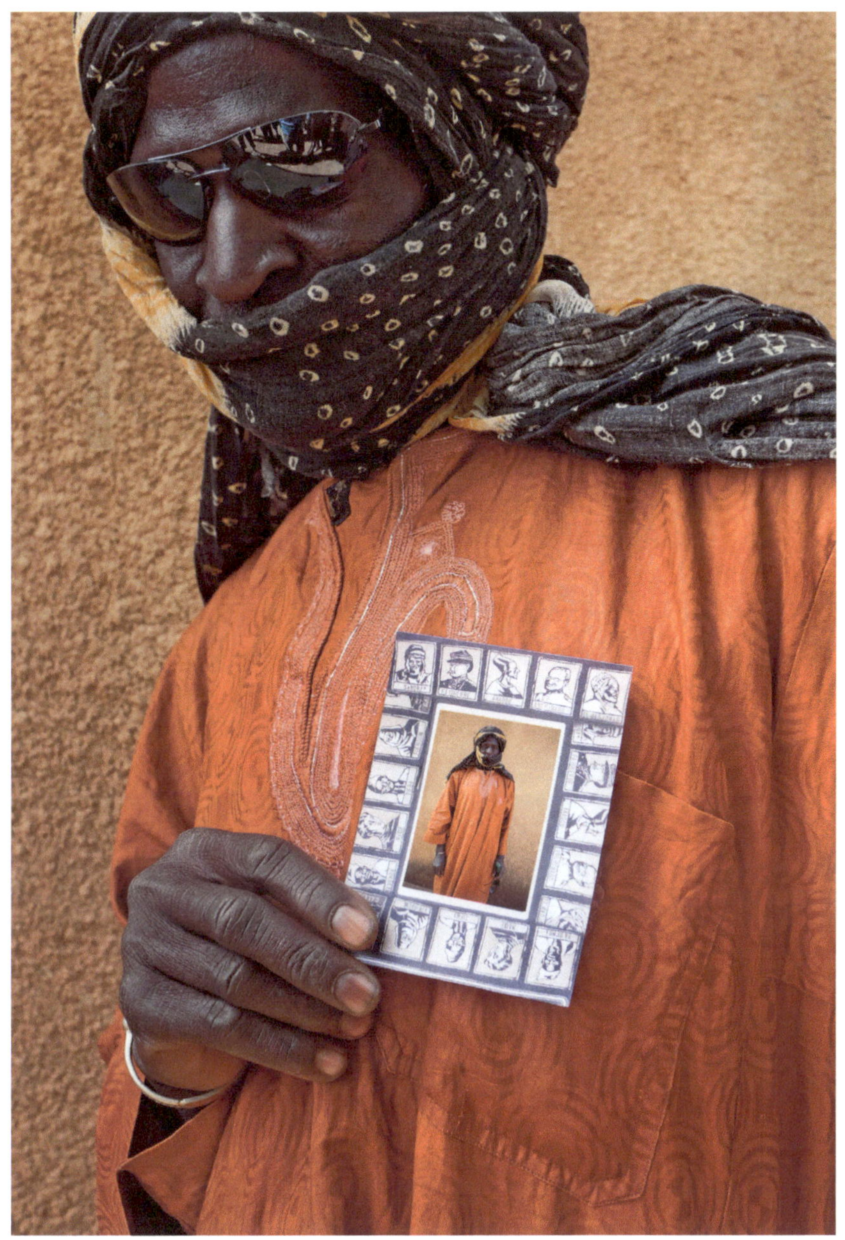

Figure 4.2. François Deschamps, *Kunja Clement, Photo-Rapide.* 2010–2011. Courtesy of the artist.

After Potoski left the CCF in 1998, no one from that institution seems to have continued his work as a cultural supporter of photographers in Bamako, especially in terms of publishing. An exhibition is open for a short amount of time and is inaccessible outside Bamako, but the catalog or book endures, allowing those who were not present to have a sense of what happened. A book of Malian press photography, *1960–2010: Notre Mali* (*Maliba k'ra anw ta yé*), was published in 2010 by AMAP, the state press agency, to mark the fiftieth anniversary of Mali's independence. (Nimis translates the Bamanankan phrase as "Great Mali has become ours").[39] The same year, two French book projects included contemporary Malian photographers. They are different in scope from Potoski's and Touré's books because they were meant to showcase contemporary Malian culture, rather than focus specifically on art photography. One, the beautifully illustrated *Novembre à Bamako*, produced by two French women, the writer Valérie Marin La Meslée and photographer Christine Fleurent, and sponsored by FNAC, covered the arts in Bamako and included pages on photographers Malick Sidibé, Alioune Bâ, Youssouf Sogodogo, Mohamed Camara, Harandane Dicko, and Salif Traoré. Samuel Sidibé, the director of the National Museum, was also included. Disappointingly, no female photographers were mentioned, though the book included a female comedian, female singers, and Adame Ba Konaré, the wife of the former president and founder of the Women's Museum.

The same year, the curator of the Bretagne Museum in France, Françoise Berretrot, spearheaded a project that focused on Malian women, "Mali au féminin" ("Feminine Mali"), and included a diaporama (a digital slide show of still photographs) by Fatoumata Diabaté. The book also showcased Sogodogo's hairstyles photographs, and included a series of portraits of Malian women living in Bretagne. More recently, German art history professor Bärbel Küster created an important web archive that includes video and transcribed interviews with numerous Malian and Senegalese photographers, conducted between 2011 and 2014, as well as excellent visual imagery and discussions of their works.[40]

Finally, the outmoded nature of analog materials caused a decline in film and paper supplies. As Europe shifted entirely to digital production, its unused film, chemicals, and cameras and other equipment were sent to Africa, supporting the CFP, for example. But after those supplies dried up, Bamako went through difficulty; few could afford a complete switch to digital photography, and the city mostly lacks high-quality digital photo labs. With the internet, however, possibilities are changing, and as digital equipment becomes higher-quality and more affordable, Bamako may see more positive changes. While one heyday of the art movement in Bamako may have temporarily passed, it is clear that these institutions had a dramatic impact on several photographers in Bamako, whose careers continue to thrive; and with the return of the biennale following the 2012 coup, it seems possible that future institutions may be founded and older ones revived.

However, significant obstacles remain to keep photography from becoming more vibrant: notably, lack of state support. In 2014, Harandane Dicko explained, "Nowadays, there's no real support for art in Mali, particularly for photography. The Malian Culture Ministry only allocates 0.45 per cent of its national budget to culture, while 80 percent of this budget is dedicated to the operations of the ministry. That shows that there's virtually no support for culture, and this is even more extreme when it comes to photography."[41] Unfortunately, the bureaucratic and corrupt nature of the Malian government willfully slows down interactions and possibilities for collaboration among individuals and institutions, replacing possible opportunities with suspicion and distrust. These obstacles seem to have affected some members of the photographic community, such that a feeling of hopelessness understandably characterizes at least some individuals' abilities to effect change. As Mali recovers from the coup, a direct result of postcolonial struggles derived from colonial imposed borders, it is impossible not to recognize the ever-present effects of the past in the difficulties of moving forward in the present. Anything that connects to Mali's bloated government runs the risk of stagnation, and in this impoverished country, there are no donors or buyers or patrons to rely on, other than Paris-based CulturesFrance.

The Bamako art world produces and reproduces knowledge and aesthetic forms through its institutions. The most fundamental form of intergenerational transformation occurs through educational institutions. French sociologist Pierre Bourdieu was not the first scholar to use the term "social capital," but his definition of social and cultural capital integrated the noneconomic assets gained through education, social class, and social standing into a Marxist economic theory. For Bourdieu, a photographic education—indeed, an education or skill set of any type—is a form of *embodied* cultural capital. By this, Bourdieu means that the knowledge learned is held in the practitioner's mind and physical capabilities or body. For a practicing photographer, such knowledge or *embodied* cultural capital accompanies two other types of cultural capital: the *objectified* state, which in this case would be defined as objects needed to make photographs—such as a camera, darkroom and equipment, printing paper, enlarger, chemicals, photography manual, and so on—and the prestige of the institution from whence the education comes, or the *institutionalized* state. In Bourdieu's supremely instrumentalized view of capitalist society, all forms of human knowledge and relationships can be transformed into power.

Bourdieu's theories help to explain and differentiate how cultural capital gained by photographers in Bamako—for example, their photographic education, and often their equipment as well—is acquired, first and foremost, through social capital. Social relations are at the heart of the transference and flow of photographic knowledge in Bamako. Moreover, the social capital operative in the field of contemporary art photography, while almost always involving international as well as local actors, operates in Malian society in a fashion similar to past studio portraiture.

Social connections of all kinds were also useful to portrait photographers in learning and plying their trade. Photographers needed familial and personal contacts to acquire cameras, equipment, and information from travels abroad.[42] Seydou Keïta noted that his uncle first brought back a camera from abroad; other photographers relied on family or friends to ship back film, as well as lenses and camera equipment, from France, other parts of West Africa, or the USSR; or to work as apprentices and to gin up business by advertising for the studio on the street. Importantly, Keïta learned photographic and printing techniques from the first African studioist in Bamako, Mountaga Dembélé. Keïta printed for Dembélé at night in exchange for knowledge and information about how to photograph. Keïta also learned about photography from Pierre Garnier, although Keïta's memoirs suggest that Garnier had a colonialist's suspicion of his assistants and therefore kept certain forms of information secret from them.

Traditionally, portrait photographers learn from being an apprentice in another photographer's studio. However, studioist Mamadou Kanté notes that, while he learned his trade from his father, he went to the USSR in 1986 to study for a year at a Soviet photography school. Photographers working today cite a number of sources of varying levels of formal education, from certificates from the new photography schools, to apprenticeships or internships in labs, studios, or press agencies, to local workshops at such art centers as Centre Soleil, to biennale workshops, and international residencies.

Prominent local individuals such as Malick Sidibé, Alioune Bâ, and Siriman Dembélé participated in mobilizing and passing on photographic education. There is always a social relationship along with the exchange of financial capital, in the payment of tuition, and the exchange of cultural capital, in the kinds of knowledges that are taught and in the time taken to learn photographic processes, concepts, and histories.

While the photography schools confer degrees, which provide their graduates with symbolic, cultural capital as well as concrete information and intangible concepts, they also supply teaching posts for several Bamako photographers. Dembélé, Bâ, and Sidibé taught at the various institutions at different times, creating a web of social interaction. I encountered photography educator Dembélé at the home of his friend, the photographer Amadou Keïta. Dembélé had formally trained in photography in Poland and France and was a recognized specialist in printing—he printed photographs for the biennale from its beginning and also printed all of Malick Sidibé's professional work. He gave me a sheet covered with handwriting and diagrams addressing the technical aspects of photography, such as where the focal point of a photograph should be. While Deschamps was interested in what he described as the "exchange" of a portrait photograph—meaning that the photographer should always offer the subject something in exchange for a picture, even if it is as small as a pleasantry or a joke—Dembélé's interest was in technically strong images.[43]

Alioune Bâ, photographer at Mali's National Museum, and until recently the president of the Association Seydou Keïta, was another photographer who mentored students at the National Museum and who guest lectured at the CFP and Promo-femme. He particularly supported female photographers, with whom he seemed to have warm relationships, again fostering the impression of social capital. A young French woman's description of her *stagiare* (stages) with Bâ demonstrates the Malian approach to learning photography, which is also evident in approaches to learning other arts, such as puppet masquerade or kora playing. The photography student, Armelle Razongles, explained how, when she came to Mali to study for a short time with Bâ, he brought her to assist his work at a marriage ceremony and had her travel to Dogon country, where she was assisted by a Dogon boy, whom she also photographed (in exchange his mother offered her some home-cooked food); she also assisted in a project teaching children photography. These are, of course, the photographic activities that Bâ and other photographers engage in. Describing her study, Razongles wrote, "Almost each of the photos realized during this short week is accompanied by a story. Each image has been guided by a discussion, listening, a smile or my participation in collective tasks. Maybe this is what real photography is! There is no photography 'in a vacuum,' but in knowing what we want to talk about."[44]

Razongles learned not only crucial technical skills (framing, lighting, etc.) but also more conceptual skills of narrative, as well as knowledge about Malian culture. One learns these skills and abilities through one's own initiative and interest, by watching and assisting masters and following along as one can.

While photography is taught at the public arts institution, the National Institute of the Arts, there is only one photography professor in residence, although other photographers like Diarra guest lecture. INA also encouraged female photography students. AMAP, the Malian press agency, can function as an educational venue as well, in that photographers can work as interns in photojournalism. To this end, many studios and color labs also make use of apprentices or interns, and this is a work-oriented form of education.

At the conservatory, American photographer François Deschamps taught four assignments over the course of an academic year. The first three involved approaches to genres: personal/family, documentary, and constructed reality. The fourth was to use one of the approaches to address the theme of that year's upcoming Bamako Biennale: sustainability.[45] Interestingly, while several students addressed expected themes such as trash disposal and the ubiquitous waste of plastic bags, others took a more optimistic and Relational approach, incorporating boys studying at a Qur'anic school or body builders exercising on the roof of a house (fig. 4.3). This example reflects the importance given to the biennale in terms of photographers creating work around its theme.[46]

Numerous photography societies are also influential in encouraging members to learn about and discuss photography, inspiring ideas about work as well as funding. There seems to be a particular emphasis on supporting these groups through formal means, with official titles and government registration, as Deschamps noted.[47] A book published in 2005 by the Rencontres, *L'Afrique en regards: Une brève histoire de la photographie* (*Africa in Perspective: A Brief History of Photography*) contains three sections: a glimpse of a world history of photography, an African history of photography written by Dagara Dakin, and a theory and technique of photography, which incorporates African photographers and technical details.

In contrast to this concerted, book-focused approach to photographic education, Mohamed Camara, the Malian star photographer who had a show at the Tate Modern while still a teenager, is perhaps the best example of the strength of social relations in catapulting him to relative fame.[48] It was his friendship with the traveling Frenchman Antonin Potoski that led to Editions L'Oeil giving Camara a camera if he promised to give them images in return. This led to Camara's series *Malian Rooms*, shown at the Tate, and to Camara's gallery representation in Paris. Interestingly, Camara was never

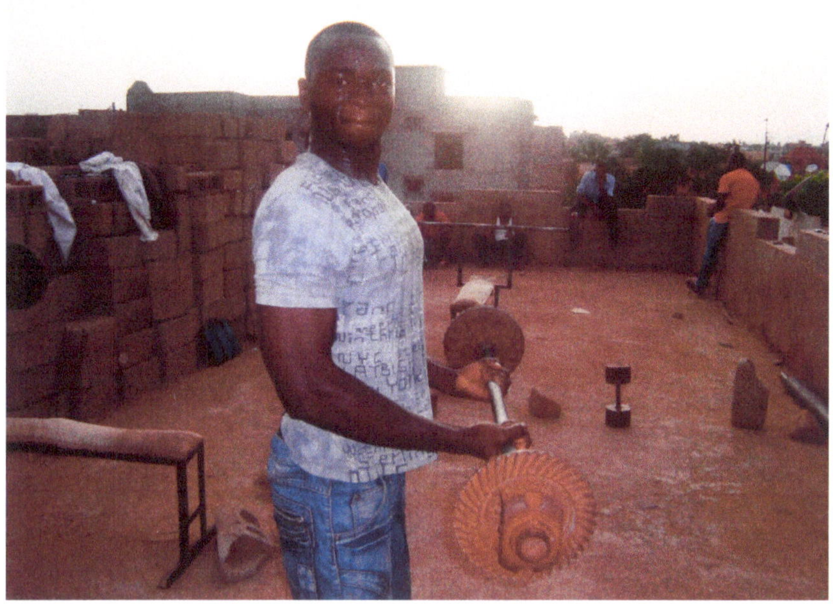

Figure 4.3. Adama Diakité, *Homme avec des haltères* (*Man with Weights*), 2011. Courtesy of the artist and Abdoulaye Kanté.

trained in the darkroom or as a technically skilled photographer like those who attended CFP: instead, his digital work has always been consistently conceptual about the image. While one could argue that Camara's success is connected to his embrace of a more internationally favored conceptual aesthetic approach rather than Mande or Malian aesthetics, Camara's style of education, in which he learned through a fadenya-inspired competitiveness ("I can do better than that!" he responded, when he saw the photographs by Dogon youth in a book by Potoski) as well as a badenya friendship with Potoski (an exchange in relation to the other), is connected both to Relation and to a Mande educational style, in which the student learns by watching and doing within the community of skilled performers, which is how griots teach their children to sing and play music.[49] This is very similar to what Bâ tells his students: to learn by doing and helping.

Social capital facilitates the flow of photographic knowledge from generation to generation, and is as crucial to art photography as it was to studio photography, although manifested differently. Born of the state's entrance into capitalist democracy, contemporary art photography participates in the political form that made it possible, cutting across ethnic and class lines to secure and exploit interpersonal relations. Contemporary art does not participate in social capital in the way that commercial portraits circulate among loved ones, and it is not commissioned by a client to circulate for sentimental, personal, and memorial reasons; rather, contemporary art is sold in galleries to clients for whom the *idea of art* means something, despite the lack of a personal relationship to the subject viewed. At the same time, books are circulated and exhibitions are held that rely on a loose network of professionals who hold varying degrees of social relations with each other.

The acquisition of the cultural capital of photographic education can be used to acquire economic capital either by way of starting a portrait business, photojournalism, or selling photographs from a gallery. Yet that cultural capital must rely on the *social* capital of the photographers in relation to their teacher, mentor, school, or studio photographer. This may be the case in every arts relationship—studio artists in the United States certainly often have close professional relationships to their mentors and teachers—but in Mali, I would argue, those relationships are even more important, perhaps because the community is small and the economic stakes are low, fostering a badenya-like culture of collaboration in the name of creativity in this new art form.[50]

Along with the official educational and archival institutions devoted to art photography, there exist several projects based on activism through photographic work with children. These projects involve the photographic intervention of Westerners into the Malian cultural sphere under the auspices of humanitarianism. International projects like the pan-European Oscura pinhole camera workshops, the American-Malian collaboration "Visual Griots," and Frenchman Antonin Potoski's projects with Dogon youth become instances of global interpenetration that bear scrutiny.[51] This type of photography is generally *not* associated with fine art, nor is it commonly discussed in art history, but it nonetheless has been encouraged by the founding of the biennale. The possible influences of this type of photography were most striking in Camara's meteoric rise to a solo exhibition at the Tate Modern in 2004 at the age of nineteen.

Bamako, then, has become an important center of African photography, aided by the close relationships of the photographic community; with the fortunate return of the biennale in 2015, 2017, and 2019 the impetus has continued. Art photography is discursively created through institutions and people interacting in a social field, creating networks of Relation. In this postcolonial city, the growing art photography movement oscillates between globalizing forces and local meanings and aesthetics, with varying outcomes that negotiate the postcolonial nature of Malian identity. While the institutions within Bamako provide concrete financial support in terms of paying jobs to a small number of photographers and arts professionals and affect a larger number of artists in enabling education and exhibition opportunities, this art world lacks what are commonly believed to be two key aspects of a functioning art world: a commercial gallery system and patronage in the form of art collectors. (Critics are arguably not needed; curators have replaced them as arbiters of taste in the global economy.) As Joanna Grabski notes in her book on Dakar's art world, *Art World City*, this remarkable situation exists in Dakar, where artists are indeed able to be successful and live on the sales of their works.[52] However, this model of an art world, based on cities like Paris in the late 1800s or 1900s and New York since the 1950s, is itself being complicated by smaller cities in the US and around the world. In other words, a gallery system is not the inevitable model; there are other possibilities for successful art worlds, although they must rely on some form of patronage or funding. The way for artists to make their living in photography can be to turn to commercial projects, such as photojournalism, which is how Daou and Diabaté support their art, or advertisement, which has become the goal of the CFP.

Despite the dearth of collectors and audience, Bamako's photographers and photographic institutions are creating new aesthetic forms that remain uniquely Bamakois. Art photography, an outgrowth of studio photography and photojournalism, offers creative possibilities to its practitioners: its aesthetics are closely connected to portraiture, linking it to the documentation of Malian culture, rife with social, local meaning; but it is also influenced by international canons introduced through photography educational systems and the exhibitions at the biennale. A new field has opened where none was before, drawing artists trained in more traditional artistic media, photographers trained in commercial professions, and those who never dreamed of becoming artists until they took up photography. With this unleashing of creative energies, new forms of memory and interaction can take place. According to Glissant, it is only through art—in a poetics free from immediate commercial drive—that new imaginaries can occur.

In *Poetics of Relation*, Glissant highlights "repetitions," in pointing to the way that an idea is taken up by different people or emerges out of different circumstances and contexts in different places. As Relation itself is always a process of becoming, not a fixed entity, it can never be proved or pinned down; only its examples can be accumulated, although such examples will never account for its full effect. The Bamakois world of art photography enables the potential for Relation through its "flood of convergences"—its network of institutions, administrators, and artists all sharing the relay of art photography as an idea, a new concept circulated among artists, professionals, and institutions. This art world is haunted always by the shadow, or perhaps more accurately the *shade*, of the biennale, which relays a sense of importance and provides the sense of confidence necessary for a fledgling art movement in an impoverished African country, along with a sense of Afropolitanism, cosmopolitanism, and future potential; at the same time, though, it is fully embodied by the active imaginaries of local producers. There is always a struggle, for Relation does not occur easily, in comfort, positive though it is. And Relation occurs from a sense of humility, against the arrogance of capitalism. This is another reason we may find Relation in Bamako, rather than in commercial art worlds like New York.

Chapter 5

Creolizing the Archive

PHOTOGRAPHERS AT THE NATIONAL MUSEUM

Against ideology content with its own company. . . . [Against] [t]hose who are the repository of the collective consciousness.
—Édouard Glissant, *Poetics of Relation*

An initially surprising aspect of the contemporary photography movement in Bamako is that four of its leading photographers work or once worked at Mali's National Museum, which houses a significant ethnographic collection of sculptures, masks, and textiles. The photographers' projects respond to their professional environment in an archival or museological manner, but subtly *creolize* the archive, in Glissantian terms, by imbuing it with a Malian sensibility that honors the appropriate context of knowledge, notes its power, and places its pleasures and burdens on the viewer.

The National Museum has long been the social hub of the Bamako Biennale and is now the administrative center as well.[1] Even while the Maison Africaine de la Photographie (MAP; African House of Photography) was the organizational apparatus for the biennale, it was in the museum's temporary exhibition space that the most significant and largest of the biennale exhibitions, the International Exhibition, was shown, while the auditorium was used for panel discussions by curators and artists. Most significantly, perhaps, in light of the sociability and discursivity of the biennale, it is under the cool shade of the museum restaurant's patio where biennale visitors gather to drink *gingembre*, eat *capitaine*, and talk and smoke. Prepaid biennale lunch buffets are served to biennale registrants. At night the museum hosts an outdoor party and during the day, large poster billboard blowups of photographs in the exhibition are displayed in the manicured park. Young, hopeful photographers and hangers-on trying to make a few centîmes also gather around the park, engaging visitors in conversations.

Despite the seemingly tenuous visible or conceptual relationships between traditional arts and contemporary photography, the National Museum as an institution has likewise played an important role in Bamako's art photography movement. Three artists—Alioune Bâ, Aboubacrine Diarra, and Joseye Tienro—are or were officially employed as photographers, while Youssouf Sogodogo formerly worked in the textiles preservation department. Sogodogo left the museum to work at Bamako's comprehensive private photography school CFP (the Cadre de la Promotion pour la Formation en Photographie), where he became director, subsequently influencing a younger generation of rising photographers. Like Sogodogo, Diarra has important influence through his position as president of the CFP, but unlike Sogodogo, he continues to still work at the National Museum. Diarra also teaches photography classes at the National Institute of the Arts (INA), the state arts college located in Bamako. Bâ, the most internationally famous of the four, was the first photographer to work in an artistic mode in Bamako, prior to the advent of the first biennale, in which he actively participated as co-organizer and photographer. Bâ was close to Seydou Keïta and served as the president of the Association Seydou Keïta until around 2010. Like Diarra and Malick Sidibé (until his death in 2016), Bâ guest lectured at various photography and arts programs in Bamako, and he particularly supported women photographers.[2] Tienro works in the museum's digital lab, supervising the digitization of the collection, and he is actively visible in his role of museum videographer during such events as the Bamako Biennale (fig. 5.1).

These photographers play or played active roles in the Bamakois photographic community as artists, teachers, mentors, administrators, and trailblazers. All of them have shown works in several biennales, and they usually also participate in various ways behind the scenes. They have all exhibited internationally, and their works have been published in Mali and France. Their prominence makes them role models who influence younger photographers, create opportunities for art photography in Bamako, and set its direction.

While at first it may be surprising to find photographers working at the National Museum because of its historical focus and its collection of tac-

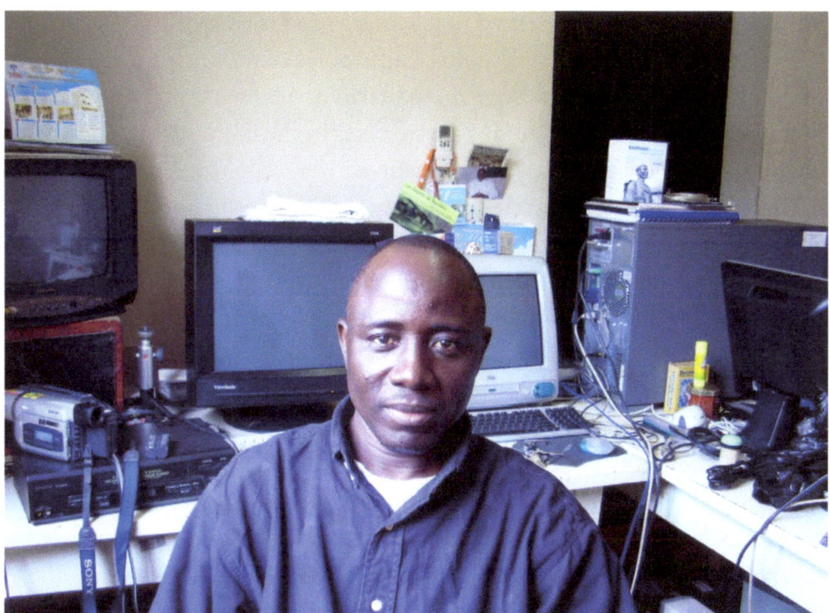

Figure 5.1. Joseye Tienro in his office at Mali's National Museum, 2006. Photo by author.

tile, often religious or power-imbued sculptures, masks, and textiles, many of whose traditions existed before colonialism, this professional focus makes sense in a Malian context. Even before the biennale was founded, the opportunities afforded by the museum's emphasis and dependence on photographs would have made it a natural magnet for the most ambitious photographers in Bamako, where an established role of "art for art's sake" photography only recently emerged. The photographers' education, access, ambition, and professional acumen enabled them to immediately be aware of the biennale, and simultaneously conferred on them an insider status.

How these photographers conceive of art photography stems in large part from their duties as official preservationists of *facen*, their nation's cultural heritage. Bodies of work by Sogodogo, Bâ, and Tienro arose from ethnographic, archival, and memorial impulses inspired by the function of the National Museum itself. In fact, their projects essentially apply the museum's historical mission to social and political aspects of the present. Sogodogo's *Hairstyles* series, Bâ's photographs of architecture, and Tienro's *Forgotten Heroes* aesthetically document the importance of culture and history. Specifically, these series emphasize the cultural significance of hairstyles and of architectural heritage, and the historical and political importance of veterans, including those who served in colonial-era wars as conscripted soldiers. The artists' attention to a changing cultural fashion (hair), a local style of building such as a *banco* mosque or an urban neo-Sudanic memorial, or the literal past embodied by veterans participates in the museum's mission of archiving, documenting, and memorializing.

Yet unlike a museum archive, in which the transmission of knowledge through didactics, brochures, and wall labels is the goal, these art photographs are not explained; their cultural meanings are available only to cultural insiders. This ethos reflects Mande ways of understanding knowledge within an individualized social context. A viewer who is not immersed in the culture cannot fully understand the meaning of the work. Thus, the photographers' projects assume a varied audience of viewers with different degrees of cultural knowledge. These photographs exercise what Glissant calls a "right to opacity," or a right to be unknown, because they show aspects of cultural heritage that become the richer for cultural knowledge on the part of the viewer, thus privileging a Malian audience, while allowing all to aesthetically view important aspects of Malian cultural heritage on a more general level.[3] Lorna Burns explains, "To acknowledge the other as opaque is to realize the existence of an unknowable otherness without assimilating all differences."[4] Glissant further explains the importance of opacity to humility and an understanding of truth as relative: "The thought of opacity distracts me from absolute truths whose guardian I might believe myself to be. Far from cornering me within futility and inactivity, by making me sensitive to the limits of every method, it relativizes every possibility of every action within me."[5] Opacity, or the unwillingness to be known, also understood as an inability to know everything about someone else (or about the world), is a crucial concept that prevents an arrogance of ignorance, and of belief that one knows an absolute truth.

In adopting opacity as an aesthetic strategy in their projects, the artists creolize the archive, transforming it with a Malian sensibility that acknowledges and appreciates that different viewers will understand their works with differing levels of knowledge. In the study of linguistics, "creole" is a term that encompasses a mixture of two or more languages that becomes a new language with its own grammar. "Creolization" is a neologism used by Glissant to exemplify the cultural mixing that is always occurring among peoples in the Caribbean.[6] I borrow the implications of "creolization" in Glissant's terminology to suggest that Sogodogo's, Bâ's, and Tienro's projects subvert the European format, or "language," of the archive to embody a Malian aesthetic.[7] These projects creolize the archive in reversing the museum's celebratory yet implicitly neocolonial ethnographic project by viewing it from the perspective of Malian citizens. They also inherently bring the museum's mission up to date by memorializing what is important in contemporary culture.[8] Creolizing the archive enables their artworks to circulate within Relation by making Malian cultural meanings aesthetically visible, and potentially accessible, to non-Malian viewers.

The influence of the museum's mission on its photographers stems from the importance placed on the status of visual and material culture in Mali. The preservation of cultural patrimony, called facen in Bamanankan, is an issue of tremendous political and artistic importance in present-day Mali. Traditional ceremonies and ways of life are changing quickly, or altogether disappearing, in the face of increasing modernity and globalization, while precious artifacts are looted and sold on the black market because of the country's extreme poverty and inability to regulate significant archeological areas.[9] Tensions between tradition and modernity inform virtually all aspects of life in Mali today, and particularly affect the roughly 14 percent of the nation's population who live in Bamako, by far the most urbanized city in Mali.[10] Such tensions present themselves in the artistic and cultural forms that are so integral to Malian identity, and thus come to the fore in photography, which participates in each realm because of its unique ability to function as both an art and a visual document.

The National Museum in Bamako is Mali's primary government institution officially devoted to the preservation of the country's varied forms of visual culture. The museum's mission statement supports the "collection, restoration, conservation and diffusion" of Mali's cultural patrimony.[11] As in most museums, photography plays an essential role in the execution of the National Museum's mission. Elizabeth Edwards notes, "The modern museum object is defined by a series of documenting photographic practices: accession photographs, conservation photographs, X-ray and infra-red photographs revealing unseen depths of the object."[12] Photographs record an artwork's original condition at the time of its accession, thus aiding conservation efforts later on, and allow conservators to see underneath layers to discover information about the object's creation. Photographs also allow objects to be archived, to be filed in data systems so that a museum employee can "view" the work without having to enter storage and risk damaging a delicate object.

At Mali's National Museum, supporting contextual photographs (and videos) also contributes to archivists' understandings of how an object functioned in its original context. For example, a photograph that shows a mask being performed in a ritual can provide useful information about the nature of the ritual, the role of the mask within the ritual, where it was performed, and for whom. Such information, combined with written documentation, can provide a sense of the mask's original life before it was accessioned. As Edwards writes, "Photographing objects was (and still is) integral and crucial to the apparatuses through which ethnographic and museological knowledge was made."[13]

Photography's peculiar qualities as a medium make it especially useful to museums, both for archiving objects and for reconstructing an object's history and the circumstances in which it was performed. Preserving the past for the sake of memory is in fact photography's most appreciated attribute. Roland Barthes claims, "It is the advent of the Photograph . . . which divides the history of the world."[14] For Barthes, our relationship to history becomes more immediate and contingent when we are able to see a photograph of a historical event. Photography has been invented, so "henceforth the past is as certain as the present, what we see on paper is as certain as what we touch."[15] For any historical project, such as a museum, photographs are crucial in attempting to re-create the past.

While the National Museum collects traditional artifacts and artworks, the ephemeral nature of performances, hairstyles, skin decorations, commemorative shrines, temporary paintings on buildings, and ritual activities, all of which are integral to the performance of and understanding of the collected objects, poses challenges to documentation and exhibition. Yet it is the *performative* nature of traditional art in Mali—its ephemeral attributes and its nonmaterial meanings—that gives masks and sculptures their power. Such performances can best be documented by photography, or increasingly by the related media of film and video (although the nonmaterial meanings and the temporal "life" of the object still vanish). Photographs of artworks are particularly useful as archival resources in recording and keeping track of a museum's objects, providing an ease of reference and comparison that video or film, as time-based media, cannot.

In Mande culture (which includes Bamana, Malinke, and Sarakole ethnicities, and which is culturally dominant in southern Mali), Téréba Togola explains that facen is "what we received from a deceased father, and, by extension, the ancestors. The *facen* (whose best equivalent in English is 'cultural heritage') comprises a vast array of tangible and intangible elements: land, wealth, ritual objects, art work, knowledge and traditions. To the Bambara and most Mande groups, the *facen* reinforces the liaison between the living and the dead (who are considered an integral part of the community). It ensures the group's cohesion and maintains its cultural identity."[16]

As in many African cultures, Mande spirituality vitally invokes the presence of ancestors. The deceased are considered spiritually present and are appealed to and appeased in various ways. History is understood as intimately connected to the present and is performed in the present through oral tales that seamlessly blend different chronologies. Kristina Van Dyke describes the precolonial Bamana worldview as operating with a genealogical view of knowledge and history—one that emphasizes fluidity, orality, the constant presence of a living history in people's imaginations, and their own personal interpretation of that history, in contrast to the fixed, static, colonial European notion of one singular linear history that exists solely in the past. Van Dyke writes, "In fact, because history is perceived to be uniquely positioned according to whomever is telling it, because it is not perceived as a linear trajectory but rather is open to selective association between present and past but always filtered through the present, with this perspective stressed, there is nothing consensual or totalizing about it."[17] Interestingly, Van Dyke's description is not dissimilar to radical postmodernist views of history as rife with ruptures, breaks, and different, competing viewpoints. That histories are written from the victors' point of view has been one of the foremost lessons of revisionist histories; certainly this was understood by people whose viewpoints were traditionally absent from the historical record. In any event, with the increase of literacy, formal education, and access to the internet, the relationship between orality and history is changing in Mali, especially for well-educated urban Bamakois photographers who combine formal education and literacy with their rich oral culture inheritance.

Numerous scholars have attempted to describe the differences between oral cultures and book-literate cultures.[18] In regard to Mande culture, Barbara Hoffman, who trained in Mali as a griot in the late twentieth century, writes:

> When attempting to explicate Mande ways of thinking about the "underside" of words, phrases, concepts, or actions, we need to take into account the "contested codes and representations" of any cultural phenomenon, and the multiple perspectives—Bakhtin's heteroglossia—that inform the production of layered meanings. To meet this challenge demands patience and much hard work, because we are not only working against the tide of our own logic, we are attempting to ferret out understandings and transform the very nature of them through the documentation in writing of ideas and meanings that are generated and sustained in the

ephemeral universe of orality. We Western scholars still have a long way to go before we can claim a firm grasp of the ontological and teleological implications of orality.[19]

In Mali, history, lineage, and culture are inextricably bound together; one cannot be imagined without the other. The facen, the cultural patrimony, reinforces relations between the present and past, between the deceased ancestors and the living, through forms of knowledge and moral authority passed on into the present. The facen also reinforces cultural identity within a society; in fact, the facen in some sense *gives* the society its particular cultural identity, as facen includes the particular forms of objects and rituals used by Bamana peoples, for example.

Malian cultural forms, or manifestations of facen in the arts, music, architecture, and religions of Mali, are celebrated both nationally and internationally. By "Malian culture," I am referring to "traditional" performances, dances, masks, sculptures, clothing, jewelry, and music performed and created by various ethnic groups as well as "modern" innovations, like pop music and studio photography.[20] A number of ethnic groups in Mali have ancient and distinctive sculptural and masking traditions whose physical remnants (objects) are preserved in the National Museum, as well as in countless museums outside Africa, like the Metropolitan Museum of Art in New York. Since sculpture was at first the only type of African art accorded attention by European and American scholars, certain Malian ethnic groups that create masks and sculptures—notably the Bamana, the Senufo, and the Dogon—were internationally recognized by museums, scholars, and collectors for over a century and are the source of many studies and publications.[21]

Mali's architecture, traditional festivals, and handmade material culture —pottery and textiles, especially bogolan cloth—are also well documented by scholars and appreciated by tourists. The ancient city of Djenne has been placed under UNESCO protection for its banco (mud-constructed) architecture, including its famous mosque, while the oldest written manuscripts in sub-Saharan Africa are under preservation in Timbuktu. The Tuareg nomads in the desert region of the Northeast are celebrated for their distinctive desert culture, dress, and camel sports, while performances and events of all sorts, such as the marionette festivals in Segou, draw researchers and tourists alike. Festivals celebrated by performances in some cases have an ancient lineage and are held for a mostly local audience. In other cases, the performances are new, or inventive variations on older performances, while the audience is made up largely of tourists, such as at the Essakane festival located about forty-five miles from Timbuktu, to which few nonlocal Malians can afford to travel. By contrast, the fishing festival at San is performed mostly for locals. Most photographers are well aware of Mali's cultural riches, as both intrinsic within the culture and also something desired by wealthy foreigners. Photographing at such cultural events is the bread and butter of many photographers' reportage work.

While cultural forms are an important source of symbolic pride for many Malians and contribute to the economic subsistence of the country, the state also emphasizes the importance of facen as a form of national ideology.[22] As Mary Jo Arnoldi notes, state-sponsored festivals attempt to inculcate notions of pride and connection to their heritage in local Malians, while the international trade in tourist art provides jobs.[23] Foreign tourism in areas like the ancient city of Djenne and treks in Dogon country also generate livelihoods among local guides and artists. Thus, photographs that depict the varied aspects of Malian culture, or "cultural photography," as I call it, have the potential to reach a wide and varied audience, both of Malians and of international tourists, and as such, the subject matter of "cultural photography" is popular indeed.

Mali's National Museum is a crucial institution with regard to issues of cultural preservation, documentation, and patrimony. The museum originated during the colonial period in 1953 as a branch of IFAN (l'Institut Français d'Afrique Noire), which was founded in 1936 in Dakar, Senegal, the center of French colonial power in West Africa.[24] Nationalized at Mali's independence, the museum was supposed to "play an important role in the scope of reinforcing national unity and contributing to the valorization of authentic culture," but that was impossible because of lack of funds.[25] In fact, the museum had virtually ceased to exist by 1976, when a renovated mission statement and new policies were developed to update the museum's function.[26] Along with the museum's reorganization, a new layout and buildings were designed by French architect Jean-Loup Pivin in a neo-Sudanic style to reflect traditional Malian banco architecture, in an attempt to recuperate the traditional process and make the museum seem more accessible to its local population.[27]

The government's choice of a French architect to redesign the National Museum highlights the postcolonial nature of the museum itself, such that the museum's architecture becomes a metonym for its ideological presence. The museum hopes to foster an appreciation of precolonial cultural traditions as a way to regain pride in Malian heritage and to reinforce a sense of national identity.[28] Arnoldi convincingly argues that the museum is a site "for constructing a national culture" and that it "has marshaled a constellation of historical memories, symbolic forms, and cultural practices in the service of this nationalistic project."[29] The museum's collections and documentation are impressive, and invaluable to preserving Mali's history.

But as Van Dyke notes, and as becomes clear when one spends time at the museum, "most Malians view it as largely irrelevant, a site for tourists."[30] The museum presents static objects from different, presumably separate cultures in vitrines supplemented by wall text. As scholars of African art recognize, this form of presentation thoroughly distorts the original context in which masks or sculptures functioned, even though it simultaneously preserves the works as objets d'art. Mali's traditional cultures utilized an oral and performative enactment of rituals through songs and ceremonies, involving music and dancing in conjunction with the appearances of sculptures or masks. A mask's power and meaning were dependent on the context in which it was performed. For example, a *komo* mask, one of the most powerful and dangerous masks of the male Bamana and Senufo komo societies, and one that is normally hidden for most of the year except to appear in a komo ceremony, has lost its power when the mask is relocated to the confines of the museum and displayed under static and constant visibility.[31] Thus, photographs and video documentation are especially powerful forms of contexualizing a mask's history (figs. 5.2 and 5.3).

In Van Dyke's description of Malian precolonial, "genealogical" history, the role of the visible is but one part of a vast system of knowledge and experience, in contrast to the European obsession with visuality as the most important way of securing knowledge.[32] Van Dyke argues that French colonialists were threatened by the radically different notions of time, materiality, and history under which traditional cultures operated. She claims that the French founded the museum to control and make sense of the oral cultures of Mali, with their vastly different genealogical and performative notions of time, history, and culture, by archiving what the French considered important and could *see*: the material objects. During the colonial period, the National Museum thus functioned as an attempt to understand and assert power over Malian cultures by collecting the physical objects left over from ephemeral and performative traditional ceremonies. This method of control was accomplished by archiving and documenting the material artifacts of Malian oral cultures. Because those artifacts were removed from their context, their meaning was severely diminished and their power was leached away.

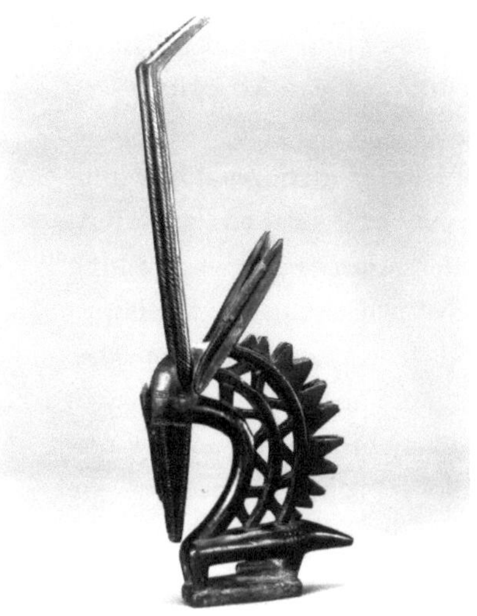

Figure 5.2. Bamana. Dance headdress (*Ci-wara kun*), late nineteenth–early twentieth century. Wood, metal, 31¾ × 13½ × 2¾ in. (80.6 × 34.3 × 7 cm). Brooklyn Museum, Gift of Rosemary and George Lois, 77.245.2. Creative Commons-BY (Photo: 77.245.1_77.245.2_PS1.jpg).

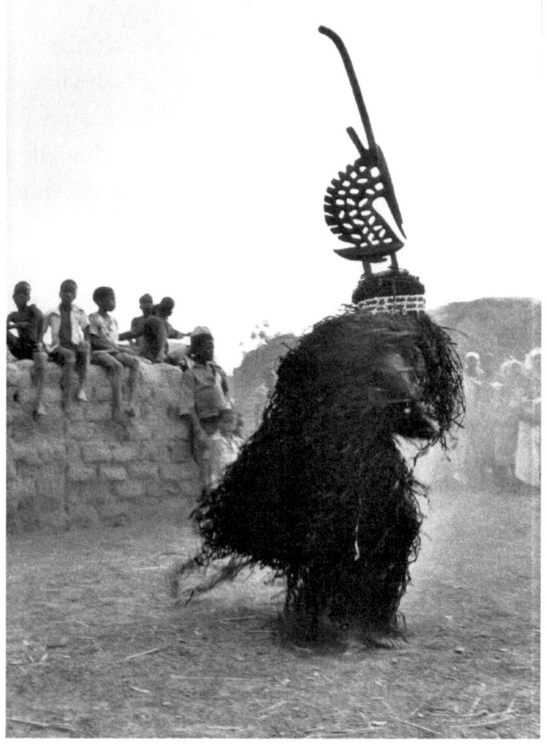

Figure 5.3. *Ci wara* dancing, early twentieth century.

The museum today still embodies the contradiction of French (and American and European) exhibition practices of African art. These display practices are very different in tenor from how Malians understood culture in the past, in that powerful objects, meant to be hidden at most times and whose visual emergences were surrounded by rituals, performances, and careful guarding of their sacred power, are now permanently visually presented as static, harmless objects in the museum. The powerful clash between precolonial Malian and colonial French worldviews is curiously reiterated here in this postcolonial museum, where the necessity of documenting patrimony for posterity conflicts with the very forms that patrimony once took. The National Museum, in its archival nature and its very essence, as a building to house and preserve material artifacts, as a site of education and cultural outreach, consigns Mali's precolonial arts to a definitive and object-specific past. In modeling itself on Western museums, the National Museum is perpetuating the archival mission of France in its attempts to collect and display the material artifacts of formerly colonized cultures, and thus to make their reception palatable to the French and to control knowledge of Africans.[33]

However, the National Museum's fundamentally contradictory, postcolonial nature does not mean that the institution is ineffectual or unimportant in the present. Though the museum may lack local adult interest, schoolchildren usually visit as part of their curriculum. For today's young Bamakois, raised in the city, many older traditional rituals are foreign to their lives. As traditional ceremonies and rituals fade away or transform beyond recognition, the museum's role becomes more and more necessary to protect the remnants of a certain history and way of life. Since its reorganization in 1976, dedicated to overturning colonial collecting policies, the museum has also focused on acquiring and exhibiting objects in media the French did not consider important, such as textiles and ceramics, and concomitantly widening its attention to acquiring pieces and documentation from underrepresented ethnic groups who did not create carved wooden sculptures, such as the Sonrai, Tuareg, Minanka, and Bobo.[34] Thus a wider spectrum of Malian culture is presently represented and preserved.

Indeed, from an international point of view, the National Museum of Mali is considered vibrant, "one of the most dynamic museums in West Africa today."[35] The museum owns a superb collection of objects and provides excellent and informative exhibitions and outreach programs. It is the nature of the museum qua museum that is fundamentally problematic.[36] While the museum has worked hard to "overcome its colonial legacy" through new outreach, collection, and exhibition policies, it could be argued that such an attempt is doomed to at least partial failure. Although the museum has "Africanized" its presentation, the museum's very structure embodies the contradiction of Western practices of exhibiting African art and, as such, embodies a postcolonial contradiction.[37]

In relation to Bamako's burgeoning photography movement, the museum at first played a somewhat ambivalent role, but has become more fully supportive since the organization of the biennale was taken over by Samuel Sidibé, the museum's director.[38] In a 2006 interview, Sidibé, who was classically trained in France as an archaeologist, was uncertain of the aesthetic value of Mali's new artistic photography and reluctant to buy contemporary works, because it was not part of the museum's historical mission, although the museum does own photographs by Keïta and Sidibé. But since he accepted the directorship, Sidibé's involvement in the biennale has encouraged the local art movement; though he speaks of the difficulty of keeping the biennale work running during the year and eleven months when it is off.[39] The National Museum has also become involved in preserving the archives of studio photographers such as Soungalo Malé. Museum employees who worked in photography, such as Diarra, Bâ, and Tienro, have access either to the darkroom or to computers for processing their personal work; thus, the museum unofficially supports their work and officially has lent its traveling exhibition hall to the biennale's International Exhibition.

Naturally, the photographers who work at the museum were well-informed about its ethnographic mission. Diarra, Bâ, and Tienro all work in the audiovisual department, where their duties include documenting, preserving, archiving, and digitizing images of the museum's extensive collection.[40] The project of digitization acts as an ongoing reminder of the importance of preserving culture, which has been a major issue since the museum's founding. Museum work also requires the photographers to travel to contemporary traditional performances and events throughout the country, in order to document the proceedings through photography and video.[41]

The archive, as a Western administrative system of organizing objects and documents that contain information, was introduced to Malian cultures by French colonialism. In its most literal and prosaic form, the archive is a regulated way of breaking down knowledge into discrete sections, which then can be grouped together by their similarities. The "rise" of the archive coincided with the nineteenth-century European anthropological project of documenting Africans and other non-Western peoples so as to "prove" European racial theories constructed to justify colonialism and European dominance. The archive as a philosophical problem of modernity has been addressed by such contemporary philosophers as Jacques Derrida, Michel Foucault, and Giorgio Agamben, among others, as a way of problematizing the historical structures through which knowledge is produced, regulated, categorized, distributed, stored, and interpreted.[42] The archive is thus viewed as a problem of modernity, created by the vast systems of social, juridical, and scientific regulation and rationalization spawned by the Western Enlightenment.

Although archives have existed for thousands of years—Derrida traces the term back to the Greeks—Thomas Richards makes a convincing case for the rapid development of archival projects in the West and what could be called an accompanying "archival mindset" during the nineteenth century that coincided with British imperialism.[43] Richards notes that the vast expansion of collections at such institutions as the British Museum benefited from the plunder supported by Britain's imperialist power. Today, museums with substantial holdings of African art often owe portions of their collections to collecting practices under colonial rule, which were often unethical.[44] But Richards also points out that when Britain did not have as much physical control over its colonies as desired, documentation of the colonies gave Britain the illusion of that control. Richards notes, "The British viewed their empire as an immense *administrative* challenge" (my italics), and it was "much easier to unify an archive composed of texts than to unify an empire made of territory."[45] The fantasy of empire was not merely supported by archival documentation of the colonies, but in a sense was *conceived of* and *validated through* collecting and organizing vast amounts of data about the territories Britain had conquered.[46] Britain's attempt at dominance through the control of knowledge can similarly be ascribed to France, although its methods of domination differed greatly.[47] Van Dyke's assertion that the National Museum functioned to control the material artifacts of Mali's cultures under colonialism, while the actual *population* was more difficult to control (especially in the legendary case of the Tuareg), makes a similar claim to Richards's about the use of colonial archival practices.

Photography's scholars have often equated the act of photographing with creating an archive. The photograph flattens any scene, portrait, or object into a two-dimensional representation that can be filed by subject, date, location, photographer, or a myriad of other categories. A performance of a mask becomes a photograph, as does an image of the mask itself. Difference is reduced to an apparent, purely formal, sameness—as Allan Sekula writes, "The archive is a vast substitution set, providing for a relation of general equivalence between images."[48] Benjamin Buchloh also notes "photography's innate structural order of the archive, its seemingly infinite multiplicity, serialization and aim for comprehensive totality."[49] Sekula addresses the historical intersection of photography with the archive in nineteenth-century Britain, where he sees the photograph as a primary tool in the categorization of the "other" (in this case, criminals). Sekula notes that, after the British Gaols Act in 1823 and Metropolitan Police Acts of 1829 and 1839, which standardized juridical procedures, "a new object is defined—the criminal body—and, as a result, a more extensive 'social body' is invented."[50] Even though photographing criminals by the police did not become a common practice until the 1860s, Sekula believes that the potential for regulation was perceived as early as the 1840s, shortly after photography was invented.[51]

If the "criminal body" was defined in London in the 1840s and assisted by the invention of photography, one can only imagine that a definition of the "colonial body" was not far behind, especially as photography traveled to sub-Saharan Africa immediately after it was announced in 1839.[52]

The "colonial body" in Mali began to be defined for the French in the early 1880s, when the first photographs of Bamako and its citizens were taken, although parts of West Africa and its peoples were photographed as early as 1840. Thus the construction of a generic African "colonial body" occurred in France at about the same time as a construction of the "criminal body" in Great Britain.[53]

While Sekula's text does not address colonialism in particular, he importantly notes the prevalence of phrenology, or the false notion that character can be determined by the shape of a person's head, as a discourse in society that shaped portrait photography in Europe and the US. This racist pseudoscience discriminated against people of color and Africans in particular on the basis of superficial physiognomy. Much early anthropological photography follows from this notion, objectifying the subject and turning him or her into a foreign and exoticized body to be studied. Such photography commonly represented Africans until local populations developed their own studios.

Projects that critique the notion of the archive have become prevalent in American and European contemporary art, following or generating the theorizing of the archive.[54] Perhaps most famous in the realm of conceptual international art are the works of German photographers Bernd and Hilla Becher. The Bechers' black-and-white, deadpan photographs formally invoke the rhetoric of the archive, in presenting a typology of obsolete structures, such as cooling towers or water towers (fig. 5.4). Each picture in a series utilizes the same lighting, viewpoint, focal length, and camera angle as almost scientific controls, thereby emphasizing the similarity among the towers, and the small variations that differentiate them. Because of the highly regulated format and presentation of the cooling towers, which are always exhibited as a series, the Bechers' project has been considered a deconstruction of the archive. Magnani writes of the Bechers' images: "It is only through their participation in a system of presentation, under the model of the archive, that the single images gain a significance which is larger than their particular instances. At the same time it is the process of ordering itself that comes under scrutiny as the implications of an abstract procedure are exposed through a mode of representation that replicates it."[55] The Bechers' reiteration of the archival format without apparent purpose thus calls attention to the paradigm of the archive and, in doing so, questions its uses and nature. As the Bechers have been exhibited internationally for several decades, this reading of their work has been reproduced in wall labels and museum information; thus their work has had an effect on how viewers knowledgeable in

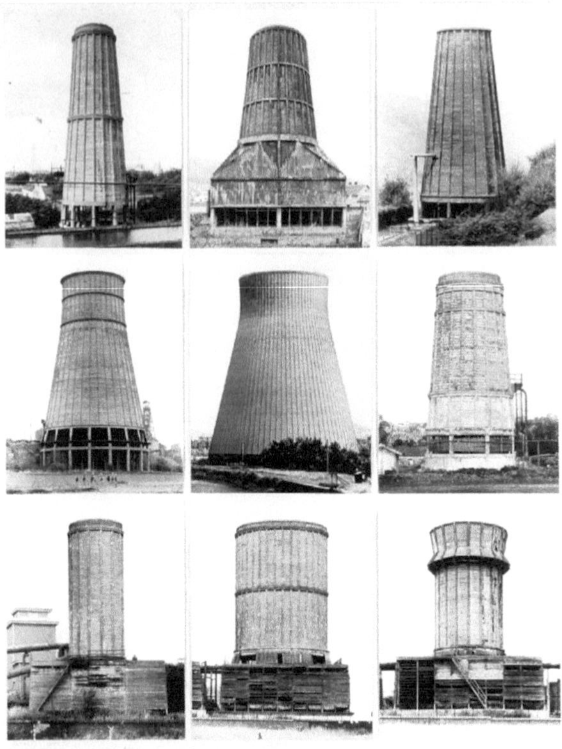

Figure 5.4. Bernd and Hilla Becher, *Cooling Towers*, 1972.

contemporary art photography—who are the primary European and American visitors to the biennale—understand such art projects. This understanding of the conceptual significance of the archive is what makes Sogodogo's, Bâ's, and Tienro's projects appreciated by a conceptually oriented international art audience, as evidenced in the publication of Sogodogo's work and the inclusion of these series in the Bamako Biennale. Yet it is not a *deconstruction* of the archive, like the Bechers' work, but a *creolization*, a transformation of the archive in an ongoing process, that Sogodogo's *Braids*, Bâ's architectural photos, and Tienro's *Forgotten Heroes* perform. They are preserving history and heritage through a Malian perspective that privileges the unknown and the individual knowledge of the viewer; it is necessarily incomplete and inconclusive. In using these Malian attributes to call attention to museologically inspired projects, these series subvert the administrative notion of the archive differently than the Bechers, instead creolizing it through appropriating its visual effect to convey knowledge of contemporary Malian culture.

Youssouf Sogodogo's project of recording girls' and women's hairstyles closely fits an archival paradigm.[56] Not coincidentally, given the contemporary art world trend of interest in archival artworks, of all Sogodogo's photographs, this series has been the most published and extensively exhibited. *The Braids of Mali* appeared in the monograph *Youssouf Sogodogo: Photographies* (2000), which accompanied an exhibition at Galerie Chab, and was included in the exhibition catalog *BKO-RAK: Photographers from Bamako and Marrakech* (1998) and in *5 Photographers from Mali* (1996).[57] Several works from the series were also shown in the 2005 Bamako Biennale's International Exhibition, the biennale's most prestigious venue. In each case, curatorial choices affected how the series is shown and understood.

Sogodogo is one of the most prominent photographers in Bamako, especially in terms of teaching. As director of the CFP, Sogodogo has influenced and supported the careers of such prominent younger photographers as Fatoumata Diabaté, Harandane Dicko, Seydou Camara, and Salif Traoré. In fact, virtually all of the younger generation of art photographers were trained at CFP, which was the most direct link to the arts-oriented approach of the biennale. Sogodogo is also an important artist in his own right, with a published monograph on his work, *Tresses du Mali* (Éditions de l'Œil, 2000), one of the few available on photographers in Mali. He has participated in a number of international and local exhibitions, including the biennale.[58] After a stint as the director of the Sahel Museum in Gao, in Mali's remote eastern desert region, Sogodogo worked as a conservator of textiles at the National Museum until becoming director of the CFP.

Like several art photographers, including Malick Sidibé, Sogodogo was originally trained in fine arts—he earned a degree in painting from the National Institute of the Arts (INA) in Bamako. Sogodogo's photographic background is unusual, however, in that he never worked in or owned a studio.[59] He took up photography while living in Gao in the 1980s, when he began to photograph the hairstyles of his daughter, her friends, his wife, and their neighbors.[60] The earliest published photographs of Sogodogo's braids are dated 1983 (fig. 5.5).[61] Thus, Sogodogo began the *Braids of Mali* series a decade before the biennale was inaugurated in Bamako, that is, before the notion of art photography began to circulate seriously among Malian photographers, which shows both the photographer's passion for the medium and for the subject, and how the Gao Museum's mission—and his own family (of huge importance in Mali)—influenced his choice of subjects.

What motivated Sogodogo to take pictures was the museological desire to preserve culture, and Sogodogo's museum employment inspired that desire, as the artist himself relates. After relocating to Bamako in 1985, Sogodogo worked as a textile conservator. Textiles and bodily adornment, including

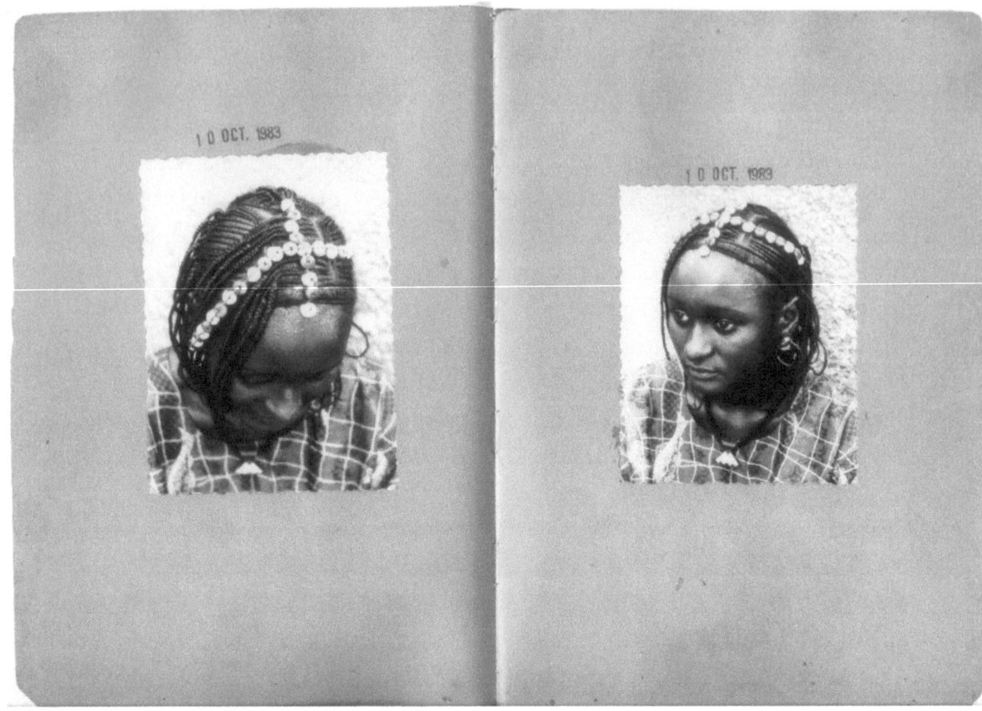

Figure 5.5. Youssouf Sogodogo, *The Gao Notebooks*, from *Youssouf Sogodogo: Photographies* (Éditions de l'Œil, 2000). Courtesy of the artist.

hairstyles, utilize abstract and decorative patterns in inventive combinations; they are usually designed and created by women and are most appreciated when worn by women. As Kerstin Pinther has remarked, both clothing (textiles) and photography act as a kind of "second skin" and both indexically stand in for the human body.[62] Before identity photos became the staple of the profession, pictures of women, dressed up to display a new outfit or hairstyle, composed the bulk of studio photography. In an interview, for example, Malick Sidibé related that a woman came into his studio to have her hairstyle photographed every time she had a new one.[63] Photographers often set up shop next door to tailors, or vice versa, demonstrating the symbiotic relationship between photography and bodily adornment in Mali.

Female beauty and adornment are vital and significant aspects of Malian culture, and hairstyle is an important component of a woman's aesthetic presentation. In *Youssouf Sogodogo: Photographies*, edited by Antonin Potoski, the Malian critic and gallerist Amadou Chab Touré discusses the importance of braiding and adornment in an accompanying essay titled "The

Heads of Women Turn."[64] Touré notes the cultural significance attached to the treatment of hair throughout an individual's life, beginning at birth: "In Malian society, the first adornment for hair is the *rasage*, the shaved head, which is the first artistic intervention authorized on the body of man. In an aesthetic ritual which accompanies the name-giving, the *rasage* signifies that hair can't grow according to its own nature. On the contrary, it should be exalted with all kinds of adornments."[65]

In Mali, the body has been a site for the expression of meaning through aesthetic manipulation. As art is inseparable from culture, so is it inseparable from the body, on and through which culture is expressed. Terence Turner notes that the "surface of the body becomes the symbolic stage upon which the drama of socialization is enacted and bodily adornment . . . becomes the language through which it is expressed."[66] It is through bodily adornment that social identities were communicated. A great deal of significance was attached to hairstyles, in particular, because the head is generally considered the locus of power, the place from which personality and intelligence emanate.[67] Many hours of effort could be put into hairstyling, and in former times, or in present-day rural areas, a particular hairdo might even take days to finish. Specific hairstyles are worn to celebrate a marriage, commemorate a death, or mark various other rites of passage.[68] Such styles vary from culture to culture. For example, as Touré explains, when a little Khassonkée girl first learns to walk, her head is decorated with little tufts of hair on the front, on the nape of the neck, and on each side of her head.[69] Various hairstyles can also signify more pedestrian meanings: in the 1950s, a shy young woman could wear a "Saturday night" hairstyle to signal her availability for a date.[70]

Just how culturally specific these meanings can be is demonstrated in a book published by a Malian press in the 1970s: *Traditional and Modern Hairstyles of Mali*, by Barthélémy and Mamadou Koné.[71] Traditional "beauty" hairstyles of different cultures are shown, such as the Bozo, Bamana, and Fulani, along with hairstyles for young brides, hairstyles to prevent divorce, and to ward off the evil eye. Children's hairstyles offer hope for a long life or help to prevent misfortune. The book also includes a wide variety of modern hairstyles not identified by ethnicity, in contrast to the traditional hairstyles.[72] Some modern styles in Mali are named after geographic locations important to the local economy, such as The Road to Koulouba, The Bend in the Niger, or The Abidjan Road. Others sites are more general—Roundabout, Waterfall, Watertower, The Work Site. Some names are conceptual (Friendship, Hope, Liberty), while others are political (Organization of African Unity,

Liberation, Négritude). Still others memorialize important events, such as The Olympic Games. One style, worn to commemorate General Charles de Gaulle, mimics the military headgear worn by the victorious Tirailleurs Sénégalais, West Africans who were conscripted into the French armies to fight in various wars, including World War II.[73] Older studio photographs show headscarves tied in the style of Versailles, Louis d'Or, Apollo II, and Marie Claire, giving concrete representations to noteworthy or fashionable political and cultural figures or institutions.[74] Modern hairstyles tend to change much more quickly than traditional hairstyles, as they carry less specific cultural meanings and are related to shifting fashion trends.[75]

Koné expresses the interrelated cultural connections among hairdressing, art, beauty, moral purpose, dignity, self-respect, and pride in one's cultural heritage. Hairdressing is an art even as sculpture is an art. It is also a language, a means of signification, a way of communication, so that the book itself, with its photographs of styles, becomes an encyclopedia. Woven through the book are references to postindependence nationalism, to "Malian" as opposed to "tribal" or ethnic identifications. National unity is the goal, expressed through the cultural form of hairstyles. This notion is made explicit later in the book: "The tribal period is over, independence and modern means of communication have enabled the races to mingle constantly."[76]

In Sogodogo's monograph, *Youssouf Sogodogo: Photographs*, the pictures of braids are divided into two series: *The Gao Notebooks* and the more polished *Braids of Mali*. The two series appear to show the progression in conceptualization from Sogodogo's first prints, taken in Gao, to a more "finished" version of the series, which also appears, with some modifications, in another book, *BKO-RAK: Photographers from Bamako and Marrakech* (fig. 5.6). (The title refers to the airline acronyms for Bamako and Marrakech.) In *The Gao Notebooks*, dates and notations that Sogodogo wrote or stamped on the backs of the photographs appear next to the images, which are remarkably similar, in pose, angle, and expression, to American yearbook photos. Some styles from *The Gao Notebooks* are named, such as *chapeau* (hat), while others are dated. (Confusingly, at least one picture appears to have been taken in Bamako, not Gao, as BKO prefaces the name of the girl, Fatoumata Tadjo, written in Bamanankan.) However, Sogodogo generally does not note his model's ethnicity, age, or name; nor does he include the name of the style. Nor does there seem to be an attempt to collect *all* of the current styles, or even one example of each variety. As a strictly museological project, then, this appears half-hearted at best.

It is the removal of these written markers of identification that renders

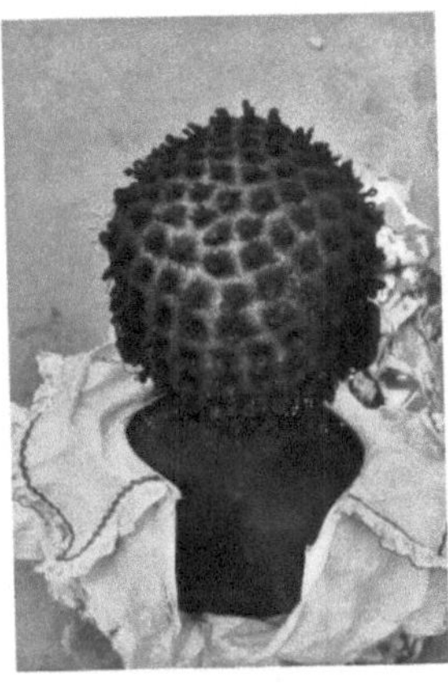

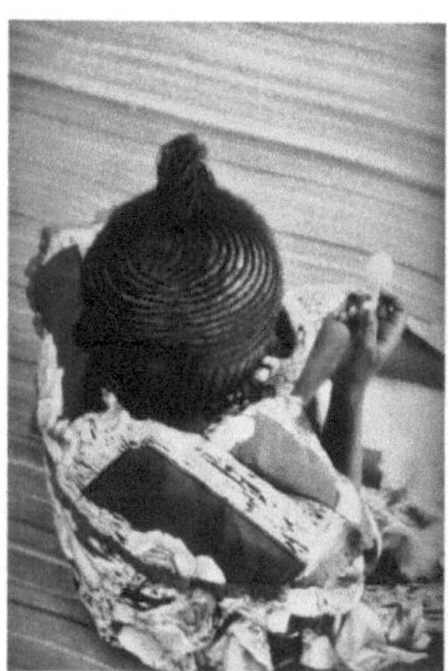

Figure 5.6. Youssouf Sogodogo, *Braids of Mali*, from *BKO-RAK* (Paris: Revue Noire, 1998). Courtesy of the artist.

the series attractive to an international audience, that distinguishes it from the obvious and unpalatable anthropological project, that makes the archive implicit and not explicit: that make the series, in a word, "art." Yet when contacted for titles of certain images for an exhibition in the US, Sogodogo easily supplied them for the photographs that named the hairstyles, such as "Little Hut in the Middle" (fig. 5.7). Thus it seems that, in prior publications or exhibitions, the lack of naming of hairstyles was a deliberate choice on the part of the publisher or curator.

While knowledge of the cultural meanings of titles is left to the viewer, the question of the obsessively comprehensive goal of an archive (ultimately always a failure) remains. Yet a description of Sogodogo's series in the 2005 biennale catalog suggests that what Sogodogo is after is *beauty*, not comprehensiveness. "You have to say that the beauty, the gentleness and the messages conveyed by those braided heads put me under their spell," says Sogodogo.[77] However, his private intention to preserve hairstyles for posterity—his apparent interest in doing so is shown by the fact that he carefully *dated* all of these images—suggests a more "museological approach" than simply an interest in beauty. Sogodogo's awareness of a broader, historical sphere, as not a personal but a broadly conceived cultural posterity, marks a difference in photographic perspective, and suggests an appeal to the universal (or at least communal) that is the province of the international artist.

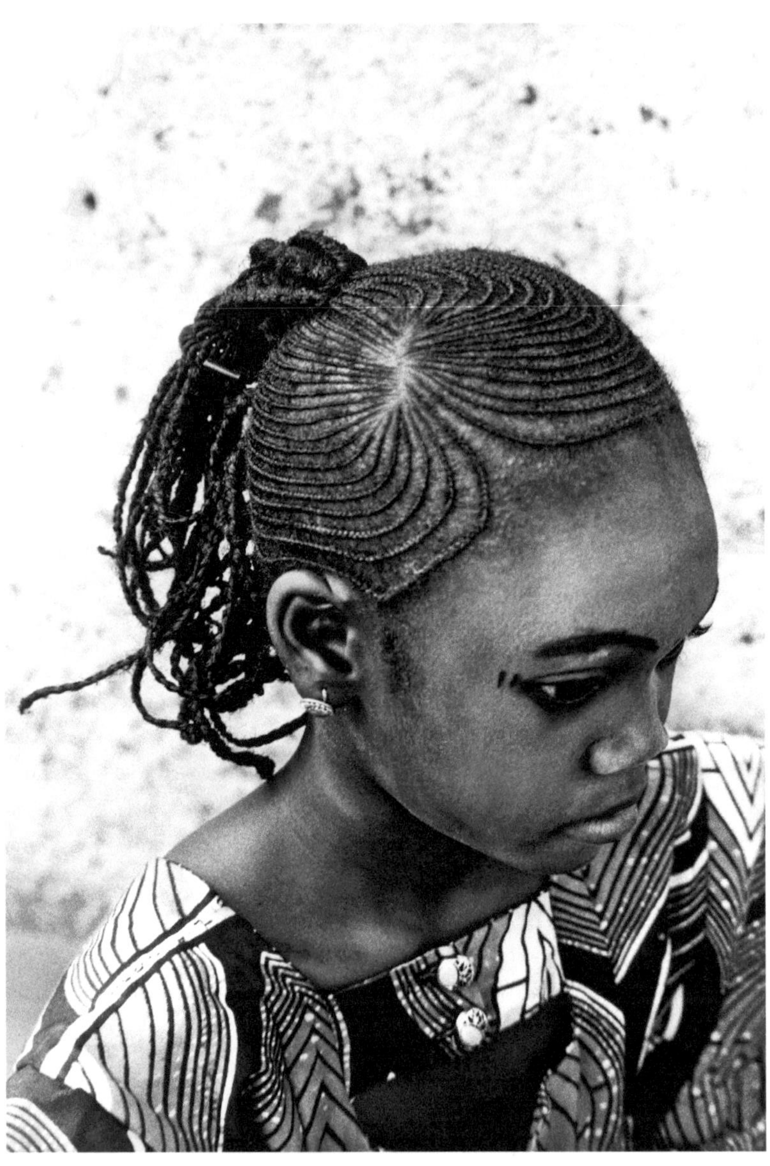

Figure 5.7. Youssouf Sogodogo, *Tiamanchtiè bougouni* (*Little Hut in the Middle*), 1997. Courtesy of the artist and Perlman Teaching Museum, Carleton College.

In contrast to Sogodogo's *Braids*, Koné's *Hairstyles* shows a wide variety of styles, contrasting traditional with fashionable, contemporary styles.[78] Whereas *Hairstyles* makes explicit the connections between culture, history, instruction, beauty, moral purpose, self-respect, citizenship, national unity, and creating pride in Mali's place in the larger, global context, *Braids* renders these connections implicit. But it still holds true that Sogodogo's photographs will operate as Koné claims in *Hairstyles*: "Historians contemplating photographs of Mali women will immediately be able to put this picture into its proper context"—something impossible for a non-Malian audience.[79]

In *The Gao Notebooks*, Sogodogo's double portraits display each side of a girl's head, the better to show off intricate asymmetrical braiding or a hairstyle's progression from front to back. This presentation shares a typological theme with photographs by anthropologists who objectified Africans, treating them as scientific examples and photographing their physical features from front and side, as one would photograph a specimen.[80] In contrast to the intentions of anthropological photography of the colonial period, however, which were to find phrenological "evidence" of supposed African inferiority or to document an exoticized people for comparative purposes, Sogodogo documents young girls' hairstyles in order to preserve an important aspect of Malian culture. He began photographing models with whom he had a personal relationship, as they were friends of his daughter.

Yet Sogodogo's project *was* ethnographic in origin: of Senufo ethnicity, Sogodogo grew up in Sikasso, in southern Mali, and he was fascinated by the beautiful hairstyles of the Songhai girls and women of Gao, a city located in Mali's northeast region. As the director of a museum, he would no doubt be very familiar with the anthropological photographs that documented many cultures' adornments, as well as objects, during and after the colonial period. But the nationalist atmosphere that has been created since Mali's independence gives Sogodogo a more privileged insider status than most foreigners would have. As a Malian museum director, Sogodogo understands the significance of hairstyles as markers of social status and stages of life, and all of the moral importance that looking beautiful carries in Malian culture. Moreover, the differences between colonial anthropologists' photos and Sogodogo's pictures can be distinguished formally, beyond the fact that some girls wear modern dress, as the girls' responses to the photographer differ. For example, an unclothed little girl, recently bathed, looks up at the viewer with a confiding and unselfconscious smile. Despite her youth, the girl's small hoop earrings and large almond-shaped eyes give her an air of sophistication. Her hair sprouts from her head in several tightly coiled shoots.

The picture is cropped at the girl's waist, and she seems to be standing comfortably, probably posed, in front of a hanging sheet, whose bottom and the edge of one side can be seen behind her. Her head is tilted a little forward, and her eyes meet the viewer's gaze, showing a sense of her personality.

In *BKO-RAK,* Sogodogo's work seems deliberately chosen to mimic the Bechers' archival strategy, as well as the more famous Nigerian photographer J. D. 'Okhai Ojeikere's hairstyles, because Sogodogo's are all similarly cropped shots from the back of the head. But this was a pointedly curated selection from Sogodogo's oeuvre, which Potoski seems to have done deliberately in order to make precisely those connections for an international audience. In fact, Sogodogo's work includes a variety of poses that often show the faces of his different models. Sogodogo also took numerous images that used an aesthetics inspired by Seydou Keïta, contrasting complex hairstyles with patterned clothing, and sometimes including a background of palm leaves or similar natural patterns.

Sogodogo's series as shown in *BKO-RAK* emphasizes the effect of picture selection to slant a series one way or another—in this case, toward an archival effect more in keeping with conceptual art photography by famous international artists, like Lorna Simpson's *Stereo Styles* (1988), which also commented on the archival nature of photography and stereotyping through appearance. The effects of cropping, presentation, and choice of images make Sogodogo's oeuvre in this book highly standardized, "archivally" standardized, which has the effect of highlighting the differences in the actual hairstyles and downplaying each individual girl's personality.

Sogodogo's visual, as opposed to oral, presentation of culture emphasizes his orientation to his own culture through his work at the museum and his educational background. The National Museum itself embodies a forceful contradiction between oral, present, genealogical culture and a European, temporal, regulative understanding of history. It is also the province of a photographer to focus on the visual. The archival approach that Sogodogo adopts tends to mimic the same scientific, documentary, archival urge that drove both anthropological and museological photography. This implication of complicity with European forms of oppression adds a frisson of tension to the series and is what makes the series resonate for an international contemporary art audience. In fact, it is possible to view Sogodogo's work as a critical response to anthropological objectification, in that he is a Malian photographer, and also in that his pictures often show the personality of the young women. By being more interested in a diversity of viewpoints and camera angles, showing women's heads in different positions, and leaving out key information, Sogodogo claims the right to opacity for himself and his subjects.

There are many layers to Sogodogo's project that speak to different audiences. It is important to understand Sogodogo's work in a Malian context, as a conscious project of preserving cultural manifestations in the face of a rapidly deteriorating loss of heritage in the postcolonial moment. His work recognizes that new forms of memory must be created and new forms of artistic tradition must be enacted, especially in Bamako where tradition is quickly losing ground. That his series also "performs" in an international context suggests the crossover between local meanings and international aesthetics.

Sogodogo's series thus creolizes the archive. Its presentation can be manipulated, as it presumably was by Potoski, to create a more or less narrow or rigidly archival effect.[81] The inclusion of such photographs as the small, smiling girl in *Braids* also provides an antidote to the regulating and objectifying gaze of the archival photograph, allowing Sogodogo to subvert the system that he has set up. Jacques Derrida notes that the term "archive" comes from the Greeks, in reference to the house where the *archons*, the city magistrates, lived.[82] Derrida connects the legality of the documents in the archive, and their power to "speak the law," with their function "of unification, of identification, of classification." According to Derrida, the archive does *not* allow for "any heterogeneity."[83] Sogodogo's *Braids* appears at first to be a unified series of pictures that identify and classify various hairstyles. Within Malian culture, these hairstyles have important meanings that contribute to social power. Yet certain pictures in *Braids* subvert the archival paradigm, which the series seems at first to embrace, by refusing to provide much identification or classification, and by including heterogeneity, such as the smiling young girl. This heterogeneity speaks to the essence of photography, which allows for infinite imagery. While Sekula notes the ability of photography to create an archive, he also comments on its disruption of the archive: "This archival promise was frustrated, however, both by the messy contingency of the photograph and by the sheer quantity of images."[84] Barthes also speaks of photography participating in the vast disorder of the world.[85] Sogodogo exploits the nature of photography to create a series that embodies a Malian worldview.

The most famous photographer at the museum, Alioune Bâ, also creolizes the archive in his photographs of traditional and postcolonial Malian architectural structures. He actually began working in an artistic mode prior to the advent of the biennale; he has exhibited in international exhibitions; and he helped implement the first biennale. He was president of the Association Seydou Keïta for many years, and in that capacity also did projects with children, including "Visual Griots," discussed in the previous chapter. Bâ says, "I first started working at the National Museum of Mali in 1981 as a public relations officer, with the task of presenting Malian culture to museum visitors."[86]

Bâ exemplifies the notion of Relation in his attitude toward his French-influenced Malian upbringing:

> When I say that I have two cultures, I consider myself to be very fortunate. I had the opportunity to go to school—a Catholic school—and my father was a lawyer. In my family, we often spoke French. My father taught me to look at the positive sides of all the cultures around us. This is what I mean by living in the middle of two cultures. I try to draw on the good sides of these cultures, and when I realized that the image that is presented of Africa around the world was limited to the more negative aspects, I decided to take it upon myself to embrace the forgotten side of Africa.[87]

Bâ's photographs of architecture stem from his practice of photographing for the National Museum, but to vastly different effect. One image shows a man either removing or picking up his sandals in front of the corrugated metal door of a banco mosque, an architectural style for which Mali is famous (fig. 5.8).[88] The man is enclosed within the shallow space of the lip, which separates the mosque from the ground, extending almost into the viewer's space at the edge of the picture plane. Wooden sticks emerging from the walls, the rough ends of beams, stipple the building's mud-cracked surface, and shadows streak down in diagonals, contrasting with the vertical stripes of the iron door. Pattern created through light and shadow diminishes focus on the man in the doorway, whose back is bent, the top of his head facing the viewer, creating distance and allowing the man to seem solitary within the shallow surface of the picture plane, as spiritual as it is ordinary. The complex pattern of striated light and shadow here speaks to similar complex patterns in the works of Keïta and Sidibé. This photograph conveys Relation through its artistic approach to an indelible aspect of Malian heritage in the contemporary moment.

By contrast, two photographs shown in the 2001 International Exhibition capture a modernist view of a new city building, the Memorial Modibo Keïta, which was built to house Keïta's archives (figs. 5.9 and 5.10).[89] The building was commissioned in the 1990s by the president of Mali's new democracy, Alpha Oumar Konaré, to commemorate Mali's first president, whose

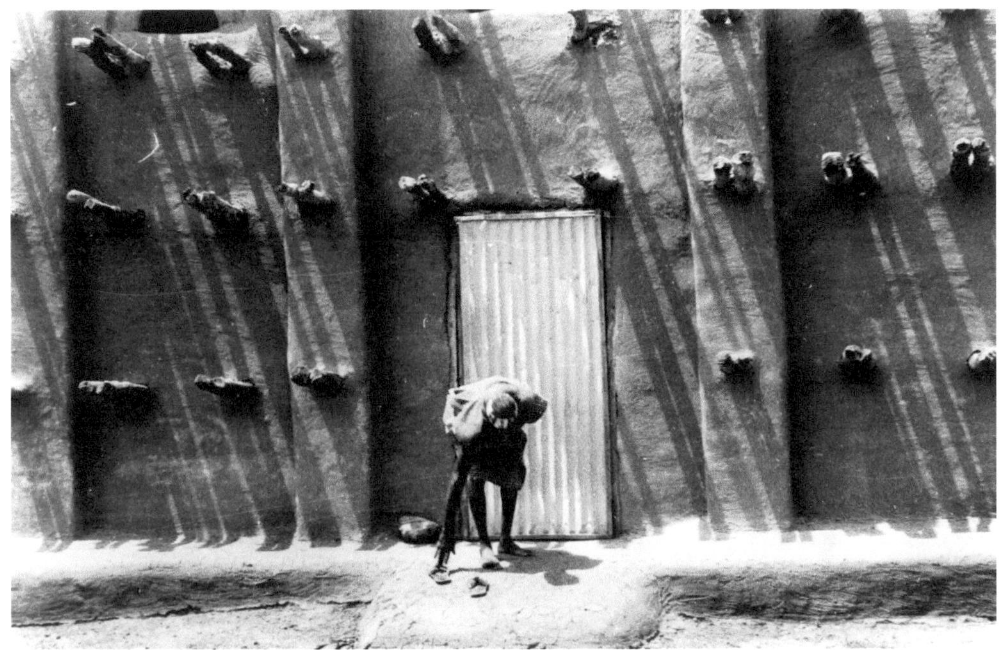

Figure 5.8. Alioune Bâ, *Mosquée de Nangoyo*, Mali, 1996. Courtesy of the artist's estate.

complex legacy included leading the fight for independence and eight years of postindependence rule as a brutal socialist dictator. Designed in a neo-Sudanic style and built by a Chinese construction company called Covec, the building complex has a plan based on Dogon imagery—the *mogonin*, or "little man," from the *kanaga* mask, a "stylized representation of a human body."[90] The Afrofuturist-looking building, with its repeated forms of flat pyramids, became the nexus of a political dispute over historical narrative, and its dedication was delayed for two years, until 1999, in order to bypass political opposition during the 1997 election. The memorial quickly became incorporated into urban life as a favored spot for taking wedding photographs, much like the National Museum's beautiful buildings and grounds.

Bâ's photographs, shown in 2001, would have reminded local viewers of the political dispute, of Modibo Keïta's legacy, and of the popular use of the grounds for wedding photos.[91] One of Bâ's images shows a man standing near a wall of shaped hedges with his back to the viewer, partly hidden by a bush. His activity is ambiguous: either he is trimming the triangular topiary shrubbery that surrounds the building, showing the human labor and cost spent in keeping up this landscape, or he is pissing, which gives a

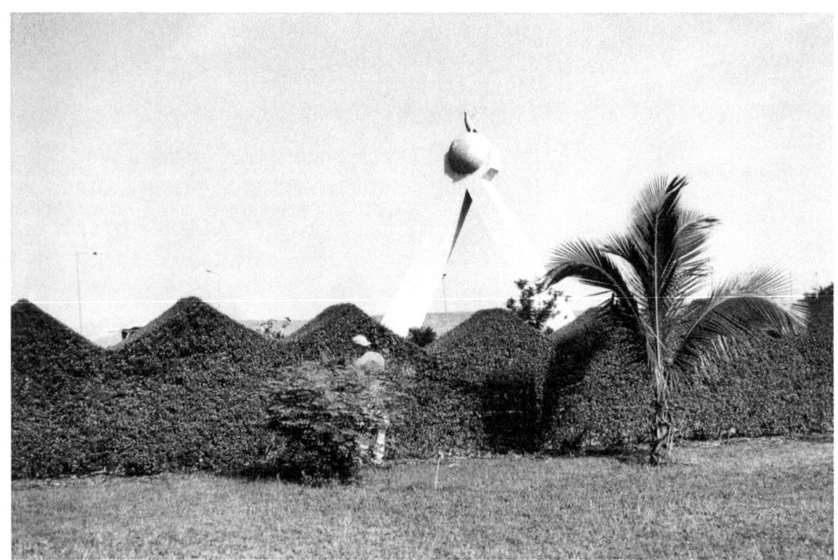

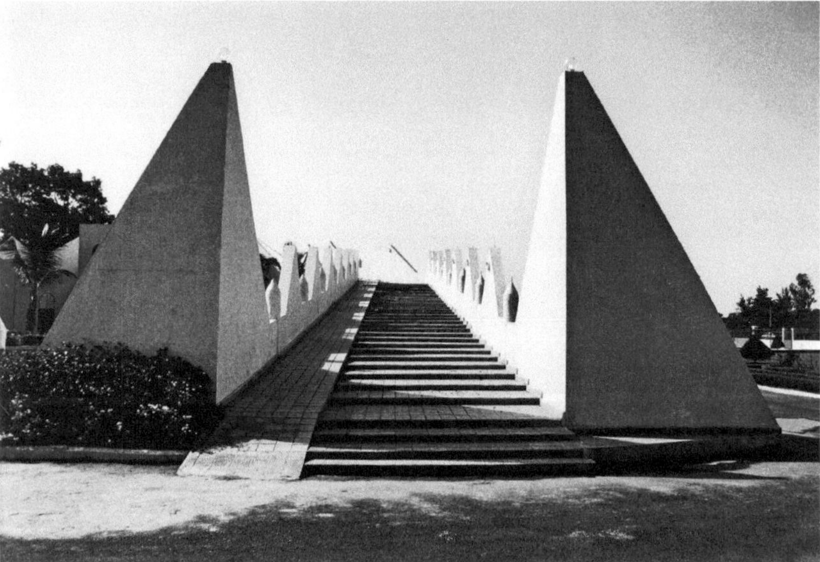

Figures 5.9 and 5.10. Alioune Bâ, Untitled and Untitled (*View of Memorial Modibo Keïta, Pyramid*), 2005. Courtesy of the artist's estate.

more critical read to the image. In the background rises the striking Peace Monument, also built in the 1990s to commemorate the peace brokered between the North and South.[92] In contrast to his image of the man before the mosque, a sign of a centuries-long religious and architectural tradition, a cultural heritage preserved and active in the present, here Bâ makes a political commentary on history through a contemporary building.[93] Another photograph by Bâ of the same building complex is empty of people, much like the building most of the time, and focuses on the base of the stairs accompanied by an apparently wheelchair-accessible ramp, although it lacks hand- or safety rails. This striking feature of accessibility, still absent in so many important buildings around the world, heralds its contemporaneity. The modernist style of the photograph suggests a familiarity with Paul Rudolph or similar architectural photographers and conveys a modernist alienation to the form that is more postcolonial than Relational in its isolated, depopulated close-ups.

Rosa De Jorio argues that the memorial contributes to and plays a role in the symbolic representation of nationalism. Yet she tempers Benedict Anderson's notion of the nation as an "integrated and coherent" imagined community with a more complex notion of the nation that acknowledges different strands and competing factions that contribute to a national imaginary, which is necessarily fractured to some extent as well as obviously ideological. "Culture is seen here as a less orderly, less cohesive construct," she explains.[94] "Within a multinational state . . . we often find not a univocal and uncontested common history but competing memories in action."[95] De Jorio's convincing analysis of the building and dedication of this monument allows us to understand Bâ's photographs as offering a divisive yet potent aspect of the imagined community of the nation. This is especially interesting in that it is a modern, alienated view, which is unusual in Malian photography. It is political and invites discourse or debate by photographing this controversial monument for the biennial theme, which was of memory.[96] Bâ utilizes his professional training to incorporate a complex representation of political divisiveness, history, and present into his image for knowledgeable locals. Yet for non-Malian viewers, the works speak more generally about the fabulous modernist architecture in African cities. On the bottom image, we see reference to modernist geometries, Afrofuturism, and architectural photography. These photographs speak differently to different audiences. To creolize the archive is to transform it and turn it into a Malian process rather than a fixed, French-inspired museum archive. While here one photo takes a position, the other is less obvious—together, the series offers layers of political commentary.

In contrast to Bâ, whose pictures consider Malian contemporary life through architecture, Tienro incorporates the notion of cultural preservation into an equally politicized arena of national history. His 2005 series, *The Forgotten Heroes* (*Les oubliés de la médaille*), documents war veterans, most of whom live in the House of Veterans (La Maison des Anciens Combattants) in Bamako.[97] Eight black-and-white photographs from this extensive series were displayed in the International Exhibition during the 2005 biennale, and three were published in the catalog, along with another that was not exhibited. This series may have been inspired by Seydou Keïta's famous portrait of a man in uniform, his cap tilted at an asymmetrical angle (see fig. 1.7). In poses similar to those struck for studio portraits, the veterans face the camera, or turn at a slight angle, with dignified, solemn expressions, wearing medals and hats that exemplify their service (figs. 5.11–5.13). One picture shows a memorial at the House of Veterans, and another shows certificates and photographs hanging on a wall there.

According to Tienro, the idea for the series came from a desire to honor his father, who is himself a veteran.[98] Tienro's series is characteristically Malian in that it begins with family—his father, his elder—and it emphasizes a respect for his elders in that he is not willing to divulge specific knowledge related to these individuals. Tienro was not sure exactly in which war his father had fought, noting that his father rarely talked about this part of his past, but Tienro believes that he fought in the Algerian War (1954–1962), in which the French conscripted Sudanese soldiers to defend Algeria's colonial status. This bitter and bloody war, in which the French freely used torture to subjugate and gain information from their prisoners, remains an ugly stain on France's history—connected, of course, to the larger evils of the history of colonialism in sub-Saharan Africa. However, Tienro stated that there is no stigma attached to Malian veterans in the Algerian War, although they fought for the French and defended colonialism in another country. This is because they were conscripted and had no choice.[99] When Tienro brought the catalog home to his father in the village of Diel-N'gosso, the photographer remarked that his father spent the whole day looking at the pictures, with the implication that his father was very moved by and proud of the series (fig. 5.13).[100]

Tienro does not currently run a studio, but he operated one in Djicoroni-Para, a neighborhood of Bamako, between 1989 and 1991, and at first glance

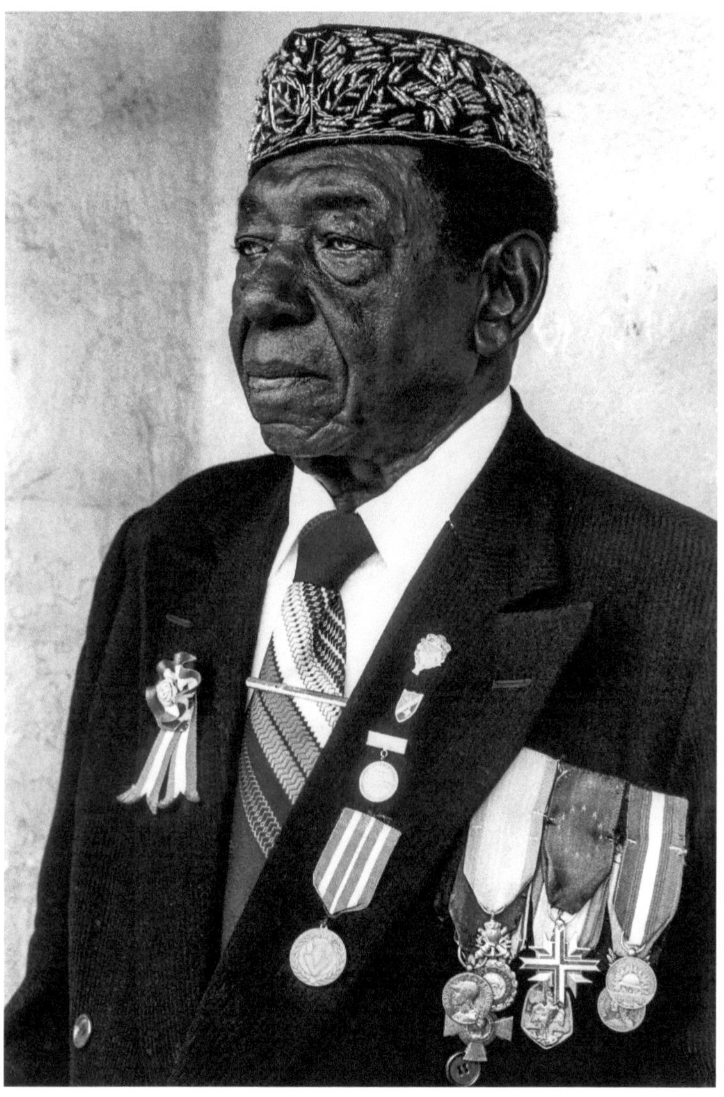

Figure 5.11. Joseye Tienro, Untitled, from *Les oubliés de la médaille* (*The Forgotten Heroes*), 2005. Courtesy of the artist and Perlman Teaching Museum, Carleton College.

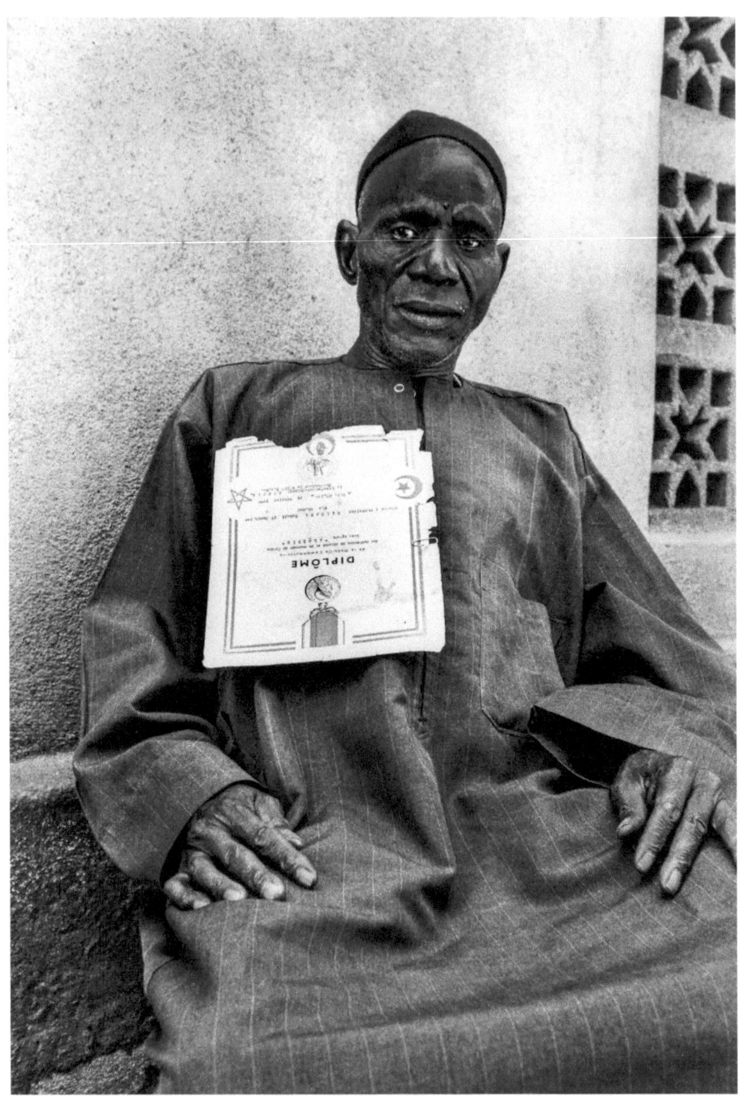

Figure 5.12. Joseye Tienro, Untitled, from *Les oubliés de la médaille* (*The Forgotten Heroes*), 2005. Courtesy of the artist and Perlman Teaching Museum, Carleton College.

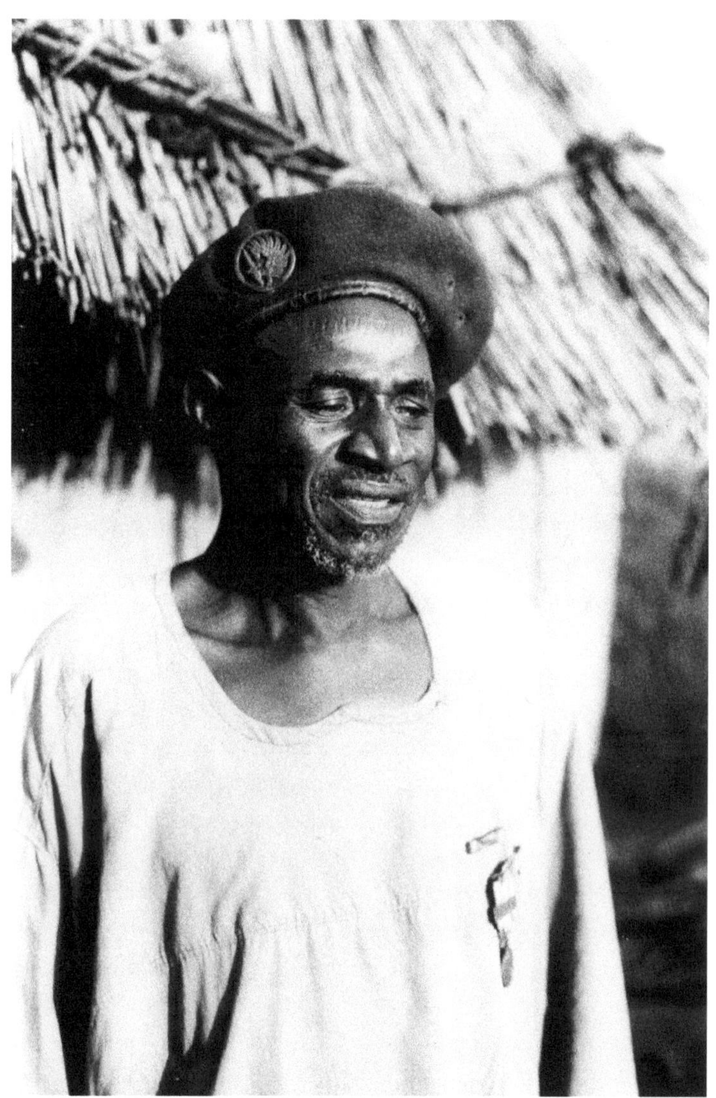

Figure 5.13. Joseye Tienro, Untitled, from *Les oubliés de la médaille* (*The Forgotten Heroes*), 2005. Courtesy of the artist and Perlman Teaching Museum, Carleton College.

The Forgotten Heroes might seem to be constituted of studio portraits.[101] The full, angled, and half-length poses of the veterans, both standing and sitting, would be common to any studio photographer's repertoire. By choosing to photograph veterans, however, Tienro emphasizes values of nationalism and patriotism in his choice of subject. Tienro described his choice for the series as a response to the rapid modernization, particularly marked in Bamako, which has resulted in young people forgetting the past and showing increasing disrespect for traditional hierarchies of age. These pictures are also archival in focusing on one specific type of subject, and they reiterate studio portrait practices.

In Tienro's series, the veterans do not smile. One man wearing a boubou and a skullcap sits against a wall in which the decorative cement openings of windows are visible behind his left shoulder. He adopts a pose that can be seen in many of Keïta's portraits of men sitting—leaning back with his knees pointing out, so that the material of the pinstriped boubou spreads across them, relaxed hands placed on his thighs (fig. 5.12). Sprague has described this same pose in portrait photographs among the Yoruba of Nigeria in the 1970s; the pictorial effect is of an imposing dignity.[102] This veteran displays his diploma on his shoulder, the writing facing him but upside-down to the viewer, in contrast to the other veterans, who wear medals and regalia. The man in the boubou seems more proud of his education than of his military service. He looks straight at the camera, which has caught him a little to the side, creating a more dynamic portrait than a straight-on view would capture. His face is composed but deeply lined, his expression unreadable. His is the only published portrait in which the sitter's eyes visibly gaze back at the viewer, giving this portrait a particular poignancy. In most of Tienro's series, like in Seydou Keïta's portraits, the men display cool and composed features, signifying the importance of reserve and control that is held in esteem in Malian culture, and emphasizing the age of the veterans and the distant era in which they fought.

In the other photographs published in the catalog, two men wear suits and ties, finely dressed for the occasion of the portrait. One, an elderly-looking man, stands in front of a building wall, which creates the effect of a plain portrait backdrop, down to the rough edges where the wall meets the crumbly earth—usually the edges of a cloth backdrop are similarly visible. His hands are as gnarled as the carved cane on which he leans. The veteran wears a round cap set at a slight angle, and his too-large jacket hangs almost to his knees. Altogether the effect is both serious and jaunty at once. Although his eyes are in shadow, his mouth is offset by a ring of white mustache and goatee. A rosette is pinned on the right lapel, while a set of six medals on the left suit-breast drag the jacket down into shadow. The white, diagonal stripe in his tie echoes the stripes on his rosette and becomes the focal point of the picture, emphasizing the odd juxtaposition of civilian dress and military medals.

The other veteran in a suit appears in a half-length bust, gazing into the distance and viewed at a side angle (fig. 5.11). Like the man with the cane, this man also wears a rosette on his right lapel and a phalanx of medals on his left breast, but pins and medals also trail down his right lapel. The man's horizontal metal tie pin visually connects the medals across his chest, echoing and offsetting the metallic thread in his tilted, African-style cap. Though his face is lined, his hair is dark, giving him the appearance of a powerful politician, or a benign dignitary. In contrast to the men in suits, one of the veterans in the series—Tienro's father—is more casually dressed and appears to have been caught in midconversation, giving the picture a snapshot appearance different from a formal portrait. His service is shown by the military beret he wears with an insignia, and a medal that can barely be seen, as the portrait angle obscures the view (fig. 5.13). He stands in front of a building with a thatched roof, as he was photographed in a village and not in Bamako.

As a series, the pictures retain a pathos implied by the title. Tienro's choice of subject in showing respect to his elders, including his father—his literal patrimony—gives a different impetus to his preservation of history than the version formally recognized by the National Museum. Tienro memorializes the figures of a modern, colonial, and postcolonial history, in contrast to preserving the artifacts from the centuries before colonialism.[103] Like Sogodogo, Tienro appears to be influenced conceptually by his work at the museum to take an archival, or museological, approach, while his formal approach appears to be influenced by studio photography. At the same time, also like Sogodogo, Tienro creates ambiguity and subverts his own archival approach by refusing to provide certain key information about his subjects, such as in which wars these heroes fought, or for what services they received their medals. In other words, although he gathers together the subjects classified under a certain type—hero—he does not provide the specific information that would make the art project become truly archival or museological. Instead, Tienro's series recognizes more generally the importance of heroes in Mande culture and preserves their portraits for history.

Although Tienro may perhaps rightly view the veterans as mostly forgotten, the heroism that Tienro alludes to is an important facet of Mande culture, and the impulse to memorialize such heroism is prolific in modern-day Bamako. Monuments and memorials to various wars and heroes in Mali's history dot virtually every intersection of the capital, becoming necessary navigational landmarks in a city notorious for its lack of street signs and decent maps. Most of these monuments are recent constructions; the government built more than twenty-five public monuments between 1995 and 2005.[104] A number of these commemorate anticolonialist heroes, political struggles (the war for independence in 1960, the recent battle for democracy in 1991), and ethnic accords (the peace agreement with the Tuareg in 1995). In other words, Mali's recent political history has been "symbolically inscribed," in Arnoldi's phrase, within the capital's own streets and intersections, despite the National Museum's emphasis on history prior to colonialism and its tendence to downplay the twentieth century. Tienro's project dovetails with this eruption of government-sanctioned political memory; but the poignancy of his subjects' expressions and poses exceeds such banal patriotism, emphasizing the individual sacrifices made by each man—their living presence a reminder of those who did not survive.

Tienro explained that his series fit the theme of the biennale—"Another World"—in that these men had lived in "another world" during their time in the military.[105] This situation is common to many African countries under colonialism, where soldiers were conscripted to fight in distant wars that had little to do with their own situations, so it is not surprising that Tienro's theme was appreciated by the biennale curators. According to Diawara, the role of the hero in Mande culture still resonates strongly in modern-day Bamako, even though the age of heroism dates back to the reign of Sundiata and the Mande empire of the thirteenth century.[106] The visual similarities to Keïta's portraits also suggest Tienro's interest in preserving history, providing dignified visions of men who are considered heroic in Mande culture, as fearless warriors, even though in today's rapidly changing era of fading memory, their exploits might be overlooked.

The projects of Sogodogo, Bâ, and Tienro stem from a museological interest in the archival preservation of cultural and political memory in pursuit of one topic—hairstyles, buildings, or veterans. At the same time, the series *refuse* classification and identification, relying on the knowledge of the viewer to identify a subject's ethnicity, social milieu, cultural history, or military affiliation with his or her specialized knowledge. This approach emphasizes a respect for the knowledge of the individual viewer and exercises the right to opacity for artists and subjects. Tienro refused to give information about his subjects' background because he was protecting their privacy; this opposed the historian's need to document and provide information for the public record. This refusal both undermines the museum's archival and anthropological ordering systems and participates in a Malian, genealogical view of history and knowledge, in which the visible is only one part of a vaster, unseen world and in which gaining knowledge is a process of a lifetime. For French viewers, this refusal of naming and classifying can be seen as subverting the ordering structure of the archive; for Malians, the viewer with the most cultural or historical knowledge is privileged. Certain markers, like the "Roundabout" hairstyle, the war that a particular medal refers to, or the complicated history of the Memorial Modibo Keïta, will be known only by Malians, or Bamakois, and even their knowledge will be imperfect in some cases. What is understood by everyone within the culture, however, is the *significance* of hairstyles and their relation to women's beauty. Likewise, it is the *importance* of male heroism in Mande culture, and the *knowledge* of Mali's difficult political changes over the past century, from colonialism to the struggle for democracy, that is understood through Tienro's and Bâ's series.

While Sogodogo's project began with an ethnographic impulse, it participates in the nationalist project of refusing to classify ethnicities, instead grouping various women's hairstyles under the general name of "Mali." Surely many Malians will be able to identify an ethnic group's style, but that connection is left to the viewer. While Tienro's project seems like a memorial, it is not clear which wars the soldiers fought in or what their roles were. Thus, for a viewer who cannot recognize the medals worn by the veterans, Tienro's project blends all heroic efforts into a more general concept of Mande heroism, while attempting to address the loss of cultural and historical memory that pervades contemporary culture in Bamako. In Bâ's architectural photos, formal interest in his approach to the fascinating and unusual architectural forms piques a non-Malian viewer's interest, but the intimate knowledge of the buildings' historical and political context is available only to a local audience. Again, as in Sogodogo's series, the ability to gather information from the photographs depends on the knowledge that the viewer already harbors. While this absence may be seen as a lack of necessary knowledge to non-Malian viewers, Van Dyke comments, "Individuals in Mande culture do not assume that everyone has equal access to or knowledge of this world. The unknown or unmarked is an important concept in its own right."[107] The idea that knowledge must be earned, and that it must come from a deep level of cultural immersion, runs through the artists' attitudes.

The paradoxical combination of archival format and Malian perspectives and aesthetics in Tienro's, Bâ's, and Sogodogo's series creolize the archival function of the National Museum where the photographers work (or worked). The Relation of the three series grows out of the reinvention and reworking of important cultural themes through the filter of photography, with its innately archival yet heterogeneous capacities. The resultant form is uniquely suited to photography, departing from a traditional, oral, and genealogical preservation of cultural history, such as that handed down through the songs of the griots. As creolized archives, these projects rely on oral history and personal and cultural knowledge—the viewer must embellish the series with his or her own dynamic addition of understanding.

Yet Sogodogo's, Bâ's, and Tienro's projects retain great local importance and can be understood as new artistic forms that are unique to the cultural and historical circumstances of present-day Mali. Through the presentation of important cultural themes—heroism, women's beauty and bodily adornment, architecture—disengaged from particular ethnicities, the works reinforce a "Malian" identity, both within Bamako and internationally. Thus, *Braids of Mali* and *The Forgotten Heroes* contribute to the implicit conflict over memory and cultural preservation that underlies the museum's mission. As such, these projects embody the debates over tradition and modernity in contemporary Mali, not only contributing to the preservation of the past but also responding dynamically to the ever-changing conditions of the postcolonial present. The problem, as has been noted for all of the art photographers, is that the local audience who would respond to these new forms of work is limited, because few Malians visit the National Museum, where both series were exhibited during the 2005 biennale. If local Malians should visit, however, the series' affinities with traditional studio photography and their cultural and sociohistorical importance would make the pictures visually and culturally accessible while remaining of fascination to an international audience.

The National Museum photographers creolize the archive because their work implies what the museum truly should be collecting if it were paying attention to contemporary concerns instead of focusing on the past. They are not deconstructing the archive as a concept—after all, they are trained to and presumably do believe in the usefulness of their professional occupation—but they are *adding* to it a Mande sensibility of the importance of contemporary culture and its concerns, as well as the incompleteness of it as a system—opacity and Mande views toward knowledge. They are also bringing in the importance of photography as its own écho-monde, a world of the appearance of things resonating among each other.

These works embody the tensions between modernity and changing traditions, present and past, that permeate contemporary Bamakois life. Further, these photographs reinforce notions of "Malian" identity, locally and on the international stage, by contributing to a nationalist understanding of history, politics, and culture. By implication, these are projects that the museum *should* commission if it is to reflect and document contemporary life. As such, the three series contribute to the implicit dialogue about national memory and cultural preservation that underlies the museum's mission, and potentially offer Relation by making Malian cultural meanings aesthetically visible, if not immediately accessible, to a non-Malian viewer.

While their projects creolize the museum's mission or the notion of the archive more generally, they also open the potential for Relation. The photographs create this potential first by subtly encouraging a viewer to do more research to find out about local meanings, like the history of the Memorial Modibo Keïta. But more importantly, Glissant believes in the power of imagination and of the poetic. By this he means that a literary or visual artwork's effect is indirect and ultimately influences the imaginaries of its audience. On viewing photographs by Sogodogo, Bâ, and Tienro, the non-Malian viewer's piqued interest could spur them to do research into local meanings. So, there is a direct possible effect on a viewer who can try to look up certain aspects of knowledge, like what a particular hairstyle might mean (although that is still difficult to find in casual research). But there is also the poetic effect, to a certain extent ineffable or incalculable, that can touch or move a viewer, who may recognize that, while this photograph may not look avant-garde in the context of global contemporary art, there is a mysteriousness, an opacity or meaning that the viewer cannot penetrate. A respect for irreducible difference—a respect for this opacity—would mean the occurrence of Relation. If a viewer sees these works and has respect for irreducible difference—a respect for opacity, for what she or he may not know—and can acknowledge the works' poetic force—then Relation occurs. Glissant notes, "We have already articulated the poetic force. We see it as radiant—replacing the absorbing concept of unity; it is the opacity of the diverse animating the imagined transparency of Relation. The imaginary does not bear with it the coercive requirement of idea. It prefigures reality, without determining it a priori."[108]

Chapter 6

Promoting Women Photographers

> In a Bambara myth of origin, after the creation of the earth and organization of everything on its surface, disorder was introduced by a woman. . . . In a word, disorder meant creativity.
> —Maryse Condé

The most striking local impact of Keïta's and Sidibé's fame is the entrance of women photographers into a profession once dominated by men.[1] While several of Bamako's male photographers have successful careers, women are also making their presence known, both locally and internationally. To understand their emergence and meaning within the new art photography movement in Mali, this chapter describes the historical and political context of the founding of Promo-femme, a school for women photographers, and explains the school's aims and curriculum as professed by its director and founder, Aminata Dembélé Bagayoko. It also examines the careers and production of five prominent former students working in various capacities, and their participation in a biennale-inspired collaboration called Tendance Floue.

Examining how women have made substantial inroads into this formerly all-male occupation demonstrates how photography in Mali is interrelated with broader discourses about sexual difference, democracy, tradition, modernity, nationalism, and patrimony. Moreover, it is here, in photographs by women, produced in the context of a patriarchal, Muslim culture and nation-state that disadvantages women politically and socially, that the potential of Relation can be realized most dramatically. I argue that understanding Luce Irigaray's feminist philosophy in dialogue with Glissant will help contextualize how women photographers in Mali engage with Relation through their professions and images.

Until the nation's transition to democracy in 1991–1992, Malian society maintained patriarchal gender roles, meaning that women did not enter male professions such as photography, although a few may have participated behind the scenes of a family-run studio. However, the newly democratic government, financially backed by Western nations, encouraged women's equality in previously unheard-of ways, particularly through the support of Adame Ba Konaré, the first president's wife and founder of Bamako's Muso Kundo (Museum for Women).

A new photographic institution that blossomed in Bamako between 1996 and 2009 was dedicated to providing young women with professional opportunities in photography. Founded and run by Malian feminist Aminata Dembélé Bagayoko, the school, Promo-femme: Center of Audiovisual Education for Young Women (Promo-femme: Centre de Formation en Audiovisuel pour Jeunes Filles), transformed the gender demographic of photographers working in Bamako while it was open, and even after it closed (fig. 6.1). Most, if not all, of the female photographers working in the city today attended this school and attribute their current status as professional photographers to its existence.

The importance of the founding of a single-gender institution to help create equality for women, like the Women's Museum founded by Adame Ba Konaré, can be understood by reference to French philosopher Luce Irigaray's feminist philosophy. Irigaray posits two different subjects (male and female), rather than the traditional universal singular subject (male), at the heart of culture and society. This acknowledgment of sexual difference is at the basis of key tenets in Malian society. Irigaray's insistence on the differences between male and female seems essentialist in that it is based on the two forms of sex found in nature. But her philosophy goes beyond a simplistic, first-wave feminist approach of celebrating female difference, because she argues that *all* of society's structures are created with the male subject at their heart, and until they are restructured to acknowledge two subjects (at least), they will remain patriarchal. Thus, in Irigaray's thought the founding of an all-female photography school like Promo-femme would further the feminist goal of equality between the sexes.

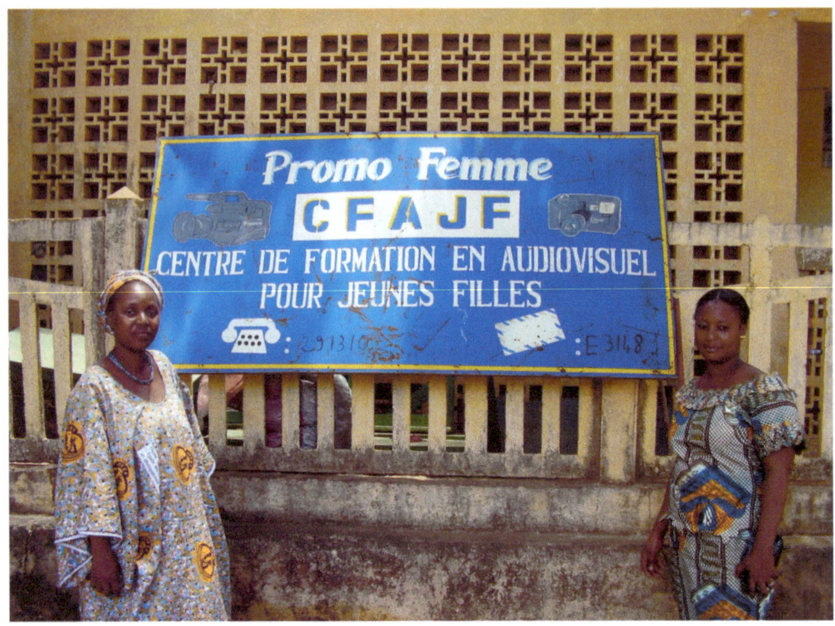

Figure 6.1. Madame Bagayoko and Kadiatou Sangaré in front of the Promo-femme building, 2006. Photo by author.

Four years after Mali's first democratic election, and two years after the first Bamako Biennale in 1994, Bagayoko established Promo-femme as a private venture, assisted by Canadian government funding.[2] Although the school initially offered a two-year program of education in the basics of film photography, Bagayoko soon recognized the inability of students to afford such a lengthy course of study, and Promo-femme then provided one single year of instruction. This program was also more opportune for mothers. Thus, Irigaray would be wholly in support of a venture like Promo-femme, which is structured around interchangeable feminist and feminine goals and ideals, differently from a male institution. During its thirteen years of operation, female students learned to shoot in black-and-white and color and to print black-and-white photographs in a chemical laboratory. Digital photography became a feature in the program as well. Prominent professional male photographers, including Malick Sidibé, Alioune Bâ, and others, often participated in teaching seminars, and in its early days the school received support from Mali's National Institute of the Arts, which includes a photography program in its curriculum.[3]

From its founding, Promo-femme actively influenced the discourse about identity, modernity, culture, and politics initiated by the new Malian art photography movement. The presence of the school created an opportunity for women to exercise power as image-makers, thereby shaping local and international perceptions about gender and photography in Mali. Although Promo-femme no longer exists, the school's graduates are slowly transforming discourses about photography, identity, and nationalism in Bamako. In addition, as working photographers, Promo-femme's graduates are negotiating female identity in Bamakois society in ways previously unavailable to them.

Examining the professions, images, and collaborative relationships of five graduates of Promo-femme who are working as photographers reveals an active arena of contestation over the roles of women pursuing professional careers in Mali's increasingly modernized and democratized society. Irigaray argues that there are multiple genders but only two sexes, suggesting that she conceives of gender as socially constructed (through the way a person identifies herself), but sees sex as biological and believes that it must be acknowledged as such.[4] Thus, there are ramifications to the shift that occurs when women, who were in the past the majority of a studio photographer's clients, and the focus of the male photographer's gaze, become photographers themselves. It is clear that the subjects often chosen by women photographers (and chosen for them in their studies by educators, for example in the CNA or at the CFP) are socially and culturally influenced by the fact of being a woman in Mali.

Nowhere in Malian society are the effects of modernity, democracy, and globalization more evident than in the increased opportunities now available to women. While Bagayoko's Promo-femme initiated a striking social change in the realm of photography, the founding of the school and the subsequent successes of its graduates emerged from broader political and societal transformations caused by the state's shift to democracy in 1992.

Professional working women in Mali must negotiate competing and coercing discourses of traditional culture(s), Islam, and the state.[5] The state's transition to democracy has promoted a rejuvenated discourse of equality between the sexes, in contradiction to the patriarchal discourses of traditional cultures and various sects of Islam, whose practices tend toward the patriarchal as they are practiced in Mali.[6] While these discourses may be hegemonic, in that they are entrenched within and sanctioned by powerful societal or governmental forces, they are not totalizing, in part because of their competing ideologies. In the spaces afforded by the conflicting agendas of democracy, Islam, and traditional societal mores, women can actively fashion their identities.[7] Obviously, the discourse of democracy provides a supportive impetus toward pursuing a photographic career; yet harmoniously melding a professional identity with societal and religious demands (often strongest in the form of familial pressure, support, or obligation) is a challenge faced by the graduates of Promo femme.

Gwendolyn Mikell has noted two important trends related to feminism in Africa: that the struggle for women's rights has been linked to times of political transitions (especially to democracy), and that feminism has been constructed around somewhat different concerns than in the US.[8] Both are true in Mali. Before colonialism, women's and men's roles were strictly defined within the various cultures that now make up Malian society. All were patriarchal, although to a lesser or greater degree. In traditional Tuareg society, for example, women had greater freedoms and power than in Bamana culture. Mande culture, which accounts for about half of the population, and whose cultural heritage predominates in postindependence Mali, traditionally denied women vital access to direct forms of power. While women still struggle for equality in Malian society, the way in which women are posited as different from men would make sense with regard to Irigaray's ideas, as women are particularly celebrated for their biological difference and ability to bear children.

Yet women are not seen as only "natural" and as excluded from culture in Malian society, as women's roles incorporate nature *and* culture, as do men's. For example, there are women griots who are as powerful and respected as male griots, in their roles as mediators, praise singers, and oral historians. There are also casted women potters who traditionally marry blacksmiths and who control the knowledge and ways of working with ceramics within their caste. The *bogolanfini* (bogolan cloth) artists are also traditionally women, and control their secret knowledge and techniques as well, including handling the nyama (power) of bogolanfini, which is related to menstruation and sexuality.[9] Malian society is therefore radically different from French society, in that Mali acknowledges the essential cultural sphere of women, which is what Irigaray seems to recommend, although women in Mali are still treated unequally in terms of polygamy, political office, and other aspects of definite power imbalances.

Theoretically, colonialism introduced an advance in women's political viability in Mali. After French women received suffrage in 1944, the National Assembly was pressured to allow similar rights to the women living in France's colonies. Thus, the right to vote in the French Sudan was extended in 1951 to any woman who had borne two children. As large families are the norm in Mali and children are highly desirable, this law affected a large proportion of the female population; and, indeed, the total number of voters in 1951 rose tremendously from previous elections as a result.[10] However, the oppression of colonialism still loomed larger than any superficial panaceas offered by the French government. In fact, the Malian women's movement began during the late colonial period and its struggles were inseparable from the liberation movement, which resulted in national independence in 1960.[11] The USRDA (Union Soudanaise Rassemblement Démocratique Africain), the French Sudan's branch of the anticolonialist movement in Francophone West Africa, offered to endorse women's emancipation as an aspect of its agenda in exchange for women's support of the liberation cause.[12] Indeed, the struggles against colonialism and neocolonialism have constituted an important facet of African feminism in general.

Irigaray's approach to feminism and sexual difference, while not currently popular in American feminist philosophy and contemporary culture because of its apparent opposition to conceptions of fluid gender, transgender, and queer identities, is useful to consider with regard to Mali, as most Malians believe the differences between men and women are ingrained and absolute, and this binary structures social life, and thus political life, to a significant degree.[13] In Mali, prominent feminist Aoua Kéita noted, in a rare example of a colonial midwife's autobiography, that the struggles were necessarily inseparable.[14] She herself had studied in France, where she must have noticed the burgeoning struggle for women's equality. Along with this experience, Kéita's traditional family background, where she observed the patriarchal power differential between men and women, and her experiences of discrimination as a professional midwife in Mali and in other African countries, heightened her feminist sensibilities.[15] Kéita was elected the first female deputy to the national assembly in the new Republic of Mali, where she worked with others to reform the marital code.[16] The national women's organization, Commission Sociale des Femmes, for which Aoua Kéita and another woman, Mariam Travélé, were responsible during President Modibo Keïta's regime, had an agenda of sexual equality and focused on women's issues.[17] However, the 1968 coup forced Aoua Kéita into exile, and in any event the commission had not contributed to a radical change in equality. The Union Nationale des Femmes du Mali (UNFM), the women's organization founded in 1974 under the dictatorship that had followed the 1968 coup, was limited by President Moussa Traoré's repressive government and was largely powerless.[18]

In contrast to the political inequality of women in postindependence

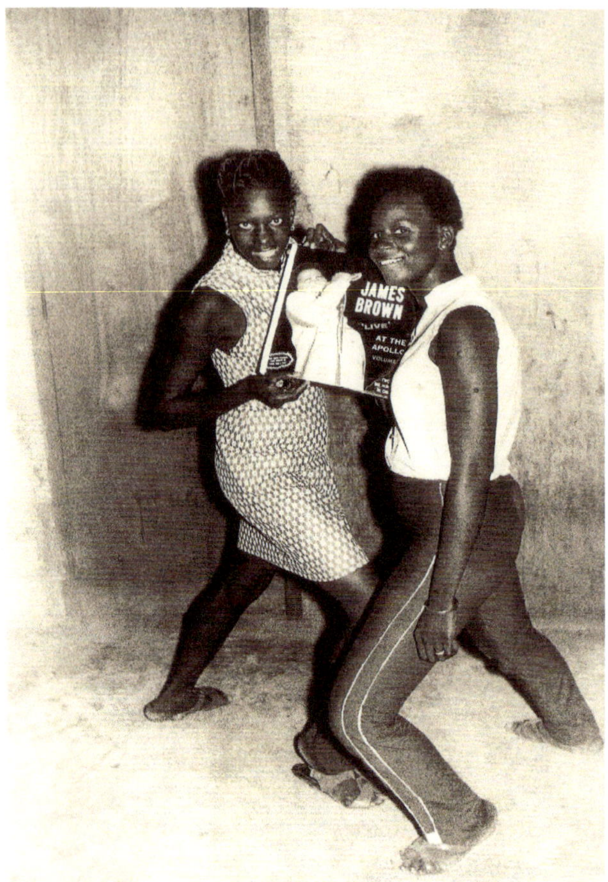

Figure 6.2. Malick Sidibé, *Fans de James Brown,* 1965. Courtesy of the artist and Jack Shainman Gallery, New York.

Mali, Malick Sidibé's portraits of the 1960s record a somewhat more nuanced social scenario, emphasizing the way in which young women, like young men, responded to the global youth movement in the newly independent socialist state (fig. 6.2). In Sidibé's pictures, girls in short skirts hold up James Brown records and participate in the parties and *grins* (social clubs) with boys. Such behavior was not sanctioned by either parents or the state, and so girls would leave home at night in traditional dress and change their clothes once they arrived at a party or a grin.

Scholar Manthia Diawara, who was a teenager living in Bamako at the time, analyzes the pan-Africanist and diasporic habitus of the postindependence era's rebellious youth movement through Sidibé's photographs. He sees the youth enacting a new form of critical independence through their identification with the 1960s global youth movement, specifically with African American rock stars like James Brown. What Diawara terms the youth's "habitus," after Pierre Bourdieu—their forms of dress (afros, bell-bottoms, and miniskirts) and "bodily dispositions"—was misunderstood by older generations and the state as neocolonial, because it did not seem authentically African and instead embraced the capitalist, imperialist West.[19] The government recognized such habitus and behavior as a danger to its hegemony, however, by sending culprits to reeducation camps. In the attempt to impose control over the bodies of young women, the three discourses of tradition, the state, and Islam were in agreement at the time, although each had its own broader, conflicting agenda.[20]

Diawara focuses on his personal experience with male friends of the era and does not discuss whether young women felt or were empowered in terms of gender equality, but Sidibé's pictures show that young women of the 1960s shared critical attitudes toward the hegemonies of the state, traditional culture, and Islam. Thus, while wearing short skirts was considered complicit with sexism by certain feminists in the American context in the 1970s, in the Malian context of the 1960s, the desire of young women to take control of their self-presentation embodies a form of feminist and antihegemonic self-assertion.[21] This becomes particularly clear when considering the cultural importance placed on women's beauty and bodily adornment in Mali, and the association of modesty with proper feminine behavior according to Islamic ideals.[22]

Within Sidibé's party and studio photographs, difference between the two sexes is highly marked; yet women seem equally enamored of pop music, dancing, and holding records, and they do the twist as energetically as their male counterparts. In a famous 1963 photo of a dressed-up brother and sister dancing together, titled *Christmas Eve*, respect can be seen in the gentle interaction between them, their heads bowed together, each of their bodies curved in an "s," with opposite feet lifted and similar smiles, his shoes contrasting with her bare feet (fig. 2.16). The innocence of their intimacy is palpable, which engenders an imaginary of equality.

After the 1991 coup, which overthrew Moussa Traoré and ushered in the new, multiparty democracy which exists today, Malian women gained empowerment and increased their participation in politics "more than ever before."[23] As the fall of the Soviet Union galvanized political transitions across Africa, Mikell notes, "the 1990s post–cold war environment provide[d] the first chance that most Africans—in particular, women of different ethnic and religious communities—have had to participate in a serious way in deciding the legal and constitutional rights of people in their own countries and the desired forms of government."[24] With democracy, modernity, and the gradual loosening of strict social hierarchies, especially in Bamako, women became able to hold political office in Mali and to work in professional positions formerly reserved for men.

In Mali, movements toward equality have been uneven. While women's rights may be constitutionally guaranteed in the new democracy, in actuality women are discouraged from equality by long-standing, patriarchal traditions dating from before colonialism. Hence, women who desire a professional career are positioned in the disjuncture between competing discourses: those that support professional and civil equality, and those that discourage women's attempts to gain more control over their lives.[25]

How can an awareness of female power or oppression within such a patriarchal and religious sociocultural context be incorporated into and expressed through an experience of Relation? As Glissant does not problematize gender specifically in his theoretical writings, the question arises whether Relation truly encompasses a feminist approach.[26] Scholar Max Hantel suggests that a feminist approach can be found within Relation if we understand it to incorporate aspects of Irigaray's philosophy of feminism as irreducible sexual difference, since *all* of Relation involves irreducible difference.

Glissant does not refer extensively to Irigaray, nor she to him.[27] But Irigaray does discuss her theory of relation in strikingly similar terms to his, as a fluid process that overcomes binaries: "Relational identity goes counter to this solipsistic, neuter, auto-logical ideal [Platonic ideal]. It contests the cleavages sensible/intelligible, concrete/abstract, matter/form, living/dead. It also refuses the opposition between being and becoming."[28] This description of relational identity parallels Glissant's notion of an identity in relation, namely, "We change, through exchange with the other." In other words, for both philosophers, identity is always in fluid transition, not settling or hardening into false binaries.

Hantel is not the only scholar to notice the similarity between Glissant and Irigaray. Michael Wiedorn argues that Glissant's view that the universalizing, rational knowledge of "Western humanism" and Enlightenment, which merely ends up reflecting itself rather than seeing the other, is "strikingly similar to Luce Irigaray's [argument] in *Ethique de la difference sexuelle* (1984), if we substitute 'the Western' for 'the masculine.' For Irigaray, masculinity has heretofore merely pretended to make contact with the feminine other, trapped in a reflexive loop of self-love that excludes woman-as-other in favor of woman-as-self, woman subjugated to and refashioned in the image of man. By the same token, the transparency of the other thus amounts to a transparency of the self to the self—one which is, moreover, a false transparency."[29] In other words, Glissant's opacity, or right to be unknown, unreadable—"we clamor for the right to opacity for everyone"—is a way of acknowledging a fundamental difference for everyone that does not re-create the other in one's own (masculine or Westernized) image. The difference is that Irigaray is positing an ideal future in which the male and female work to understand and appreciate their differences and in which all political and social structures are created with at least two sexes in mind; in this idealized or utopian future, racism is no longer an issue.[30] Reading Glissant's notion of Relation with Irigaray in mind enables us to see how female photographers in Mali are envisioning and enacting a feminist imaginary, instead of reflecting a masculine conception of what women should be.

Although the social and political conditions that allowed the school Promo-femme to flourish were created by Mali's transition to democracy, Bagayoko was the primary force behind the school's founding. In the most obvious sense, Bagayoko's capabilities, her passion, acumen, and insight, and her training as a female educator, enabled her to single-handedly change photography's gender demographic in Bamako. Madame Bagayoko, as she was called by her students, was not herself a photographer, but worked first in the public sector as the director of an *école supérieure* after receiving an advanced degree in social services.[31] Promo-femme grew out of and was supported by the Association for Women's Education and Community Support (AFFAC), of which Bagayoko was also the president.[32] The organization's first programs involved the traditional female arts of dyeing, sewing, and bogolan cloth making, which underwent a revival in the 1980s and 1990s because of its use by the fashion designer Chris Seydou, and ironically is practiced now in Bamako mostly by men.[33]

According to Bagayoko, her initial aim was to encourage young women to earn money through any type of profession. Bagayoko noticed that young men in Bamako were drawn to photography when faced with unemployment, which is very high in the city, because it is relatively cheap to acquire a camera, and working as an itinerant photographer requires little capital.[34] It was the noticeable lack of women photographers that caused Bagayoko to found Promo-femme; she was also quick to apprehend the importance of the Bamako Biennale's inauguration in 1994, both in attracting international attention and in increasing the opportunities and popularity of photography in Bamako. Bagayoko thus founded Promo-femme with the aim of providing professional options for young women through photography.

The Promo-femme website further explained Bagayoko's reasons for opening the school, as well as her ultimate objectives for the project.[35] The school was "concerned with multiplying the domains of education for young Malian women who have not, for various reasons, continued their studies."[36] The website noted that, since young men without education can make a good living from their work as photographers, it would be worthwhile introducing young women to this path by providing them with a good education.[37] The school's advertisement pamphlet makes clear Bagayoko's acumen in positioning her school with relation to Bamako's reputation as the center of African photography due to the biennale. Here she clearly states that the aim of the school was to change the gender demographic of photographers in the city, and she acknowledges its success in already beginning to do so: "Until recently in Mali, photography was considered a profession reserved solely for men. With the creation of the center, Promo-femme, and the education of the first female photographers, this opinion is now a distant memory. More and more young women occupy the milieu of Malian photography. Bamako is the capital of African photography, and all opportunities are available to young women photographers to take their place. To do this, the center will create a partnership with any services that are open to the development of this profession."[38] In 2006, according to its promotional literature, the stated aims of Promo-femme were to:

- diversify the opportunity of education of young Malian women who have not had the chance to continue their studies;
- educate three hundred young women, by the year 2007, in photography and videography; and
- perfect the work of graduates and of other women who already work in audiovisual media.[39]

Other short-term goals were to increase the capacities of the center by acquiring more equipment, and to make presentations to the public to assure the school's ability to finance itself. A longer-term project was to create three photography agencies, and the eventual aim was to make Promo-femme a multifunctional center for various professions by 2010. Sadly, the school was closed for lack of funding before these goals were reached. Bagayoko's goals for her students and for the school nevertheless show an admirable and ambitious program for encouraging equality by providing women photographers with training and ultimately jobs in Bamakois society, while still acknowledging their difference as women in society, and thus creating a Relational context in Irigaray's terms.

During its brief life, the school was highly successful in educating female photographers. From its opening in 1996, the center claimed to have trained an impressive number of young women (177), of whom about one-third were still working in photography in 2006.[40] A dozen were working at ORTM, the national radio and television station.[41] More than twenty worked for communication agencies in Bamako, such as television stations or newspapers. One graduate worked for the press, took nearly all of the reportage photos for the Ministry of the Promotion of Women, Children, and the Family, and thus covered the First Lady of Mali at the time, Madame Touré Lobo Traoré. One graduate was working for the mayor of the District of Bamako and documented all of the events of the district with photography or video. More than thirty were making photographic or video reportages for marriages, baptisms, graduations, and other types of events, while five opened their own studios. Unfortunately, many who did not give up their cameras were obliged to stay in training with the owners of studios, where they earned nearly nothing. Thus, Promo-femme hoped to create three photography agencies in order to support these women economically.[42] Bagayoko actively helped her students continue their education and professions after graduation by placing them in internships throughout the city and arranging exhibitions for them.[43] Through the network of her graduates and in connection with other institutions, Bagayoko thus created viable professions for her students.

In Bamako, while Bagayoko and Promo-femme were most instrumental in supporting women photographers, other institutions and individuals—male photographers, administrators, and teachers—also contributed to supporting female photographers in their nascent careers.[44] For example, Bamako's other private photography school, the Centre de Formation en Photographie (CFP), pursued equality of the sexes by ensuring that each incoming class of students was half female. The CFP also assigned projects that encourage an ideology of equality, while acknowledging the differences between women and men in society. In 2003, Kadiatou Sangaré, Diabaté, and Alimata dite Diop Traoré all participated in a CFP-sponsored exhibition titled *Women Looking at Women*.[45] Seven female photographers from the school joined female interlocutors to interview and photograph famous women in Bamako.[46] By pairing the CFP students, fledgling professionals, with journalists and women who already had made their names and careers, the CFP encouraged the students to view the professionals as role models and perhaps even mentors. The CFP's Swiss origins—the school was run by Helvetas at the time—may have provided the original impetus for equal treatment, but admirably the school kept the policy despite its transition to Malian tenure. While the teachers at CFP were male, the director, Youssouf Sogodogo, was very supportive of Diabaté, and in 2006 she worked in the school as an assistant teacher.[47]

At the government-run National Institute of the Arts (INA), female students were also encouraged to undertake photographic training. While it is likely that women, like men, were first admitted to INA under the auspices of traditional arts, several final theses by women working in photography received the highest marks in the class.[48] In addition to institutional encouragement for women in photography, some individual male photographers have also taken on young women as protégées, helping them to exhibit their work.[49] Many of the more prominent older male photographers received their training in the USSR or in France, which may have influenced their supportive attitudes toward women.[50] Importantly, Malick Sidibé was supportive of women photographers, judging by his willingness to give lectures at Promo-femme and to display the work of Ouassa Sangaré, among others, outside his studio during the 2005 biennale.[51] Youssouf Sogodogo commented that the occasion of Diabaté's winning the AFAA prize (granted by the Association Française d'Action Artistique, the government organization that funds the Bamako Biennale) would act as a wake-up call to male photographers, proving that women photographers can outshine men.[52] The support of male photographers and of institutions run by men clearly exemplifies Irigaray's theory that women and men must equally work to understand each other.

Youma Fall, a curator active in Senegal, in an essay on three Senegalese women artists in the Dak'art 2006 catalog, asked a crucial question of African women artists with regard to structural patriarchy and sexism: "Do they have access to the channels of dissemination of contemporary production?"[53] In this regard, a model of sexual equality existed from the beginning of the biennale, in that it was born as the brainchild of French female photographer Françoise Huguier, who invited Bernard Descamps to join her in its organization, along with male Malian photographers Alioune Bâ, Racine Keïta, and Django Cissé. Only two women, both white South Africans, Jenny Gordon and Ingrid Hudson, were exhibited in that first biennale, but the exhibition has become decidedly more inclusive since 1994. Curator Simon Njami spoke specifically of having feminism and the equality of women as an agenda; during his directorship of four editions, Michket Krifa, an Algerian woman, curated an Algerian press photography section (in which a surprising four out of nine photojournalists were women) in the 2005 biennale.[54] In that biennale, women were represented as well as (or better than) they were in typical American museum exhibitions: almost one-third (eleven out of thirty-seven) of the artists in the International Exhibition were female. Krifa went on to cocurate, with Laura Serani, the 2009 and 2011 exhibitions. In 2015, Nigerian curator Bisi Silva, also now deceased, a cocurator under Njami's directorship, became the sole curator, and the first black, continent-based female curator. Continuing this encouraging trend, curatorship went to a German Cameroonian woman, Marie-Ann Yemsi, in 2017, with the title *Afrotopia*. The efforts of women in the French office that directs the biennale have also been significant; in general, women have played an important role in the biennale, and their influence is increasing.

While the Encounters have increasingly encouraged women in the profession, Malian photographers have a long history to overturn. Studio photography in Mali traditionally depended on strictly defined masculine and feminine roles, and women typically comprised the bulk of a photographer's clients.[55] For example, Tanya Elder relates that, in the course of a day, photographer Sorry Kouyaté took "eight photographs of children, six photographs of couples, five of men and fifty-six pictures of women, either on their own or together with friends."[56] While studio photographs are taken to commemorate major events and holidays, and to record familial relations and friendships, aesthetic occasions, like acquiring a new dress or hairstyle, also serve as a pretext for visiting a studio. In fact, it is so common that many photographers deliberately set up shop next to tailors, or vice versa. In Mali, as in much of West Africa, women are particularly celebrated for their looks, as the Malian author of a photography book on hairstyles explains, identifying "that most authentic of our possessions" as "the traditional, pure beauty of our women."[57] Women spend a good deal of time, energy, and money on decorative adornments—beautiful dresses, jewelry, hairstyles, and henna patterns for the palms and feet—and often have a picture taken to record a new hairstyle or a newly tailored outfit.[58]

The mark of a good studio photographer in Mali is to not only capture but enhance a woman's beauty. Diawara notes that Seydou Keïta's photography performed two functions: "a decorative one that accentuates the beauty of Bamakoises and a mythological one wrapped up with modernity in West Africa."[59] A woman's beauty shows her sophistication, her urbanity, and her modernity. "For women, Keïta's camera was a guarantee of beauty, fulfilling the truth of their being Bamakoise. His portraits were said to make any woman beautiful, giving her a straight, aquiline nose, emphasizing her jewelry and make-up, and capturing a sense of her modernity through the attention paid to her high-heeled shoes and handbag."[60] A studio photographer plays an active part in constructing the woman's beauty, by posing her in a certain way, providing modern props and a fashionable cloth backdrop, and using lighting effects and sometimes even retouching. When viewing a Keïta photograph, the quality of the shot is obvious. Women are caught in fascinating poses, their skin glows, and their clothing is arranged to glamorous effect. Indeed, the now-famous phrase that Keïta repeated to his female clients when instructing them to pose was "You look beautiful like that."

A male studio photographer's social acumen was necessary to successfully interact with female clients, notes Elder.[61] Flattery and flirtation are crucial skills practiced by photographers to encourage a female client to comfortably reveal her most beautiful and engaging self. Meanwhile, the photographer must also exercise diplomacy in negotiating the business relationship in a way that is not threatening to a woman's husband.[62] In other words, flattery and flirtation must remain superficial, at a professional level, for the photographer to achieve the best business results. Elder also describes one particular photographer's way of working a party, where he singled out one beautiful woman to photograph, and thereby (in his words) incited envy in the rest, who then demanded his attention.[63] In a society with strict heterosexual norms, such gendered conventions reveal the inherent bias faced by female portrait photographers, who cannot be expected to as successfully manipulate the flirtatious photographer/client relationship. Instead of relying on the traditional, masculine model of such an interaction, then, a woman photographer must invent her own model to successfully charm women clients.

Thus, it is perhaps not surprising that only one of Promo-femme's graduates whom we interviewed, Penda Diakité, chose to open her own studio (fig. 6.3).[64] Diakité opened Studio Photo: Afrique Vision in 2002, close to her home in the Lafiabougou neighborhood of Bamako, three years after finishing her study at Promo-femme.[65] Following graduation, she had pursued several internships—six months at Studio Prophoto in the Hippodrome neighborhood and three months at the National Center for Health Education and Information.[66] Diakité also spent six months at Lion Photo, a reputable Korean color lab in downtown Bamako that handles much of the work for itinerants, where she gained experience in "point of view" (framing the shot), miniportraits, and identity photos.[67] She also participated in several

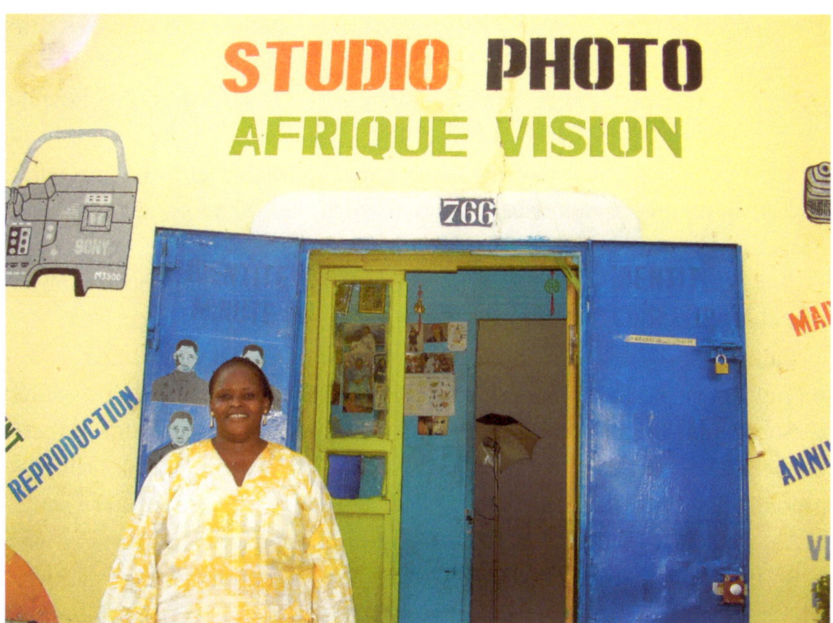

Figure 6.3. Penda Diakité in front of her studio, 2006. Courtesy of author.

workshops at Centre Soleil d'Afrique, including one that focused on digital training, and her work was displayed at Galerie Chab in an exhibition titled *Colors of Women* in 2003. Diakité's curriculum vitae advertised reportage in weddings, baptisms, conferences, and other ceremonies.[68]

According to Diakité, her initial desire to attend Promo-femme occurred when she first heard an advertisement for the school on the radio. She asked her father to let her attend, but he told her she was crazy (literally, "You are sick").[69] However, she remained firm in her aspiration, and when she asked her father again several months later, he relented and agreed to pay the fee.[70] Diakité evinces a strong determination that attests to the difficulty of becoming a woman photographer in Bamako. She related a telling anecdote about a client who thought that her male assistant was the photographer, and gave her a hard time on discovering that she was the studio owner; eventually she won him over and he allowed her to photograph him.[71] Diakité's power in doing so shows the help of Promo-femme support and of her determination to create equality for women.

The desire of the sitter to create an "improved" identity—in other words, the wish fulfillment motive—is a consistent theme in much African studio photography. The collaboration between the photographer and subject in the creation of the sitter's idealized identity has often been noted. In Keïta's case, Lamunière notes, "While the photographers' role was to fulfill their sitters' wishes, they also asserted their artistic will. Keïta describes how his sitters selected the pose they wanted, but says he felt that he always knew which one was better."[72] Sitters contributed by dressing up for a picture, and bringing prestigious or beloved items with them. Photographers offered props and encouraged sitters to pose in an attractive stance.[73]

But times have changed in Bamako. While older studio photographers, like Hamidou Maïga and Malick Sidibé, used painted backdrops, patterned or painted backdrops are no longer in use. In 2006, all of the studio photographers in Bamako owned large photographic color backdrops, which they bought at a local store. (One photographer, artist Mamadou Konaté, deliberately uses abstractly painted or tie-dyed backdrops because they are unique.) Common themes were elaborate gardens, with fountains and sculptures, a lake with a mansion in the background, green topiary gardens with palm trees and mirrored reflecting ponds, a conservatory rose garden with a white wicker rocking chair.[74] Almost all of the backdrops that I observed were dominated by blues and greens, with a prevalence of water imagery and lush vegetation. As half of Mali is composed of the Sahara Desert and the Sahel, a subdesert zone, and even the southern areas like Bamako are parched most of the year, the backdrops serve as refreshing views which remove the subject from the dust and heat, the difficult geographical conditions that aggravate the country's poverty. The backdrop provides a fantasy of wealth in picturing luxurious or vacation-oriented landscapes. Some backdrops even combine elements signifying vacation paradises that are geographically dislocated; one showed a Polynesian sculpture against a brick wall on mown green lawns, where the location seemed unclear. Heike Behrend has noted, with regard to studio photography in Likoni, Kenya, that the function of the backdrop is to project an imaginary space of cosmopolitan leisure and escape, rather than to depict a seamless illusionistic scene, and Diakité's studio photographs similarly create this type of imaginary projection.[75]

Yet the notion of identity creation and its attendant mythology seems, in this era, somewhat overinflated. In the Bamako studios that I visited, the commercial poster backdrops seemed the only part of the experience that suggested a different identity, but they were rarely used. In fact, one photographer said that only rural people—considered country bumpkins, he implied—still use the poster backdrops, because a newcomer to the city believes that, if he or she sends such a picture back to the village, people will believe it is "real." Thus, it seemed that a sophisticated city dweller would not choose to be photographed in front of the backdrops. This was only one photographer's anecdote, however, which is belied by the portraits that Penda Diakité showed me. Her young clients, possibly friends, may have been playing with the backdrops in full knowledge of that older convention. In any event, most clients preferred the *fond abstrait*, or plain white backdrop, for identity portraits. If in the 1950s "having one's portrait taken by Keïta signified one's cosmopolitanism," today the commercial backdrop seems to signify modernity and urbanity for rural villagers, but to indicate a lack of sophistication among Bamakois themselves.[76] This distinction highlights the vast difference in amenities, education, and attitude between the capital and the countryside in Mali.[77]

In Bamako, the amount of time a person spends posing has also been much reduced from the 1950s, when Seydou Keïta was most active. Keïta relates that he would spend up to an hour posing someone (which seems likely to be an exaggeration unless it was for a special commission, since it does not mesh with his story of lines of people waiting outside his studio on a Saturday), while I observed various studio photographers pose a sitter, and was posed myself by several, in all of one or two minutes.[78] Presumably advanced technology, like automatic focus and lighting, have decreased the posing time, especially for photographers working with digital cameras, since the waste of film is no longer a concern.

Though most portraits I observed were taken for identity purposes, once I saw a mother bring in a baby girl with a new doll in packaging, clearly bought for the occasion of the photograph, and another young woman who changed her blouse in the studio for the occasion. Thus the tradition of bringing in valued items for a picture, and being concerned with dress, still seemed present. The uses that a studio photograph is put to once it is taken home may also contribute to the identity creation of an individual, as in the past. For example, a wedding photograph may be displayed on the wall of a couple's living room, contributing to the memory of a presumably happy day and further strengthening the couple's bond.

Interestingly, Diakité's studio photographs do not betray a noticeable difference from the pictures of other studios in Bamako. She owns several of the commercial photo backdrops popular at other studios I visited, and has experimented with text banners that crisscross her backdrops. One, which shows text that reads "Happy New Year, 2003," shows a turquoise pool, behind which palm trees, the ocean, and striking rock formations suggest a tropical paradise. One portrait shows an anonymous young woman wearing a Western-style tight jean skirt and a close-fitting gold blouse, with mod leather shoes, giving her a fashionable, modern, and young look. Diakaté's posing of her friends is crucial to Relation in a feminist sense, for Irigaray argues that it is especially in woman-to-woman relationships where women can support each other and find a new language for equality. Irigaray especially mentions familial relationships, which is interesting because Diakité's young daughter (in 2006) accompanied us to the studio, and her mother was clearly modeling for her a feminist way of being in the world.

In another photo by Diakité, two friends sit back to back on the floor, posed in a way that shows their warmth for each other while displaying a sense of fun and informality (fig. 6.4). Normally people do not sit on the floor as it is considered undignified. In the photo, the two friends sit in front of a color poster backdrop of a lush topiary garden, behind which meanders a wide and glassy green river. The women both wear slacks and tank tops, again showing their modernity, although the woman on the right is more "dressed up"—that is, she wears a formal blouse, while the woman on the left wears a tank top with letters on the front. Both have removed their shoes, and the woman on the right has placed her shoes neatly in front of her, pointed to the right. This placement of the shoes is seen in several of Seydou Keïta's portraits as well, suggesting that the women are pictured as if at home and that they desire to show off their fine shoes. The juxtaposition

Figure 6.4. Penda Diakité, studio portrait, 2006. Courtesy of the artist and Perlman Teaching Museum, Carleton College.

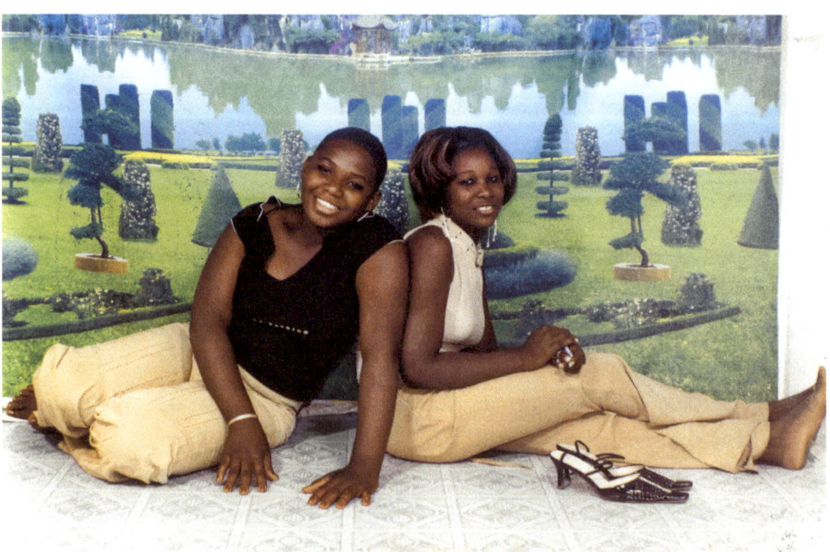

of this attribute with the "park" in the backdrop suggests that the backdrop was chosen more for its decorative qualities than to convey an attempt at "realism." As Diakité's pictures use the backdrop, it may be more preferable to young people. Then again, since these were pictures that Diakité had on hand, they may have been of friends.[79]

Diakité's work has appeared in several publications and exhibitions, but she explained that most of her art photographs unfortunately were lost in a fire in 2005. She cited portrait photographers Malick Sidibé and Seydou Keïta as important influences, Sidibé especially. She said that he shows what we would not otherwise know without photography.[80] Diakité seems to echo Barthes's sentiment: "Perhaps we have an invincible resistance to believing in the past, in History, except in the form of myth. The Photograph, for the first time, puts an end to this resistance: henceforth the past is as certain as the present, what we see on paper is as certain as what we touch."[81] Like Keïta and Sidibé before her, Diakité participates in the continuation of a vernacular, community-oriented preservation of an individual's past. But through the viewer's knowledge that the photographer is a woman, and through the lively poses of her subjects, Relation can potentially occur, especially as a viewer realizes the odds of a woman being a studio photographer in Mali.

For the other women interviewed, opening a studio was not an immediate goal. Kadiatou Sangaré (no relation to Ouassa Sangaré) held an internship at a national language school in Bamako called Institut des Langues Abdoulaye Barry (ILAB).[82] Sangaré, like Traoré and Diabaté, attended CFP after Promo-femme.[83] Her job illustrates the indelible connection between photography and cultural identity and speaks to the importance of photography as a visual language that transcends specific oral and written languages within a particular cultural context.

ILAB provides instruction and transcription in Mali's many languages, including very difficult languages like the Dogon dialects or obscure languages spoken by only a small population. The school is thus an important resource for national and international scholars of Malian culture. ILAB's photographers illustrate brochures and photograph the various villages, clothing, and hairstyles of different ethnic groups in order to provide cultural awareness in the service of language-learning. Hence, a photographer's job at ILAB is similar to the work of the National Museum's photographers, but the images are used for the purpose of teaching and preserving a language rather than for the preservation of objects or ephemeral ceremonies.

Issues of languages, of tremendous importance in Africa, are hotly debated in postcolonial studies. The question of whether an author writes in an ethnic or former colonial language determines the writer's audience, but also, unfairly, is sometimes used to pinpoint the author's position on a spectrum of perceived "authenticity." Photography appears to evade this conundrum, operating superficially as a universal language; but, as this book demonstrates, images carry different meanings for different audiences. In the context of ILAB, photographs serve to facilitate linguistic knowledge, working with cultural knowledge to preserve history. The ILAB photographer's job, to "illustrate" a living language, emphasizes the inseparability of language from culture, of visual effects from mental constructs. And as Mali's democracy has succeeded largely because of decentralization, the celebration of diverse languages takes on political importance. The Malian government's goal since the 1990s—to appreciate and preserve the nation's diverse cultures, while assuaging ethnic disputes—is furthered by ILAB. Sangaré's job emphasizes the importance that photography plays in contributing to the national dialogue about cultural identity versus national identity, democracy, and decentralization. Languages are especially important within Relation; while Glissant is most interested in creole languages that form through cultural exchange, the mission of the ILAB is also important in terms of preserving and making accessible older and hard-to-access languages.

The one series that Sangaré showed was of a Christian ceremony that she had taken while a student at the CFP. These pictures were typical of such reportage, including individual portraits and the overall ceremony. Christianity is growing in Bamako, but the exoticism of the subject seemed to make it a popular one for a number of photographers. One photograph by Sangaré shows a man wearing a commemorative Dutch-wax shirt printed with two photographs, presumably of religious leaders, one of whom looks like an Orthodox patriarch. The competing faces, each turned in a different direction, creates a striking image. Knowledge of the sex of the photographer extends the possibility of Relation to the viewer, but this image does not in and of itself necessarily suggest Relation; it is the context of Sangaré's work within her job of making different linguistic dialectics available for study through a communication of images that here seems Relational.

Like Kadiatou Sangaré, Alimata dite Diop Traoré worked as an unpaid intern, but at the Malian government press agency, AMAP (Agence Malienne de Presse et de Publicité). Founded in 1992, after the transition to democracy, AMAP grew out of the press agency ANIM (Agence Nationale d'Information Malienne), which was the organ of the socialist government and was founded after independence in 1960.[84] A number of ANIM's photographers studied in the German Democratic Republic (East Germany) and Czechoslovakia. ANIM issued from a photographic archive service created in 1956 by two Frenchmen.[85] Photographs printed by ANIM did not appear with the photographer's by-line, and the same is true today for AMAP, except for certain AP photos.[86] Like most press agencies in socialist, postindependence Africa, ANIM followed the official party line and did not criticize the state.[87] By the mid-1990s, the number of photographers at AMAP had dwindled to six.[88] Today AMAP has only a few working photographers. The staff, including all of the reporters, was composed of men, except for Traoré, which suggests the challenges she faces as a young woman new to the field.

Traoré studied at the CFP after graduating from Promo-femme in 2003, and her curriculum vitae notes a three-month internship at ORTM. Traoré received family support for her choice of profession—both of her parents have been unusually understanding and supportive, especially her mother. She also cited the role model of an aunt who had also been a photographer, though the aunt had since left the country.[89] Traoré works with a digital camera and is able to make use of the technology available to her at the AMAP offices, which includes a computer.

Traoré's series here focuses on women and children in Missira, a Bamako neighborhood.[90] Her pictures have an off-the-cuff aesthetic, a sense of humor that suits the attention-grabbing techniques necessary for a photojournalist. Her work plays on strong, often humorous visual contrasts, which often take the form of visible tensions between modernity and tradition. In one picture by Traoré, a woman stops on the street to adjust her headscarf and looks severely at the camera, while behind her looms a young man on a motorbike. The open sewers that run next to the road are visible. Another shows little boys running with their arms full of firewood. A third picture shows a toothless older woman smiling sweetly as she passes by a wall with a painted advertisement of a young woman selling juice with ad text in French, which most women in Mali cannot read (fig. 6.5). The old woman carries wash utensils in a basin on her head, and her wizened arm reaches up as the painted girl's young arm reaches down, framing the older woman's head. The contrast between the wizened, hard-working older woman and the cheery, attractive girl in the advertisement would be heart-wrenching if not for the older woman's pleased grin. All of these pictures capture daily life in Bamako, where such juxtapositions, such signs of French influence and affluence, constantly intermingle with local traditions and poverty. Yet what makes these photographs enable Relation, rather than creating a post-

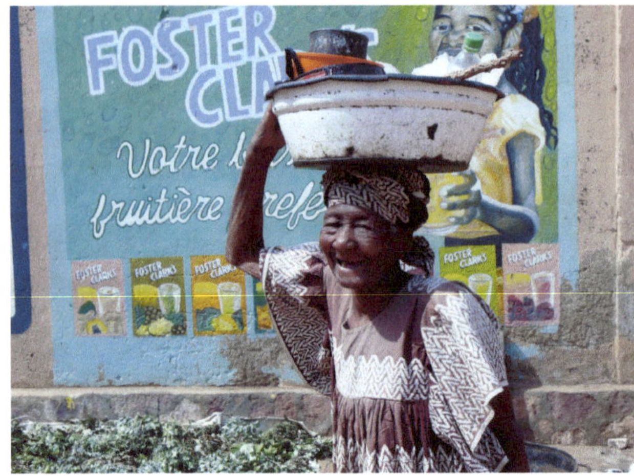

Figure 6.5. Alimata dite Diop Traoré, *Foster, Missira District*, 2006. Courtesy of the artist and Amadou Keïta.

colonial critique, is their celebratory embrace of these juxtapositions, whose subjects do not seem unhappy. Traoré's focus on women and children emphasizes the importance of family, which is key to Malian social life, and also creates possibilities for a different, feminist imaginary, in Irigaray's terms, on the part of viewers, and on the part of the subjects, especially the children, who are photographed by a woman rather than a man.

While on a path to a career as a photojournalist, Traoré also exhibits photographs as art. Traoré said, "I dream of being a great artist, a star if you like, who exhibits all over the world."[91] She also said that she had been fortunate in having supportive parents, especially her mother, and that if she had to choose between getting married and her career, she would choose a career. This was a question apparently asked of every female photographer interviewed for this news story, which shows the extreme importance placed on a woman's marrying and bearing children in Malian society.

While women fight for equality and the right to work outside the home in traditionally male professions in Africa, marriage and motherhood are still generally seen as of paramount importance.[92] Pringle comments, "The ability of educated, middle-class Malian women to compete effectively with men is still limited, yet on balance it compares favorably with the situation in the United States and many other developed countries."[93] However, most women in Mali maintain their identity as "female" and differentiate themselves from men, in contrast to the US, where women in positions of power have asserted their equality on the basis of *not* differentiating themselves from men. Turittin notes that Aoua Kéita often praised her fellow feminists

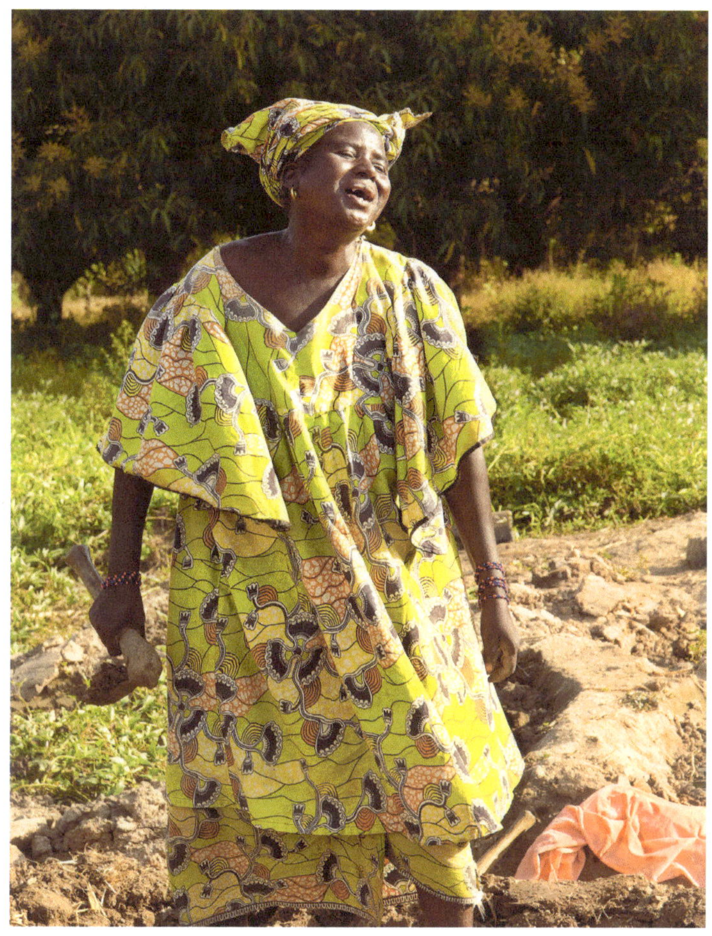

Figure 6.6. Alimata dite Diop Traoré, *J'aime la vie* (*I Love Life*), from the series *Le quotidien des femmes* (*The Daily Lives of Women*), 2008. Courtesy of the artist, Amadou Keïta, and Perlman Teaching Museum, Carleton College.

for their militancy *and* their attractiveness, reminding them of their valuable identity as childbearing women.[94]

Irigaray provides a different model for understanding the place of women in Malian society that is not dependent on a masculine logic that women must be like men in order to succeed. She writes: "In order to question the universal subject, it is necessary to approach another logic. The only logic that can assure a rational and universal foundation is that which starts from the reality of two genders, masculine and feminine. Such a logic compels us to rethink, theoretically and practically, the subjective constitution as well as the one of the individual or collective world. The *one* no longer remains here the visible or invisible, conscious or unconscious paradigm, which governs rational organization; this organization henceforth takes into consideration the existence of two subjects, irreducible one to the other."[95] While in Mali women are still subordinated to a hierarchical order, the acknowledgment of the two sexes is present and does exist. Ending sexism through ending the hierarchical order, rather than by trying to make women follow the male model, seems a possibility for the future of Mali. Women photographers who work against the grain of a sexist and hierarchical culture, often to celebrate women's lives and importance within the performative and agricultural communities in Mali, are fighting against this hierarchical system but still giving force to their feminine-feminist vision.

This irreducible appreciation for difference can be seen not only in Malian photographs but also in the gender makeup of the new generation of photographers. Alimata Traoré engages difference as a theme in her recent series, *The Everyday Life of Women* (fig. 6.6). The studies in color and form reveal the particularities of Malian life: a woman works in a field, an older woman wrapped in blue rests on a banco building (fig. 6.7), a mentally ill woman on the street sits among the woven plastic bags ubiquitous in Africa. Traoré's deliberate inclusion of this woman is part of the variant experience of life; allowing the mentally ill to inhabit the streets if they choose is a striking difference between cities in Africa and those in Europe or the US. Here, the circumstances of Traoré as a woman, as well as the theme and aesthetics of the series, contribute to a sense of Relation—a "rebellious consciousness" that shows a woman's view of a world in which men have most of the legal and unseen power.[96] While respect for difference is arguably a "Malian" characteristic, it was also noticeably encouraged by ideas about gender equality and through specific assignments at the photography schools that sprang up in Bamako. An appreciation for difference also governs the curatorial spirit of the biennale exhibitions, if not the administration. Thus these

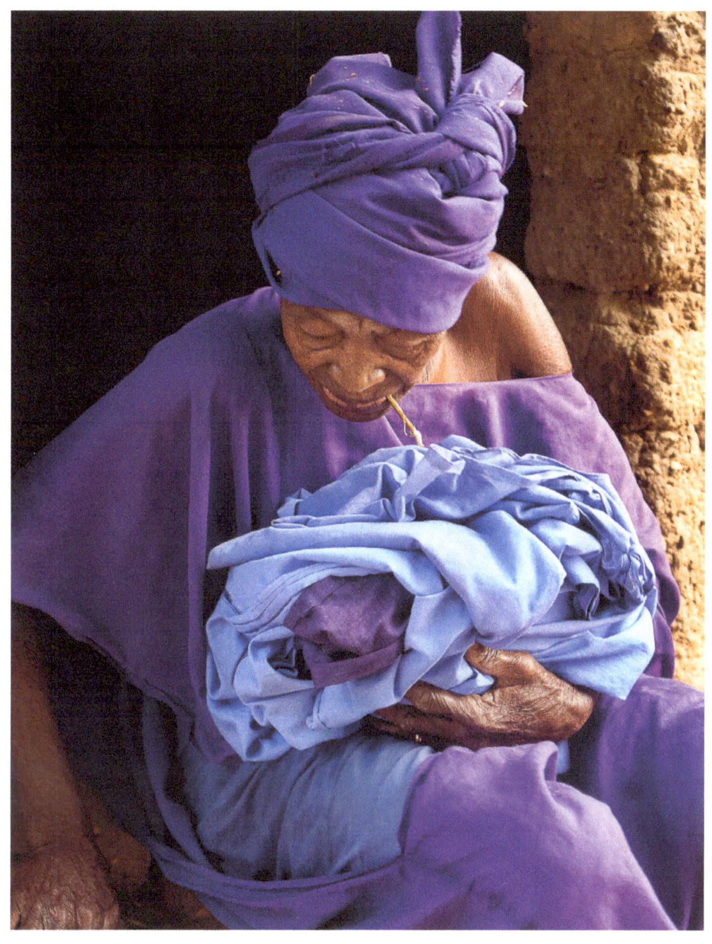

Figure 6.7. Alimata dite Diop Traoré, *La tristesse* (*Sadness*), 2008. Courtesy of the artist and Amadou Keïta.

works specifically respond to the circumstances created by the biennale, intermixing local ideas with outward interests in an example of Relation.

While Traoré has exhibited as an artist, her work tends toward the photojournalistic. By contrast, Ouassa Pangassy Sangaré, who also did reportage, wanted to be known as an artist. She was among the first students to attend Promo-femme, and in 2006 she was the most internationally established of the five women. She has traveled and worked widely in West Africa and Europe, as well as across Mali. Sangaré used both film cameras and digital, and branched out into video and film as well. She worked with a number of prominent male photographers, such as Alioune Bâ and Amadou Baba Cissé, and she cited Bâ, Malick Sidibé, and Mamadou Konaté as mentors and teachers. Sangaré contributed work to several editions of the biennale in the "Off" exhibitions and was included in the 2005 biennale as one of an international roster of photographers who had participated in a master class held in Bamako in February 2005.[97] Sangaré acted as a mentor and support for younger female photographers like Alimta Traoré.[98] Together with Penda Diakité and another Promo-femme student, Awa Fofana, she created a short-lived agency for women photographers with the help of the arts collective Centre Soleil, in 2002.[99]

The works by Sangaré that I saw typically focused on women. One photo

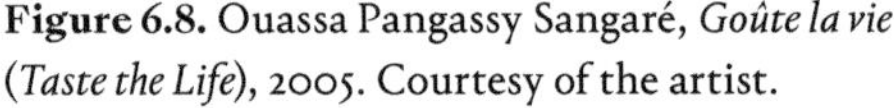

Figure 6.8. Ouassa Pangassy Sangaré, *Goûte la vie* (*Taste the Life*), 2005. Courtesy of the artist.

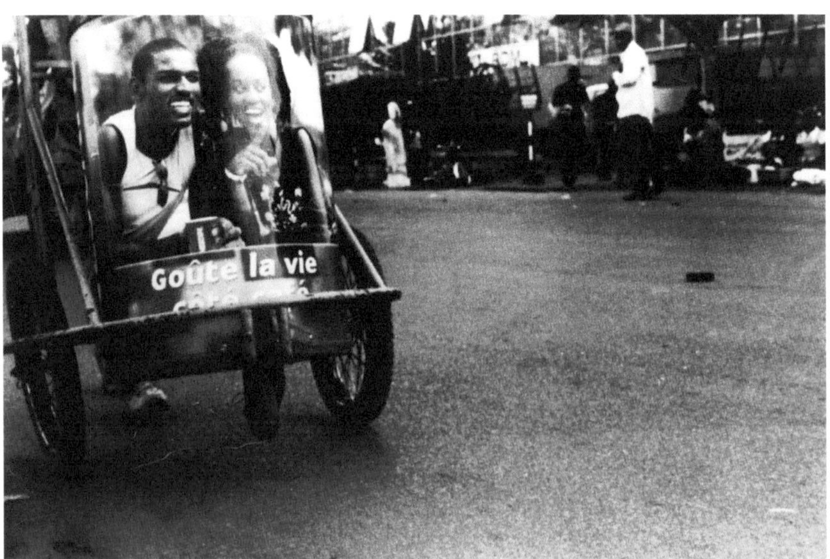

showed a close-up of an albino woman who had troubled skin. Albinos suffer great discrimination in Mali, although the prominence of the renowned albino singer Salif Keïta is helping to make people a little more comfortable with the condition.[100] Sangaré wanted to expose the difficulties of the woman's ailment, a subject later taken up in Mali by French photographer Alain Turpault and Malian photographer Seydou Camara. This was one of very few photographs that critically examined social or political problems in Mali.[101] While this could be partly the legacy of decades of a government-censored press, it seemed also an aspect of Malian culture to downplay the difficulties of life and to celebrate beauty, as the studio photographers do. In two other pictures, it is possible to see Sangaré's concern with social realities, which embodies a postcolonial critique, rather than a sense of Relation. One example shows someone pushing a coffee dispenser down the street, showing a glossy advertisement of a happy, attractive, and well-off young couple enjoying "the taste of life" (fig. 6.8). The emptiness of the street opposite the coffee pusher, which takes up much of the picture, belies the joy the couple feels in their taste of life. In the other picture, a very young baby is sleeping on a pile of cloths (a clever way to keep the baby safe while the mother attends to a task nearby). Still, the image of the small baby left by itself on the ground, and the title, *We, the Children,* suggests that Sangaré identifies not only herself, but some kind of community, with this image.

On the day of our second interview in June 2006, Sangaré was critical about the difficulties she faced as a woman in her profession. She was heading to France to participate in a workshop with Konaté and other photographers, so it seemed that her career was progressing despite her troubles, but she explained that the emotional and psychological difficulties of being a female photographer were weighing on her. Like the other women photographers, Sangaré had received familial support in her choice of profession. Sangaré's father was himself an amateur photographer and had given her a camera at the age of twelve or thirteen. However, she related that few male photographers took her seriously as a woman and that it was harder to find work and exhibitions.[102] Sangaré's images, with their critical eye toward capitalism and advertising, also seem less Relational and more connected to a postcolonial critique.

In 2006, Ouassa Sangaré was the best-known of this cohort of women photographers, but by 2018 the most famous female photographer in Mali was Fatoumata Diabaté.[103] Diabaté won the AFAA prize for young artists at the 2005 biennale while she was a twenty-five-year-old student at the CFP, where she was a protégée of its director, Youssouf Sogodogo. During an interview in 2006, while she was a student at the CFP, she explained, "The CFP has become a symbol of my life. I'm here all the time. I don't lack anything for my profession here: I can develop, I can print, I can learn." After finishing her education at Promo-femme, Diabaté became discouraged because it was difficult to take photographs in her neighborhood and to do photojournalism, but education at the CFP made a dramatic difference in her abilities to take photographs professionally.[104]

The award honored her series on the Tuareg, a nomadic ethnic group who live in the Sahara desert in northern Mali.[105] Four pictures from Diabaté's Tuareg series were exhibited as a selection from the Bamako Biennale in *Lens of Life*, also curated by Simon Njami and on exhibition at the Museum of the African Diaspora in San Francisco, from May 18 to September 23, 2007, the first selection of the biennale to travel to the United States. In one, Diabaté shows a woman holding her finger to her lips, as if to keep in evil words (fig. 6.9). The high-contrast shape of her body and headwrap echo the tents behind her, pale in the desert light. As the Tuareg have historically held a conflictual relationship with southern Mali, this series addresses Relation in its sympathy toward cultural similarities and differences. In an interview in 2010, Njami spoke of his decision to award Diabaté the prize as a deliberate act of feminist support. Diabaté acknowledges the importance of Promo-femme on her career on her website: the first sentence in "About" states, "J'ai fait mes premiers armes au Centre de Formation Audio Visuelle Promo-femmes, ce q'il m'ouvrit les portes du Centre de Formation en Photographie de Bamako (CFP) entre 2002 et 2004" (I got my career start at Promo-femme, which opened the doors to the CFP, where I studied between 2002 and 2004).[106]

After graduation, Diabaté spent the summer of 2006 in Bordeaux, France, participating in a photography workshop, and she explained how winning the AFAA prize had changed her life.[107] While Diabaté's mother had always supported her unconventional choice to pursue photography, her father had not understood her passion or professional goals—that is, until Diabaté won the prize. Winning the prize showed him that her work was taken seriously by others, which changed his own attitude, and he became supportive of her career.[108]

In a similar series to the Essakane project in traveling to a different culture and landscape within Mali, Diabaté also participated in a project called "Mali au féminin" ("Feminine Mali"), which involved photographing women and girls in Dogon country and in Bamako. In comparison to Alain Amet, a male French photographer whose work was shown with Diabaté's

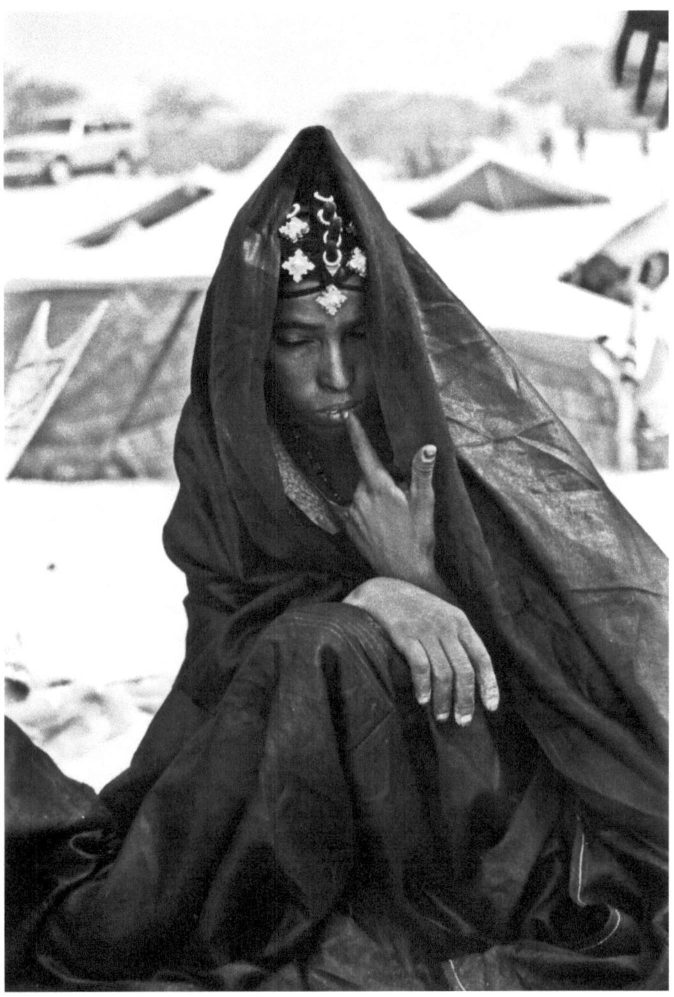

Figure 6.9. Fatoumata Diabaté, *Touaregs, en gestes et en mouvements* (*Touareg Series, Gestures and Movements*), Timbuktu, 2005. Courtesy of the artist and Patrice Loubon Gallery.

in "Mali au féminin," her pictures convey a sense of intimacy, often through close-ups. The women in Diabaté's photographs appear either unselfconscious or deliberately posed and aware of the artist; both approaches convey an outward dignity and inward interiority. Diabaté's photos include ethnographic "type" images, for example of a "Peul woman," with a child looking back at the photographer in a photo titled *Exchange of Gaze* ("type" photographs being so prevalent in the history of the country and in postcard and tourist images that they seem unavoidable). But Diabaté also uses a wide range of aesthetics, including images blurred through movement, soft focus, dust, or shadows; asymmetric compositions, close-ups, and the centering of the figure to convey interest. Diabaté's color photos also emphasize pattern and similar tonal values, which makes them complicated or difficult to understand visually, suggesting a blending of Mande aesthetics with the kind of modernist clarity that Diabaté was trained in at the CFP. For example, in *Fish Seller,* the titular subject's upper body creates a strong pyramidal shape in the composition, reinforcing the strong four-point cross created by her fists on a metal scale, but her clothes and the background and shadows create a visual complexity across the picture's surface (fig. 6.10). Interestingly, Diabaté's images are all of women and girls, in contrast to many landscapes and architecture photos by Amet, who was photographing for the Museum Bretagne and seemed especially fascinated with the Dogon landscape and architecture. Amet's photographs have a standard, recognizable "photojournalist" aesthetic. Diabaté's focus on women, especially in the context of the book and exhibition, emphasizes women's difference from men but celebrates their abilities and individuality, suggesting an imaginary of equality in Irigaray's sense.

While familial relationships are obviously important to photographers, the social relationships between the Promo-femme graduates also created an atmosphere of mutual support. The women often worked together on collaborative projects and maintained ties with Promo-femme's founder, Bagayoko, to further their professional capacities. Thus social capital, which is important in most Malian endeavors, seemed to be especially important for, and well utilized by, women photographers, to support their forays into the masculine-dominated world of photography. Promo-femme contributed to the careers of its graduates not only through its photographic education but also by creating an informal network among its students.

A number of Promo-femme graduates also participated in two biennales through one of its most exciting "Off" projects, the Cinéma Numérique Ambulante (CNA; Moving Digital Projection). The CNA was created by a Eu-

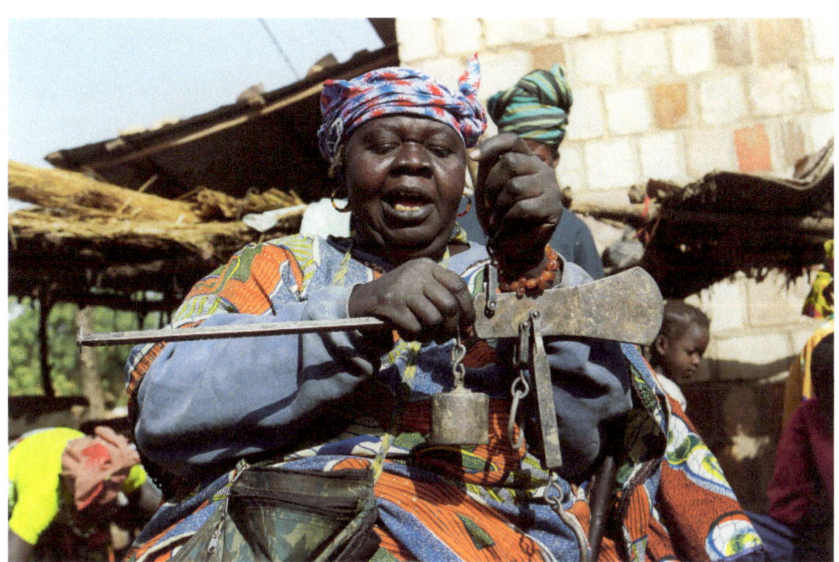

Figure 6.10. Fatoumata Diabaté, *Vendeuse de poisson* (*Fish Seller*), *Mali au féminin*, 2010. Courtesy of the artist and Patrice Loubon Gallery.

ropean organization that recruited local Bamakoise photographers to enter a neighborhood and take digital photographs of residents during the day. Those images were projected that same night on the side of a neighborhood building for a local audience.[109] While the biennale is largely an exclusive affair, catering to international artists, curators, and arts professionals, the CNA, which operates during the opening week of the biennale, engages with the local urban population in a manner similar to the studio portraits whose impetus sparked the biennale in the first place; the project is remarkable for its attempt to incorporate the general public into the biennale and for bringing photography "to the street." The impromptu slideshow articulates the neighborhood's own importance for itself, reflecting images of residents in their urban spaces back to themselves in an act that surprises, delights, and potentially empowers.

Presumably women were included in the CNA because Tendance Floue both recognized the need to support women photographers and realized that women might see and take photographs differently through their embodied experience. In the 2005 biennale, as part of the Contours organized by local parties and the Maison Africaine de la Photographie (African House of Photography), Cinéma Numérique Ambulant collaborated with the photographer Meyer of the collective Tendance Floue to create Studio-

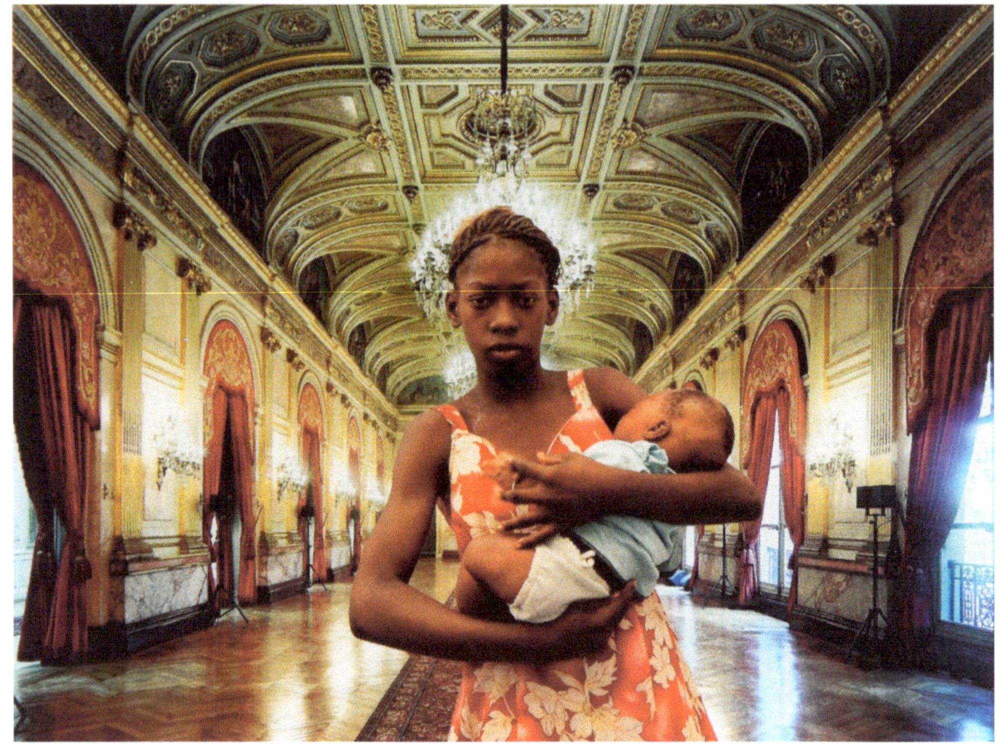

Figure 6.11. Ouassa Pangassy Sangaré, Cinéma Numérique Ambulant (CNA), Quartier de Niaréla, Bamako, 2005. Courtesy of Tendance Floue via Christian Lambert.

photo Numérique Ambulant (SNA). Five Promo-femme students—Alimata Traoré, Diabaté, Oussa Sangaré, Kadiatou Sangaré, and Awa Fofana—participated in the SNA. The group created a project called "25 quartiers de Bamako, 5 photographes femmes" ("25 Neighborhoods in Bamako, 5 Female Photographers").[110] Unfortunately, the women are not named on Meyer's website or on the CNA website.

The project involved two types of photographing. The women photographers went out in pairs. One woman would use a drop cloth and a laptop, setting up an impromptu studio to photograph portraits of locals. The subject would then choose his or her backdrop from a catalog of images created by the collective Tendance Floue, and the background would be Photoshopped behind the person's image (fig. 6.11).[111] This is the same process found in digital photo studios in Bamako, except that in the studio that I visited, the backdrop was actually part of a computer program and thus used standard, “globally accessible” backdrops. In the case of the SNA, the backdrops available were more varied and interesting because they were views shot by Tendance Floue photographers. As Meyer notes, the project was similar to contemporary studio traditions, but simply allows for more options and variety, as the photo backdrops for sale in the market and used by local studio photographers are similarly nonspecific and deal with the signification of “elsewhere.”

The other type of photographing, taking place at the same time as the portraits in the neighborhoods, contrasts with the photo portraits. The other woman of the pair would enter the neighborhood and take pictures of residences and people. These were reportage and were not (apparently) Photoshopped. Both sets of photographs were edited each day by the pair of women photographers and Meyer, and then projected at seven o’clock in the evening on the walls of the neighborhood. This was a very successful venture, and audiences varied from five hundred to two thousand people.

The CNA returned as the SNA (Studiophoto Numérique Ambulant) in the 2011 (ninth) biennale to set up photo studios in the neighborhoods. For this project, a photo studio was actually set up on the grounds of the National Museum, and two young women were operating it; however, they appeared rather dispirited by the heat and lack of interest in their project, which was probably deemed jejune by most biennale visitors, many of whom now view studio photography as out of date, or retro (it entered the fine art world about twenty-five years ago, after all). The gap between fine art—the biennale, with its pretensions to sophistication—and local culture could be felt. Still, the images projected in the cinemas this time used only a brightly colored backdrop. While the CNA 2005 images resonated with poetry and absurdity (depending on the choice of backdrop), these bright backdrops call to mind the colorful sense of life in Mali, and the flatness of the backdrops conveys a certain seriousness. The clothing and features of the participants are highlighted (fig. 6.12). Removed from context, set off against bright colors, they suggest a heterotopia to the world—these figures in their brilliantly colored no-space are set into Relation, with their neighborhood audience as well as biennale visitors.

The response to the CNA projects was enthusiastic—dozens of people crowded the seating before the projections (figs. 6.13–6.15). Documentary images of the event show people surging forward with excitement in seeing themselves and their neighbors projected on the wall. Here the individual portrait is made public and returned to the individual in a communal context. The communal sharing of image production and viewing activated by

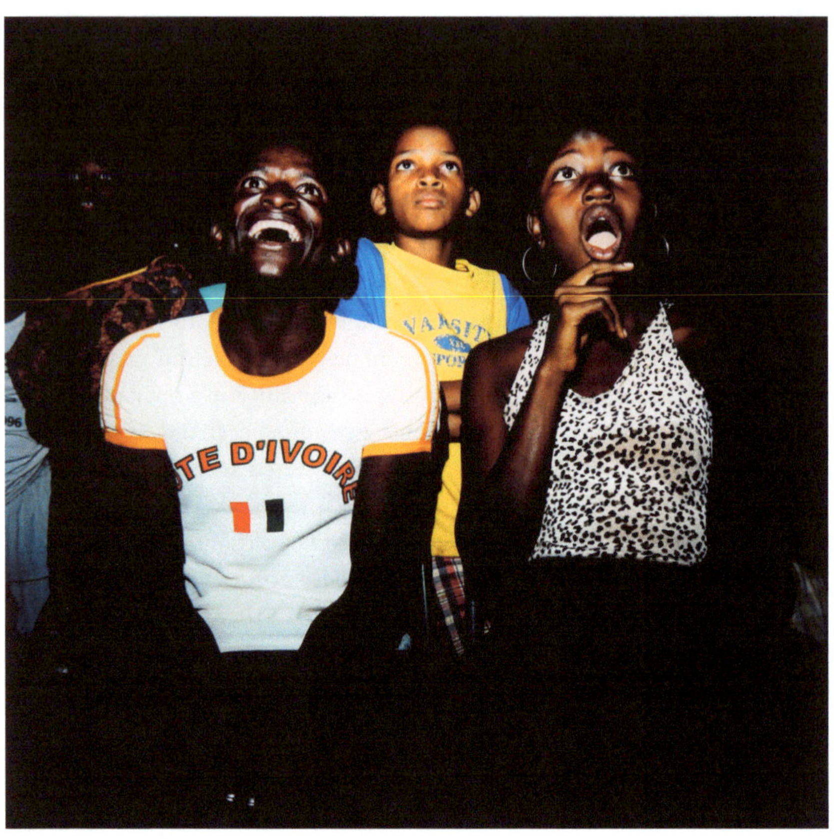

Figure 6.12. Meyer, CNA, Quartier de Niomiriambougou, *Mon frére lumière*, Bamako, 2005, People Watching CNA. Courtesy of Tendance Floue via Christian Lambert.

Figures 6.13, 6.14, and 6.15 *(opposite)*. Ouassa Pangassy Sangaré, Cinéma Numérique Ambulant (CNA), Quartier de Niaréla, Bamako, 2005, Portraits with photo-shopped images, backdrops from catalogue of Tendance Floue.

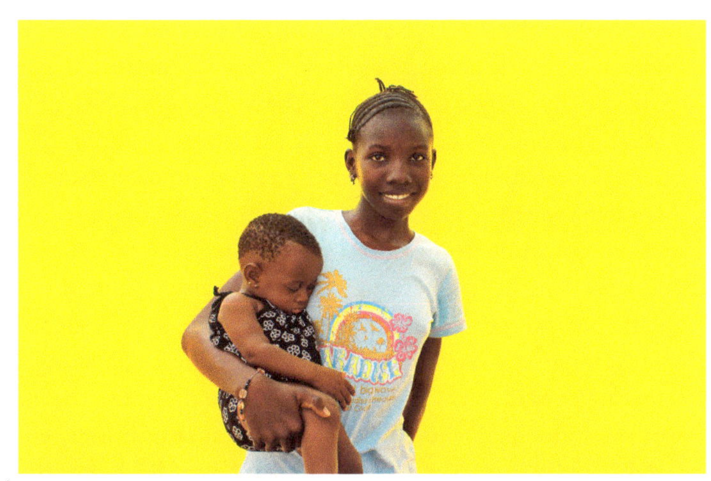

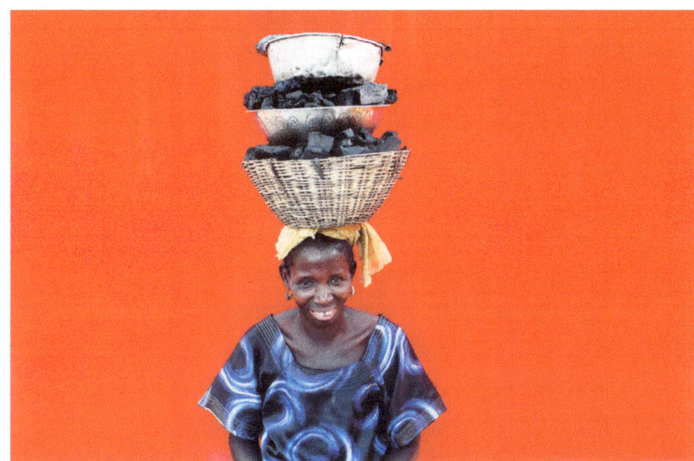

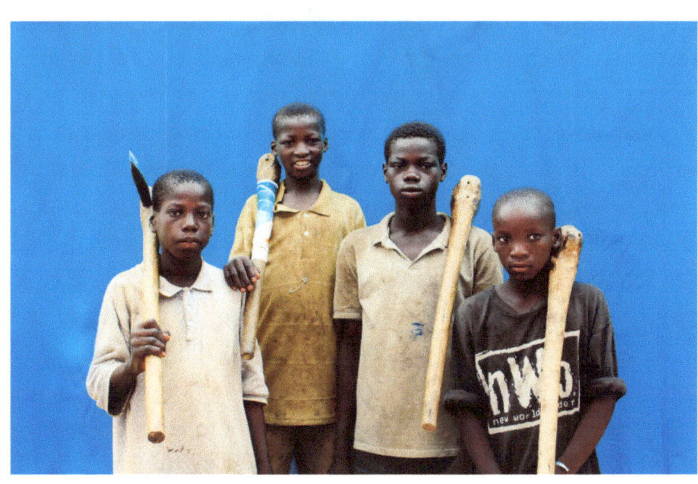
nWo.

the CNA creates a form of social capital not unlike the creation and circulation of studio portraits by photographers like Seydou Keïta in the 1940s and 1950s—the very photographs that inspired the founding of the biennale. Of all the photography projects in Bamako, CNA is the most similar to the original intent of the portrait photographs by Keïta and Sidibé in its sociological effects, if not in its aesthetic form, in returning portraiture to its celebratory, social function. But while studio portraiture in the past was preferred by female clients operating in collaboration with the gaze of the male photographer's camera, here women collaborate with everyone in the neighborhood to create images shared in a festive night (with live music), blending the performative nature of Malian traditional arts with the delight in the indexical presence of the individual, shared communally. In this project, Glissant's Relation and Irigaray's sense of relational identity are both operative, creating a feminist imaginary that is influenced through Tendance Floue, yet that speaks indelibly of contemporary, urban Malian culture, while celebrating women's influence as image-makers and appreciating sexual difference.

While the emergence of women into the Bamakois photographic community is unprecedented and exciting, there is no "feminine" aesthetic in the pictures that I was shown, and the photographs by women did not seem to share any particular traits in common. The one commonality that I noticed was that women are encouraged, usually by their school's agendas but also sometimes by their professions and personal interest, to focus especially on women and children as subjects. However, this is not an uncommon topic for male photographers as well; it seems to stem from the cultural circumstances that made women the primary clients of studio photographers—that is, the gender divisions in Malian society: women's childbearing role is emphasized above all other potential roles, so women take pride in their beauty as representative of their fertility. However, when schools like Promo-femme and the CFP encourage female photographers to take women as subjects, usually those have been in order to celebrate strong, professional women who work outside the home in important leadership and cultural positions, such as in an exhibition I saw in 2006 at the Centre Culturel Français.

The art photography movement's liminal status between traditional modes of reportage and studio portraiture and the presence of the biennale and feminist approaches brought in by Canadian, Swiss, and French institutions, as well as supportive men in the Bamako photography movement, have contributed to affording women increased opportunities in photography. Bagayoko's influence as the founder of Promo-femme was the crucial basis of the opening up of opportunities, which were furthered by the coop-

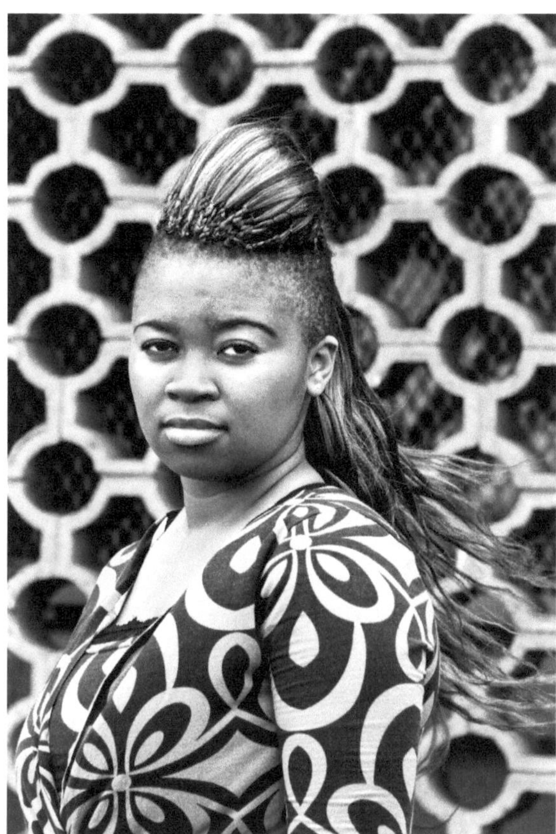

Figure 6.16. Zanele Muholi, *Lynette Mokhooa, KwaThema Community Hall, Springs, Johannesburg*, 2011. © Zanele Muholi. Courtesy of Stevenson, Cape Town/Johannesburg and Yancey Richardson, New York.

eration and support the school's graduates provide each other. The personal qualities of resourcefulness, strength, and determination to succeed of these women, along with familial support as they have broken into a traditionally male profession, must also be emphasized. Photography's qualities as a medium—its versatility in various capacities, from illustrating language texts, to recording weddings, to illustrating the newspaper and becoming an art—also contribute to its becoming an important professional opportunity for women.

While women in Mali may have received limited international recognition as of yet, this situation is bound to change, provided the biennale continues to function and promote African photographers. Especially with the more recent iterations of the biennale, curated first by Laura Serani and Michket Krifa, and then Bisi Silva and Marie-Ann Yemsi, African women are becoming more prominent in the field of photography; notably, South African photographer and LGBTQ activist Zanele Muholi is now one of the most famous photographers from the continent. Muholi's work is owned by such major global art museums as MoMA in New York—where, interestingly enough, their portraits that mimic West African studio photographs in their use of bust-length portraits, patterned clothes, and backdrops (in this case a poured-cement decorative wall) prevail. In marked contrast, however, Muholi's portraits are a form of collaborative visual activism, in that the artist deliberately photographs lesbians and transgender individuals with their full consent and participation in proud and dignified poses (fig. 6.16).

Whether Malian women photographers will ever be able to embrace such progressive subjects remains to be seen. For in Mali, as scholar Tal Tamari explains, "the long-standing Manding belief that a woman owes full obeisance to her husband and that her children's moral qualities—and correlatively, success in life—are largely dependent on her own . . . is so ingrained in Bamana culture that it actually appears in school textbooks prepared by the Ministry of Education."[112] In the epigraph to this chapter, Maryse Condé, a woman Caribbean writer of the same generation as Glissant, turns a Bambara myth of origin on its head and attributes all creativity to women. Photographers like Penda Diakité, Kadiatou Sangaré, Ouassa Sangaré, Alimata Traoré, and Fatoumata Diabaté are similarly overturning photographic conventions of gender, both in terms of who is pictured, how they are pictured, and who is taking the photograph, to create a Malian feminist imaginary in Relation with the world.

Chapter 7

Errantry, the Social Body, and Photography as the Écho-monde

The thought of errantry is a poetics, which always infers that at some moment it is told. The tale of errantry is the tale of Relation.
—Édouard Glissant, *Poetics of Relation*

The most famous art photographer of Bamako, in terms of markers of global art world success, occupies a unique place in Bamako's art scene. Perhaps because he grew up in Abidjan, in neighboring Ivory Coast, and moved back to his birthplace of Bamako as a teenager, or perhaps for other reasons, Mohamed Camara's (b. 1983) circumstances and art are an exception among the Bamakois photographers. Camara broke into the global art scene with a solo show at London's Tate Modern in 2004 at the age of nineteen. Since then, he has participated in numerous biennales and workshops in France. Because he embraces the journey between Mali and France, often making cultural difference the subject of his work, in a seemingly light-hearted fashion that can at times be strikingly poignant, his work can be characterized as *errance*, or errantry, in Glissantian terms.[1]

For Glissant, movement and rootlessness are key to Relation. Improvising on Gilles Deleuze's concept of the rhizome, Glissant emphasizes his belief that any culture that makes claim to a rootedness, either to a land (place) or an essence (religious, cultural, or mythic) becomes an empire, exerting or attempting to exert force not only over others, but also creating a false arrogance among the people within its own culture through reference to the necessarily exclusionary nature of this root.[2] Errantry is the way by which rootlessness is accomplished; errantry describes a search, a journey, which is neither rooted in its beginnings or ends (like an arrow shot from a bow that falls after a straight flight), nor involves the repetition of circularity and return characteristic of nomadic social forms of organization, based on cyclical seasons. Camara's birth in Ivory Coast, his teenage years spent in Bamako, and his journeys to live and work in different parts of France are not nomadic; rather, they epitomize an errant search, as a close analysis of his photographs' aesthetic and conceptual concerns will show.

Camara found his way to art photography through an encounter with the young Frenchman Antonin Potoski. The story is that Camara and other teens were passing around the book of Dogon photographers that Potoski had recently published.[3] Camara said that he could take photographs as well as the Dogon youth. So, Potoski contacted the publisher of the book, Éditions de l'Œil, who agreed to lend Camara a digital camera if he would use it. The press subsequently published Camara's pictures in 2002, accompanied by a poetic text by Colette Fellous.[4] *Chambres maliennes* (*Malian Rooms*), as they were titled, was exhibited in 2002 at Galerie Chab in Bamako and at Pierre Brullé Gallery in Paris as part of the Paris Photo Month, included in the 2003 Bamako Encounters, traveled to Italy as part of *Africalia*, and ended up in a solo exhibition at the Tate in 2004.[5]

When Camara received the camera from the publisher, he began to take pictures on the street, but quickly discovered that passersby became angry, as it is considered impolite to take someone's picture without permission in Mali.[6] Camara also worried that his camera would be stolen. Therefore, he turned to photographing the rooms in his family's and friends' compounds. Compounds in Mali consist of rooms or small buildings clustered around a central, open courtyard, whose entrances and windows are covered only by curtains and shutters. The pictures for which the young artist earned his solo exhibition at the Tate were poetic takes on these shabby, luminous, blue-painted rooms, with pictorial interest playing off the light entering through transparent curtains.

Camara's pictures juxtapose the everyday and the mysterious, revolving around the intimacy, privacy, and openness in these scenes. We catch glimpses of young men and women obscured by curtains or netting, seen through windows, shadowed in doorways, asleep or lost in thought, seemingly oblivious to the camera. A naked woman poses with arms outstretched,

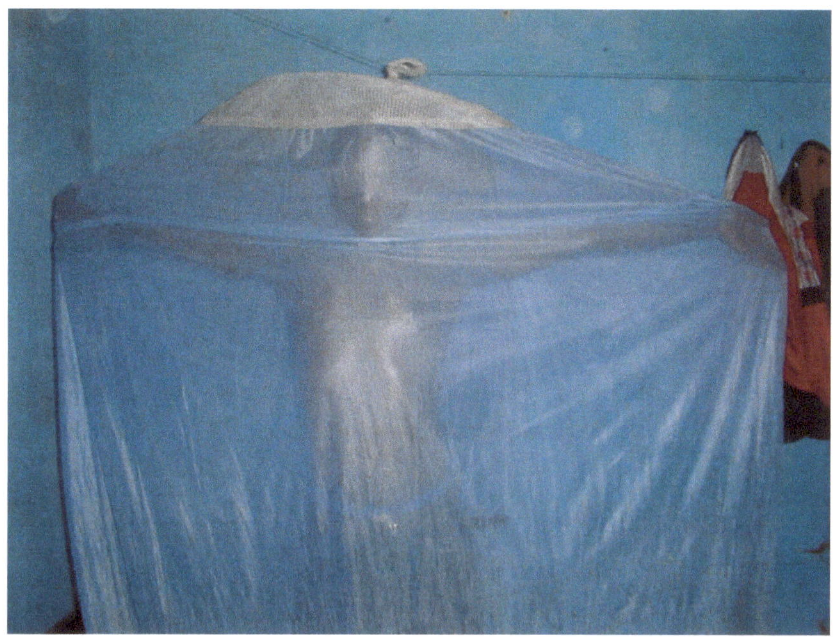

Figure 7.1. Mohamed Camara, *Alou joue sous la moustiquaire, Chambre malienne 23 (Alou Plays under the Mosquito Net, Malian Rooms)*, Bamako, 2002–2003. Courtesy of the artist and Galleri James Flach.

veiled in an ectoplasmic mosquito net whose top bobs above her head (fig. 7.1). The rich, deep blues of painted rooms play a supporting role; this is a common color in Bamako, according to Camara because it is the cheapest. The interiors are places for dreaming, half-clothed, while outside fully dressed people walk purposefully, ride bicycles, or hold up a soccer ball, framed by the dark windows and floating curtains. The obvious poses—a boy seen through netting, the girl in the mosquito net, the hand in the window—blend with the seemingly unposed, such as the man looming in the doorway holding a dead squirrel, wearing ragged shorts. The vase of flowers on the ground next to a sleeping woman recalls nineteenth-century portrait props, while the floating soccer shirt hung in the window contrasts with the gently blowing ruffled edges of patterned, translucent door curtains. The pictures are sensual yet modest; sex is imminent but just beyond view.

Camara's view of a teenager's desires, an interior dream world caught halfway between childhood and the prosaic responsibilities of adulthood, struck an international chord. The Tate exhibited the *Chambres maliennes* as well as twenty new photographs and a video. Among all of the Malian art photographers, Camara's work is the most connected to global art world concerns. His two films are especially conceptual: from inside a room, one watches a door sill with curtains hanging above it for minutes at a time; the film combines several doorways in slow sequence: sometimes the curtains blow or are parted by people passing through. Another film, called *The Dream of a Young Provençal*, begins with a blond young man with his eyes closed, head bowed into a handful of lavender; he is then shown lying down with sprigs of lavender all over him. The camera, using double exposure, then wavers and walks us through a blurry field of lavender. It then returns to the young man lying down, pans slowly over his sleeping body, pans up directly over his head as if the viewer is rising to the ceiling, and becomes blurry again, disorienting the viewer, and then the young man returns into focus below. The film ends as it began, with the young man smelling the lavender with his eyes closed. The last shot lingers on his face as his eyes remain closed. Both films evince a confident conceptual approach, and yet equally evince a strong Malian aesthetics. The first captures a sense of patience felt very much in Mali, as well as showing the doorways both as metaphors and real spaces at the same time. The second also seems Malian in spirit, in its fascination with cultural regionalism—the young Provençal is enveloped in the famous lavender landscape from which his culture and background emerge. It is also fascinating in that the young man is arguably objectified—he is sleeping, and the film is sensual, if not overtly sexual—hence, in taking this young Frenchman as its docile subject, the work performs a reversal of the filmic gaze so often perpetrated on Africans by Europeans; also, hints of a homoerotic gaze would encourage a Relational approach for some viewers.

It was partly the originality of Camara's subjects that earned his work attention at the Tate Modern, which was at the time actively seeking African practitioners to exhibit. Few in the London art world had seen the blue interiors of homes in Mali. But it was just as much his whimsical, humorous, and sometimes dreamy or poignant aesthetic, and the fact that urban teens were taken seriously as people with their own interiorities, rather than objectified as subjects of a *National Geographic* type of photography, that made Camara's photos attractive. Like Sidibé's portraits of self-consciously stylish urbanites, Camara's rooms showed a mood and subject that a young, hip London art world could identify with, yet in a setting and with props and poses that were striking and unusual. This series thus enables Relation by celebrating youthful desires and fantasies, instead of focusing on the high unemployment rate for youth in Bamako, for example, as Salif Traoré did in the 2009 biennale.

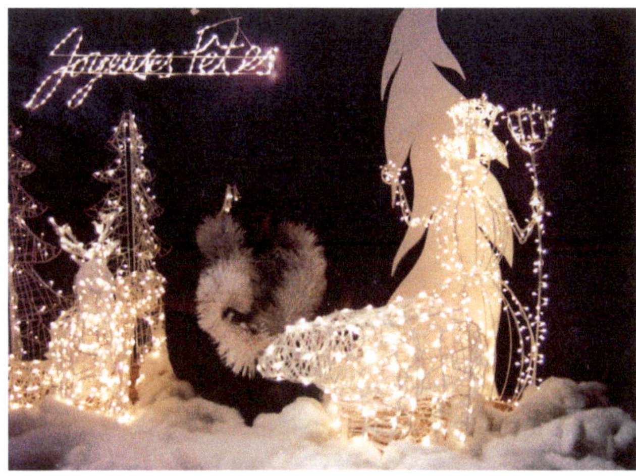

Figure 7.2. Mohamed Camara, *Christmas Cactus 1: In My Dreams in Bamako It Was Christmas*, 2001–2002. Courtesy of the artist and Galleri James Flach.

While Camara's earlier series present an internationally recognizable view of teenagers in Bamako, locally rooted in a poetics of place, his more recent work addresses the changes in perception his international travels have afforded him. More obviously staged, retaining the odd and yet touching campiness of the dreamlike setting, but to a heightened degree, Camara's later works playfully capture the ironies of foreign culture experienced as difference in a series called *Christmas Cactus* (2004). *Help Help M. Blachère, Tarzan Is Caught in His Lianas,* shows the artist bare from the waist up and wrapped in a blue vine of Christmas lights. He walks through a tangle of these glowing vines, which dangle and hang from trellises in a staged setting reminiscent of a department store's back room. The Jean-Paul Blachère Foundation has supported Camara and other photographers in Mali, so Camara's title mocks the often neoprimitivizing, patronizing air of such foundations as AFAA. He also suggests that the "lianas" that "Tarzan" is caught in, or perhaps the troubles that Africa is caught in, are products of the glitzy, superficial, capitalist West. In another picture, Camara sits in baggy basketball shorts and no shirt in an arching throne of strung lights, again reminiscent of a department store display. A lit Santa with goofy, giant shoes lurks behind Camara, whose figure is darkly silhouetted against his throne, and strung lights and tree branches animate the scene. In a third, Camara, barely visible, peeps out from a white feather boa, sitting bemusedly on the floor next to a silvery, lit Christmas tree, snowman, and reindeer, while above him the words *Joyeuses Fêtes* are written in lights (fig. 7.2). In *The Cactus of Siberia: Mohamed and the Mountains*, he stands in skintight blue trunks and sneakers outside on a porch against a backdrop of snowy mountains, in a clever play on the phrase supposedly uttered by the prophet Mohamed—"If the mountains will not come to Mohamed, Mohamed will come to the mountains." This expression does not actually originate in the Qur'an—it comes from a mocking story in Francis Bacon's *Essays* (1625)—but it seems likely that Camara is using it in its pop culture meaning. All of these pictures play on the disjuncture between religious, cultural, and literal climates, highlighting the exoticism of snowy, Christian France in all of its glamour and superficial rituals. As Betsy Wing notes, "*Errance,* for Glissant, while not aimed like an arrow's trajectory, nor circular and repetitive like the nomad's, is not idle roaming, but includes a sense of sacred motivation."[7] Here and in other images Camara questions religion, exotic Christian rituals in particular, through an emphasis on his Muslim heritage (figs. 7.3–7.5).

Camara continues his humorous approach, combined with a kind of magical realism, in his series *Some Mornings*, shown in the 2007 Bamako Encounters. This series includes works such as *Some Mornings Are Not Like Others* (fig. 7.3), in which a young man emerges from a mosquito-net covered mattress on the floor to discover water bags laid in a grid before him, like enormous, lozenge-shaped jewels. The interior and use of the mosquito net recall the early series *Malian Rooms*, but with a magical realist twist. *Some Mornings She Is the First to Begin the Journey to the Window* (fig 7.4) shows a woman's form half dissolved by light in a room with an ultra-chic lamp and high-end design chair, transitioning from solid to translucent. *Some Mornings I Thank My God* shows the artist sitting; above his upraised left hand floats a neon red heart with a double image of two people outlined within. *Some Mornings My Cousin Plays Tricks That I Don't Understand* (fig 7.5) shows a lumpy black figure standing on two small human legs, attenuated arms tied between a

(*opposite*)

Figure 7.3. Mohamed Camara, *Certains matins pas comme les autres, Certains matins* (*Some Mornings Are Not Like Others*), 2005. Courtesy of the artist and Galleri James Flach.

Figure 7.4. Mohamed Camara, *Certains matins, elle est la première à commencer la journée à la fenêtre, Certain matins* (*Some Mornings She Is the First to Begin the Journey to the Window*), 2005. Courtesy of the artist and Galleri James Flach.

Figure 7.5. Mohamed Camara, *Certains matins, ma cousine me fait des trucs que je ne comprends pas, Certains matins* (*Some Mornings My Cousin Plays Tricks That I Don't Understand*), 2005. Courtesy of the artist and Galleri James Flach.

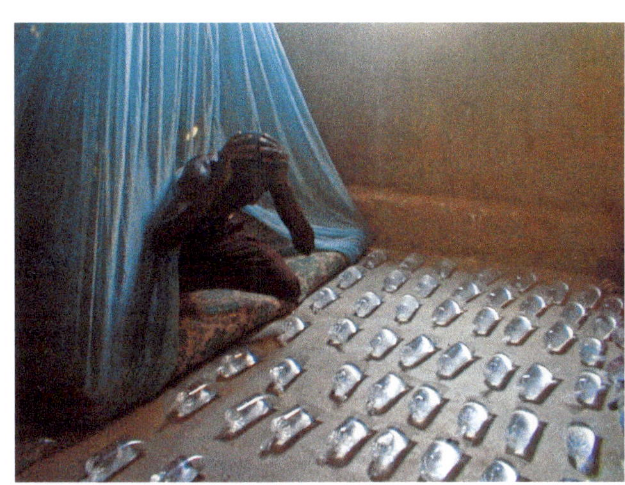

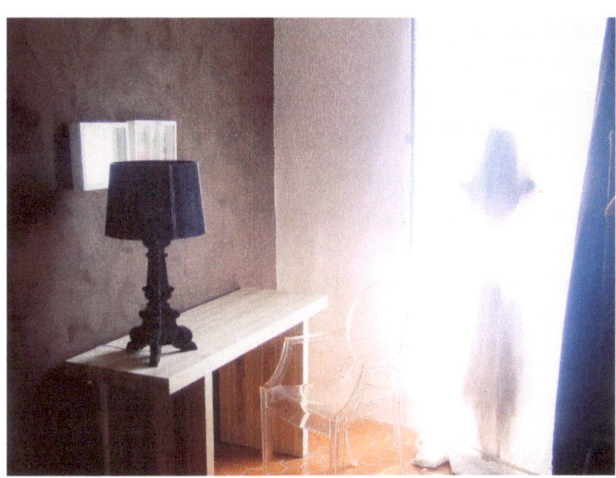

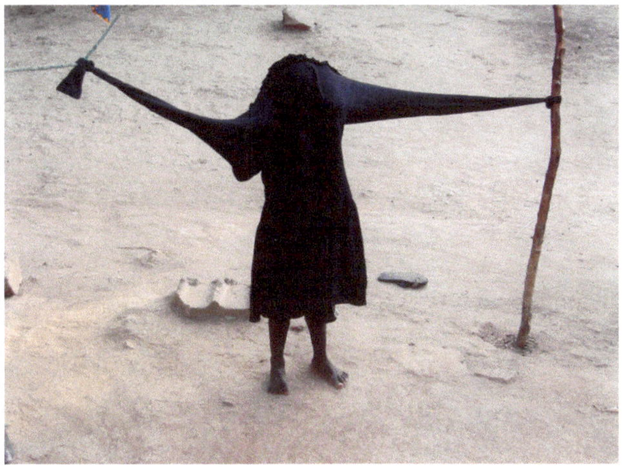

post and a clothesline. The title helps us realize it is a small child with her black dress pulled up over her head and her sleeves covering her hands, but the child looks like a *boli* figure come to life. (A boli is a monstrous, abstract [*informe*] Bamana object made from cotton wrapped around a wooden armature and applied with mud and blood that has apotropaic functions and nyama, or life-force. Camara is not of Bamana ethnicity, but boli figures are part of common knowledge in Mali.) In a 2010 series, Camara inserted photographs—usually portraits—into bags of water, commenting on photography's relationship to its past technologies and to memory, suggesting the way memory gradually disintegrates in one's mind, such as in *I Retain Our Memories* (fig 7.6). Camara's work is interesting in its variation on themes, such as interiors, the mosquito net, and water bags, that increase in conceptual interest. Camara was for years the only artist in Mali who created imaginary scenes in a knowing or lightly ironic way, and his work anticipated the art world by a decade, with its low-tech magical humor and absurdity that is transculturally effective, crossing religion with a neon heart, high design with soap opera kitsch and beautiful light. This series blends fantasy and reality through acknowledged tricks of the camera, of the pose and props, and of Photoshop; what gives it absurdity, humor, and poignancy is the combination of these elements with narrative (fig. 7.6).

Some critics might claim that Camara's difference from his cohort in terms of his training, or lack thereof, and his conceptual approach could mean that Relation is not conveyed through his work—that since his work is appreciated by an international audience, his work is therefore somehow co-opted or only a sign of market taste. But I would argue that there is no *one* right way of being in Relation or of showing Malian cultural approaches or Mande aesthetics. These are still celebratory images, not critical; they are quite different from those of other African photographers; and they convey Mande values, just in a different valence and perhaps to a different audience.

Like Camara, Fatoumata Diabaté created a series that conveys *errance* in celebrating the contemporary youth culture of her Afropolitan friends and youth. Diabaté's series *Sutigi—à nous la nuit* (*The Night Belongs to Us*, 2013) shows mostly young women, and a few men, out on the town in Bamako and other West African cities (fig. 7.7).[8] Diabaté notes,

> It brings us back to youth and its frivolity and desire of liberty. . . . I wanted to immortalize my youth through those modern outfits I like to wear at night, or even to go out in my neighborhood with friends. Then, I've started taking pictures of my friends. . . . Through this series, I try to

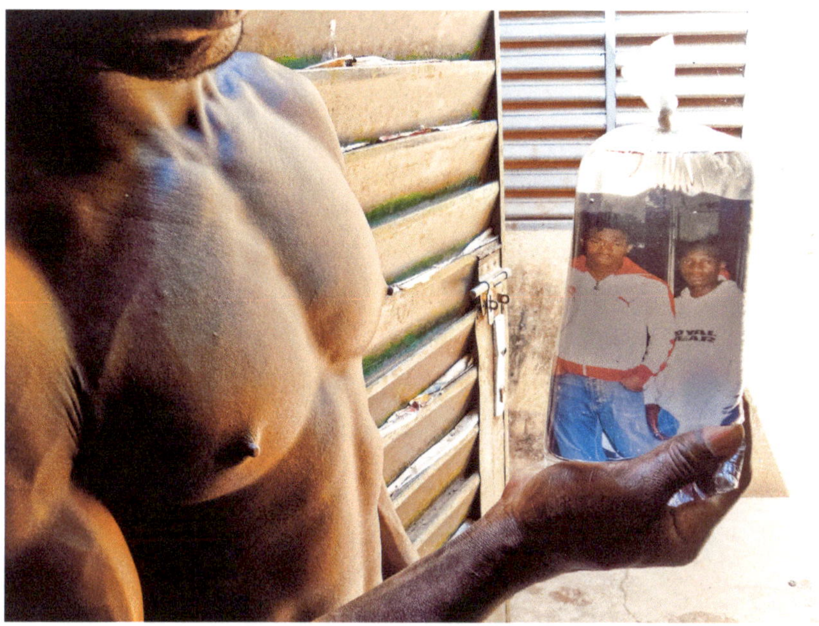

Figure 7.6. Mohamed Camara, *Je retiens nos souvenirs* (*I Retain Our Memories*), 2010. Courtesy of the artist and Galleri James Flach.

> showcase a way of living, an importance to appearance that is specific to some young people. It's like a testimony of my own time, as you can see when you pay attention to their ease in front of the camera. Us, young people, feel better at night than during the day.[9]

In this series, Diabaté makes use of dìbi, the obscurity of nighttime, to highlight the difference between the experience of contemporary youth and their elders. As Diabaté recounts, the series is clearly meant to evoke the party shots of Malick Sidibé in the 1960s in an attempt to convey glamor, excitement, frivolity, and fashion among her peers, in a society in which marriage and children—adult responsibilities—will soon prevail. Slinky dresses with untied long neck straps, a busty show of barely contained cleavage, a boyish portrait of the artist herself in a bicycle cap and a revealing, angled-cut top; these photographs by Diabaté are unabashedly sexy, which has undoubtedly been a province of photography formerly reserved for male photographers in Mali. In these photos, women take control of their own sexuality and presentation for a female photographer's gaze. These photos of women and men suggest Irigaray's Relational identity, in which women appear as women but also as they would like to be seen, in control of their

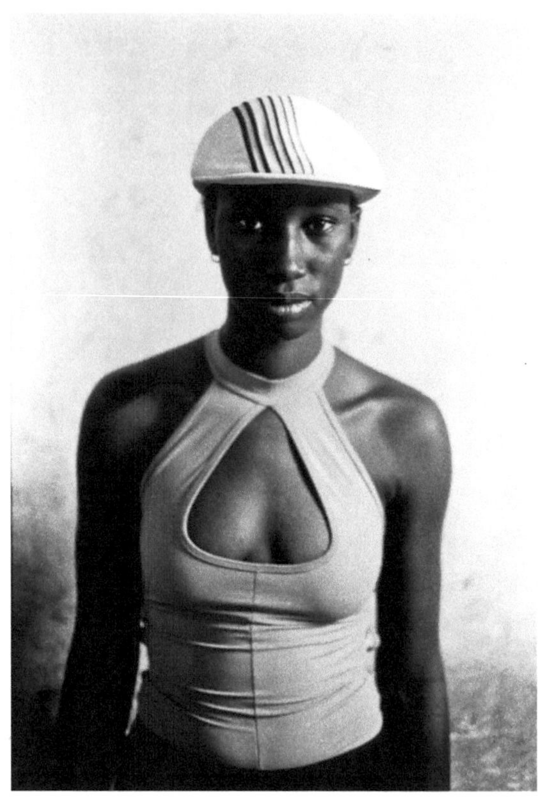

Figure 7.7. Fatoumata Diabaté, *Sutigi—à nous la nuit* (*The Night Belongs to Us*), 2012. Courtesy of the artist and Patrice Loubon Gallery.

sexuality and meeting the viewer's gaze with confidence. The series *Sutigi*, like Camara's series, also conveys Glissant's notion of errantry. Diabaté traveled through numerous countries in West Africa to capture a youthful aesthetic and spirit specific to young people. The celebration of the glamour and beauty of these youth, belied by hardships, is not superficial but a form of liberated imaginary, a future potential that offers more than women may have been able to dream of in the past: an acknowledgment of the fleetingness of time passing and a way of becoming a cosmopolitan person (fig. 7.8).

Like Camara and Diabaté, many Bamakois art photographers have continued studio portraiture's fascination with the "social body," or the way in which an individual's body in Mali is always imagined in a social context, with resulting communal implications.[10] The importance of the body, and especially of the communal body, ties this work closely to Relation and the Mande emphasis on community. Artists Mamadou Konaté (b. 1959), Emmanuel Daou, Alioune Bâ (b. 1959), and Seydou Camara exhibit a diversity of aesthetic approaches toward the theme of the body as a display of socially

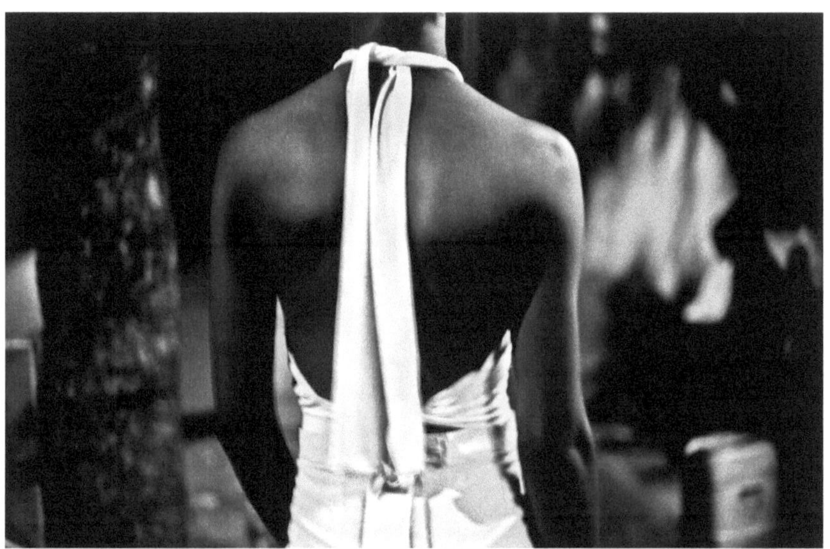

Figure 7.8. Fatoumata Diabaté, *Sutigi—à nous la nuit (The Night Belongs to Us)*, 2012. Courtesy of the artist and Patrice Loubon Gallery.

understood signs, a locus of memory, and a site of desire, but also a site of moral instruction.

Galerie Chab published a book of Mamadou Konaté's *Everyday Finery*, a series of close-ups of everyday objects, including a ring with his initials, which took on a curious beauty and significance through framing, lighting, and distortion. Another series that Konaté found successful was taken at San for a local fishing festival. These black-and-white images convey dramatic angles and moments in the festival, which is an important cultural event. More striking works by the artist feature close-ups that emphasize intimate aspects of the body. A work by Mamadou Konaté, a close-up of a Songhai woman's facial scarification, separates aesthetic signification from the body of the woman (fig. 7.9).[11] Focusing in on a particular mark of distinction, beauty, and communal belonging, Konaté's work comments on a kind of universal modernist photography with a particularity devoted to cultural belonging. The woman's identity becomes a communal mark rather than an individual face, emphasizing the focus on the body as conveyor of social cohesion.

Konaté also seems to comment on excision or scarification in a photograph of a girl with closed eyes, the shadow of a rusty razor crossing her face. He verified that it was a razor, although he did not explicitly say that this work was about excision. The girl's eyes are closed, as if she is avoiding the

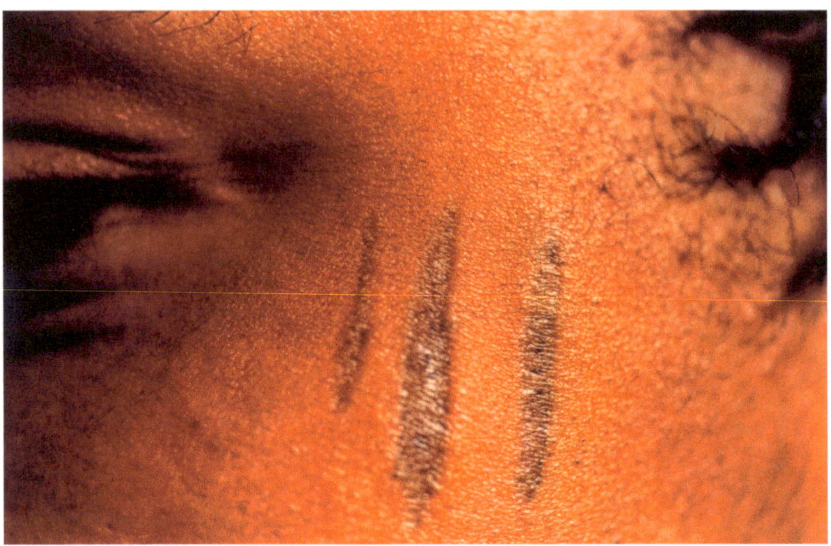

Figure 7.9. Mamadou Konaté, *Scarifications*, 1998. Courtesy of the artist.

pain or dreaming. Unlike Daou's series on the Dafing, this work seems more pointedly critical of female genital excision. Another of Konaté's curious series was for the 2011 biennale, "Sustainable World," which focused on environmental concerns. He shows children holding seedlings in red-and-white cartons, which match one boy's shorts. The children are posed and seem unaware of the camera; an older boy with red shorts sits in the center, head bowed to read a page open on his lap, presumably schoolwork, and is flanked by a younger girl and boy facing each other; yet the children do not look at each other. The series refers to the efforts against desertification—the famed "Green Wall" initiated in 2007 by the African Union to plant trees along the edge of the Sahel. Yet the curious lighting and use of the actual trees makes the series waver between symbolism and reality; it seems somewhat otherworldly. Instead of focusing on damage to the environment caused by pollution, as so many photographers did in that biennale, Konaté uses symbolism to create a sense of optimism, which resonates with the optimism of Relation. Konaté here contributes to an imaginary of the future in which today's children will better care for the earth.

In Bakary Emmanuel Daou's series on West African pictographs, the artist combines the corporeal aspect of Malian culture—using the body to convey communal signs—with an interest in the oldest written human form of communication, pictographs (fig. 7.10). In Mali, women's bodies

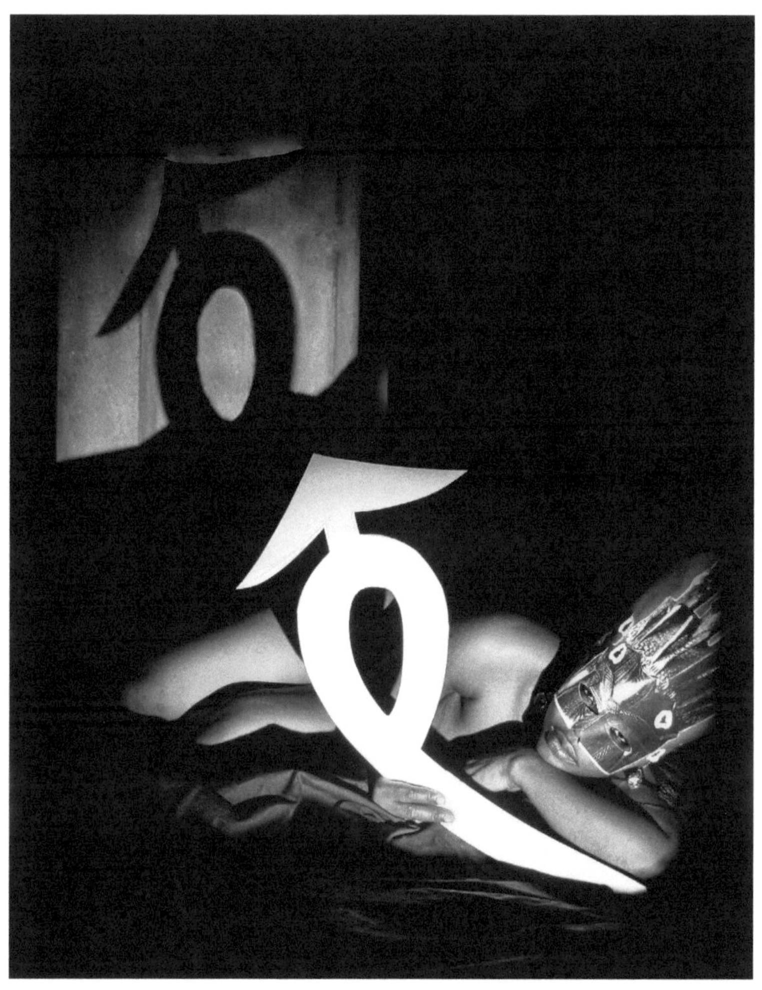

Figure 7.10. Emmanuel Daou, *La confidence—signes et symboles* (*The Secret—Signs and Symbols*), 2006. Courtesy of the artist.

traditionally bear aesthetic and communicative adornment, such as in the hairstyles worn by women in Youssouf Sogodogo's photographs. He explains that he uses the attractive female body to draw attention to the pictograph and the desire to communicate.[12] Here the voluptuous female model holds a cardboard pictograph that Daou says West Africans use in the market to communicate across linguistic barriers. This example surely bespeaks Relation, as Glissant notes that Relation is spoken multilingually.[13]

Daou's models wear obviously constructed masks that signify "Africa" to a global audience. This casual aesthetic makes clear Daou's symbolism. Like studio portraiture, in which clients appear with props not their own, the "props" Daou uses are meant to be taken not literally but symbolically. This gives the series a low-tech, postmodern look, much like the visible edges of the studio photographs printed from old negatives—edges that would have been cropped out for the clients. But Daou's masks also convey a specifically local meaning. The masks resemble N'tomo society masks, with their flat foreheads and multiple prongs. The difference is that whereas N'tomo masks were worn by boys during initiation into adulthood, here they are worn by women who symbolize the sexual possibilities of male adulthood.

Daou continued to play with the idea of symbolic masks in his eerie series *In the Time of Ebola*, which was shown in the 2015 biennale. In these photographs, medical workers in white wear strange masks mimicking animal masks or mustard gas masks, made out of a blue, spongy medical material. In one image they carry spray bottles menacingly as they advance on a man who holds his hands up. In another image, shot in front of the Independence Monument, two figures address a third lying down, who may be a corpse. Daou's commentary was on West African people's fear of medical workers during the recent Ebola outbreak; its point, according to Bisi Silva, was to help educate and warn against future outbreaks.[14] These images contain an element of opacity or mystery, and instead of documenting the horrors of the outbreak, as so many in the press did at the time, they remind viewers of the events in the hopes of encouraging a different response in the future.

In contrast to the multilingual nature of Daou's pictograph series, Alioune Bâ's series *Corps écriture* (*Body Writing*) displays phrases handwritten in French on a model's body, ranging from Malian aphorisms to the artist's own poetry (figs. 7.11 and 7.12). The very letters trace the curve of the body, bumping over lumps of bony shoulder blades ("Money can buy a bed but not sleep") and curving to embrace a pregnant belly ("Vestibule of the stars"). The theory of creolization from which Relation emerged stemmed in part from Glissant's interest in the Creole languages of the Caribbean,

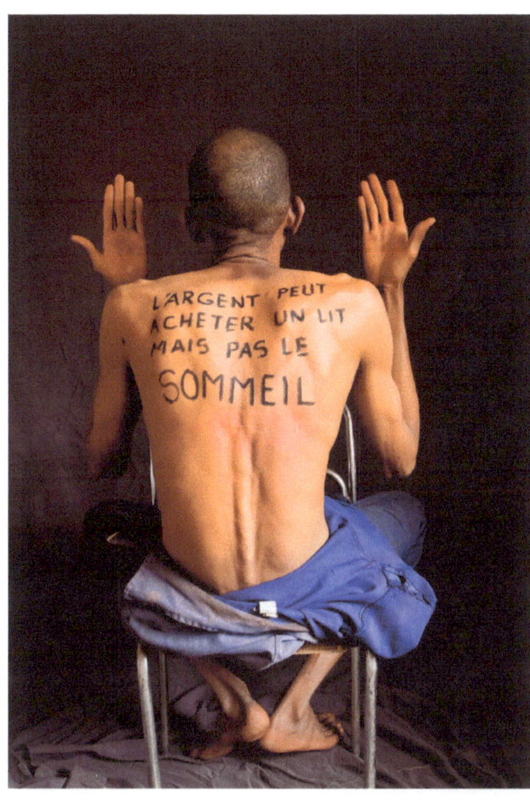

Figure 7.11. Alioune Bâ, *L'argent peut acheter un lit* (*Money Can Buy a Bed but Not Sleep*), *Corps écriture* (*Body Writing* series), 2008. Courtesy of the artist's estate and Perlman Teaching Museum, Carleton College.

Figure 7.12. Alioune Bâ, *Vestibule des étoiles* (*Vestibule of the Stars*), *Corps écriture* (*Body Writing* series), 2008. Courtesy of the artist's estate and Perlman Teaching Museum, Carleton College.

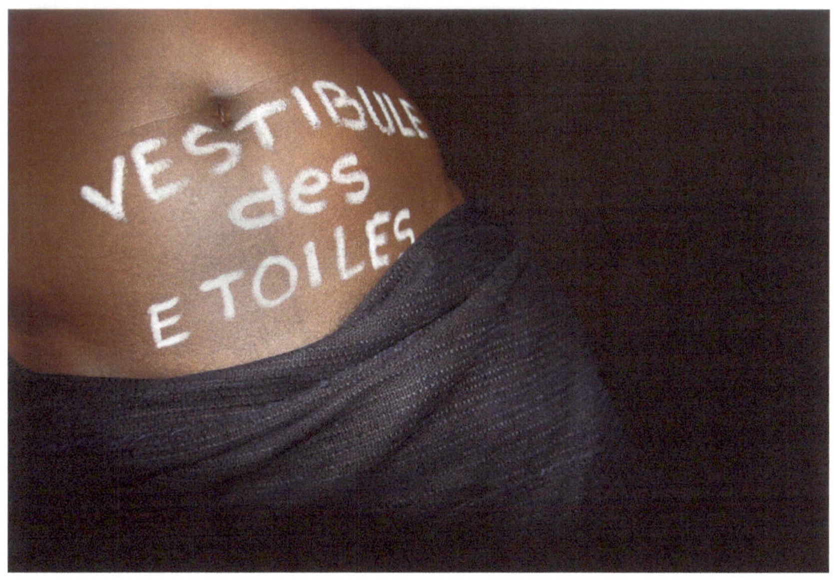

extending as a metaphor from linguistics to a broader cultural analysis. The French language was a vehicle for colonial oppression in Martinique, and the Creole language that developed among the slaves from different cultures in Africa, allowing them to communicate with each other, resisted the domination of the French language by mixing its vocabulary with African grammatical structures, creating unexpected phonetics to convey hidden meanings that evaded and resisted the oppression of the master. Unlike English, French adheres to strict vocabulary rules: the French Academy decides on whether new words and phrases, such as colloquialisms, are allowed into the language. This rigid top-down governance of new terminology surely also affects contemporary Francophone writers' sense of French as a hierarchical power structure.[15] Glissant's creolized vocabulary and poetic language, his neologisms such as "chaos-world," and his writing offered in Martiniquan speech rhythms thus subvert French domination.[16] Bâ's use of French rather than Bamanankan, the most commonly spoken language in Mali, signals the artist's desire to communicate both to a mostly male Malian audience and to the Francophone audience of the biennale. But the works also suggest the way in which the French language is imposed on the communal body and yet is shaped by it, thus using language in a way that resists domination.

A respect for irreducible difference most powerfully characterizes Relation, and this definition of Relation coincides with many aspects of contemporary photography in Mali, beginning with the respect for difference of opinion and worldview, which is a highly valued quality. For example, when I asked photographers whether there is such a thing as "Malian photography," all of them responded with a bemused negative, and it was reiterated that each artist has his or her own creative vision. The artists implied that it would be disrespectful to place limitations on a photographer's vision by fitting his or her work into a national or cultural mold. The photographer's view that one individual's way of understanding the world may not correlate with the next individual's worldview displays a fundamental respect for difference, and indeed is consistently listed as characteristic of a Malian attitude. This attitude was striking, given the smallness of the art photography community and the singular nature of its influences (Keïta's and Sidibé's studio photographs).[17]

Bâ, who grew up speaking French, asserts that he feels he belongs to two cultures—both Mali and France. He uses photography to explain each culture to the other, and particularly to show France all of the wonderful aspects of Mali (and hence Africa) that they might not otherwise see. His

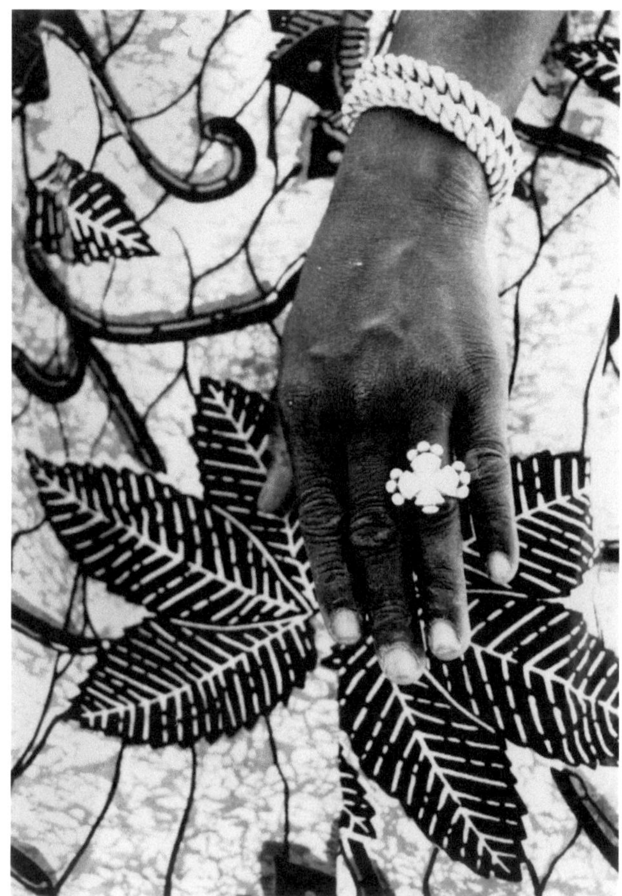

Figure 7.13. Alioune Bâ, Untitled (*Tégé-Mains* [*Hands*]), 1997. Courtesy of the artist's estate.

series of hands shows a hennaed hand with a braceleted wrist, the beautiful lace of a sleeve against a hand, and a hand with a ring against the flattened patterned backdrop of a woman's dress. The ring functions as a metonymically displaced center of the patterned flower (fig. 7.13). The use of close-up and cropping makes these works modernist in vein, yet also Malian in their aesthetic and indexical focus on clothing, henna, and jewelry.

Similarly, a sympathetic, nonreductive acknowledgment of difference—the irreducible difference of Relation that "respects the particular qualities of the community in question"—is seen in *Bibiana*, a series of portraits of people with albinism by the younger photographer Seydou Camara.[18] Camara's decision to portray albinos as ordinary people has an important social purpose, conveying a respect for difference that is communally inclusive. His portraits remain connected to the individuality of West African studio portraiture in their subjects' direct gaze and engagement with the viewer, their quotidian qualities and posed but unstudied thoughtfulness. Camara shows an unwillingness to patronize his subjects; he does not universalize or exoticize albinism.[19] Instead, the series acknowledges the individuality and unique appearance of each human being, which is a key aspect of Relation.

Another striking series by Seydou Camara, which includes aspects of art and reportage, focuses on the manuscripts of Timbuktu. This series was commissioned when restorers were working on the Timbuktu manuscripts, and became even more significant after the coup, when thousands of manuscripts were spirited out of the library in Timbuktu and removed to safety, away from the religious extremists destroying sacred heritages and histories. The series was shown in the 2015 biennale. In one striking photograph, pages of a book curl up and rise out of the darkness. They are placed on a wood block or a saddle; it's hard to tell. The support on which they lie is obscured by darkness, but small tassels shine faintly in the gloom. The top page is rendered illegible in its tight writing and its curled form, reminiscent almost of a parchment scroll instead of the vellum it likely is. Here the word is light and light is the word. The lit page emerging from darkness suggests knowledge saved from extremist impulses and religion gone awry; the page itself remains opaque and mysterious in its meaning. This work, Camara's most haunting photograph, signals the extreme danger to an ancient African heritage, when Timbuktu was a place of revered education, power, and peace, of tolerance. From another photograph we become aware of the camera's viewpoint. The pages take center place, blurring our vision, as the edges of the pages, thin as grass blades, become thickened into visual obstructions. The frame becomes the view. Photography reminds us of itself; the books remind us of how the manuscripts enclose information, yet keep their secrets for only those knowledgeable enough to understand. The pages look like shiny feathers; they are bluish gray with age. In the back we see a crisp blue tile. The modern grid contrasts with the weighty presence of the past, its texture and its nature. These photographs beautifully capture the importance of this treasured Malian heritage while allowing viewers both to glimpse the historical heritage, yet keep its real sense of opacity in that the volumes are complex and contain much hidden knowledge.

Several years older than Seydou Camara, the photographer Harandane Dicko, who was a colleague of Fatoumata Diabaté's at the CFP, has been shown in significant exhibitions in Mali and abroad. Éditions de l'Œil has published a chapbook on his mosquito net series, and an image was included in Erin Haney's survey book *Photography and Africa*.[20] He also participated in several biennales and in a collaborative project between the British Museum and Bamakois photographers. (Bâ was the previous photographer collaborating with the British Museum.) Dicko's mosquito net series involved a sociocritical aspect, where he worked with a French photographer after learning from him in a workshop, and traveled through the country photographing people with mosquito nets, to raise awareness of using them in order to avoid malaria and other mosquito-borne illnesses. While these black-and-white photos are playful, they speak to important issues. Another series that builds on the portrait tradition was made by photographing people in the rearview mirror of his motorbike while riding through West African cities. These images both speak to the interest in the social body and still consider the human figure in its urban, social context; similarly, they partake in the errance of Camara's and Diabaté's travels, and they speak in a visual language of repetition and variation through the visual use of the motorbike's lens, which gives them round or rectangular frames within the photograph and create dìbi, or blurriness and obscurity, by capturing the different valences within the mirror and outside the frame.

While the National Museum photographers are significant, their approach also speaks to a broader interest in what I call "cultural photography" promulgated by the photography schools, CFP, and Promo-femme. This genre of photography emphasizes the culturally distinctive aspects of Malian culture, both for local interest as seen in photojournalism and individual photographers' projects, and for external publication and interests. Amadou Keïta was a photographer who in 2006 had not yet exhibited in a biennial, but he was ambitious and since then has participated in several. While he showed many photographs, including studio portraits, three series stood out for their striking aesthetics, their subject matter, and their originality. They convey Relation through a mixture of emphasis on Mande culture and internationally influenced aesthetics.

One that was especially striking shows a woman painting her house (fig. 7.14). She is wearing a light-colored head wrap and steadies herself against the pale wall with her left hand above her head, while her right hand makes the finger marks. Within the dark design of radiating finger marks, her lighter hand with gleaming fingers is barely visible. Another from the same series shows a steer with long horns standing before the house on which the woman paints. You can see the checkered marks she has created and her head, white before the finger marks, which crown and ring her head. This photograph is extremely striking, perhaps because information on this type

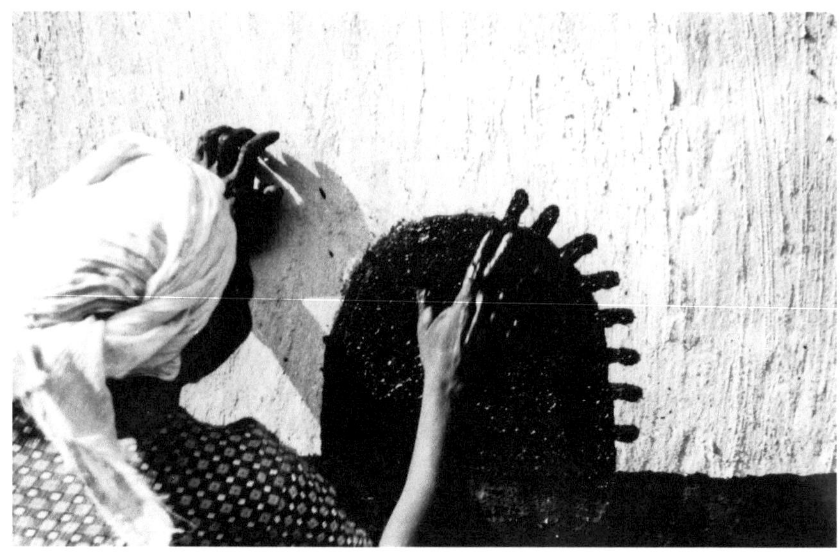

Figure 7.14. Amadou Keïta, Untitled, 2005.
Courtesy of the artist.

of wall painting seems completely lacking, but also because of the photographer's eye in capturing the metonymy of the woman painting on the wall; the play of light and shadow; the formal presence; and the wall's texture, which is reiterated sideways in the folds of the woman's head wrap, whose asymmetry becomes an important formal element in its embellishment or decoration. The woman's work is half finished, in process. Her fingers are visible against the blackness of her painting by the sheer gloppy shininess of the paint itself. This is modernist photography's aesthetics, but given over to the process of a practice that is so deeply rural and feminine that there is *no research on the subject*; yet Keïta made a photograph of it that glamorized and heroicized this action in black-and-white. Even the sunlight on her back and the shadow her head wrap casts on her shoulder, the obscure darkness of her face creates an image that resonates with opacity against the clarity, and the rough hot texture of the wall.

A series on women making pottery was shot as a possible financial opportunity connected to a European patron interested in pottery as tourism. Pottery is made by women of the *jeli* caste. These photographs have a modernist aesthetic, using close-up, cropping, and pattern to become formal plays of repetition and geometric pattern, but they always remain recognizable as cultural studies of the women's work. The pots gleam. A third series also showed Amadou Keïta's modernist interests in how a close-up or a telephoto lens can stretch space and features into abstraction, which was unusual among the photographers in 2006, as was his willingness to work in color. He took several photographs of boats on the Niger River, and the rich brown earth in contrast to the greenish blue of the water turned into an abstraction. At the time, color had been used successfully only by Mohamed Camara, and the other photographers dismissed his aesthetic and his process. In the past decade, however, with digital advancements, it has become as ubiquitous as black-and-white.

Art photographs are also sold as postcards in the National Museum gift shop and in the expensive hotels. These contrast with tourist postcards of women in "traditional" clothing, in a dance or performance, with a line of women dressed all the same, without tops and barefoot, wearing beads and long strip skirts. One art postcard by Alioune Bâ shows a woman's hand with a ring resting on a slim waist, where modernist close-up and cropping are used to show a silvery pattern a little bit like snakeskin and the woman's hand with pointy fingernails.[21] Mamadou Konaté's scarification postcard and a postcard of a girl's hairstyle by Youssouf Sogodogo are also available.

Django Cissé, called the "postcard photographer" of Bamako, was one of the cofounders of the biennale. At that time he was highly successful in his practice, making images not only for postcards but also on government-issued postage stamps. Thus the biennale was, from the beginning, composed of a variety of attitudes toward photography, acknowledging the importance of Malian cultures to Malians, the importance of the foreigner's touristic view of Mali's cultures, and photography's vital, insidious role in tourism. Christraud Geary and others have analyzed the way that African "image worlds" were circulated through European postcard views taken by colonial photographers.

Cissé's postcards document the visual culture that tourists want to see, such as a young girl in traditional Fulani dress and adornment, with giant gold earrings and dark-inked tattoos around her mouth, wearing bogolan cloth and balancing a large white bowl on her head. The postcard is titled *Young Milk Seller* (fig. 7.15). In this sense of presenting "types," Cissé's postcards follow the lineage of postcards sold by Simon Fortier and other French image-makers in the late nineteenth and early twentieth centuries.[22] However, his postcards still differ from those anthropological types in small but noticeable ways, which suggest a Mande aesthetic. For example, many of the views of types are slightly off-center, such as the milk seller, and she looks a little bit like she's moving. She also engages the viewer directly, head-on,

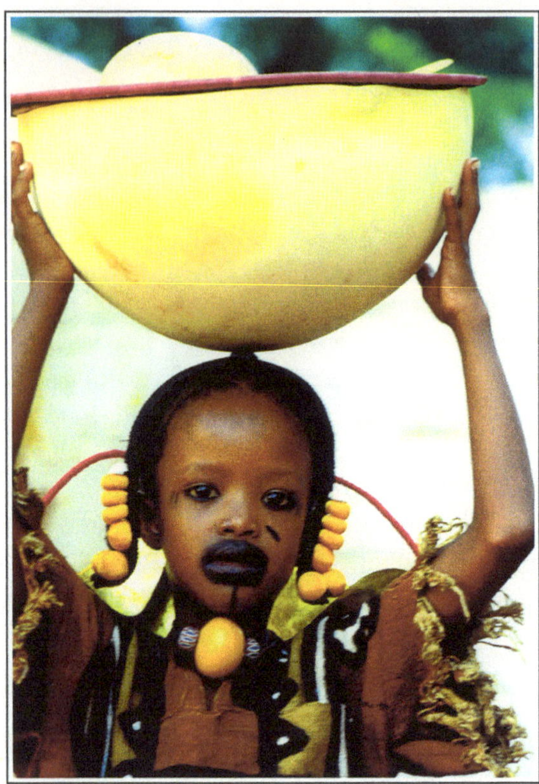

Figure 7.15. Django Cissé, *Young Milk Seller*, ca. 2004. Courtesy of the artist.

although presumably he would have had to bend down to get a picture of her head on the same level as the viewer. His photos suggest a visual interest in asymmetry, and while the subjects' pictures are anonymous and stereotyped, they often look relaxed and comfortable in the photographer's presence. His postcards often capture scenes that would not likely appear in a European photographer's "touristic" lens, such as an older man and woman sitting together chatting on a doorstep. In stark contrast, available for sale at the postcard office in 2005–2006 were aerial photographs of villages or the river taken by a French photographer, which support Christopher Pinney's assertion that the colonial (or neocolonial) gaze attempts to spatially flatten and control its subject.[23]

Four collages in the tourist office in Bamako that use photographs by Cissé especially capture the Mande aesthetic of repetition and variation. Each is composed of a view that is then montaged with other views, and these montages are repeated horizontally four or five times. For example, in one, Dogon masqueraders appear on cliffs in the Bandiagara escarpment, but are montaged with a view of pirogues on the river. These images highlight the most dramatic elements of Malian visual culture from a tourist's point of view; the repetition makes them seem endless, as if they exist through time. Many of Cissé's photographs were included in the tourist office's book titled *Mali: An Authentic Africa*. These include each geographic tourist location, but retain a sense of Cissé's aesthetic, seen in his inclusion of aspects of Mali that a French photographer would likely not capture. Overall, though, these tourist photographs signal "Malianness" within a restricted vision of what encapsulates "authentic" Mali, which means essentially unmodernized, except in Bamako, which in the book is celebrated for its modern look. The complicated relationship of cultural festivals revived by the socialist dictatorship in the 1960s is elided here, as is the touristic interest in eliding differences between dances for tourists and formerly ritualistic, politically and religiously significant dances. That being said, tourism is an important economy in Mali and has to some extent preserved aspects of traditional dances and performances as a living force, while changing their context.[24]

This genre of cultural photography is exemplified in the works of numerous photographers. Amadou Keïta's series on women potters behaves according to a museum's logic but was shot at the behest of a potential European customer. Django Cissé is the photographer of postcards and of the fascinating photo-collage that resides in Bamako's city tourist office, which is, literally, tourist art. Mamadou Konaté's fishing series at San is sold as fine art and was exhibited in a biennale. As Alioune Bâ told the visiting French photography student to go to cultural festivals and to travel around Mali while photographing, and to talk to people; this is the basis for a photographic education in Mali. Bâ emphasizes the importance of knowing what one is photographing. This was also Françoise Huguier's approach when she made her series based on Leiris's Dakar-Djibouti trip; it is also part of the CFP training, resulting in Fatoumata Diabaté's series on the Tuareg, and it is what the museum photographers do as part of their jobs. Such an "ethnographic" approach stems from Mali's rich cultural history. Before the advent of the biennale, Cissé was already making a living selling postcards based on Mali's cultural treasures. While this could be seen as tourist photography, it is more complicated than that, since Mali has pride in its own cultural forms—so this form of photography, though it may to some extent stem from colonial interests and have an ethnographic and touristic component, is also creolized, like the National Museum photographers' works, through indigenous concerns.

While Malian cultural values and historical circumstances enable the possibilities of Relation, the medium of photography, specifically used to create art, enables the Bamakois artists to fully embody a poetics of Relation. The chaos of the world is ordered and disordered by this strange replication of itself into images, into an image-world. Photography, in its wild multiplicity, instantaneity, and indexicality could be seen as Glissant's écho-monde, the resonance of things among things, a visual echo of the surface appearances of the world. Glissant explains that écho-monde is a culture. For Glissant the natural and the cultural are intertwined and inseparable; there is no distinct biology separate from human action. Photography in Mali particularly emphasizes this interconnection in its almost constant focus on the human body, which is culturally adorned and modified in a variety of ways.

Here Relation's affinity with the peculiar medium of photography becomes clear. As "Relation is movement,"[25] so are photographs movement: as reproducible slivers of a particular time and place, they move through history. Now more than ever before they appear almost everywhere, updating us constantly on what the world is doing. Glissant was prescient when he said, "Let us repeat this, chaotically: Relation neither relays nor links afferents that can be assimilated or allied only in their principle, for the simple reason that it always differentiates among them concretely and diverts them from the totalitarian—because its work always changes all the elements composing it, and, consequently, the resulting relationship, which then changes them all over again."[26] An afferent is a nerve carrying a message toward the central nervous system. This could also describe photography, which is always concretely differentiated by a second or split second of time. Yet photography as a medium avoids the totalitarian—there is no *photograph* that can represent all photographs, or that can stand in for photography as a generality. As Roland Barthes says, a photograph is never of itself—it is always of its referent: "The Photograph belongs to that class of laminated objects whose two leaves cannot be separated without destroying them both: the windowpane and the landscape, and why not: Good and Evil, desire and its object: dualities we can conceive but not perceive (I didn't yet know that this stubbornness of the Referent in always being there would produce the essence I was looking for)."[27] As photography becomes increasingly digitized, its movement becomes ever more noticeable. The reproducibility of the same image (even though it always involves a tiny bit of digital information loss) contributes to photography's circulation in Relation. The reproducibility of photographs is what makes it the medium of Relation par excellence.

Celia M. Britton writes, "Relation is, among other things, a principle of narration: what is 'related' is what is *told*. And it is also what is *relayed* from one person to another, forming a chain or network of narrative 'relations.'"[28] In the era of the signaletic, according to Mette Sandbye, photography relays narrative instantly, and in ways that are manifold in meaning, so that the recipient cannot necessarily know what the images mean.[29] They are usually accompanied by text for clarification: social media is the era of the immediate postcard to no one and everyone at the same time. As Britton explains, "Relayed language is a strategy of diversity . . . [that] resist[s] the oppressively singular authority of what Mikhail Bakhtin calls the 'monologic text,' [to] put in its place a plural text made up of a number of different contributions or versions, in which no one person has control of the whole story."[30] This description sounds exactly like photography in its varied versions that no one can completely control.

Britton also notes that Relation is against the idea that individuals are the origin of their language. Relayed language is not an inherent and essential part of identity; it is collectively shared and takes on meaning only through others, through which it also changes: "Relayed language implies, in contrast, that language is passed around a number of subjects and also that there are 'relays' intervening between subject and language."[31] In Britton's terms, then, photography can be understood as a relayed language, in that photographs, while looking the same, can have vastly different meanings for different viewers, as Malian photographs do.[32]

This is not to say that *all* photography is necessarily in Relation. But photography has the potential to be a *relayed language*. The internet drastically changes the opportunities for Malian images to be seen, especially for a photographer like Amadou Keïta, and also has been instrumental in enabling exhibitions to be curated across distances and also across economic differences. *Snap Judgments* at the International Center of Photography printed in high quality a number of works by African photographers who could not necessarily afford it, and this was done in *Photographing the Social Body* at Carleton College as well. The internet helps not only with the coordination of the biennale and the cost of putting it on, but also in enabling exposure of the works, especially in photography (which is not as much the case with painting, drawing, sculpture, or installation, in which the viewer's presence of the original objects is needed or at least desired). The internet enables interested people to learn about the biennale and follow it online, and the web also offers new platforms and older issues of digitized magazines.

Malian art photographers take an aesthetic approach to representing the world: they portray the "real" in utilizing the indexical nature of photography (a photograph is always of someone or something that exists in the world), but combine photography's inherent documentation with their creative imaginations. As the Bamako artists use photography to artistically convey its most beloved use—that of representing the human body, the site of individual and communal identity—they pay homage to the studio tradition that opened the way for their art. This medium-specific approach is consistent with Glissant's own novels, which draw on the historical situation of Martinique and France to convey stories of his own imagination, yet thematically speak to human experience. He insists on the connection between knowledge and poetics, on the importance of imagination intertwined with history, stating: "The highest point of knowledge is always a poetics."[33]

Mali is now struggling with the violent after-effects of the coup that ended two decades of peaceful democracy in 2012. Although the Rencontres returned in 2015, society is still affected by the attempted secession of the North and its unfortunate collaborations with jihadist terrorist elements. Through their varied emphases on social interactions, the tolerance and celebration of difference, the importance given to personal and national memory, and the traditional values of moral didacticism, the photographs discussed here commemorate the period of peaceful democracy that ushered in the biennale itself. Above all, the poetics of these photographs embody Relation in their "lightness of vision," offering us, their viewers, the opportunity to see another part of the world in its particularity, its irreducibly human difference.[34] These photographs bring us into Relation, offering a chance to change our identities and thus, perhaps, the world.

Conclusion

Embodying Relation describes and theorizes the rise of an art photography movement in Bamako since the early 1990s. Glissant's concept of Relation provides an alternative approach to understanding the dynamics of exchange between the local and global circumstances of the emergence of art photography and its subsequent growth within the city. The entrance of Keïta's and Sidibé's portraits into the global art world and the inauguration of the biennale resulted in diverse effects. Through Glissantian neologisms of opacity, creolization, errantry, and écho-monde in connection with Mande and Malian aesthetic, social, and cultural tropes, this book considers circumstances that encompass the shift in Keïta's and Sidibé's postcelebrity work, as each photographer returned to a practice that he had long given up; the effect on African and American artists of the Keïta or Sidibé studio portrait "look"; the complex and changing relationship of the biennale to its Malian constituents; the blossoming of art world institutions and professions in Bamako; the archival projects of the National Museum photographers emphasizing cultural and historical preservation in a museological manner; interventions on behalf of youth through the medium of photography; the professionalization of women photographers; the meteoric rise of Mohamed Camara's playful and pensive gambits; and the more measured but culturally substantive ascendance of Fatoumata Diabaté's attentive projects, as well as other Malian photographs that continue an emphasis on the communal social body underlying art photography stemming from the older portrait tradition.

Photography in Mali has always been imbricated in the city's social and cultural history. The medium was invented in France and England and introduced to the Sudan by the French military and missionaries as a blatant tool of subjugation, and as an aid to colonization and religious conversion. When Malian studio photographers took up the medium in the 1930s, they instead emphasized the social and performative aspects of photography. The performance of posing for a studio photograph, and the subsequent print's circulation among family and friends, which contributes to the creation of social capital, or a sense of badenya community, shows that studio photography is embedded in social processes, conveying modern Mande aesthetics and values under French colonial rule. Mande aesthetic values permeate colonial-era studio portraits, giving a visual cultural force to the politics of decolonization. Black diaspora aesthetics come into play after independence, as clients look beyond Mali's borders for inspiration in both fashion and worldview.

The shift to art photography out of studio portraiture's rise to international fame means that international influences on artistic photography are more present than ever, such that the photographic projects examined here convey Malian social values and Mande aesthetics in a potential process of Relation. The art photographers working in Bamako operate within a highly postcolonial society and are affected by the neocolonial structure of the biennale, yet their art photographs celebrate contemporary culture and privilege Malian viewers and Mande aesthetics. Their circumstances and projects—the *processes* they create and in which they participate—have origins arising from various intersecting and overlapping histories: of photography in Mali, of colonialism, of tourist art, of archiving practices of traditional art, of modern art. All of these impulses have coalesced in the new institution of the Bamako Biennale. Through careful examination of the specific forms, processes, and circumstances of various photographic projects, I show how Glissant's poetics of Relation manifests in complex and specific ways.

The professionalization of female photographers is the most dramatic change that the coming of the biennale and the art photography movement have created. The efforts of Aminata Bagayoko and her students to change the gender demographic in photography has had important ramifications for the Bamakois community, even as it reflects the upheavals that democracy has created in society. These women photographers are living the effects of positive changes in society and are furthering those changes with their choices and determination. In this case, both local and foreign institutions, spearheaded by such women as Bagayoko and Huguier, supporting such determined photographers as Fatoumata Diabaté, are beneficial in encouraging gender equality among photographers, and photography by women provides for new perspectives, subjects, and ways of creating Relation.

But as women enter the profession and as Mali struggles politically, the future of the art photography movement and of the Bamako Encounters is at stake. Both are subject to tenuous political conditions, whether local or global, and also to the changes that photography undergoes as digital images and cell phone pictures become ever more present. Will a resolution eventually be worked out between the biennale and its Malian hosts? A recorded conversation printed in the 2015 biennale catalog among CAMM's director Abdoulaye Konaté, the National Museum director Samuel Sidibé, and the MAP director Moussa Konaté shows Abdoulaye Konaté pressing hard for more influence and responsibility, as Sidibé and Moussa Konaté criticize the government's administration. Until art photography becomes as culturally meaningful for the general public as studio portraiture once was—which seems possibly only with a shift to Malian themes possibly enabled by the digital revolution—the local significance of the biennale seems likely to be restricted to a small but powerfully committed number of individuals, while its pan-African importance will likely continue apace. Excitingly, in 2019, the French ceded administrative and curatorial control of the Biennale to the Malian state, while providing half of the financial support.

As ubiquitous digitization changes photographic practices across the world, from an emphasis on unique images to an immediate presentness, or what Mette Sandbye calls the "signaletic" function of photography, all of these projects may recede into an atemporal present in which the overwhelming image flow knows no bounds, leaving only scattered traces.[1] This makes it even more important for this fragile history to be documented, enticing viewers especially to notice the Mande aesthetics and values that permeate the Malian art photography movement and its institutions.

The art photography movement in Bamako disrupts normative readings of global contemporary art with a locally inflected aesthetic understanding that still operates with opacity in the larger art world. Glissant's emphasis on the fluidity and ever-changing nature of Relation is crucial to understanding art in a way that is less subject to art market fluctuations and more concerned with the imaginaries such photographs might provide. Many scholars of the contemporary African art world do not appreciate the biennale because of its neocolonial aura; scholars also deride the importance of Keïta and Sidibé, claiming that other West African photographers were equally salient. But the complexity of biennale effects, and the emergence of Keïta's and Sidibé's works *as contemporary art* in global art exhibitions, have given rise to a local art movement that is rhizomatic and in constant exchange with foreign influences, while drawing on Mali's illustrious cultural heritage. Glissant's notion of Relation offers a theoretical apparatus for understanding the relationship between the local and the global as mutually informing the other and creolizing each other on the level of aesthetics. Thus Malian art photographs embody a unique culture in dialogue—in Relation—with the world.

Glissant asserts that we can measure what kind of overturnings will be necessary in our sensibilities by changing our poetics.[2] In the appreciation of difference and in seeking alternatives to the incessant, corporatizing pressures of globalization, in Mali's hope for moving beyond its impoverished circumstances, civil strife, and corrupt government, the modest yet potent visions of Malian art photographers celebrate their preservation of culture and heritage through new aesthetic forms, conveying optimism for the future through their Mande aesthetics and their Relational imaginaries.

Notes

Introduction

Epigraph: Édouard Glissant, *Poetics of Relation*, trans. Betsy Wing (Ann Arbor: University of Michigan Press, 1990), 20.

1 "La série *Sutigi* Renvoie au bel âge de la jeunesse caractérisée par l'insouciance et le désir de liberté." Fatoumata Diabaté, "*Sutigi: À nous la nuit,*" *Afrique en visu,* June 21, 2014, http://www.afriqueinvisu.org/sutiki-a-nous-la-nuit,942.html.

2 See Érika Nimis, "Yoruba Studio Photographers in Francophone West Africa," in *Portraiture and Photography in Africa,* ed. John Peffer and Elisabeth L. Cameron (Bloomington: Indiana University Press, 2013), 107.

3 Mande cultures make up over half of Mali's population and are especially concentrated in Bamako and the southern region of Mali. "Mande" is a term used to designate a number of different ethnic groups, including the many Bamana people. I do not use "Mande" interchangeably with "Mali," but the Mande groups do dominate the culture and languages of the southern region of Mali and especially of Bamako, although the nation is a mosaic of ethnicities and the city draws people from across the country.

4 See Barbara G. Hoffman, "Secrets and Lies: Context, Meaning, and Agency in Mande," *Cahiers d'Études Africaines* 38, no. 149 (1998).

5 In fact, Keïta and Sidibé were just two of many studio photographers working across West Africa.

6 Originally titled "Rencontres de la Photographie Africaine," the biennale has occurred every two years, with two exceptions—a three-year gap between 1998 and 2001, and a four-year gap between 2011 and 2015 because of the 2012 coup.

7 Mali's first democratically elected president, Alpha Oumar Konaré, had a doctorate in history and especially supported the biennale.

8 That trend is now disintegrating as a shift to digital makes high-quality color as accessible as black-and-white, and as black-and-white film becomes increasingly unavailable.

9 I use the term "global conceptualism" to encompass "idea-based art" that, while having a material and formal meaning, draws on a history of concerns that stem from Duchamp's readymades to Warhol's Brillo boxes to contemporary installation, video, and mixed-media art. See Alexander Alberro and Blake Stimson, eds., *Conceptual Art: A Critical Anthology* (Cambridge, MA: MIT Press, 1999); and Jane Farver et al., *Global Conceptualism: Points of Origin, 1950–1980s* (New York: Queens Museum of Art, 1999).

10 See Candace M. Keller, "Visual Griots: Identity, Aesthetics, and the Social Roles of Portrait Photographers in Mali," in Peffer and Cameron, *Portraiture and Photography in Africa*. Mande incorporates the Bamana as well as numerous other ethnic groups, including Dyula, Malinke, Somono, Bozo, and Wasuluka.

11 Manthia Diawara, "Talk of the Town: Seydou Keïta," in *Reading the Contemporary: African Art from Theory to the Marketplace*, ed. Olu Oguibe and Okwui Enwezor, 236–242 (Cambridge, MA: MIT Press, 1999).

12 Celia M. Britton, *Édouard Glissant and Postcolonial Theory: Strategies of Language and Resistance* (Charlottesville: University Press of Virginia, 1999), 14.

13 See Homi Bhabha, "Of Mimicry and Man: The Ambivalence of Colonial Discourse," *October* 28 (Spring 1984), and *The Location of Culture* (London: Routledge, 1994). See also Gayatri Spivak, *A Critique of Postcolonial Reason: Toward a History of the Vanishing Present* (Cambridge, MA: Harvard University Press, 1999).

14 This interdisciplinary aspect of being a literary writer and a philosopher connects to Négritude, which as a philosophy grew out of poetry; to African heritage, in that oral traditions of poetry include philosophy; and to French culture, in such examples as Simone de Beauvoir, Simone Weil, Jean-Paul Sartre, and Albert Camus.

15 Fanon traveled to Mali and met President Modibo Keïta. He was impressed by histories of the great empires, including the Mali Empire. Frantz Fanon, *Black Skin, White Masks*, trans. Charles Lamm Markman (New York: Grove, 1967); Frantz Fanon, *Studies in a Dying Colonialism*, trans. Haakon Chevalier (London: Earthscan, 1959).

16 Younger Afro-Francophone philosophers include Achille Mbembe, Felwine Sarr, Jean Godofroy Bidima, and Seloua Luste Boulbina.

17 See, for example, Ulrich Loock, "Opacity," *Frieze*, November 7, 2012, https://frieze.com/article/opacity; Teju Cole, "A True Picture of Black Skin," *New York*

Times, February 18, 2015, https://www.nytimes.com/2015/02/22/magazine/a-true-picture-of-black-skin.html.

18 Édouard Glissant and Hans Ulrich Obrist, *100 Notes–100 Thoughts / 100 Notizen–100 Gedanken*, dOCUMENTA (13) (Ostfildern, Germany: Hatje Canz, 2012), 5.

19 See agnès b., *Collection agnès b.*, text by Édouard Glissant and Felix Hoffmann (Zurich: JRP/Ringier, 2016).

20 Césaire was first a student and then a teacher at the same high school in Martinique that Glissant and Fanon attended in the 1930s, although he was not Glissant's teacher. Both Césaire and Glissant incorporate new ways of thinking about and celebrating identity in relation to African heritage. Glissant differs from Césaire in the diminished importance of Africa, and in embracing a postmodern sense of constant exchange as constitutive of identity. See John E. Drabinski, "Aesthetics and the Abyss: Between Césaire and Lamming," in *Theorizing Glissant: Sites and Citations*, ed. John E. Drabinski and Marisa Parham (London: Rowman, 2015).

21 Édouard Glissant, *Philosophie de la Relation* (Paris: Éditions Gallimard, 2009), 66; translated and quoted by Michael Wiedorn in his article "Glissant's *Philosophie de la Relation*: 'I have spoken the chaos of writing in the ardor of the poem,'" *Callaloo* 36, no. 4 (Fall 2013): 903.

22 J. Michael Dash, *Édouard Glissant* (New York: Cambridge University Press, 1995), 145, 158.

23 "[*Relation*] takes notions of *errance*, *métissage* and creolisation to a new global level" (Dash, *Édouard Glissant*, 179). H. Adlai Murdoch writes, "Indeed, the Caribbean arguably provides the engendering locus of Glissant's key principles of *Relation*, creolization, and opacity." H. Adlai Murdoch, "Édouard Glissant's Creolized World Vision: From Resistance and *Relation* to *Opacité*," *Callaloo* 36, no. 4 (Fall 2013): 877.

24 Glissant, *Poetics of Relation*, 5.

25 Glissant, *Poetics of Relation*, 8.

26 Celia M. Britton, "Globalization and Political Action in the Work of Édouard Glissant," *Small Axe 30* 13, no. 3 (2009): 9.

27 Glissant, *Poetics of Relation*, 58. *Relation* is not specific to race, in contrast to Négritude.

28 The great empires that spread throughout the region in the middle ages created cultural continuity, which was ruptured by the transatlantic slave trade, fueling intra African slavery.

29 Manthia Diawara's film *Édouard Glissant: One World in Relation* (K'a Yéléma Productions, 2009) was screened at Cornell University in 2010, followed by a panel discussion with Glissant, Diawara, and art historian Salah Hassan; at the annual meeting of the African Studies Association in 2013, in Baltimore; and at the Pérez Art Museum Miami, October 1, 2015, with a discussion by Diawara. "Art Talk: Manthia Diawara on 'Poetics of Relation'" (video), Pérez Art Museum Miami, posted November 9, 2015, http://www.pamm.org/blog-tags/edouard

-glissant. *One World in Relation* was included in the 2015 exhibition *Capital: Debt—Territory—Utopia* at the Hamburger Bahnhof in Berlin.

30 See Laila Pedro, "For Those in Peril on the Sea: Seeing Édouard Glissant in Miami," *Brooklyn Rail*, September 2015, https://brooklynrail.org/2015/09/art/for-those-in-peril-on-the-sea-seeing-douard-glissant-in-miami.

31 Stuart Hall, an Anglophone critical theorist born in Jamaica, describes the "shock of the 'doubleness' of similarity and difference" between Martinique and Jamaica, for example, in Stuart Hall, "Cultural Identity and Diaspora," in *Colonial Discourse and Post-colonial Theory: A Reader*, ed. Patrick Williams and Laura Chrisman (New York: Columbia University Press, 1994), 396.

32 Britton, *Édouard Glissant and Postcolonial Theory*, 11.

33 Britton, *Édouard Glissant and Postcolonial Theory*, 11.

34 Glissant, *Poetics of Relation*, 8.

35 In contemporary Mali, jokes about slavery abound to ease social relations on this historical sore point. Greetings also assume a familial relationship. Malian culture is famous for hospitality, tolerance of difference, and an emphasis on the use of discussion to solve problems.

36 Britton, *Édouard Glissant and Postcolonial Theory*, 11.

37 Dash, *Édouard Glissant*, 176–177.

38 Glissant, *Poetics of Relation*, 19.

39 For a thorough comparison of postcolonial theory to Relation and a discussion of Kwame Anthony Appiah's essay, "Is the Post- in Postmodernism the Post- in Postcolonial" (*Critical Inquiry* 17, no. 2 [1991]), see Allison Moore, "A Lightness of Vision: The Poetics of *Relation* in Malian Art Photography," *Social Dynamics* 40, no. 3 (2014: 538–555, https://doi.org/10.1080/02533952.2014.991181).

40 See, for example, Walter J. Ong, *Orality and Literacy: The Technologizing of the Word* (London: Methuen, 1982); Andrew Shryock, *Nationalism and the Genealogical Imagination: Oral History and Textual Authority in Tribal Jordan* (Berkeley: University of California Press, 1997). For Mali, see Hoffman, "Secrets and Lies"; Kristina Van Dyke, "The Oral-Visual Nexus: Re-thinking Visuality in Mali" (PhD diss., Harvard University, 2005).

41 J. Michael Dash, "Writing the Body: Édouard Glissant's Poetics of Re-membering," *World Literature Today* 63, no. 4 (Autumn 1989): 609.

42 "The body becomes the threshold of consciousness between self and world, self and other." Dash, "Writing the Body," 612.

43 Dash, "Writing the Body," 612; Dash, *Édouard Glissant*, 145.

44 Celia Britton explains that, by the 1990s, Glissant "increasingly writes as though the values of *Relation*, chaos and diversity have in fact already prevailed." Britton, *Édouard Glissant and Postcolonial Theory*, 9.

45 Gyan Prakash, "Postcolonial Criticism and Indian Historiography," *Social Text*, nos. 31/32 (1992): 8.

46 This discussion is complicated by Jean-Loup Amselle's assertion that Bamana was an ethnicity constructed by the French that encompassed a class of people who were formerly peasants or slaves, and who were animist rather than Mus-

lim. Jean-Loup Amselle, *Mestizo Logics: The Anthropology of Identity in Africa and Elsewhere* (Palo Alto, CA: Stanford University Press, 1998).

47 Diawara, *One World in Relation.*

48 For example, when a foreigner visits Mali to do research, he or she is given a family name.

49 For a list of many of these relationships, see Rachel A. Jones, "'You Eat Beans!': Kin-Based Joking Relationships, Obligations, and Identity in Urban Mali" (honors thesis in Anthropology, Macalester College, 2007), 59, http://digitalcommons.macalester.edu/cgi/viewcontent.cgi?article=1001&context=anth_honors.

50 "At a time when 'ethnic cleansings' and genocide are depressingly prevalent around the world, *cousinage* is an invaluable means of defusing potential conflicts." Rhéal Drisdelle and Charlie Pye-Smith also note "Mali's deep-rooted concern with its past." Rhéal Drisdelle and Charlie Pye-Smith, *Mali: A Prospect of Peace?* (Oxford, UK: Oxfam, 1997), 9–10.

51 Unlike in many African nations, Mali's political parties have not been allowed to form around the basis of ethnic groups, and Mali's ethnic tolerance has often been cited as an important reason for its relatively stable democracy.

52 H. Adlai Murdoch, "Glissant's *Opacité* and the Re-conceptualization of Identity," in Drabinski and Parham, *Theorizing Glissant*, 21–22.

53 Postcard production came later, in the 1900s.

54 Valérie Loichot writes, "If Édouard Glissant devised the concept of *Tout-Monde* (*Whole-World*), he also cultivated a *Tout-Art* (*Whole-Art*). Glissant's aesthetic practice and philosophy consist in highlighting connections between artistic production in geographically discrete parts of the world; in encouraging mixed media creations and performances; in establishing friendships between the critic and the artist; and in relinquishing human production to the agency of plants or water." Valérie Loichot, "Le tout-art d'Édouard Glissant," *Contemporary French and Francophone Studies* 20, nos. 4–5 (2016): 558.

55 Betsy Wing, "Glossary," in Glissant, *Poetics of Relation*, xxii. "Imaginary" is not meant in Jacques Lacan's sense.

56 This Carleton College exhibition, *Photographing the Social Body: Malian Portraiture from the Studio to the Street*, was shown at MAP in 2015 during the biennale.

57 Amadou Chab Touré has since left Bamako and currently runs the art space Carpe Diem in Ségou.

58 See Valérie Marin La Meslée and Christine Fleurent, *Novembre à Bamako* (Marseille: Le Bec en l'Air Éditions, 2010); Françoise Berretrot, ed., *Mali au féminin* (Montreuil: Éditions de l'Œil/Édition Musée de Bretagne, 2010).

59 *Only* the title of this exhibition catalog is in Bamankan; the rest is in French.

60 Wanda M. Corn, *The Great American Thing: Modern Art and National Identity, 1915–1935* (Berkeley: University of California Press, 1999), xiv.

61 See William J. Foltz, *From French West Africa to the Malian Federation* (New Haven, CT: Yale University Press, 1965), 10. See also Mary Jo Arnoldi, "Overcoming a Colonial Legacy: The New National Museum in Mali, 1976 to the Present,"

Museum Anthropology 22, no. 3 (1999), and "Bamako, Mali: Monuments and Modernity in the Urban Imagination," *Africa Today* 54, no. 2 (Winter 2007).

62 Robert Maxwell Pringle, *Democratization in Mali: Putting History to Work*, Peaceworks, no. 58 (Washington, DC: United States Institute of Peace, 2006), 16, http://www.usip.org/pubs/peaceworks/pwks58.html.

63 "It is imagined because the members of even the smallest nation will never know most of their fellow-members. . . . It is imagined as a community, because . . . the nation is always conceived as a deep, horizontal, comradeship." Benedict Anderson, *Imagined Communities: Reflections on the Origin and Spread of Nationalism* (London: Verso, 1983), 7.

64 Photographers only seemed interested in work by people they *knew* personally.

65 Thus Gayatri Spivak asks if the "subaltern" can ever, actually, speak. Gayatri Spivak, "Can the Subaltern Speak?," in *Marxism and the Interpretation of Culture*, ed. Cary Nelson and Lawrence Grossberg, 271–313 (Chicago: University of Illinois Press, 1988).

66 The Carleton exhibition *Photographing the Social Body* was translated into French on its website thanks to the efforts of Carleton professor Chérif Keïta and his students. Carleton College, last updated September 9, 2019, https://apps.carleton.edu/museum/socialbody/.

67 See interview with Abdoulaye Konaté, Samuel Sidibé, and Moussa Konaté in the 2015 biennale catalog.

68 Chika Okeke-Agulu, *Postcolonial Modernism: Art and Decolonization in Twentieth-Century Nigeria* (Durham, NC: Duke University Press, 2015).

69 Malian photography could be understood as participating in contemporaneity, like Aboriginal Dream paintings are, as Terry Smith describes the term in 2006. Terry Smith, "Contemporary Art and Contemporaneity," *Critical Inquiry* 32, no. 4 (Summer 2006).

70 As Glissant notes, "Sometimes, by taking up the problems of the Other, it is possible to find oneself." Glissant, *Poetics of Relation*, 18.

71 Glissant and Obrist, *100 Notes—100 Thoughts*, 5.

Chapter 1. Unknown Photographer

Chapter epigraph: Malick Sidibé, quoted in Malick Sidibé and Simon Njami, "The Movement of Life: A Conversation with Simon Njami," in *¡Flash Afrique! Photography from West Africa*, ed. Gerald Matt and Thomas Mießgang (Vienna: Kunsthalle Wien, 2001), 95. *Section epigraph:* Érika Nimis, *Photographes de Bamako de 1935 à nos jours / Photographers in Bamako from 1935 to the Present* (Paris: Éditions Revue Noire, 1998), 5.

1 In the 1950s in Mali, Négritude was a philosophical force of liberation embraced by the nation's educated elites and espoused by Mali's future president and resistance leader, Modibo Keïta.

2 Sources differ on the date of Magnin's trip to Bamako.

3 *In/Sight*'s inclusion of sub-Saharan and North African artists of all races, and its

inclusion of various genres such as portrait, art, and ritual photographies, as well as a section on the South African journal *Drum*, broke open assumptions about what constitutes "African photography" several years before the third Bamako Biennale in 1998 did the same.

4 Margarett Loke, "Inside Photography," *New York Times*, July 11, 1997, https://www.nytimes.com/1997/07/11/books/inside-photography.html.

5 As Candace Keller has pointed out, Magnin's book on Sidibé focuses on his party and beach scenes in order to differentiate his work from Keïta's.

6 Sidiki Sidibé, Malick's cousin and a former apprentice, said he took some of the famous reportage pictures. Malick did not acknowledge Sidiki's authorship, and Sidiki has not complained out of custom and politeness. Sidiki Sidibé, interview by author with assistance of Bakary Sidibé, digital recording, Bamako, Mali, June 16, 2006. It was typical studio practice in Europe and the US for the studio owner to take credit for all of the pictures. Candace Keller states that this was also the case in Mali. See Keller, "Framed and Hidden Histories: West African Photography from Local to Global Contexts," *African Arts* 47, no. 4 (Winter 2014).

7 The term is popular in literature on Keïta, although inappropriate, uncritically paralleling the "discovery" of Africa by European explorers.

8 Cape Town Month of Photography Festival 1999, *100XC: Photography in South Africa* (Cape Town: South African Centre for Photography at University of Cape Town and University of Cape Town Press, 1999). See Geoffrey Grundlingh, ed., *Cape Town Month of Photography Festival* (Cape Town: South African Centre for Photography, University of Cape Town, 2002).

9 Ann M. Shumard, *A Durable Memento: Portraits by Augustus Washington, African American Daguerreotypist* (Washington, DC: National Portrait Gallery, 1999), 11.

10 Jürg Schneider, "Portrait Photography: A Visual Currency in the Atlantic Visualscape," in Peffer and Cameron, *Portraiture and Photography in Africa*, 40–45.

11 Christopher Pinney, "Notes from the Surface of the Image: Photography, Postcolonialism and Vernacular Modernism," in *Photography's Other Histories*, ed. Christopher Pinney and Nicolas Peterson (Durham, NC: Duke University Press, 2003), 203.

12 Tanya Elder, *Capturing Change: The Practice of Malian Photography, 1930s–1990s* (Linköping, Sweden: Linköping University Press, 1997), 55–60.

13 Aimé Césaire, "From *Discourse on Colonialism*," in Williams and Chrisman, *Colonial Discourse and Post-colonial Theory*, 177. See full text in Aimé Césaire, *Discourse on Colonialism* (New York: Monthly Review Press, 1972).

14 Eleanor M. Hight and Gary D. Sampson, "Introduction: Photography, 'Race,' and Post-colonial Theory," in *Colonialist Photography: Imag(in)ing Race and Place*, ed. Eleanor M. Hight and Gary D. Sampson (New York: Routledge, 2002), 1.

15 Hight and Sampson, "Introduction," 1.

16 Susan Sontag, *On Photography* (New York: Farrar, Straus and Giroux, 2001), reiterated in Christraud M. Geary, *In and Out of Focus: Images from Central Africa, 1885–1960* (Washington, DC: National Museum of African Art, Smithsonian

Institution, and Philip Wilson, 2002). See also Deborah Poole, *Vision, Race, and Modernity: A Visual Economy of the Andean Image World* (Princeton, NJ: Princeton University Press, 1997).

17 John Tagg, *The Burden of Representation: Essays on Photographies and Histories* (Minneapolis: University of Minnesota Press, 1988), 165.

18 Nimis, *Photographes de Bamako*, 7–13. The area that is now Mali underwent various name changes under colonialism, finally settling on French Sudan in 1920. So as not to confuse matters, I refer to the area the French entered in the early 1880s, and eventually colonized, as the French Sudan.

19 Nimis, *Photographes de Bamako*, 7.

20 Nimis, *Photographes de Bamako*, 8.

21 Variously called Soninke, Ghana, or Wagadu, 300–1200; Mali, circa 1230–1600; and Songhai, founded 800, freed from Malian Empire in 1430, and destroyed in 1591.

22 Elder, *Capturing Change*, 63.

23 Nimis, *Photographes de Bamako*, 15.

24 Also known as Mountaga Kouyaté, according to Michelle Lamunière. See Lamunière, *You Look Beautiful Like That: The Portrait Photographs of Seydou Keïta and Malick Sidibé* (Cambridge, MA: Harvard University Art Museums, 2001; New Haven, CT: Yale University Press, 2001), 22.

25 Reproduced in Lamunière, *You Look Beautiful Like That*, 23. Patterned backdrops are also seen in earlier Senegalese portrait photos; Dembélé was likely the first to use it in Bamako, as he was the first African photographer to practice in the city.

26 Elder, *Capturing Change*, 77. Lamunière also notes that the first West African photographers were elites, usually part of a mixed society of Africans and Europeans (*You Look Beautiful Like That*, 14).

27 André Magnin, ed., *Seydou Keïta* (Zurich: Scalo, 1997), 11.

28 Elder, *Capturing Change*, 76.

29 Dembélé cited in Elder, *Capturing Change*; interview with André Magnin in Magnin, *Seydou Keïta*, 9.

30 Lamunière, *You Look Beautiful Like That*, 24; Magnin, *Seydou Keïta*, 9. Regarding Garnier's withholding of crucial knowledge, Elder states, "He [Pierre Garnier] kept the printing process and later the film developing process hidden from African photographers" (*Capturing Change*, 71).

31 Lamunière, *You Look Beautiful Like That*, 24. Dembélé found a particular manual that he obtained in France very helpful for photographic information, according to Elder (*Capturing Change*, 73–75).

32 See Agnès de Gouvion Saint-Cyr, "Antoine Freitas," in *Anthology of African and Indian Ocean Photography*, ed. N'goné Fall and Pascal Martin Saint Léon (Paris: Éditions Revue Noire, 1998), 18–19; see also Elder, *Capturing Change*, 79.

33 Geary, *In and Out of Focus*, 112.

34 Nimis, *Photographes de Bamako*, 56.

35 Mahmood Mamdani, *Citizen and Subject: Contemporary Africa and the Legacy of Late Colonialism* (Princeton, NJ: Princeton University Press, 1996).

36 Diawara, "Talk of the Town," 236.

37 Lauri Firstenberg, "Postcoloniality, Performance, and Photographic Portraiture," in *The Short Century: Independence and Liberation Movements in Africa 1945–1994*, ed. Okwui Enwezor, 175–179 (Munich: Prestel, 2001).
38 Arjun Appadurai, "The Colonial Backdrop," *Afterimage* 24, no. 5 (March–April 1997): 4.
39 Amilcar Cabral, "National Liberation and Culture," paper presented at Syracuse University, February 20, 1970, quoted in Peter Childs and R. J. Patrick Williams, eds., *An Introduction to Postcolonial Theory* (London: Prentice Hall, 1997), 57.
40 Bruce S. Hall, "Bellah Histories of Decolonization, Iklan Paths to Freedom: The Meanings of Race and Slavery in the Late-Colonial Niger Bend (Mali), 1944–1960," *International Journal of African Historical Studies* 44, no. 1 (January 2011): 65.
41 Manthia Diawara refers to Pierre Bourdieu's notion of habitus with regard to Malick Sidibé's photographs; the habitus of Keïta's subjects is different but equally resistant to colonialism within their historical context.
42 Jack Goody, *The Interface between the Written and the Oral* (Cambridge: Cambridge University Press, 1987), 170. In her discussion of Mande culture, Barbara Hoffman says, "In our Western, teleological ways of thinking, such an idea is perplexing. How can you have a story that is "true" if it does not conform to some original version of itself?" Hoffman, "Secrets and Lies," 97.
43 Mary Jo Arnoldi, *Playing with Time: Art and Performance in Central Mali* (Bloomington: Indiana University Press, 1995), 121.
44 James S. Brink, "Dialectics of Aesthetic Form in Bamana Art," in *Bamana: The Art of Existence*, ed. Jean-Paul Colleyn (New York: Museum for African Art; Zurich: Museum Rietberg/Snoeck-Ducaji & Zoon, 2001), 238.
45 Brink, "Dialectics," 238.
46 Keller notes, "In my research experience, those words were not used to discuss and evaluate photography and associated visual imagery. Thus, they have been excluded from this discussion." Candace Keller, "Visual Griots: Identity, Aesthetics, and the Social Roles of Portrait Photographers in Mali," in Peffer and Cameron, *Portraiture and Photography in Africa*, 403n76.
47 Keller, "Visual Griots," 389.
48 Keller, "Visual Griots," 389.
49 Keller, "Visual Griots," 389.
50 Tal Tamari, "'Hady': A Traditional Bard's Praise Song for an Urban Teenager," *Research in African Literatures* 38, no. 3 (Fall 2007).
51 John Picton writes, "Textiles [in Africa] have been proved historically to be of greater significance than sculpture." John Picton, "Desperately Seeking Africa" (review of *Africa Explores*, New York, 1991), *Oxford Art Journal* 15, no. 2 (1992): 108.
52 See Pinney, "Notes from the Surface of the Image."
53 Pinney, "Notes from the Surface of the Image."
54 Monni Adams, "Beyond Symmetry in Middle African Design," *African Arts* 23, no. 1 (November 1989). Keller, "Visual Griots: Social, Political, and Cultural Histories in Mali through the Photographer's Lens" (PhD diss., Indiana University, 2008), 328.
55 Ninety percent of clients were women. Elder, *Capturing Change*, 221–222.

56 Isolde Brielmaier makes a similar point in her essay "Mombasa on Display: Photography and the Formation of an Urban Public, from the 1940s Onward," in Peffer and Cameron, *Portraiture and Photography in Africa*, 253–286.

57 See Teju Cole's review of Ojeikere, Sidibé, and Keïta, "Portrait of a Lady," *New York Times*, June 24, 2015.

58 Keller, "Visual Griots," 389.

59 For an elaboration on the concepts of fadenya and badenya, see Charles S. Bird and Martha B. Kendall, "The Mande Hero: Text and Context," in *Explorations in African Systems of Thought*, ed. Ivan Karp and Charles S. Bird, 13–26 (Bloomington: Indiana University Press, 1980).

60 Bird and Kendall, "The Mande Hero," 14.

61 Bird and Kendall, "The Mande Hero," 15.

62 Stephen Wooten, *The Art of Livelihood: Creating Expressive Agri-Culture in Mali* (Durham, NC: Carolina Academic Press, 2009).

63 Geoffrey Batchen, "Vernacular Photographies," in *Each Wild Idea: Writing, Photography, History* (Cambridge, MA: MIT Press, 2001), 78.

64 David Halpern, *Social Capital* (Cambridge, UK: Polity, 2005), 4.

65 Pascal Imperato believes that this is due in part to ample land shared among a relatively small population for cooperative, beneficial uses (herding and farming). Pascal Imperato, *Mali: A Search for Direction* (Boulder, CO: Westview, 1989), 81–82. Pringle attributes Mali's interethnic tolerance to national pride in the Mali Empire, and the legend of King Sundiata, who gave back the twelve Malian kings their staffs in order to allow them to each rule over his own land, although Sundiata was emperor over all. Pringle, *Democratization in Mali*, 13–14.

66 Elder, *Capturing Change*, 74.

67 Anthony O'Connor, *The African City* (New York: Africana, 1983), 21–22.

68 Batchen discusses the relationship of vernacular photography to personal memory in "Vernacular Photographies" and in *Forget Me Not: Photography and Remembrance* (New York: Princeton Architectural Press, 2004).

69 Patrick R. McNaughton, *A Bird Dance near Saturday City: Sidi Ballo and the Art of West African Masquerade* (Bloomington: Indiana University Press, 2008).

70 Forced labor was banned by a law put forth by several Francophone West Africans, Houphouët-Boigny, Césaire, and Senghor. Universal voting rights were allowed in 1956. Frederick Cooper, *Africa since 1940: The Past of the Present* (Cambridge: Cambridge University Press, 2002), 78.

71 Shown in the 1996 biennale were Kélétigui Touré (b. 1922), who was born in Kayes and was an itinerant photographer; Adama Kouyaté (b. 1927), who opened a studio in Ségou; Hamadou Bocoum (1930–1992), a teacher in Mopti who opened his studio in 1956; El Hadj Tidjani Sitou (b. 1933), a Nigerian photographer in Mopti who opened a studio in 1971; and El Hadj Bassirou Sanni (1937–2000), a Nigerian photographer who settled in Mopti in 1962. His son Latifu Sanni (b. 1951) is also a photographer. See Louis Mesplé, ed., *2èmes Rencontres de la Photographie Africaine*, trans. Jed English (Paris: Extrait de Cimaise no. 244, 1996). Thanks to Candace Keller for sending me a copy of the second biennale catalog and alerting me to the exhibition she curated of El Hadj Tidjani Sitou's

works at Indiana University in 2007. Shown in the 1998 biennale were Félix Diallo, the only photographer in Kita from 1955 to 1975; the Traoré brothers; and Touré M'Barakou (1922–1992), the first photographer in the Gao region. See Louis Mesplé, ed., *Ja Taa! Prendre l'image: 3e Rencontres de la Photographie Africaine, Bamako, 1998* (Arles: Actes Sud, 1998), 35–37. Thanks to Madame Coulibaly Diawara, who procured a copy of the exhibition catalog for me. Another still-practicing studioist, Hamidou Maïga (b. 1932), worked in Timbuktu in the 1950s. He eventually left and settled in Bamako, where he has worked since 1973. Hamidou Maïga, interviews by author with assistance of Bakary Sidibé, digital recordings, Bamako, Mali, July 12 and 17, 2006. Also see Amadou Chab Touré, *Hamidou Maïga, photographie les "Tomboctiens"* (Bamako: Galerie Chab, 2000).

72 Nimis, *Photographes de Bamako*, 11.

73 Elder, *Capturing Change*, 77.

74 Sakaly's son Youssouf Sakaly runs a studio in Bamako today.

75 Érika Nimis, "The Golden Age of Black-and-White in Mali," in Fall and Saint Léon, *Anthology of African and Indian Ocean Photography*, 115. St. Louis had daguerreotype studios since 1860. Meïssa Gaye was born in 1892 and seems to have begun photographing in the 1910s, while Mix Gueye opened a studio in the 1930s. Frédérique Chapuis, "The Pioneers of St. Louis," in Fall and Saint Léon, *Anthology of African and Indian Ocean Photography*, 50–52, 54.

76 André Magnin, ed., *Malick Sidibé*, trans. Simon Pleasance and Fronza Woods (Zurich: Scalo, 1998), 36.

77 Manthia Diawara, dir., *Édouard Glissant: One World in Relation* (K'a Yéléma Productions, 2009).

78 See Léopold Sédar Senghor, "Negritude," in *Senghor: Prose and Poetry*, ed. and trans. John Reed and Clive Wake (London: Oxford University Press, 1965), 97–105.

79 Imperato, *Mali*, 130.

80 Imperato, *Mali*, 60.

81 Imperato, *Mali*, 60–61. The rebellion ended in 1964, but the harsh treatment by the Keïta government left a troubled legacy for further relations between the state and the Tuareg.

82 Imperato, *Mali*, 62.

83 Imperato, *Mali*, 87–89.

84 Elder, *Capturing Change*, 81–84.

85 Elder, *Capturing Change*, 89.

86 Elder, *Capturing Change*, 89.

87 The police archives are not accessible. Candace Keller was told by various sources within Bamako that the negatives had burned in a fire. Keller, personal communication, May 2006.

88 For a full discussion of apprentices and authorship, see Keller, "Framed and Hidden Histories."

89 Manthia Diawara, "The Sixties in Bamako: Malick Sidibé and James Brown," in *Malick Sidibé—Photographs* (Gothenburg, Sweden: Hasselblad Center; Göttingen, Germany: Steidl, 2003), 14–22.

90 Candace Keller, "'Visual Griots': Identity, Invention and Style, One Aspect of

the Social Role of Portrait Photographers in Mali." Paper presented at conference, Portrait Photography in African Worlds, University of California, Santa Cruz, February 3–4, 2006.

91 Sidibé and Njami, "The Movement of Life," 94.

92 Nimis, *Photographes de Bamako*, 87–88.

93 A number of photographers I spoke to in Bamako referred to commercial photographers as "social photographers."

94 President Keïta was elected democratically in 1961, but the status of the election was suspect.

95 Konaré was elected to a second five-year term in 1997, and then stepped down—a new precedent of following the legal term limit and ending the "life presidency" so common to African countries, and formerly common in Mali. Konaré was replaced by Amadou Toumani Traoré (ATT), the general who orchestrated the 1991 coup. ATT won the most recent elections as well.

96 In 1995 Alpha Oumar Konaré utilized Mali's 1970 UNESCO convention to protect Mali's cultural heritage.

97 Rosa De Jorio, "Politics of Remembering and Forgetting: The Struggle over Colonial Monuments in Mali," *Africa Today* 52, no. 4 (Summer 2006): 82.

98 Arnoldi discusses the Konarés's emphasis on "*le devoir de memoire*, the responsibility to remember" (Arnoldi, "Bamako, Mali," 11).

99 According to the photographers in Bamako, Keïta is published widely because he carefully preserved his negatives, not because his work is of higher quality than others. Some find his photographs too busy because of the clashing patterns.

100 For aesthetic reasons, Keïta's exhibited photos were culled from many thousands of negatives, as Keller has noted (conversation with author, 2006)

101 Svend E. Sokkelund and Tanya Elder, *Hamadou Bocoum* (Copenhagen: Fotografisk Center and Copenhagen Capital of Culture, 1996).

Chapter 2. Malian Portraiture

Epigraph: Glissant, *Poetics of Relation*, 1.

1 In *Postcolonial Modernisms: Art and Decolonization in Twentieth-Century Nigeria* (Durham, NC: Duke University Press, 2015), Chika Okeke-Agulu remarks on how the emergence of contemporary African art on the global scene is often portrayed in art criticism as if African modernism had not occurred—how it seems to emerge from nowhere, in an ahistorical vacuum.

2 One of Keïta's most famous photographs was of the Mallarméan dandy with a flower in his hand and a pen in his breast pocket. Regarding photography's shift from documentary to verité, see Okwui Enwezor, "Documentary/Vérité: Bio-Politics, Human Rights and the Figure of 'Truth' in Contemporary Art," *Australian and New Zealand Journal of Art* 5, no. 1 (2004).

3 John Peffer made this comment at the *Beyond the Frame* symposium's postsymposium roundtable. *Beyond the Frame: Contemporary Photography from Africa and the Diaspora,* symposium held at Walther Collection and Columbia University, October 22, 2016.

4 I discovered this gem in a copy of the original issue saved in the art history office of CUNY Graduate Center. It has since been published and written on.

5 This essay was subsequently reprinted in *In/Sight*'s catalog in 1996, two decades after those photographs had been taken, to accompany the exhibition of Keïta's and Sidibe's works, among others. Clare Bell et al., eds., *In/Sight: African Photographers, 1940 to the Present* (New York: Guggenheim Museum, 1996).

6 Érika Nimis documented the influence of Yoruba photographers on West African portraiture; El Hadj Tijani Àdìgún Sitou is a Yoruba photographer working in Mali in the 1960s and 1970s. Nimis, "Yoruba Studio Photographers in Francophone West Africa."

7 For a thorough discussion of artists of color working in New York see Kellie Jones, *Eyeminded: Living and Writing Contemporary Art* (Durham, NC: Duke University Press, 2011).

8 As Jerry Saltz notes, Roberta Smith (his wife, who preceded him into the profession of art criticism) was the only major critic to appreciate the 1993 Whitney Biennial. Jerry Saltz, "Jerry Saltz on '93 in Art," *New York Magazine*, February 1, 2013, http://nymag.com/arts/art/features/jerry-saltz-1993-art/.

9 Collectif, *Magiciens de la Terre* (Paris: Centre Georges Pompidou, 1992).

10 While CAAC has been criticized for its support of non-MFA-holding, craft-trained, or in some cases folk artists, it gave visibility to African artists and concerns.

11 In the preface to *Orientalism* (New York: Vintage Books, 1979), Edward W. Said describes Foucault's ideas and methods as fundamental to his critique, and Spivak translated Derrida's seminal *Of Grammatology*. Jacques Derrida, *Of Grammatology*, trans. Gayatri Chakravorty Spivak (Baltimore: Johns Hopkins University Press, 1976).

12 Abigail Solomon-Godeau, "Playing in the Fields of the Image," in *Photography at the Dock: Essays on Photographic History, Institutions, and Practices*, 86–102 (Minneapolis: University of Minnesota Press, 2003), 88.

13 Jeff Wall, "Marks of Indifference: Aspects of Photography in, or as, Contemporary Art," in *Reconsidering the Object of Art: 1965–1975* (exhibition catalog), ed. Ann Goldstein and Anne Rorimer, 247–267 (Los Angeles: Museum of Contemporary Art, 1995); Rosalind Krauss, "Photography's Discursive Spaces: Landscape/View," *Art Journal* 42, no. 4 (Winter 1982); and Solomon-Godeau, "Playing in the Fields of the Image."

14 As Fredric Jameson noted, Warhol initiated a postmodernist critique in the art world. See Jameson, *Postmodernism, or, The Cultural Logic of Late Capitalism* (Durham, NC: Duke University Press, 1991).

15 See Douglas Eklund, *The Pictures Generation: 1974–1984* (New York: Metropolitan Museum of Art, 2009).

16 Douglas Crimp, "Photographic Activity of Postmodernism," *October* 15 (Winter 1980); Craig Owens, "The Discourse of Others: Feminists and Postmodernism," in *The Anti-aesthetic: Essays on Postmodern Culture*, ed. Hal Foster, 57–82 (Seattle: Bay Press, 1983).

17 Solomon-Godeau, "Playing in the Fields of the Image," 86–87.
18 See Geoffrey Batchen, "Does Size Matter?," *Camerawork: Journal of Photographic Arts* 30, no. 2 (Fall/Winter 2003).
19 After his death, Mapplethorpe's photographs were projected onto the Corcoran by friends to protest the cancellation of his exhibition in 1989, and artist Simon Attie was projecting "ghosts"—photographs of the former inhabitants of Jewish neighborhoods—onto present-day buildings in Berlin.
20 Batchen notes the relationship between Keïta's originals and his gallery prints in "Does Size Matter?"
21 According to Rips, the printer for the 2006 exhibition at Sean Kelly Gallery, Charles Griffin, stated that he had never seen a vintage photograph by Keïta. Griffin also prints photographs for Cindy Sherman and Hiroshi Sugimoto. Michael Rips, "Who Owns Seydou Keïta?," *New York Times*, January 22, 2006, section 2, 33.
22 Rips, "Who Owns Seydou Keïta?" The possibly vintage prints I saw at Association Seydou Keïta in Bamako in November 2005 were matted in such a way that I was unable to verify the studio stamp on the back; they were slightly orange-tinted, low-contrast, and seemed water-damaged. I was also shown Keïta's negatives in the summer of 2006. Vintage prints by other studio photographers of the same era vary between low and high contrast.
23 Rips, "Who Owns Seydou Keïta?"
24 Candace Keller, personal communication, April 1, 2012.
25 Candace Keller, personal communication, April 1, 2012.
26 Diawara, "The Sixties in Bamako."
27 "Thus, to say that Sidibé's photographs are 'Black photographs' . . . is to affirm his participation in the 1960s in shaping the new and universal look of the youth of African descent" (Diawara, "The Sixties in Bamako," 19).
28 Michelle Lamunière, interview with Seydou Keïta assisted by Baba Maiga, trans. Lia Brozgal, in Lamunière, *You Look Beautiful Like That*, 47.
29 Teju Cole, "Maestro Sidibé," Africa Is a Country, April 15, 2016, https://africasacountry.com/2016/04/maestro-sidibe.
30 Diawara, "The Sixties in Bamako," 11.
31 Diawara, "The Sixties in Bamako," 12.
32 Keïta's and Sidibé's works are sometimes displayed with little contextual background. The press release for Sean Kelly indicates biases as well as factual truth, mentioning the props and bedspread backdrops, but also stating that clients in this 90 percent Muslim country arrived wearing their "Sunday best."
33 Julia Kristeva's theory of intertexuality helps to highlight the differences in context and reception between the studio photographs and their reprints from the same negatives.
34 Glissant, *Poetics of Relation*, 144.
35 Sidibé and Njami, "The Movement of Life," 96.
36 Sidibé and Njami, "The Movement of Life," 96.
37 Dorothea E. Schulz, "Music Videos and the Effeminate Vices of Urban Culture in Mali," *Africa* 71, no. 3 (2001).

38 Malick Sidibé, interview by author, Bamako, Mali, November 22, 2005; Malick Sidibé, interview by author with assistance of Bakary Sidibé, digital recording, Bamako, Mali, June 20, 2006.

39 In Mali there is an expectation that those who earn wealth will share it, particularly with their large extended families; Sidibé is exemplary in this regard.

40 Other images in the series show women wearing only skirts with their breasts exposed. While women in Mali dress this way in rural areas, Huguier's photographs show a lack of awareness of the exoticizing history of these images and her own complicity in publishing them. *National Geographic* recently issued an apology for publishing these types of images.

41 Keller notes that "Huguier's text [*Secrètes*] is part of Studio Malick's archival collection" but asserts, "It is difficult to ascertain the direction of influence between these two artists." Keller, "Visual Griots: Social, Political, and Cultural Histories in Mali through the Photographer's Lens" (PhD diss., Indiana University, 2008), 476n1922.

42 Shortly before his death, Ojeikere's work was shown in the Fifty-Fifth Venice Biennale in 2013, revitalizing an interest in African photography and repositioning the discourse around his work as art.

43 Keller argued for this reading in her dissertation, "Visual Griots," and an earlier paper (also titled "Visual Griots") on the same topic.

44 Malick Sidibé, interview by author, Bamako, Mali, June 20, 2006.

45 Keller, "Visual Griots: Social, Political, and Cultural Histories in Mali through the Photographer's Lens," 363–364.

46 Malick Sidibé, interview by author, Bamako, Mali, November 22, 2005.

47 Malick Sidibé, "Prints and the Revolution" (photographs), *New York Times Magazine*, April 1, 2009, http://archive.nytimes.com/www.nytimes.com/slideshow/2009/04/01/magazine/20090405-style-slideshow_index.html.

48 Bisi Silva, "8th Encounters of Bamako, African Photography Biennale," *Artforum*, February 2010, 221–222.

49 Eve MacSweeney, "Sunday Best," *Harper's Bazaar*, May 1998.

50 "The extent of Keïta's involvement is unclear: *Bazaar*'s fashion editor selected the models, backdrops, and clothes, and the constraints of the magazine format may have determined some aspects of the composition and camera angle." Elizabeth Bigham, "Issues of Authorship in the Portrait Photographs of Seydou Keïta," *African Arts* 32, no. 1 (Spring 1999): 65.

51 MacSweeney, "Sunday Best," 174.

52 "Mali—Gross Domestic Product per Capita in Current Prices," Knoema, accessed July 17, 2018, https://knoema.com/atlas/Mali/GDP-per-capita.

53 Diawara notes how the legend of the heroic Sundiata Keïta and his empire still operates in the imaginations of many Malians today; young men who emigrate to France live for their acclaim as heroes when they return to the Mande world. See Manthia Diawara, "Return Narratives," in *In Search of Africa*, 86–119 (Cambridge, MA: Harvard University Press, 2000).

54 Bigham, "Issues of Authorship," 65.

55 Image in Bigham, "Issues of Authorship," 67.

56 "Because of the Indonesian prototype, these cloths became known as wax prints, although in reality no wax as such ever comes anywhere near them." John Picton, "Colonial Pretense and African Resistance: Commemorative Textiles in Sub-Saharan Africa," in Enwezor, *The Short Century*, 161.

57 For a fascinating discussion of the many forms that bogolan has taken, see Victoria Rovine, *Bogolan: Shaping Culture through Cloth in Contemporary Mali* (Washington, DC: Smithsonian Institution Press, 2001).

58 Dorothea E. Schulz, "Competing Sartorial Assertions of Femininity and Muslim Identity in Mali," *Fashion Theory* 11, nos. 2/3 (2007): 260, 275–276.

59 Bigham, "Issues of Authorship," 58.

60 Geoffrey Batchen, "Vernacular Photographies," *History of Photography* 24, no. 3 (2000): 79.

Chapter 3. Biennale Effects

Epigraph: Glissant, *Poetics of Relation*, 178.

1 Michael Wiedorn, *Think Like an Archipelago: Paradox in the Work of Édouard Glissant* (Albany: SUNY Press, 2018), xv.

2 See Jeanne Mercier, "Les Rencontres Africaines de la Photographie, Bamako 2005" (MA thesis, École des Hautes Études en Sciences Sociales, 2006).

3 By 2006, Cissé was not active; a photographer named Moussa Sacko owned the postcard shop near the post office. Harouna Racine Keïta had his own studio, Labo Photo, but gave up photography for cinema soon after the biennale was founded. He worked with American scholar Susan Vogel and National Museum director Samuel Sidibé in shooting a film on *ci wara* masks that was displayed in 2011 with a ci wara exhibition on loan from the Quai Branly Museum in Paris, which had objects "collected" (stolen) from the Dakar-Djibouti trip.

4 Erin Haney and Jennifer Bajorek, "Eye on Bamako: Conversations on the African Photography Biennial," *Theory, Culture and Society* 27, nos. 7–8 (2010).

5 Simon Njami, ed., *Mémoires intimes d'un nouveau millénaire: IVes Rencontres de la photographie africaine, Bamako, 2001* (Paris: Éditions Eric Koehler, 2001).

6 Mercier, "Les Rencontres Africaines de la Photographie"; Marie Lortie, "Colonial History, Curatorial Practice and Cross-cultural Conflict at the Bamako Biennial of African Photography (1994–2007)" (MA thesis, Carleton University, Ottowa, Canada, 2008), 1.

7 Huguier's title, *On the Traces of Phantom Africa*, refers to the French surrealist ethnographer Michel Leiris's famous book *L'Afrique fantôme* (1934; repr., Paris: Gallimard, 1988), journal entries and photographs published after his travels in 1931–1933 on the Mission Dakar-Djibouti as Marcel Griaule's secretary-archivist. Huguier's photographs taken while she followed in Leiris's footsteps are the subject of her exhibition and book, *Sur les traces de l'Afrique fantôme* (Paris: Maeght

Éditeur, 1990). Huguier's photographs follow Leiris's in their exoticization of African subjects.

8 Édouard Glissant, *Poetic Intention*, trans. Nathalie Stephens with Anne Malena (Callicoon, NY: Nightboat, 2010).

9 In 1969 he was beginning to theorize "Relation." Glissant, *Poetic Intention*, trans. Nathalie Stephens with Anne Malena (1969; repr., Callicoon, NY: Nightboat, 2010), 122.

10 It is characteristic of Glissant to take seriously white writers writing about people of color and to be aware of the nuanced values of their production; he argues that Faulkner's African American characters have opacity because Faulkner understood that he could not properly understand their culture and lives. Huguier's project of tracing Leiris's steps seems consistent with French attitudes of the 1990s toward Africa, seen for example in Jean Hubert-Martin's curatorship of the Pompidou's *Magiciens de la terre*.

11 I borrow from T. J. Demos's idea of institutional effects in his dissection of the multiple and contradictory effects of the Tate Modern. See T. J. Demos, "The Tate Effect," in *The Global Art World: Audiences, Markets and Museums*, ed. Hans Belting, Andrea Buddensieg, and Peter Weibel, 78–87 (Karlsruhe: ZKM, Center for Art and Media, 2009).

12 See Chantal Mouffe, "Democratic Politics in the Age of Post-Fordism," in "The Art Biennial as a Global Phenomenon: Strategies in Neo-political Times," special issue, *Open* 16 (2009): 36–37. For a complete discussion, see Ernesto Laclau and Chantal Mouffe, *Hegemony and Socialist Strategy: Towards a Radical Democratic Politics* (London: Verso, 2001). For more discussion of labor in the contemporary (American) art world, see Lane Relyea, *Your Everyday Art World* (Cambridge, MA: MIT Press, 2013).

13 Curator Bisi Silva made the 2015 biennale free for Malians.

14 See International Center of Photography (ICP)'s 2014 exhibition *What Is a Photograph?*, curated by Carol Squiers, https://www.icp.org/exhibitions/what-is-a-photograph.

15 Moussa Kalapo works for the Archive of Malian Photography project headed by Candace Keller. See the Archive of Malian Photography website, http://amp.matrix.msu.edu, accessed November 28, 2018.

16 Mercier, "Les Rencontres Africaines de la Photographie," 12. The MAP now houses the archives from the Archive of Malian Photography project, which holds studio but not art photography.

17 Caroline A. Jones, "Biennial Culture: A Longer History," in *The Biennial Reader: An Anthology on Large-Scale Perennial Exhibitions of Contemporary Art*, ed. Elena Filipovic, Marieke Van Hal, and Solveig Øvstebø, 66–87 (Bergen: Bergen Kunsthall, 2010), 83.

18 Lucie Touya, interview by author, Paris, July 2010.

19 Richard Vine, "Report from Mali: The Luminous Continent," *Art in America* 92, no. 9 (October 2004): 69.

20 Second Rencontres exhibition catalog, n.p.

21 This connection likely stems from the transference from commercial, vernacular studio photos to videos, of weddings in particular; this fluidity between mediums has obviously been exacerbated in the digital age worldwide.

22 Keller, "Visual Griots: Social, Political, and Cultural Histories in Mali through the Photographer's Lens," 697.

23 In 1972 it was officially named FESPACO.

24 This is an avenue for further research beyond the scope of this book. Donor countries to FESPACO include Burkina Faso, Denmark, Finland, France, Germany, Netherlands, Sweden, and the People's Republic of China; there are myriad international donor organizations.

25 Simon Sheikh, "Marks of Distinction, Vectors of Possibility: Questions for the Biennial," in "The Art Biennial as a Global Phenomenon," special issue, *Open* 16 (2009): 70.

26 Pascal Gielen, "The Biennial: A Post-institution for Immaterial Labor," in "The Art Biennial as a Global Phenomenon," special issue, *Open* 16 (2009).

27 Nikos Papastergiadis and Meredith Martin, "Art Biennales and Cities as Platforms for a Global Dialogue," in *Festivals and the Cultural Public Sphere*, ed. Liana Giorgi, Monica Sassatelli, and Gerard Delanty, 45–62 (New York: Routledge, 2011), 46.

28 Papastergiadis and Martin, "Art Biennales and Cities as Platforms," 48.

29 Anthony Gardner and Charles Green, "Biennials of the South on the Edges of the Global," *Third Text* 27, no. 4 (August 2013).

30 The *Tout-monde* for Glissant means the whole world, in opposition to globalization—it is like *mondialité*, or worldliness. Hans Ulrich Obrist and Asad Raza, eds., *Mondialité: The Archipelagos of Édouard Glissant* (Paris: Éditions Skira, 2017), 297.

31 FESPACO began in 1969.

32 Thomas Fillitz, "The Biennial of Dakar and South-South Circulations," *Artl@s Bulletin* 5, no. 2 (2016): article 6; Joanna Grabski, *Art World City: The Creative Economy of Artists and Urban Life in Dakar* (Bloomington: Indiana University Press, 2017); Elizabeth Harney, *In Senghor's Shadow: Art, Politics, and the Avant-Garde in Senegal, 1960–1995* (Durham, NC: Duke University Press, 2004).

33 Grabski, *Art World City*.

34 Lortie, "Colonial History, Curatorial Practice and Cross-cultural Conflict."

35 Mary Jo Arnoldi, "Youth Festivals and Museums: The Cultural Politics of Public Memory in Postcolonial Mali," *Africa Today* 52, no. 4 (Summer 2006): 56. She notes, "The performing arts were an especially potent resource in the creation of an official national culture because many troups within the country already had a strong emotional investment and commitment to these arts" (56).

36 Arnoldi, "Youth Festivals," 63.

37 Simon Njami, interview by author, Paris, July 2010.

38 See CulturesFrance website (now Institut Français), accessed July 29, 2008, and August 2016, http://www.culturesfrance.com/africa-creating/afrique-en-creations-by-discipline/p016.html.

39 Information pamphlet from AFAA's office in Paris, August 2005, titled *Afrique en*

créations/The AFAA—A User's Guide, 2. The countries that benefit from the aid are included in the ZSP (Zone de solidarité prioritaire).

40 According to an unnamed source, this consolidation, later enacted by a Sarkozy appointee, was the goal of Olivier Poivre d'Arvor, the director of AFAA from 1999 to 2010. In "Eye on Bamako," Haney and Bajorek note that the fact that photographers in the biennale were able to accurately recite the dates and name changes of these shifts shows how critical these governmental reorganizations were. However, as the French government organized their travel to the biennial, it is unsurprising that non-Malian artists would have noticed name changes.

41 Institut Français, accessed July 17, 2016, https://www.if.institutfrancais.com/en.

42 See Donald Morrison and Antoine Compagnon, *The Death of French Culture* (Cambridge, UK: Polity, 2010), 112–113. Compagnon notes similar unbending, hierarchical behavior when CulturesFrance worked with the New York Public Library to coordinate a writer's panel. I noticed this top-down approach first-hand in working on an African exhibition at the International Center of Photography with AFAA to bring Francophone African artists to the opening (*Snap Judgments*, 2006).

43 Lortie, "Colonial History, Curatorial Practice and Cross-cultural Conflict."

44 She writes, "I am convinced that cultural and artistic practices could play an important role in the agonistic struggle because they are a privileged terrain for the construction of new subjectivities." See Mouffe, "Democratic Politics," 40.

45 See also Haney and Bajorek, "Eye on Bamako."

46 Gradual recognition in the limited scholarly literature has been granted to Malian photographers Alioune Bâ, Django Cissé, and Racine Keïta (according to Amadou Chab Touré), who participated in the planning of the biennale.

47 Sakaly's and Sitou's works have been included in other exhibitions and major archiving projects, thanks largely to the efforts of their surviving families, American scholar Candace Keller, Moussa Konaté, and François Deschamps, but Hamadou Bocoum's work has seemingly disappeared. Candace Keller and the Archive of Malian Photography have received research grants from the British Library and the National Endowment for the Humanities, which have enabled the archiving projects of Mamadou Cissé, Abdourahmane Sakaly, Malick Sidibé, Adama Kouyaté, and Tijani Sitou. Candace M. Keller, webpage, "Grants and Fellowships," accessed November 20, 2019, http://candacemkeller.com/grants-fellowships/.

48 All of the Malian exhibitions were coordinated by Mesplé, Sokkelund, or Oscura.

49 Mercier, "Les Rencontres Africaines de la Photographie," 17. Konaté is the best-known contemporary artist from Mali.

50 The first two biennales did not have titles; the middle four, all directed by curator Simon Njami, of Cameroonian descent, have been in French, as were the two directed by an Italian, Laura Serani, and a French Algerian, Michket Krifa. *Telling Time* (2015) was actually in English. Antawan Byrd, Yves Chatap, and Bisi Silva, eds., *Telling Time: Rencontres de Bamako Biennale Africaine de la Photographie* (Tenth Biennale), English and French ed. (Heidelberg: Kehrer, 2016).

51 Mercier, "Les Rencontres Africaines de la Photographie," 18.

52 The Contours were funded by PSIC (Programme d'Appui et de Valorisation des Initiatives Artistiques et Culturelles) and were run by Amadou Chab Touré. Mercier, "Les Rencontres Africaines de la Photographie," 19.

53 According to Amadou Chab Touré, Antonin Potoski, a French photographer who worked at the Centre Culturel Français from 1996 to 1998, encouraged Konaté to experiment with abstraction. Touré, interview by author, Bamako, 2006.

54 Mercier, "Les Rencontres Africaines de la Photographie," 18–20. Mercier recounts that it was impossible for her to gain access to archives or records about the biennale at the Maison Africaine de la Photographie, and I experienced the same problem. I was told that there are no archives—for example, records of artists who exhibited or their works, or photocopies or digital images of them.

55 Paul O'Neill, *The Culture of Curating and the Curating of Culture(s)* (Cambridge, MA: MIT Press, 2012), 61.

56 O'Neill, *The Culture of Curating and the Curating of Culture(s)*, 20–21.

57 The organizers invited photographers from the black community in Great Britain. Other themes have been "Sacred Rites, Profane Rites" ("Rites sacrés / rites profanes") (2003), "Another World" ("Un autre monde") (2005), and "In the City and Beyond" ("Dans la ville et au-dèla") (2007).

58 To be precise, Njami's phrase for himself was "loose item." Njami, interview by author, July 2010, Paris.

59 The 2001 exhibition catalog—Njami, *Mémoires intimes d'un nouveau millénaire*, 92—echoes the humble tone of *Anthology of African and Indian Ocean Photography*. They note that Abdoulaye Konaté sent out the research mission (94).

60 Njami, *Mémoires intimes d'un nouveau millénaire.*

61 In this short biennale catalog essay, Magnin says, "Exhibitions devoted to Keïta were first held in France in 1993. In 1994, the Cartier Foundation for Contemporary Art presented a personal exhibition on the occasion of Paris Photo Month, revealing him to specialist and the general public alike" (24). This essay says he worked for Surete National from 1962 to 1977, but his relatives ran the studio until 1977, when he "closed shop." Exhibition catalog for 2003 biennale. Simon Njami, ed., *Ves Rencontres de la Photographie Africaine, Bamako 2003: Rites sacrés / Rites profanes* (Paris: Éditions Eric Koehler, 2003).

62 Exhibition catalog for 2003 biennale, "New Momentum," 5.

63 Susanna Denholm Wing, "Constitutional Dialogues: Participation and Citizenship in the Transition towards Democracy in Mali, 1991–1999" (PhD diss., UCLA, 2000), 126.

64 Wing, "Constitutional Dialogues," 62.

65 Wing, "Constitutional Dialogues," 70.

66 "Questions are submitted to an honorary jury, read by individuals at the forum, and broadcast on radio and television. Ministers are expected to respond directly to the questions posed." Wing, "Constitutional Dialogues," 125.

67 Wing, "Constitutional Dialogues," 69–70, 126.

68 Wing, "Constitutional Dialogues," 215.

69 Documenta 11 took place in 2002. Given that Okwui Enwezor was the first African curator, it is likely Konaté was aware of Documenta 11, and it is certain that Njami was.

70 For 2001, Amadou Chab Touré, who had recently opened the only photography gallery in Bamako, the titular Galerie Chab, organized a "Photo Street" for the "Offs." Mercier, "Les Rencontres Africaines de la Photographie," 19.

71 Amadou Sow, interview by author with assistance of Bakary Sidibé, digital recording, July 5, 2006.

72 This was based on observation of the biennale proceedings—the group was so small that everyone met each other—and from numerous conversations with local taxi drivers.

73 Geoffrey Batchen emphasizes the problematic nature of photography's reproduction in his scholarship. See, in particular, "Latent History," *Art in America* 96, no. 2 (February 2008); 54–57; and "Dreams of Ordinary Life: *Cartes-de-visite* and the Bourgeois Imagination," in *Image and Imagination*, ed. Martha Langford, 63–74, 266–268 (Montreal: McGill-Queen's University Press & Le Mois de la Photo, 2005). The Cinéma Numérique Ambulant (Traveling Digital Cinema, or CNA), discussed in chapter 6, has also been an important attempt to involve the local community, although it is considered part of the "Contours."

74 This would also seem to have been a choice of the curators, since usually photo studios stamp the name of the studio on the back of the prints.

75 Youssouf Sogodogo, interview by author with assistance of Bakary Sidibé, digital recording, Bamako, Mali, July 8, 2006.

76 Moussa Konaté, n.p., in *Bamako 2007, Dans la Ville et au-dela.*

77 "Outlines events are implemented by decentralized cultural operators whose projects are selected after a call for proposals launched by the Maison Africaine de la Photographie (MAP)." Samuel Sidibé, "contours/outlines," in *Bamako 2007 VIIIes Rencontres Africaines de la Photographie: Dans la ville et au-dela*, ed. Simon Njami (Paris: Marval, 2007), 164–165.

78 Samuel Sidibé, "contours/outlines," 164–165.

79 "L'hôpital Sominé Dolo de Mopti / The Sominé Dolo Hospital of Mopti," in Njami, *Bamako 2007 VIIIes Rencontres Africaines de la Photographie*, 188–189.

80 Exhibition catalog for 2009 biennale (which had information about 2007): Michket Krifa and Laura Serani, eds., *Rencontres de Bamako 2009: Biennale Africaine de la Photographie: Frontières* (Nantes: Actes Sud; Paris: CulturesFrance, 2009) (*Borders*), 316.

81 Samuel Sidibé, untitled note in Krifa and Serani, *Rencontres de Bamako 2009*, 9.

82 Olivier Poivre d'Arvor, Sophie Renaud, and Paul de Sinety, untitled note in Krifa and Serani, *Rencontres de Bamako 2009*, 8.

83 This exhibition owed collaboration to Magnin and Picto.

84 Michel Foucher, "Africa and the Play of Borders," in Krifa and Serani, *Rencontres de Bamako 2009*, 23.

85 Achille Mbembe, "The Seed and the Silt," in *For a Sustainable World: Rencontres de Bamako African Photography Biennale*, 9th ed., eds. Michket Krifa and Laura Serani (Arles: Actes Sud; Paris: Institut Français, 2011), 28. "Most vernacular knowledge

was useful only in relation to this endless labour of restoration. In this context, agriculture, for instance, was above all a system of healing arts. It was understood that the environment was a force in itself. One could work, transform and control it only in accord with it and not by setting oneself against it, through fragments of action scattered in time and in space." Mbembe, "The Seed and the Silt," 27–28.

86 Mbembe, "The Seed and the Silt," 27–29.

87 Samuel Sidibé, "For a Sustainable Biennial," in Krifa and Serani, *For a Sustainable World*, 14.

88 Sidibé, "For a Sustainable Biennial," 15.

89 Fatoumata Diabaté, *L'homme en animal*, in Krifa and Serani, *For a Sustainable World*, 70.

90 Ananias Léki Dago, "Workshop/Mali Bamako: The Mali Version," in Krifa and Serani, *For a Sustainable World*, 344.

91 "UNICEF au Mali," UNICEF, accessed September 5, 2016, https://www.unicef.org/mali/.

92 See Vine, "Report from Mali," 69.

93 Articles about the biennale in each paper were always by these authors: *L'Essor*, M. Konaté; *Les Echos*, Amadou Sidibé; and *Le Républicain*, Assane Koné.

94 Emmanuel de Roux, "Rites, hommages et découvertes aux Rencontres de Bamako," *Le Monde*, October 31, 2003; and "Bamako, bric-à-brac," *Libération*, October 27, 2003, 33–34.

95 Nicolas Michel, "Honneur aux artists de l'image," *Jeune Afrique—L'Intelligent*, October 12/18, 2003; Charlotte Cans, "Un havre de culture à Bamako," *Jeune Afrique—L'Intelligent*, October 5/11, 2003.

96 The review was published in October 2004, almost one year after the exhibition.

97 Holland Cotter, "Out of Adversity, Visions of Life," *New York Times*, April 15, 2012, http://www.nytimes.com/2012/04/15/arts/design/salif-diabagate-and-other-artists-struggle-in-africa.html?action=click&contentCollection=Art%20%26%20Design&module=RelatedCoverage®ion=EndOfArticle&pgtype=article.

98 It is unlikely Cotter was allowed to choose the images for the paper.

99 Silva said that her main objective with this edition was to engage locals—an approach that directly addressed past criticisms that the festival had pandered to foreign visitors, rather than prioritizing local communities. Charlotte Jansen, "Art in a Time of Terror: Mali's Photo Festival Makes Defiant Return," *Guardian*, December 31, 2015, https://www.theguardian.com/world/2015/dec/31/mali-bamako-photography-biennial-returns.

100 Jansen, "Art in a Time of Terror."

101 Bisi Silva, "100 Écoles / 10 000 Étudiants," in Byrd, Chatap, and Silva, *Telling Time*, 328–329.

102 Dagara Dakin (DD), "Aboubacar Traore *Inchallah* (2015)," in Byrd, Chatap, and Silva, *Telling Time*, 226.

103 Yves Chatap, "Moussa Kalapo *La métaphore du temps* (2015)," in Byrd, Chatap, and Silva, *Telling Time*, 92.
104 Bisi Silva and Yves Chatap, "Mali Jaw," in Byrd, Chatap, and Silva, *Telling Time*, 320–321.
105 Byrd, Chatap, and Silva, *Telling Time*, 327.
106 In contrast to the Bamako biennale, Léki Dago's first Rencontres du Sud (Abidjan, 2000) was nationally focused, according to Haney and Bajorek, "Eye on Bamako."
107 See Hansi Momodu-Gordon and Guilhem Monceaux, "Les Rencontres de Bamako, 1994–2015," in Byrd, Chatap, and Silva, *Telling Time*, 415–416.
108 The Depth of Field photographers who met at the 2001 Bamako Biennale were Kelechi Amadi-Obi, Uchechukwa James-Iroha, Toyosi Zaynab Odunsi, Amaize Ojeikere, Emeka Okereke, and Toyin Sokefun-Bello. Amaize is the son of J. D. 'Okhai Ojeikere, whose work I discuss briefly in chapter 5. After meeting at the 2001 Bamako Biennale, four future members started the collective in their hometown of Lagos, an instance of how the biennale promotes fruitful connections among participants.
109 Okwui Enwezor, *Snap Judgments: New Positions in Contemporary African Photography* (Göttingen, Germany: Steidl, 2006).
110 Sionne Neely, "'Preserving Memory as Future': An Interview with Aida Muluneh," Accra Alt Radio, May 22, 2013, https://accradotalttours.wordpress.com/2013/05/22/preserving-memory-as-future-an-interview-with-aida-muluneh/.
111 T. J. Demos, "Sammy Baloji and Alice Seeley Harris" (review of show at Autograph ABP/Rivington Place, London), *Artforum*, May 2014, 315.
112 Haney and Bajorek, "Eye on Bamako."
113 The Radisson Blu Hotel was attacked by terrorists on November 20, 2015, a week after the Encounters opened. One hundred seventy hostages were held temporarily and over twenty people killed. Most biennale visitors had already left Bamako.
114 Marian Nur Goni, "What Happened during the Addis Foto Fest #2?," Africultures, April 9, 2013, http://www.africultures.com/php/index.php?nav=article&no=11453.
115 Patrick Chabal and Jean-Pascal Daloz, *Africa Works: Disorder as Political Instrument* (Bloomington, IN: International African Institute, 1999).
116 Chabal and Daloz, *Africa Works*.
117 "Indeed, one of the most widespread complaints about contemporary biennials is their lack of connection to the 'local' audience, but this often takes the form of a positivity of the social: that social relations and identities in a specific context are given and whole if not holy, that the local audience is a singular group with essential qualities and shared agencies" (Sheikh, "Marks of Distinction," 74).
118 Sheikh, "Marks of Distinction," 74.

Chapter 4. Bamako Becoming Photographic

Epigraph: Glissant, *Poetics of Relation*, 45.

1 Wiedorn, *Think Like an Archipelago*.

2 Diawara, "Talk of the Town," 236. Gosselin uses the idea of "mestizo logic" (see Amselle, *Mestizo Logics*). She writes, "This particular hybrid construction of ethnicity . . . allows me to argue that in urban Mali, excision is to be understood in relationship to a (southern) 'Malian' culture—as opposed to for instance a 'Bamanan,' 'Mandinka' or 'fulbe' culture. The crystallization of differences that is enshrined in the latter approach is more of an inheritance from a colonial administration that had a need to classify in order to govern more firmly, than an accurate reflection of a historically fluid socioscape." Claudie Gosselin, "Campaigning against Excision in Mali: Global and Local Hierarchies, Hegemony and Knowledge" (PhD diss., University of Toronto, 2001), 55.

3 See O'Connor, *The African City*, 32–34.

4 See Moussa Dembélé, "French Colonization and Urban Evolution in Djenne and Bamako," in *Globalization and Urbanization in Africa*, ed. Toyin Falola and Steven J. Salm, 217–247 (Trenton, NJ: Africa World Press, 2004), 241.

5 In Abderramane Sissako's 2006 film *Bamako*, the photographer videos a wedding, which occurs as a counterpoint to a legal tribunal, the main event of the film.

6 Michel Foucault, *Archaeology of Knowledge*, trans. A. M. Sheridan Smith (New York: Pantheon, 1972), 48–49; Pierre Bourdieu, *The Field of Cultural Production: Essays on Art and Literature*, ed. Randal Johnson (New York: Columbia University Press, 1993). While Bourdieu used such universal notions as "the state," recent work in African scholarship suggests that African states are formed differently, with different agents and workings of power.

7 Pierre Bourdieu. *The Social Structures of the Economy*, trans. Chris Turner (Cambridge, UK: Polity, 2005).

8 V. Y. Mudimbe, "*Reprendre*: Enunciations and Strategies in Contemporary African Arts," in *Africa Explores: 20th Century African Art*, ed. Susan Vogel, 276–287 (New York: Center for African Art, 1991), 280.

9 V. Y. Mudimbe, "African Art as a Question Mark," *African Studies Review* 29, no. 1 (1986): 3–4.

10 *Nyama* is often translated as "life-force."

11 Sarah C. Brett-Smith, *The Making of Bamana Sculpture: Creativity and Gender* (Cambridge: Cambridge University Press, 1994), 24.

12 Brett-Smith, *The Making of Bamana Sculpture*, 24.

13 Brett-Smith, *The Making of Bamana Sculpture*, 25.

14 Sarah C. Brett-Smith, *The Silence of the Women: Bamana Mud Cloths* (Milan: 5 Continents Editions, 2014).

15 See Krauss, "Photography's Discursive Spaces."

16 The landmark text edited by Nelson Graburn, *Ethnic and Tourist Arts: Cultural Expressions from the Fourth World* (Berkeley: University of California Press, 1976), was the first major study of tourist arts. The same year, *African Arts* devoted an

issue to the discussion of authenticity, a crucial turning point in the study of tourist art. Christopher Steiner's Marxist approach considers tourist art largely as a function of economic practice in *African Art in Transit* (Cambridge: Cambridge University Press, 1994), while Bennetta Jules-Rosette discusses tourist art in terms of semiotics, describing the market as a system which gives meaning to objects as "a process of communication and exchange." Jules-Rosette, *The Messages of Tourist Art: An African Semiotic System in Comparative Perspective* (New York: Plenum Press, 1984), 361. Philip L. Ravenhill includes a chapter on the Baule *colon*, a type of tourist art, in *Dreams and Reverie: Images of Otherworld Mates among the Baule, West Africa* (Washington, DC: Smithsonian Institution Press, 1996). Sidney Kasfir explores the contradictions in the study of African authenticity, an issue inextricably intertwined with tourist art, in "African Art and Authenticity: A Text with a Shadow," *African Arts* 25, no. 2 (April 1992). See also Ruth B. Phillips and Christopher B. Steiner, eds., *Unpacking Culture: Art and Commodity in Colonial and Postcolonial Worlds* (Berkeley: University of California Press, 1999), which includes Graburn's response to his original 1976 essay: "Epilogue: Ethnic and Tourist Arts Revisited."

17 Imperato, *Mali*, 94.

18 Paul Ramey Davis, "A Social History of Painting in Bamako, Mali, 1930s–1980s" (PhD diss., Indiana University, 2012).

19 According to Youssouf Traoré, the Audio/Visual Section was initiated in 1976, when he began teaching there as the photography professor. Candace Keller, email to author, August 20, 2008; Youssouf Traoré, interview by author with assistance of Bakary Sidibé, digital recording, Bamako, Mali, July 4, 2006.

20 Érika Nimis, "Mali's Photographic Memory: From Outsider Readings to National Reclaiming," *Visual Anthropology* 27 (2014): 402.

21 The CAMM is financed by the European Union and by PSIC.

22 In 2006, Touré started incorporating painters as well as photographers. In 2010, he moved his gallery to Segou and retitled it Carpe Diem.

23 None of the women had studied at INA, although INA now teaches women as well as men. All of the women first attended Promo-femme.

24 Usually the exhibitions document traditional culture, rather than contemporary photography. Chapter 5 further discusses the importance of the National Museum and its photographers.

25 Moussa Konaté wrote a letter for me to begin my research in Mali and was consistently generous with his time and with what archives were available. In 2015, Cherif Keïta, Laurel Bradley, and I sent the exhibition *Photographing the Social Body: Malian Portraiture from the Studio to the Street* to the Maison Africaine de la Photographie during the 2015 biennale.

26 Photography is relatively cheap, but many photographers in Bamako can't afford the materials to print their work.

27 Helvetas has been active in Mali since 1977.

28 The CFP does all of the printing for Malick Sidibé and in 2005 did the printing for the biennale as well. Lamentably, this did not occur in subsequent biennales.

29 CFP website, http://bamako-cfp.org/spip.php?article25 (no longer active).

30 François Deschamps, interview by author, November 2013.
31 For further discussion of women photographers and Promo-femme, see chapter 6.
32 Konaté's works were shown in *Africa Remix* (2006) at the Centre Georges Pompidou in Paris and *Divine Comedy: Heaven, Purgatory, and Hell Reconsidered by Contemporary African Artists* (2015) at the Smithsonian National Museum of African Art, Washington, DC; his work is owned by the Metropolitan Museum of Art in New York. See Simon Njami, ed., *Africa Remix: L'art contemporain d'un continent* (Paris: Centre Georges Pompidou, 2005).
33 He also exhibits European photographers and was planning to start showing Senegalese and other West African photographers.
34 Okwui Enwezor and Chika Okeke-Agulu, *Contemporary African Art since 1980* (Bologna: Damiani, 2009), 21.
35 This was when Deschamps taught at the conservatory on a Fulbright fellowship.
36 François Deschamps, phone interview, November 10, 2013.
37 François Deschamps, phone interview, November 10, 2013. His website describes the projects at length: http://francoisdeschamps.net.
38 Alioune Bâ, interview by author, Bamako, Mali, March 21, 2011.
39 Nimis, "Mali's Photographic Memory," 401.
40 For the web archive, edited by Bärbel Küster and Clara Pacquet, that includes video and transcribed interviews with numerous Malian and Senegalese photographers, see "Photography and Orality: Dialogues in Bamako, Dakar and Elsewhere," http://dakar-bamako-photo.eu/en/home.html.
41 Küster and Pacquet, Harandane Dicko section of "Photography and Orality" archive, accessed October 14, 2019, http://dakar-bamako-photo.eu/en/harandane-dicko.html.
42 Elder, *Capturing Change*, 74.
43 Deschamps was limited in teaching technique by the lack of facilities, so the format of the course was conceptual. Siriman Dembélé, interview by author with the assistance of Bakary Sidibé, digital recording, July 2006.
44 "Chaque image a été guidée par une discussion, une écoute, un sourire ou encore une participation de ma part aux tâches collectives. Peut-être qu'il s'agit là de ce qu'est vraiment la photographie ! On ne photographie pas 'dans le vide' mais bien en connaissant ce dont on veut parler." Armelle Razongles, "Afrique in visu," January 10, 2011, http://www.afriqueinvisu.org/metier-de-photographe-suivez-le,548.html.
45 François Deschamps, phone interview by author, November 10, 2013.
46 This was also emphasized in interviews with numerous participating Malian photographers.
47 François Deschamps, phone interview by author, November 10, 2013.
48 Jonathan Jones, "Boy Done Good," *Guardian*, October 6, 2004, http://www.guardian.co.uk/culture/2004/oct/06/1.
49 The book of photographs by Dogon children is Antonin Potoski, *Les Dogons par les Dogons* (Montreuil: Éditions de l'Œil, 2001).

50 There is not a sense of cutthroat competition. The financial gain realized by Galerie Chab and the CFP suggest that the situation could change if it involved more economic capital.

51 Oscura was included in two biennales. "Visual Griots," a project conducted by Shawn Davis for the American-based Academy for Educational Development in collaboration with Alioune Bâ, Amadou Sow, and the NGO Association Vigne, initiated photographic workshops for children in the villages of Damy and Kouara, showing the resulting prints at Association Seydou Keïta during the 2005 Bamako Biennale. The project traveled to Washington, DC, New York, and the Fowler Museum in Los Angeles. See Shawn Davis, "Visual Griots of Mali: Empowering Youth through the Art of Photography," *African Arts* 39, no. 1 (Spring 2006).

52 See Grabski, *Art World City*.

Chapter 5. Creolizing the Archive

Epigraph: Glissant, *Poetics of Relation*, 201.

1 The control of the biennale was shifted from Moussa Konaté at the Maison Africaine de la Photographie (MAP) to Samuel Sidibé, the director of the National Museum, for the 2009 biennale.

2 Bâ's career actually began before the biennale was founded, as he first exhibited his work at the Hôtel de l'Amitié in Bamako in 1990, and then in France and Denmark in 1993.

3 "We clamor for the right to opacity for everyone." Glissant, *Poetics of Relation*, 194.

4 Lorna Burns, "Politicising Paradise: Sites of Resistance in Cereus Blooms at Night," *Journal of West Indian Literature* 19, no. 2 (2011). Also cited in Murdoch, "Glissant's *Opacité*," 20.

5 Glissant, *Poetics of Relation*, 192.

6 Glissant uses it in contrast to *creolité*, a term used in 1989 by the Martiniquan writers Jean Bernabé, Patrick Chamoiseau, and Raphaël Confiant in *Éloge de la creolité* (Paris: Gallimard, 1993), which was a response to concerns with Négritude. Creolization is an ongoing process of change and transformation.

7 Earlier works by Alioune Bâ also incorporate a museological approach, but his more recent series extends into a more conceptual vein discussed in chapter 7. Aboubacrine Diarra's works are briefly discussed in chapter 3, but his work is not often published or exhibited.

8 To my knowledge these works are not actively collected by the National Museum. In a 2006 interview, Samuel Sidibé showed disinterest in collecting art photography because the museum's mission is historical; however, in the past fourteen years this may have changed.

9 Because of Mali's economic poverty and the voracious international antiquities market, the looting of undocumented archaeological finds and treasured or forgotten objects reached an emergency crisis in the early 1990s. In 1995 the issue became so urgent that Mali became the first African country, in fact the first

non-Western nation, to submit a request for the protection of cultural property under the 1970 UNESCO Convention. See Maria Papageorge Kouroupas, "U.S. Efforts to Protect Cultural Property: Implementation of the 1970 UNESCO Convention," *African Arts* 28, no. 4 (Autumn 1995): 33.

10 Calculated from statistics in 2015 (Bamako's population) and 2017 (overall population).

11 "Le musée a pour mission la collecte, la restauration, la conservation et la diffusion du patrimoine culturel national." Originally from website no longer functioning: National Museum, Mali, http://www.museenationaldumali.org.ml/historique.html. See Observatory of Cultural Practices in Africa (OCPA) website, *OCPA News*, no. 177 (March 26, 2007), https://ocpa.irmo.hr › OCPA_News_No177_20070326.

12 Elizabeth Edwards, *Raw Histories: Photographs, Anthropology and Museums* (Oxford, UK: Berg, 2001), 77.

13 Edwards, *Raw Histories*, 51.

14 Barthes, *Camera Lucida*, trans. Richard Howard (New York: Farrar, Straus and Giroux, 1981), 88.

15 Barthes, *Camera Lucida*, 88.

16 See Téréba Togola, "The Rape of Mali's Only Resource," in *Illicit Antiquities: The Theft of Cultures and the Extinction of Archaeology*, ed. Neil Brodie and Kathryn Walker Tubb, 250–256 (London: Routledge, 2002), 250–251. Now deceased, Togola was Mali's national director of cultural heritage.

17 Van Dyke, "The Oral-Visual Nexus," 49.

18 Scholars in the past privileged the written over the oral culture, which is not my judgment. My approach to the study of Malian photographers, most of whom are well educated in several languages, including French and Bamanankan, is to attempt to understand the competing and cooperating effects of strong oral traditions within highly literary, educated approaches to visual culture.

19 Hoffman, "Secrets and Lies," 99.

20 The terms "traditional" and "modern" are problematic, because traditional may refer to a changing tradition that was only fixed to a particular time and convention through Western collecting practices, and many "modern" forms hold elements of tradition. The terms "nineteenth-century precolonial," "colonial," and "postcolonial" may make more sense in terms of locating these traditions chronologically.

21 Because of the international popularity of these sculptural traditions, an industry in "airport art," or sculptures and masks made for tourists, is lively and present today. In Bamako, masks and sculptures can be bought at the Artisanat in the Grand Marché (the market that spreads across the center of downtown Bamako) and in upscale boutiques in neighborhoods where development workers live. Founded during colonial rule to support the making of traditional crafts, the Artisanat is now under the aegis of the Ministry of Tourism.

22 Pringle writes, "Arguably the single most important factor in Mali's democratization process: the sense of pride that the Malians have in their own history." Pringle, *Democratization in Mali*, 13.

23 Mary Jo Arnoldi, "Youth Festivals and Museums: The Cultural Politics of Public Memory in Postcolonial Mali," *Africa Today* 52, no. 4 (Summer 2006): 55–75.

24 The Musée Soudanais de Bamako functioned as a temporary holding center for objects on their way to Dakar.

25 "Il devait jouer un rôle important dans le cadre du renforcement de l'unité nationale et contribuer à la valorisation d'une culture authentique." National Museum of Mali, accessed October 13, 2007, http://www.museenationaldumali.org .ml/historique.html (website no longer exists; a mirror site from Geocities, October 2009, is https://www.oocities.org/infomali/Musee/collecti.htm).

26 Van Dyke, "The Oral-Visual Nexus," 82; Arnoldi, "Overcoming a Colonial Legacy," 28.

27 Arnoldi, "Overcoming a Colonial Legacy," 29. Pivin contributed to the early editions of the Bamako Biennale and also contributed to the additions.

28 Arnoldi, "Youth Festivals," 55–56.

29 Arnoldi, "Youth Festivals," 55.

30 Van Dyke, "The Oral-Visual Nexus," 78. Also see Arnoldi, "Overcoming a Colonial Legacy," 29. School groups appear to be the only consistent Malian visitors.

31 Arnoldi, "Overcoming a Colonial Legacy," 35.

32 See Martin Jay, *Downcast Eyes: The Denigration of Vision in Twentieth-Century French Thought* (Berkeley: University of California Press, 1993). Jay shows how recent French philosophers have criticized this visual emphasis, a legacy of the Enlightenment.

33 Museums like the British Museum and the American Museum of Natural History are particularly egregious in this manner; Mali's National Museum's display is much closer to the Metropolitan Museum of Art's display, as it lacks contextualizing models or approaches of any sort.

34 Arnoldi, "Overcoming a Colonial Legacy," 29–31.

35 Arnoldi, "Overcoming a Colonial Legacy," 28.

36 By contrast, Van Dyke praises the "culture banks" in more remote Malian villages, in which villagers deposit objects but their meanings are kept within the community, and the community has a say over how those objects are presented to tourists. Van Dyke, "The Oral-Visual Nexus," 2.

37 Van Dyke, "The Oral-Visual Nexus," 83. However, Arnoldi notes that in the 1976 reorganization of collection policies, the definition of the object to be collected was widened to include its associated documentation. Arnoldi, "Overcoming a Colonial Legacy," 31.

38 Samuel Sidibé, interview by author with assistance of Bakary Sidibé, digital recording, Bamako, Mali, June 14, 2006.

39 Samuel Sidibé, interview by author, Bamako, Mali, March 21, 2011.

40 In the interest of limiting the scope of this project, I asked them only about photography. Racine Keïta is the only photographer I know of who also works creatively in video, but there are surely others.

41 Preserving culture through photographs is not solely the province of the National Museum. Studio photography has done the same, in a manner much more integrated with societal norms, values, and desires, since the first studios opened

in the 1930s. Michelle Lamunière writes, "The fact that images privately commissioned for domestic settings were often shared with the larger community conferred special status on photographers as creators and guardians of visual memory" (Lamunière, *You Look Beautiful Like That*, 13). Candace Keller has argued that many studio photographers in Bamako even conceive of themselves as "visual *griots*." The griot, in Mande culture, is an oral historian who comes from a particular caste and who relates a selective history through traditional means, in performances and praise songs for the ruling caste. In my own research, I found that few photographers conceived of themselves as "visual griots" (and some were offended at first at the suggestion, because the freeborn/noble caste looks down at griots); after an explanation, some photographers acknowledged that the role of the photographer in preserving memory had a similar function to that of a griot. Keller asserts that Malick Sidibé had become aware of this term used to describe his work and used it with pride. For the complications around discussions of ideas in Mande culture and American researchers, see Barbara Hoffman, an American scholar who worked in Mali for over twenty years and underwent training as a (real) griot. She writes: "Mande words are polysemic; a great sensitivity to and understanding of context is required to be assured of communicative competence. . . . One implication for researchers asking the question, 'What does this mean?' is that it must be understood that the response will be an indication of what is meant at that time, in that place, by that speaker replying to the particular person asking the question. We should not be surprised to see that the same question evokes a different response under another set of circumstances; in Mande ways of speaking, meaning is as fluid as the changing social circumstances of its production." See Hoffman, "Secrets and Lies," 99.

42 See Charles Merewether, ed., *The Archive: Documents of Contemporary Art* (Cambridge, MA: MIT Press, 2006).

43 Thomas Richards, *The Imperial Archive: Knowledge and the Fantasy of Empire* (London: Verso, 1993).

44 The sacking of Benin City in 1897, which finalized the process of bringing the region that would become Nigeria under British rule, and which resulted in the looting of the Benin bronzes now housed in the British Museum and the Metropolitan Museum of Art, is one of the most egregious examples. For more on the relationship between Great Britain's perception of Africa and Britain's collection and exhibition policies of African material culture, see Annie E. Coombes, *Reinventing Africa: Museums, Material Culture and Popular Imagination in Late Victorian and Edwardian England* (New Haven, CT: Yale University Press, 1994).

45 Richards, *The Imperial Archive*, 1, 4.

46 Richards makes a strong case regarding the 1885 Berlin Conference, the infamous high point of the "Scramble for Africa," which resulted in the African map's division among fourteen European nations. These boundaries remained theoretical for a good decade or two after the conference, until the various European powers were able to defeat local African governments with improved weapons and armies inoculated against disease. In what Richards views as Britain's

ultimate fantasy, the collection of factual information from the colonies and other territories was meant to be unified into a single fount of comprehensive knowledge. According to Richards, "This supplanting of power by the force of knowledge is one of the hallmarks of the twentieth century." Richards, *The Imperial Archive*, 7.

47 France used complicated networks of administrative systems to rule its territories in West Africa, where it arbitrarily divided, documented, and archived its subjects. While "the imperial archive was [only] a fantasy of knowledge collected and united in the service of state and Empire," this "fantasy" held great importance among colonial administrators. Richards, *The Imperial Archive*, 4.

48 Allan Sekula, "The Body and the Archive," *October* 39 (Winter 1986): 17.

49 Benjamin Buchloh, "Gerhard Richter's Atlas: The Anomic Archive," in *The Archive: Documents of Contemporary Art*, ed. Charles Merewether, 85–102 (London: Whitechapel, 2006), 85.

50 Sekula, "The Body and the Archive," 4–6.

51 Sekula, "The Body and the Archive," 5.

52 Larry W. Yarak discovered an entry in the Elmina Journal in the National Archives, The Hague, Archief van de Nederlandsche Bezittingen ter Kuste van Guinea, which told of a Captain Bouet who made a daguerreotype on shore. See Yarak, "Early Photography in Elmina," *Ghana Studies Council Newsletter*, no. 8 (Spring/Summer 1995): 9–11, http://www.ghanastudies.com/gsa/gsc_newsletter_8.pdf.

53 Nimis, *Photographes de Bamako*, 7.

54 Hal Foster, "Archival Impulse," *October*, no. 110 (Fall 2004); Okwui Enwezor, *Archive Fever: Uses of the Document in Contemporary Art* (Göttingen, Germany: ICP/Steidl, 2008).

55 See Gregorio Magnani, "Ordering Procedures: Photography in Recent German Art," *Arts Magazine* 64 (March 1990): 82.

56 This is based on the works that I saw by Sogodogo. He did not show me unpublished works. The hairstyle series are also the most-often-published works.

57 *BKO-RAK* also includes works by Malians Amadou Traoré, Mamadou Konaté, students of a prytaneum in the town of Kati, Mali, and the Moroccan artist Hicham Benohoud. Antonin Potoski, who published a book of Dogon photography and helped Mohamed Camara, was also the impetus behind these three publications. Antonin Potoski, ed., *BKO-RAK: Photographes de Bamako et de Marrakech* (Paris: Éditions Revue Noire, 1998).

58 His work also appears in *BKO-RAK* and Berretrot, *Mali au féminin*.

59 Youssouf Sogodogo, interview by author with assistance of Bakary Sidibé, digital recording, Bamako, Mali, July 8, 2006. In an interview, Sogodogo explained that he took his photos to a local studio, who said they weren't any good, but when he took them to Malick Sidibé, he said they were excellent.

60 Sogodogo said that he was attracted by the cultural differences of the region. Youssouf Sogodogo, interview by author with assistance of Bakary Sidibé, digital recording, Bamako, Mali, July 8 and 15, 2006.

61 Antonin Potoski, ed., *Youssouf Sogodogo: Photographies* (Montreuil: Éditions de l'Œil, 2000), unpaginated.

62 Kerstin Pinther and Julia Ng, "Textiles and Photography in West Africa," *Critical Interventions* 1, no. 1 (2007).
63 Lamunière, *You Look Beautiful Like That*, 37.
64 Amadou Chab Touré, "Les têtes des femmes tournent," in Potoski, *Youssouf Sogodogo*, n.p.
65 Touré, "Les têtes des femmes tournent," p. 1 of text.
66 Terence S. Turner, "The Social Skin," in *Not Work Alone: A Cross-cultural View of Activities Superfluous to Survival*, ed. Jeremy Cherfas and Roger Lewin, 112–140 (London: Temple Smith, 1980), 112. Quoted in Mary Jo Arnoldi and Christine Mullen Kreamer, *Crowning Achievements: African Arts of Dressing the Head* (Los Angeles: Fowler Museum of Cultural History, UCLA, 1995), 10.
67 Arnoldi and Kreamer, *Crowning Achievements*, 9–10.
68 "Special hair styles and head-wear often figure prominently in rituals for major life passages such as birth, coming of age, marriage, and funerals" (Arnoldi and Kreamer, *Crowning Achievements*, 15). See also Esi Sagay, *African Hairstyles: Styles of Yesterday and Today* (London: Heinemann, 1983).
69 Touré, "Les têtes des femmes tournent," p. 2 of text.
70 Touré, "Les têtes des femmes tournent," p. 4 of text.
71 Barthélémy Koné and Mamadou Koné, *Coiffures traditionnelles et modernes au Mali/Traditional and Modern Hairstyles of Mali* (Bamako: Éditions Populaires du Mali, n.d.). A short text accompanying each photograph provides basic information about the hairstyle, such as its name and sometimes its local meaning. The book is written in French, English, and German, and *not*, significantly, in Bamanankan; thus it was clearly published for an international audience and for elite, well-educated Malians. (Although it exhorts women, few women could read French in the 1970s.) Yet it remains for the Malian historian to contextualize the photographs.
72 In West Africa in general, Arnoldi notes, "Many popular hair styles are given local names that relate them to contemporary events or highlights local notions of modernity." Arnoldi and Kreamer, introduction to *Crowning Achievements*, 24.
73 "There is a hairstyle worn in memory of General de Gaulle. It imitates the military headdress of the Tirailleurs Sénégalais when they returned home in triumph." Koné and Koné, *Coiffures traditionnelles*, 15, 158.
74 While the book states that photography and text are by Mamadou Koné, it is unclear whether some of the older pictures, clearly studio photographs, originated from the author's own studio.
75 "Hair styles and hats that are not associated with ritual contexts often undergo the most rapid transformations responding to the dynamics of fashion and taste." Arnoldi and Kreamer, introduction to *Crowning Achievements*, 24.
76 Arnoldi and Kreamer, introduction to *Crowning Achievements*, 49.
77 Simon Njami, ed., *VIes Rencontres Africaines de la Photographie, Bamako 2005: Un autre monde* (Paris: Éditions Eric Koehler, 2005), 38.
78 While it is possible that Sogodogo was familiar with Koné's book, I did not see it in any of Bamako's bookstores, nor at the National Museum, which would be the most likely venue for it. Sogodogo has asserted that he was unfamiliar with

Nigerian photographer J. D. 'Okhai Ojeikere's similar black-and-white photographs of hairstyles. While Ojeikere was exhibited in Nigeria and Switzerland in 1995, he became well known only about five years later, when Magnin published a monograph on his work and he began to exhibit widely. André Magnin, ed., *J. D. 'Okhai Ojeikere* (Arles, France: Actes Sud, 2000).

79 Koné and Koné, *Coiffures traditionnelles*, 4.

80 It is likely that Sogodogo would have seen a similar style of photographs in the Gao Museum.

81 Sogodogo stated that Potoski chose the images for the exhibitions. Sogodogo, interview by author, Bamako, Mali, June 8, 2006.

82 Jacques Derrida, *Archive Fever: A Freudian Impression*, trans. Eric Prenowitz (Chicago: University of Chicago Press, 1998), 2–3.

83 Derrida, *Archive Fever*, 2–3.

84 Sekula, "The Body and the Archive," 17.

85 Barthes, *Camera Lucida*, 7.

86 Alioune Bâ, interview conducted in Bamako, National Museum of Mali, by Bärbel Küster, Marleine Chedraoui, Judith Rottenburg, and Janine Schöne, February 16, 2011, posted in "Photography and Orality: Dialogues in Bamako, Dakar and Elsewhere" archive, http://dakar-bamako-photo.eu/en/alioune-ba.html.

87 Alioune Bâ, interview conducted in Bamako, National Museum of Mali, by Bärbel Küster, Marleine Chedraoui, Judith Rottenburg, and Janine Schöne, February 16, 2011, posted in "Photography and Orality: Dialogues in Bamako, Dakar and Elsewhere" archive, http://dakar-bamako-photo.eu/en/alioune-ba.html.

88 The city of Djenne, famed for its banco architecture, is a UNESCO heritage site, and the Djenne mosque is a world-famous building.

89 Because of the political dispute, the museum ended up broadening its mission, since the party that owned most of the archives would not donate them. See Rosa De Jorio, "Narratives of the Nation and Democracy in Mali: A View from Modibo Keïta's Memorial," *Cahiers Études Africaines* 172 (2003).

90 De Jorio, "Narratives of the Nation."

91 De Jorio says that some people were upset about the money spent, others were proud of the beautiful building, and that it became the spot for holding weddings (De Jorio, "Narratives of the Nation," 833n12).

92 De Jorio and Arnoldi both note the program of new buildings under the presidency of Alpha Oumar Konaré. See De Jorio, "Narratives of the Nation"; Mary Jo Arnoldi, "Symbolically Inscribing the City: Public Monuments in Mali, 1995–2002," *African Arts* 36 (2003): 56–65, 95–96.

93 The Djenne mosque was destroyed in 1830 but rebuilt; other mosques have existed for centuries.

94 De Jorio is referring to J. R. Llobera's discussion of Catalan history in J. R. Llobera, "The Role of Historical Memory in Catalan National Identity," *Social Anthropology* 6, no. 3 (1998). Cited in De Jorio, "Narratives of the Nation," 828.

95 Llobera, "The Role of Historical Memory in Catalan National Identity," 828.

96 Njami, *Mémoires intimes d'un nouveau millénaire.*

97 Elsewhere I refer to the *Les oubliés de la médaille* series as *The Forgotten Medal-*

Winners, but the translation *The Forgotten Heroes* conveys Tienro's description of the series. Tienro asked permission of veterans at the house and visited four times during the shooting of the series. He described his work at the National Museum as preserving culture. Joseye Tienro, interview by author with assistance of Bakary Sidibé, digital recording, Bamako, Mali, July 1, 2006.

98 Tienro, interview by author, July 1, 2006.

99 After Mali achieved its independence in 1960, the Malian government was highly critical of France's war with Algeria.

100 Tienro, interview by author, July 1, 2006.

101 Tienro, interview by author, July 1, 2006. See also Njami, *VIes Rencontres Africaines de la Photographie, Bamako 2005*, 120.

102 Sprague argues that this pose conveys the traditional Yoruba aesthetic characteristics of *jijora*, *odo*, and *ifarahon*. "The concept of *jijora*—mimesis at the midpoint—implies the work should exist somewhere between complete abstraction and individual likeness. . . . *Odo*, depiction midway between infancy and old age, at the prime of life . . . and *ifarahon* 'visibility,' implies clarity and definition of form and line, and a subsequent clarity of identity." Stephen F. Sprague, "Yoruba Photography: How the Yoruba See Themselves," in *Photography's Other Histories*, ed. Christopher Pinney and Nicolas Peterson, 240–260 (Durham, NC: Duke University Press, 2003), 246. Nigerian photographers often traveled to other countries and participated in the spread of studio photography across West Africa, according to Érika Nimis: see Nimis, "Nigeria: The Photographic Giant," *Africultures*, May 31, 2001, http://africultures.com/nigeria-the-photographic-giant-5534/.

103 Although the International Exhibition was held in the temporary exhibition hall of the National Museum with the museum's permission, the museum's director and staff did not participate in any of the biennale's selection procedures.

104 Arnoldi, "Symbolically Inscribing the City," 56.

105 Tienro, interview by author, July 1, 2006.

106 Diawara, *In Search of Africa*, 88–94.

107 Van Dyke, "The Oral-Visual Nexus," 42.

108 Glissant, *Poetics of Relation*, 192.

Chapter 6. Promoting Women Photographers

1 In her study of studio and itinerant photographers conducted in the towns of Mopti, Segou, and Kayes between 1993 and 1996, Tanya Elder notes one female photographer, Fanta Sidibé, among fifty-six photographers interviewed. The biennale was founded in Bamako in 1994, and Promo-femme was founded in Bamako in 1996, i.e., during the time of her study; Elder does not state whether either of these institutions influenced Sidibé's career choice. See Elder, *Capturing Change*, 96.

2 Aminata Dembélé Bagayoko, interview by author with assistance of Bakary Sidibé, digital recording, Bamako, Mali, July 25, 2006. The school was formally

approved by the Malian government in 1998 according to the information pamphlet provided by Promo-femme, July 25, 2006.

3 Bagayoko, interview by author, July 25, 2006.

4 Danielle Poe says Irigaray offers "a continuous critique of static understandings of sex and gender." Poe, "Can Luce Irigaray's Notion of Sexual Difference Be Applied to Transsexual and Transgender Narratives?," in *Thinking with Irigaray*, ed. Mary C. Rawlinson, Sabrina L. Hom, and Serene J. Khader, 111–128 (Albany: SUNY Press, 2011), 112. In Irigaray's philosophy, sexual difference is more fundamental than racial difference because there is no biological construction of race—race is an entirely social construct with real, lived effects, as Charles Mills argues. See Charles Mills, *Blackness Visible: Essays on Philosophy and Race* (Ithaca, NY: Cornell University Press, 1998), 46–50. Irigaray is not unaware of the effects of racism in the world, but she understands those effects as entirely constructed through human social structures of power, rather than as being rooted in a natural or biological necessity. There is no genetics of race.

5 Erika Wilson, "Navigating Competing Discourses: Narratives of Womanhood in Bamako" (MA thesis, Simon Fraser University, 2000).

6 While women's equality has been nominally on the Malian political horizon since independence, in actuality women have held little political power, and patriarchal traditions remained largely in place socially. See Gosselin, "Campaigning against Excision," 51–52.

7 Wilson, "Navigating Competing Discourses," 13.

8 Gwendolyn Mikell, "African Feminism: Toward a New Politics of Representation," *Feminist Studies* 21, no. 2 (Summer 1995). She writes, "The greater willingness of African women to embrace feminist politics and gender representation in the 1990s is traceable to the current national crises and political transitions which have been occurring throughout the continent over the past fifteen decades." Mikell, "African Feminism," 408.

9 In the urban context of Bamako the bogolan techniques have been appropriated by mostly male, contemporary artists who are unable to imbue their works with nyama.

10 Susanna Denholm Wing, "Constitutional Dialogues: Participation and Citizenship in the Transition towards Democracy in Mali, 1991–1999" (PhD diss., UCLA, 2000), 6–7.

11 Jane Turrittin, "Aoua Kéita and the Nascent Women's Movement in the French Soudan," *African Studies Review* 36, no. 1 (April 1993).

12 Turittin, "Aoua Kéita," 74. USRDA was the Sudanese limb of the Rassemblement Démocratique Africain.

13 However, according to Danielle Poe, "Irigaray's complex understanding of sexual difference as natural, cultural, spiritual, and morphological can help us interpret transsexual narratives." Poe, "Can Luce Irigaray's Notion," 111.

14 Turittin, "Aoua Kéita," 63.

15 Turittin, "Aoua Kéita," 66.

16 Turittin, "Aoua Kéita," 63.

17 Gosselin, "Campaigning against Excision," 51.

18 Imperato, *Mali*, 89. Also cited in Gosselin, "Campaigning against Excision," 52.

19 Diawara, "The Sixties in Bamako," 11, 12.

20 Diawara, "The Sixties in Bamako," 15.

21 Dressing like Americans also suggests Malian identification with the United States' nascent civil rights movement, which was itself influenced by African independence movements.

22 Schulz, "Competing Sartorial Assertions," 261.

23 Turrittin, "Aoua Kéita," 85. Turrittin comments that in 1993, two women were elected ministers in the democratic government.

24 Mikell, "African Feminism," 409.

25 Wilson, "Navigating Competing Discourses," 13. Susanna Denholm Wing notes the strength of traditional law in outweighing constitutional law. Wing, "Women's Rights in West Africa: Legal Pluralism and Constitutional Law," abstract for paper presented at American Political Science Association Annual Meeting, Boston, MA, 2002.

26 Glissant's female characters in his novels allow him to explore gendered constructions in nuanced and complex ways, according to Celia Britton. Nzegwu explains by reference to white feminist philosopher Sandra Harding: "The use of gender as an explanatory scheme elevates the discourse to the level of feminism because its built-in assumptions are calibrated to detect constructions of masculinity and femininity as well as of female oppression." Nkiru Nzegwu, *Family Matters: Feminist Concepts in African Philosophy of Culture* (Albany: SUNY Press, 2006), 8–9, 17–32; Sandra Harding, "Women as Creators of Knowledge," *New Environments* 32, no. 6 (1989).

27 They were contemporaries and were born two years apart.

28 Stephen Pluhacek and Heidi Bostic, "Thinking Life as Relation: An Interview with Luce Irigaray," *Man and World* 29, no. 4 (October 1996): 353.

29 Wiedorn, *Think Like an Archipelago*, 38.

30 Glissant's philosophy is either more radical, in that he sees everyone as irreducibly different—in which case there could be presumably as many sexes as there are human beings—or it could be more conservative with regard to sexual difference, in that he does not see sex as particularly important in constituting difference, which would not be a sufficiently feminist approach.

31 Bagayoko, interview, July 25, 2006.

32 Association pour la Formation Féminine et Appuis Communautaires (AFFAC) is an NGO that was founded in 1989 to create professions for educated and illiterate women who lack familial support.

33 See Rovine, *Bogolan*.

34 See Koné, "La photographie en tant que moyen de lutte contre le chômage," Rapport de Fin des Cycles, Institut National des Arts, Mali, 2006.

35 Promo-femme website, accessed July 18, 2018, http://promofemme.courantsdefemmes.org/index.html.

36 "L'idée de création d'un Centre de formation en audiovisuel est venue dans un soucie [*sic*] de multiplier les domaines de formations des jeunes filles maliennes

qui n'arrivent pas, pour diverses raisons à continuer leurs études. Pour cette catégorie de filles au Mali il n'existait que des Centres de coutures et de teintures. De ce fait nous avons estimé qu'étant donner que les garçons photographes, sans formation, vivent bien de leur travail, pourquoi ne pas introduire les jeunes filles dans cette voie avec une bonne formation." "Historique du centre," Promo-femme website, accessed August 30, 2007, http://promofemme.courantsdefemmes.org/historique.html.

37 Promo-femme information pamphlet, *Notes techniques sur le centre Promo-femme*, obtained July 2006.

38 "Jusque'à une date récente au Mali, la photographie était considérée comme un métier réservé aux hommes exclusivement. Avec la création du centre Promo-femme et la formation des premières filles photographes, cette opinion n'est plus qu'un lointain souvenir. Les jeunes filles occupent de plus en plus le milieu de la photographie malienne. Bamako étant la capitale de la photographie africaine, toutes les opportunités sont à la porté des jeunes filles photographes pour se faire de la place. Pour ce faire, le centre a tissé des relations de partenariat avec tous les services qui oeuvrent pour le développement de ce métier." Promo-femme, *Notes techniques.*

39 "Diversifier l'offre de formation des jeunes filles maliennes qui n'ont pas eu la chance de continuer leurs études"; "Former d'ici l'an 2005 deux cent (200) jeunes filles à la photographie et vidéographie"; "Assurer le perfectionnement des sortantes et des autres femmes qui travaillent déjà dans l'audiovisuel." "Présentation de Promo-femme," Promo-femme website, accessed July 18, 2018, http://promofemme.courantsdefemmes.org/presentation.html.

40 Promo-femme, *Notes techniques.*

41 Office de Radiodiffusion-Télévision du Mali.

42 Promo-femme, *Notes techniques.*

43 For example, Fatoumata Diabaté and Alimata Traoré both participated in a show on the subject of "colonial buildings" held at the Musée du District de Bamako in 2002.

44 In her discussion of Malian feminism, Turittin suggests that, during the struggle for liberation, there were two types of feminists, female and male. According to Turittin, female feminists are motivated by dissatisfaction with their inequality and their life situation, while male feminists are motivated by a more general desire for the greater good of society. Turittin, "Aoua Kéita," 61. This is a somewhat false distinction, in that women are motivated by more than personal desire and often seek broad social change, while men are also often motivated personally through relationships with particular women. Nevertheless, Turittin highlights the point that a feminist movement *does* generally include, if not require, the support of men.

45 "Regards de femmes sur des femmes."

46 Youssouf Sogodogo, interview by author, notes, Bamako, Mali, November 20, 2005.

47 Fatoumata Diabaté, interview by author and Bakary Sidibé, digital recording, Bamako, Mali, July 27, 2005.

48 Sarah C. Brett-Smith has written that women bogolan dyers acquire and express knowledge in their works differently from male sculptors. Women learn knowledge in a more abstract method that is contingent on context. See Brett-Smith, "The Knowledge of Women," in *Anthropologies of Art*, ed. Mariet Westermann, 143–163 (Williamstown: Sterling and Francine Clark Art Institute, 2005). I am grateful to Youssouf Traoré, the photography professor at INA, for telling me about these students and lending me their theses to read. Traoré, interviews by author, digital recordings, Bamako, Mali, July 4 and 14, 2008. See Koné, "La photographie . . . contre le chômage"; Siaka Sanogo, "Rôle de la photographe dans la sauvegarde des masques et statuettes Senoufo au Musée National" (Rapport de Fin des Cycles, Institut National des Arts, Mali, 2006); and Nana Flama Samake, "La photographie documentaire en tant que moyen d'identification et de classification des objets au Musée National" (Rapport de Fin des Cycles, Institut National des Arts, Mali, 2006).

49 Alioune Bâ, who works at the National Museum, has taught women in techniques of video and photo, and Amadou Sow at the House of African Photography was helping to coordinate an exhibition that included Alimata Traoré. Amadou Baba Cissé worked with the French woman Elisabeth Towns on Oscura, and had traveled on a photo shoot with Ouassa Sangaré. Harandane Dicko and Fatoumata Diabaté, both of whom are protégés of Sogodogo, have traveled and worked together in and outside Mali.

50 While male photographers whom I interviewed generally acknowledged the ability of women to be photographers, several informal, objectifying discussions of women among certain male photographers did not suggest an attitude of respect or equality. My presence as a woman presumably influenced responses.

51 Sidibé's generosity is well known. Another example is his support of biennale photographers by displaying their work outside his studio, which is sure to receive well-placed international visitors during the biennale week—even though Sidibé himself does not feel that "art" photography is good photography.

52 Sogodogo, interview by author, July 8, 2006.

53 Youma Fall, "Of Some Women in the History of Art in Senegal," in *Dak'Art 2006, 7ème biennale de l'art africain contemporain: Afrique Entendus, Sous-entendus et Malentendus / Seventh Biennial of African Contemporary Art: African Agreements, Allusions and Misunderstandings*, ed. Yacouba Konaté (Dakar: Secrétariat Général de la Biennale de l'Art africain contemporain de Dakar, 2006), 72/76. Fall notes that only a third of the applications for Dak'art 2006 were submitted by women, and only a sixth of the final participating artists chosen for the exhibition were female.

54 Njami also curated the seventh biennale, which was held in November 2007.

55 Elder, *Capturing Change*, 221.

56 Elder, *Capturing Change*, 221–222.

57 Koné and Koné, *Coiffures traditionnelles*, 4.

58 This practice is common across West Africa. In Dakar, the practice is given a name, *sañse*, when women have photographs taken of themselves in elegant dress and then display these pictures in albums and frames. See Hudita Nura Mustafa, "Portraits of Modernity: Fashioning Selves in Dakarois Popular Photography,"

in *Images and Empires: Visuality in Colonial and Postcolonial Africa*, ed. Paul S. Landau and Deborah D. Kaspin, 172–192 (Berkeley: University of California Press, 2002), 172.

59 Bamako is known for its beautiful women—"*A Bamako les femmes sont belles* in the words of the popular song" (Diawara, "Talk of the Town," 242).

60 Diawara, "Talk of the Town," 236.

61 Elder, *Capturing Change*, 221–223.

62 Jean-François Werner, "Les tribulations d'un photographe de rue africain," *Autrepart* 1 (1997): 136–137; also cited in Elder, *Capturing Change*, 223.

63 Elder, *Capturing Change*, 222.

64 According to Promo-femme's pamphlet, only five graduates in total have opened a studio of their own. Admittedly, opening a studio is a much more expensive venture than simply becoming an itinerant photographer, as it requires overhead costs such as rent, electrical bills, equipment, and laboratory supplies.

65 Fatoumata Diabaté related that another graduate of Promo-femme, Awa Fofana, also runs a studio. Diabaté, interview by author and Bakary Sidibé, digital recording, Bamako, Mali, July 27, 2006. Several other female studio owners were listed in a citywide directory of photographers and artists. The CFP is committed to having an equal number of male and female students. Sogodogo, interview by author, notes, Bamako, Mali, November 20, 2005.

66 Centre National d'Information d'Education pour la Santé (CNIES).

67 Lion Photo was opened in 1993 by Kim Chi Noun according to Nimis, *Photographes de Bamako*, 91.

68 The emphasis on baptisms seems strange in a predominantly Muslim country, but was common to many photographers' resumes. Indeed, Christian ceremonies seemed to be a focus of interest for a number of photographers, perhaps because they are so unusual. Christianity is also growing in popularity in West Africa.

69 "Tu es malade." Penda Diakité, interview by author and Bakary Sidibé, digital recording, Bamako, Mali, July 8, 2006.

70 Diakité, interview by author, July 8, 2006.

71 Diakité, interview by author, July 8, 2006.

72 Lamunière, *You Look Beautiful Like That*, 32.

73 In Yoruba studios, subjects can be posed and then framed as if on television. See Marilyn Hammersley Houlberg, "Feed Your Eyes: Nigerian and Haitian Studio Photography," *Photographic Insight*, no. 1 (Winter–Spring 1988): 4. In Kenya, Likoni Ferry photographers create a mélange of backdrop materials (banners, posters, plastic flowers, and the like) that disconnect the subject from any specific place, projecting the subject into a "global" space. Heike Behrend, "'Feeling Global': The Likoni Ferry Photographers of Mombasa, Kenya," *African Arts* 33, no. 3 (Autumn 2001): 76.

74 The photographer Amadou Traoré placed his own white wicker chair for the sitter in front of the pictured wicker chair.

75 These backdrops are likely created by digital means.

76 "It registered the fact that the sitter lived in Bamako, had seen the train station, the big market, and the central prison, and went to the movies [all located near

his studio]: in short, it signified that the sitter was modern." Diawara, "Talk of the Town," 236.

77 Many city dwellers travel back and forth to their home villages.

78 Lamunière, *You Look Beautiful Like That*, 24.

79 This idea was suggested by Bakary Sidibé.

80 Penda Diakité, interview, July 12, 2006.

81 Barthes, *Camera Lucida*, 87–88.

82 Amadou Waïgalo, "15e anniversaire du décès d'Abdoulaye Barry: Les langues nationales pour affermir la decentralization," *Afribone.com*, October 2, 2006, www.afribone.com/article.php3?id_article=4546. Abdoulaye Barry devoted his life to politics and was a professor of Bamanankan at the National Institute of the Arts. The language institute was founded in 1991, the year of democracy.

83 Alimata Traoré and Fatoumata Diabaté also attended CFP (formerly Helvetas).

84 Pascal Martin Saint Léon and Jean-Loup Pivin, "The Official Agencies," in Fall and Saint Léon, *Anthology of African and Indian Ocean Photography*, 198. Nimis contends that AMAP was created in 1960 and makes no mention of ANIM. Nimis, *Photographes de Bamako*, 97.

85 Dagara Dakin, "La presse et la photographie (1960–1990)," in *L'Afrique en regards: Une brève histoire de la photographie*, ed. Martin van der Belen, 66–73 (Trézélan, France: Filigranes Éditions, 2005), 68.

86 Dakin, "La presse et la photographie (1960–1990)."

87 Dakin, "La presse et la photographie (1960–1990)."

88 Nimis, *Photographes de Bamako*, 97.

89 Alimata dite Diop Traoré, interview by author and Bakary Sidibé, digital recording, Bamako, Mali, July 21, 2006.

90 Traoré exhibited in *Women Looking at Women*, which may have contributed to her interest in photographing women and children. At Promo-femme as well, the students were encouraged to do projects on various women's professions.

91 "Je rêve déjà d'être une grande artiste photographe, une star si vous voulez, qui va exposer dans tous les pays du monde! J'avoue que si un jour je devais choisir entre un homme et ma carrière de photographe, je choisirais ma carrière." Alimata dite Diop Traoré, "Regard de Femmes" (interview), *Afriphoto*, November 23, 2003, http://www.afriphoto.com/index.asp.

92 Mikell, "African Feminism," 412. Another trend Mikell noted in terms of African feminism is that marriage and motherhood are considered of vital importance in many if not all African countries.

93 Pringle, *Democratization in Mali*, 39.

94 Turittin, "Aoua Kéita," 84.

95 "Certainly, this reality of the *two* has always existed. But it was submitted to the imperatives of a logic of the *one*, the *two* being reduced then to a pair of opposites not independent one from the other. Moreover, the duality was subordinated to a genealogical order, a hierarchical order, in space and in time, which prevented considering the necessity of the passage to another mode of thinking, and of living." Pluhacek and Bostic, "Thinking Life as Relation," 344.

96 Glissant, *Poetics of Relation*, 139.
97 Njami, *VIes Rencontres Africaines de la Photographie, Bamako 2005*, 195.
98 Alimata dite Diop Traoré, interview by author and Bakary Sidibé, digital recording, Bamako, Mali, July 21, 2006.
99 I was unable to interview Awa Fofana because she was not in Bamako in the summer of 2006.
100 It used to be Bamana tradition to sacrifice an albino in times of great trouble.
101 Yacouba Dembélé had taken pictures of a boy climbing into a big trash bin, and people cooking food near the open sewers (common), while Amadou Baba Cissé, who was mentioned in the introduction, took pictures of condoms.
102 Kadiatou Sangaré, interview by author with assistance of Bakary Sidibé, digital recording, Bamako, Mali, July 24, 2007.
103 Fatoumata Diabaté, interview by author and Bakary Sidibé, digital recording, Bamako, Mali, July 27, 2006.
104 Diabaté, interview by author and Bakary Sidibé, July 27, 2006.
105 I use the name "Tuareg" because that is the title of the series; however, the people call themselves Tamasheq, or Kel-Tamasheq ("people who speak Tamasheq").
106 The phrase *fait mes premieres armes* translates literally as "picked up my first weapon," but means "cut my teeth" or "started my career."
107 A number of prizes are awarded at the biennale, and this one was specifically awarded by Association Française d'Action Artistique (now CulturesFrance), which funds and runs the biennale.
108 Diabaté, interview by author and Bakary Sidibé, July 27, 2006.
109 Fatoumata Diabaté, Ouassa Pangassy Sangaré, Kadiatou Sangaré, Alimata Traoré, and Awa Fofana participated.
110 Njami, *VIes Rencontres Africaines de la Photographie, Bamako 2005*.
111 For more on Tendance Floue, see the collective's website, http://tendancefloue.net/meyer/series/portraits-decales/.
112 Tamari, "'Hady,'" 89. Hantel asserts, "The *chaos-monde* starts with irreducible sexual difference." Max Hantel, "Toward a Sexual Difference Theory of Creolization," in Drabinski and Parham, *Theorizing Glissant*, 99.

Chapter 7. Errantry, the Social Body, and Photography

Epigraph: Glissant, *Poetics of Relation*, 18.

1 "While *errance* is usually translated as 'wandering,' 'errantry' seems better suited to Glissant's use of the word, and there is precedence in translations of Césaire. *Errance*, for Glissant, while not aimed like an arrow's trajectory, nor circular and repetitive like the nomad's, is not idle roaming, but includes a sense of sacred motivation." Betsy Wing, translator's notes, in Glissant, *Poetics of Relation*, 211.
2 Deleuze differentiates between plants that have a single root and plants that grow in a biologically rhizomatic fashion, with many shallow roots or nodes that spread under the earth's surface and grow outward horizontally. This metaphor is modified by Glissant to allow for the abolition of any roots; creolization is the

process of transmutation, the mixing of people from other places, along with the murder of indigenous people of the Caribbean islands, which serves as a literal instance of this social-philosophical concept.

3 Colette Fellous, *Mohamed Camara: Photographe* (Montreuil: Éditions de l'Œil, 2002).

4 Fellous, *Mohamed Camara*.

5 The Jean-Paul Blachère Foundation also supported the publication or the artist, as Blachère is thanked in the book.

6 This public antipathy to photography is not new: Seydou Keïta also mentioned that, when he first began photographing in the 1940s, "to take photos like that in the street caused all sorts of problems." Magnin, *Seydou Keïta*, 9. Other photographers whom we interviewed also alluded to this problem, in particular, Alimata dite Diop Traoré.

7 Betsy Wing, translator's notes, in Glissant, *Poetics of Relation*, 211.

8 She later expanded the series to other cities.

9 Fatoumata Diabaté, "Sutigi—The Night Is Ours," Facebook, accessed July 18, 2018, https://www.facebook.com/africareframed/photos/?tab=album&album_id=502936053159266.

10 See Allison Moore, *Photographing the Social Body: Malian Portraiture from the Studio to the Street* (Northfield, MN: Pearlman Teaching Museum, Carleton College, 2012).

11 Mamadou Konaté, interview by author, Bamako, Mali, November 2011.

12 Emmanuel Daou, interview by author, Bamako, Mali, July 28, 2006.

13 Glissant illustrates *Poetics of Relation* with pictographs.

14 Vickey Hallet, "Ghost Towns, Surreal Ebola Docs, Hip Hats: It's Africa's Big Photo Show," *National Public Radio*, December 5, 2015, https://www.npr.org/sections/goatsandsoda/2015/12/05/457141714/ghost-towns-surreal-ebola-docs-hip-hats-its-africas-big-photo-show.

15 The Francophone writers include Césaire, who developed Négritude with Léon Damas and Léopold Senghor, and fellow Martinican Frantz Fanon, a student of Césaire's. Glissant also responds to French philosophers like Sartre (whose connection to the Négritude poets is well known) and the Algerian-born Derrida, philosopher of *différance*, well as the Creolité writers whom Glissant influenced: Jean Bernabé, Patrick Chamoiseau, and Raphaël Confiant.

16 Celia Britton's book focuses on "Glissant's exploration of the role that language plays in resisting colonial domination." Britton, *Édouard Glissant and Postcolonial Theory*, 10.

17 This contains a paradoxical twist in that it is "Malian" to deny a universal "Malian-ness." While it may also be "American" to acknowledge diversity, I assert that citizens of some nations, such as France, Germany, and Japan, *do* expect a specific national similarity.

18 Glissant, *Poetics of Relation*, 75.

19 In contrast to *Bibiana*, see Pieter Hugo, *Albino Project* (2002–2003); Alain Turpault, *Children of the Moon* (2007); Gustavo Lacerda, *Albinos* (2009–2012). See Moore, "A Lightness of Vision."

20 Erin Haney, *Photography and Africa* (London: Reaktion, 2010).
21 I also noticed this photograph framed on the wall of the office of Centre Soleil.
22 David Prochaska, "Fantasia of the Photothéque: French Postcard Views of Colonial Senegal," *African Arts* 24, no. 4 (October 1991).
23 Pinney, "Notes from the Surface."
24 See Christopher B. Steiner, "Authenticity, Repetition, and the Aesthetics of Seriality: The Work of Tourist Art in the Age of Mechanical Reproduction," in Phillips and Steiner, *Unpacking Culture*, 87–103.
25 Glissant, *Poetics of Relation*, 171.
26 Glissant, *Poetics of Relation*, 172.
27 Barthes, *Camera Lucida*, 6.
28 Britton, *Édouard Glissant and Postcolonial Theory*, 164.
29 Mette Sandbye, "It Has Not Been—It Is: The Signaletic Transformation of Photography," *Journal of Aesthetics and Culture* 4, no. 1 (2012).
30 Britton, *Édouard Glissant and Postcolonial Theory*, 164.
31 Britton, *Édouard Glissant and Postcolonial Theory*, 164.
32 Britton, *Édouard Glissant and Postcolonial Theory*, 183.
33 Glissant, *Poetics of Relation*, 140.
34 The recognition of the other is "an aesthetic constituent, the first edict of a real poetics of Relation." Glissant, *Poetics of Relation*, 29–30.

Conclusion

1 Sandbye, "It Has Not Been—It Is."
2 "Mesure qu'il faudra de renversements dans les sensibilités . . . non par leçon de morale, mais par changer nos poétiques." Glissant, *Poetics of Relation*, 134; translated by Michael Wiedorn in "Go Slow Now: Saying the Unsayable in Édouard Glissant's Reading of Faulkner," p. 193, in *American Creoles: The Francophone Caribbean and the American South*, ed. Martin Munro and Celia Britton, 183–196 (Liverpool: Liverpool University Press, 2012).

Bibliography

Adams, Monni. "Beyond Symmetry in Middle African Design." *African Arts* 23, no. 1 (November 1989): 34–103.

Afrique et Caraïbes en Créations (formerly Afrique en Créations) website. Accessed July 29, 2008. http://www.culturesfrance.com/africa-creating/afrique-en-creations-by-discipline/p016.html.

Alberro, Alexander, and Blake Stimson, eds. *Conceptual Art: A Critical Anthology.* Cambridge, MA: MIT Press, 1999.

Amselle, Jean-Loup. *Mestizo Logics: The Anthropology of Identity in Africa and Elsewhere.* Palo Alto, CA: Stanford University Press, 1998.

Anderson, Benedict. *Imagined Communities: Reflections on the Origin and Spread of Nationalism.* London: Verso, 1983.

Appadurai, Arjun. "The Colonial Backdrop." *Afterimage* 24, no. 5 (March/April 1997): 4–10.

Appiah, Kwame Anthony. "Is the Post- in Postmodernism the Post- in Postcolonial?" *Critical Inquiry* 17, no. 2 (1991): 336–357.

Arnoldi, Mary Jo. "Bamako, Mali: Monuments and Modernity in the Urban Imagination." *Africa Today* 54, no. 2 (Winter 2007): 3–24.

Arnoldi, Mary Jo. "Overcoming a Colonial Legacy: The New National Museum in Mali, 1976 to the Present." *Museum Anthropology* 22, no. 3 (1999): 28–40.

Arnoldi, Mary Jo. *Playing with Time: Art and Performance in Central Mali*. Bloomington: Indiana University Press, 1995.

Arnoldi, Mary Jo. "Symbolically Inscribing the City: Public Monuments in Mali, 1995–2002." *African Arts* 36 (2003): 56–65, 95–96.

Arnoldi, Mary Jo. "Youth Festivals and Museums: The Cultural Politics of Public Memory in Postcolonial Mali." *Africa Today* 52, no. 4 (Summer 2006): 55–75.

Arnoldi, Mary Jo, and Christine Mullen Kreamer. *Crowning Achievements: African Arts of Dressing the Head*. Los Angeles: Fowler Museum of Cultural History, UCLA, 1995.

Association Française d'Action Artistique. *Afrique en créations/The AFAA—A User's Guide*. Paris: AFAA, 2005.

b., agnès. *Collection agnès b*. Text by Édouard Glissant and Felix Hoffmann. Contributions by Hans Ulrich Obrist, André Magnin, Clément Dirié, Kenneth Anger, Futura, Jonone, Harmony Korine, and Jonas Mekas. Zurich: JRP/Ringier, 2016.

Barthes, Roland. *Camera Lucida*. Translated by Richard Howard. New York: Farrar, Straus and Giroux, 1981.

Batchen, Geoffrey. *Burning with Desire: The Conception of Photography*. Cambridge, MA: MIT Press, 1999.

Batchen, Geoffrey. "Does Size Matter?" *Camerawork: Journal of Photographic Arts* 30, no. 2 (Fall/Winter 2003): 6–12.

Batchen, Geoffrey. "Dreams of Ordinary Life: *Cartes-de-visite* and the Bourgeois Imagination." In *Image and Imagination*, edited by Martha Langford, 63–74, 266–268. Montreal: McGill-Queen's University Press and Le Mois de la Photo, 2005.

Batchen, Geoffrey. *Each Wild Idea: Writing, Photography, History*. Cambridge, MA: MIT Press, 2001.

Batchen, Geoffrey. *Forget Me Not: Photography and Remembrance*. New York: Princeton Architectural Press, 2004.

Batchen, Geoffrey. "Latent History." *Art in America* 96, no. 2 (February 2008): 54–57.

Batchen, Geoffrey. "Vernacular Photographies." In *Each Wild Idea: Writing, Photography, History*, 56–80. Cambridge, MA: MIT Press, 2001.

Batchen, Geoffrey. "Vernacular Photographies." *History of Photography* 24, no. 3 (2000): 262–271.

Beckley, Bill, ed. *Uncontrollable Beauty: Toward a New Aesthetics*. New York: Allworth, 1998.

Behrend, Heike. "'Feeling Global': The Likoni Ferry Photographers of Mombasa, Kenya." *African Arts* 33, no. 3 (Autumn 2001): 70–77, 96.

Behrend, Heike. "Photo Magic: Photographs in Practices of Healing and Harming in East Africa." *Journal of Religion in Africa* 33, no. 2 (2003): 129–145.

Behrend, Heike, and Tobias Wendl. *Snap Me One! Studiofotografen in Afrika*. Munich: Münchner Stadtmuseum and Prestel, 1998.

Bell, Clare. "Introduction." In *In/Sight: African Photographers, 1940 to the Present*,

edited by Clare Bell, Okwui Enwezor, Danielle Tilkin, Octavio Zaya, and Olu Oguibe, 9–14. New York: Guggenheim Museum, 1996.
Bell, Clare, Okwui Enwezor, Danielle Tilkin, Octavio Zaya, and Olu Oguibe, eds. *In/Sight: African Photographers, 1940 to the Present.* New York: Guggenheim Museum, 1996.
Bernabé, Jean, Patrick Chamoiseau, and Raphaël Confiant. *Éloge de la créolité: In Praise of Creoleness.* Paris: Gallimard, 1993.
Berretrot, Françoise, ed. *Mali au féminin.* Montreuil: Éditions de l'Œil/Édition Musée de Bretagne, 2010.
Bhabha, Homi. *The Location of Culture.* London: Routledge, 1994.
Bhabha, Homi. "Of Mimicry and Man: The Ambivalence of Colonial Discourse." *October* 28 (Spring 1984): 125–133.
Bigham, Elizabeth. "Issues of Authorship in the Portrait Photographs of Seydou Keïta." *African Arts* 32, no. 1 (Spring 1999): 56–67, 94.
Bird, Charles S., and Martha B. Kendall. "The Mande Hero: Text and Context." In *Explorations in African Systems of Thought,* edited by Ivan Karp and Charles S. Bird, 13–26. Bloomington: Indiana University Press, 1980.
Blier, Suzanne. "Enduring Myths of African Art." In *Africa: The Art of a Continent: 100 Works of Power and Beauty,* edited by Tom Phillips, 26–32. New York: Solomon R. Guggenheim Museum, 1996.
Bourdieu, Pierre. *The Field of Cultural Production: Essays on Art and Literature.* Edited by Randal Johnson. New York: Columbia University Press, 1993.
Bourdieu, Pierre. *Photography: A Middle-Brow Art.* Translated by Shaun Whiteside. Stanford, CA: Stanford University Press, 1996.
Bourdieu, Pierre. *The Social Structures of the Economy.* Translated by Chris Turner. Cambridge, UK: Polity, 2005.
Brett-Smith, Sarah C. "The Knowledge of Women." In *Anthropologies of Art,* edited by Mariet Westermann, 143–163. Williamstown, MA: Sterling and Francine Clark Art Institute, 2005.
Brett-Smith, Sarah C. *The Making of Bamana Sculpture: Creativity and Gender.* Cambridge: Cambridge University Press, 1994.
Brett-Smith, Sarah C. *The Silence of the Women: Bamana Mud Cloths.* Milan: 5 Continents Editions, 2014.
Brielmaier, Isolde. "Mombasa on Display: Photography and the Formation of an Urban Public, from the 1940s Onward." In *Portraiture and Photography in Africa,* edited by John M. Peffer and Elisabeth Lynn Cameron, 253–286. Bloomington: Indiana University Press, 2013.
Brink, James S. "Dialectics of Aesthetic Form in Bamana Art." In *Bamana: The Art of Existence,* edited by Jean-Paul Colleyn, 237–242. New York: Museum for African Art; Zurich: Museum Rietberg/Snoeck-Ducaju & Zoon, 2001.
Britton, Celia M. *Édouard Glissant and Postcolonial Theory: Strategies of Language and Resistance.* Charlottesville: University of Virginia Press, 1999.
Britton, Celia M. "Globalization and Political Action in the Work of Édouard Glissant." *Small Axe,* no. 30 (vol. 13, no. 3) (2009): 1–11.

Buchloh, Benjamin. "Gerhard Richter's Atlas: The Anomic Archive." In *The Archive: Documents of Contemporary Art*, edited by Charles Merewether, 85–102. London: Whitechapel, 2006.
Buckley, Liam. "Portrait Photography in a Postcolonial Age: How Beauty Tells the Truth." Paper presented at the conference Portrait Photography in African Worlds, University of California, Santa Cruz, February 3–4, 2006.
Buckley, Liam. "Self and Accessory in Gambian Studio Photography." *Visual Anthropology Review* 16, no. 2 (Fall/Winter 2000–2001): 71–91.
Buckley, Liam. "Studio Photography and the Aesthetics of Postcolonialism in the Gambia, West Africa." PhD diss., University of Virgina, 2003.
Burns, Lorna. "Politicising Paradise: Sites of Resistance in Cereus Blooms at Night." *Journal of West Indian Literature* 19, no. 2 (2011): 52–67.
Byrd, Antawan, Yves Chatap, and Bisi Silva, eds. *Telling Time: Rencontres de Bamako Biennale Africaine de la Photographie* (Tenth Biennale). English and French ed. Heidelberg: Kehrer, 2015.
Cans, Charlotte. "Un havre de culture à Bamako." *Jeune Afrique—L'Intelligent*, October 5/11, 2003.
Cape Town Month of Photography Festival, 1999. *100XC: Photography in South Africa.* Cape Town: South African Centre for Photography at University of Cape Town and University of Cape Town Press, 1999.
Césaire, Aimé. *Discourse on Colonialism.* New York: Monthly Review Press, 1972.
Césaire, Aimé. "From *Discourse on Colonialism.*" In *Colonial Discourse and Postcolonial Theory*, edited by Patrick Williams and Laura Chrisman, 172–181. New York: Columbia University Press, 1994.
Chabal, Patrick, and Jean-Pascal Daloz. *Africa Works: Disorder as Political Instrument.* Bloomington, IN: International African Institute, 1999.
Chapuis, Frédérique. "The Pioneers of St. Louis." In *Anthology of African and Indian Ocean Photography*, edited by Ngoné Fall and Pascal Martin Saint Léon, 48–67. Paris: Éditions Revue Noire, 1998.
Chatap, Yves. "Moussa Kalapo *La métaphore du temps* (2015)." In *Telling Time: Rencontres de Bamako Biennale Africaine de la Photographie (Tenth Biennale)*, English and French ed., edited by Antawan Byrd, Yves Chatap, and Bisi Silva, 92. Heidelberg: Kehrer, 2015.
Childs, Peter, and R. J. Patrick Williams. *An Introduction to Postcolonial Theory.* London: Prentice Hall, 1997.
Clifford, James. *The Predicament of Culture: Twentieth-Century Ethnography, Literature, and Art.* Cambridge, MA: Harvard University Press, 1988.
Clifford, James. *Trade Routes: Travel and Translation in the Late Twentieth Century.* Cambridge, MA: Harvard University Press, 1997.
Collectif. *Magiciens de la Terre.* Paris: Centre Georges Pompidou, 1992.
Condé, Maryse. "Order, Disorder, Freedom, and the West Indian Writer." In "Post/Colonial Conditions: Exiles, Migrations, and Nomadisms," special issue, *Yale French Studies* 83, no. 2 (1993): 121–135.
Coombes, Annie E. *Reinventing Africa: Museums, Material Culture and Popular Imagi-*

nation in Late Victorian and Edwardian England. New Haven, CT: Yale University Press, 1994.
Coombes, Sam. *Édouard Glissant: A Poetics of Resistance.* London: Bloomsbury, 2018.
Cooper, Frederick. *Africa since 1940: The Past of the Present.* Cambridge: Cambridge University Press, 2002.
Corn, Wanda M. *The Great American Thing: Modern Art and National Identity, 1915–1935.* Berkeley: University of California Press, 1999.
Crimp, Douglas. "The Photographic Activity of Postmodernism." *October* 15 (Winter 1980): 91–101.
CulturesFrance (formerly Association Française d'Action Artistique, or AFAA, now Institut Français) website. Accessed July 29, 2008. http://www.diplomatie.gouv.fr/fr/actions-france_830/action-culturelle_1031/les-instruments_11307/france-culturesfrance_11308/index.html.
Dago, Ananias Léki. "Workshop/Mali Bamako: The Mali Version." In *For a Sustainable World: Rencontres de Bamako African Photography Biennale,* 9th ed., edited by Michket Krifa and Laura Serani, 344. Arles: Actes Sud; Paris: Institut Français, 2011.
Dakin, Dagara (DD). "Aboubacar Traore *Inchallah* (2015)." In *Telling Time: Rencontres de Bamako Biennale Africaine de la Photographie (Tenth Biennale),* English and French ed., edited by Antawan Byrd, Yves Chatap, and Bisi Silva, 226. Heidelberg: Kehrer, 2015.
Dakin, Dagara (DD). "La presse et la photographie (1960–1990)." In *L'Afrique en regards: Une brève histoire de la photographie,* edited by Martin van der Belen, 66–73. Trézélan, France: Filigranes Éditions, 2005.
D'Arvor, Olivier Poivre, Sophie Renaud, and Paul de Sinety. Untitled note. In *Rencontres de Bamako 2009: Biennale Africaine de la Photographie: Frontières,* edited by Michket Krifa and Laura Serani, 8. Nantes: Actes Sud; Paris: CulturesFrance, 2009.
Dash, J. Michael. *Édouard Glissant.* New York: Cambridge University Press, 1995.
Dash, J. Michael. "Writing the Body: Édouard Glissant's Poetics of Remembering." *World Literature Today* 63, no. 4 (Autumn 1989): 609–612.
Davis, Paul Ramey. "A Social History of Painting in Bamako, Mali, 1930s–1980s." PhD diss., Indiana University, 2012.
Davis, Shawn. "Visual Griots of Mali: Empowering Youth through the Art of Photography." *African Arts* 39, no. 1 (March 2006): 70–83.
De Jorio, Rosa. "Narratives of the Nation and Democracy in Mali: A View from Modibo Keita's Memorial." *Cahiers Études Africaines* 172 (2003): 827–855.
De Jorio, Rosa. "Politics of Remembering and Forgetting: The Struggle over Colonial Monuments in Mali." *Africa Today* 52, no. 4 (Summer 2006): 79–106.
Dembélé, Moussa. "French Colonization and Urban Evolution in Djenne and Bamako." In *Globalization and Urbanization in Africa,* edited by Toyin Falola and Steven J. Salm, 217–247. Trenton, NJ: Africa World Press, 2004.

Demos, T. J. "Sammy Baloji and Alice Seeley Harris" (review of show at Autograph ABP/Rivington Place, London). *Artforum* 52, no. 9 (May 2014): 315.

Demos, T. J. "The Tate Effect." In *The Global Art World: Audiences, Markets and Museums*, edited by Hans Belting, Andrea Buddensieg, and Peter Weibel, 78–87. Karlsruhe, Germany: ZKM, Center for Art and Media, 2009.

De Roux, Emmanuel. "Bamako, bric-à-brac." *Libération*, October 27, 2003, 33–34.

De Roux, Emmanuel. "Rites, hommages et découvertes aux Rencontres de Bamako." *Le Monde*, October 31, 2003.

Derrida, Jacques. *Archive Fever: A Freudian Impression*. Translated by Eric Prenowitz. Chicago: University of Chicago Press, 1998.

Derrida, Jacques. *Of Grammatology*. Translated by Gayatri Chakravorty Spivak. Baltimore: Johns Hopkins University Press, 1976.

Diabaté, Fatoumata. *L'homme en animal* (artist note and photo series). In *For a Sustainable World: Rencontres de Bamako African Photography Biennale*, 9th ed., edited by Michket Krifa and Laura Serani, 70–73. Arles: Actes Sud; Paris: Institut Français, 2011.

Diawara, Manthia. "The Competing Sartorial Assertions: Malick Sidibé and James Brown." In *Malick Sidibé—Photographs*, 8–22. Gothenburg, Sweden: Hasselblad Center; Göttingen, Germany: Steidl, 2003.

Diawara, Manthia. "Return Narratives." In *In Search of Africa*, 86–119. Cambridge, MA: Harvard University Press, 2000.

Diawara, Manthia. "Talk of the Town: Seydou Keïta." In *Reading the Contemporary: African Art from Theory to the Marketplace*, edited by Olu Oguibe and Okwui Enwezor, 236–242. Cambridge, MA: MIT Press, 1999.

Diawara, Manthia, dir. *Édouard Glissant: One World in Relation*. Film. K'a Yéléma Productions, 2009.

Drabinski, John, and Marisa Parham, ed. *Theorizing Glissant: Sites and Citations*. London: Rowman and Littlefield International, 2015.

Drisdelle, Rhéal, and Charlie Pye-Smith. *Mali: A Prospect of Peace?* Oxford, UK: Oxfam, 1997.

Edwards, Elizabeth. *Raw Histories: Photographs, Anthropology and Museums*. Oxford, UK: Berg, 2001.

Edwards, Elizabeth, ed. *Anthropology and Photography 1860–1920*. New Haven, CT: Yale University Press, 1992.

Eklund, Douglas. *The Pictures Generation: 1974–1984*. New York: Metropolitan Museum of Art, 2009.

Elder, Tanya. *Capturing Change: The Practice of Malian Photography, 1930s–1990s*. Linköping, Sweden: Linköping University, 1997.

Enwezor, Okwui. *Archive Fever: Uses of the Document in Contemporary Art*. Göttingen, Germany: ICP/Steidl, 2008.

Enwezor, Okwui. "Documentary/Vérité: Bio-Politics, Human Rights and the Figure of 'Truth' in Contemporary Art." *Australian and New Zealand Journal of Art* 5, no. 1 (2004): 11–42.

Enwezor, Okwui, ed. *The Short Century: Independence and Liberation Movements in Africa 1945–1994*. Munich: Prestel, 2001.

Enwezor, Okwui. *Snap Judgments: New Positions in Contemporary African Photography.* Göttingen, Germany: Steidl, 2006.

Enwezor, Okwui, and Chika Okeke-Agulu. *Contemporary African Art since 1980.* Bologna: Damiani, 2009.

Fall, N'goné, and Pascal Martin Saint Léon, eds. *Anthology of African and Indian Ocean Photography.* Paris: Éditions Revue Noire, 1998.

Fall, Youma. "De quelques femmes dans l'histoire de l'art au Sénégal / Of Some Women in the History of Art in Senegal." In *Dak'Art 2006, 7ème biennale de l'art africain contemporain: Afrique Entendus, Sous-entendus et Malentendus / Seventh Biennial of African Contemporary Art: African Agreements, Allusions and Misunderstandings,* edited by Yacouba Konaté, 69–76. Dakar: Secrétariat Général de la Biennale de l'Art africain contemporain de Dakar, 2006.

Fanon, Frantz. *Black Skin, White Masks.* Translated by Charles Lamm Markman. New York: Grove, 1967.

Fanon, Frantz. *Studies in a Dying Colonialism.* Translated by Haakon Chevalier. London: Earthscan, 1959.

Farver, Jane, Luis Camnitzer, Rachel Weiss, and László Beke. *Global Conceptualism: Points of Origin, 1950–1980s.* New York: Queens Museum of Art, 1999.

Fellous, Collette. *Mohamed Camara: Photographe.* Montreuil: Éditions de l'Œil, 2002.

Fillitz, Thomas. "The Biennial of Dakar and South-South Circulations." *Artl@s Bulletin* 5, no. 2 (2016): article 6.

Firstenberg, Lauri. "Postcoloniality, Performance, and Photographic Portraiture." In *The Short Century: Independence and Liberation Movements in Africa 1945–1994,* edited by Okwui Enwezor, 175–179. Munich: Prestel, 2001.

Firstenberg, Lauri, and John Peffer, eds. *Translation/Seduction/Displacement: Postconceptual and Photographic Work by Artists from South Africa.* Portland: Institute of Contemporary Art at Maine College of Art, 2000.

Foltz, William J. *From French West Africa to the Malian Federation.* New Haven, CT: Yale University Press, 1965.

Fondation Arabe pour l'image website. Accessed September 9, 2008. http://www.fai.org.lb/CurrentSite/index.htm.

Foster, Hal. "Archival Impulse." *October,* no. 110 (Fall 2004): 3–22.

Foster, Hal, ed. *The Anti-aesthetic: Essays on Postmodern Culture.* Seattle: Bay Press, 1983.

Foucault, Michel. *Archaeology of Knowledge.* Translated by A. M. Sheridan Smith. New York: Pantheon, 1972.

Foucher, Michel. "Africa and the Play of Borders." In *Rencontres de Bamako 2009: Biennale Africaine de la Photographie: Frontières,* edited by Michket Krifa and Laura Serani, 23. Nantes: Actes Sud; Paris: CulturesFrance, 2009.

Gardinier, David E. "The Impact of French Education on Africa, 1817–1960." *Proceedings of the Meeting of the French Colonial Historical Society* 5 (1980): 70–82.

Gardner, Anthony, and Charles Green. "Biennials of the South on the Edges of the Global." *Third Text* 27, no. 4 (August 2013): 442–455.

Gattegno, Agnès. "Bamako: L'art africain en capitale." *Magazine Air France* 103 (November 2005): 76, 96–114.

Geary, Christraud M. *In and Out of Focus: Images from Central Africa, 1885–1960.* Washington, DC: National Museum of African Art, Smithsonian Institution, and Philip Wilson, 2002.

Gielen, Pascal. "The Biennial: A Post-Institution for Immaterial Labor." In "The Art Biennial as a Global Phenomenon," special issue, *Open* 16 (2009): 8–17.

Glissant, Édouard. *Philosophie de la Relation.* Paris: Éditions Gallimard, 2009.

Glissant, Édouard. *Poetic Intention.* Translated by Nathalie Stephens with Anne Malena. Callicoon, NY: Nightboat, 2010.

Glissant, Édouard. *Poetics of Relation.* Translated by Betsy Wing. Ann Arbor: University of Michigan Press, 1997.

Glissant, Édouard, and Hans Ulrich Obrist. *100 Notes—100 Thoughts / 100 Notizen—100 Gedanken.* dOCUMENTA 13. Ostfildern, Germany: Hatje Canz, 2012.

Goni, Marian Nur. "What Happened during the Addis Foto Fest #2?" *Africultures*, April 9, 2013. http://africultures.com/what-happened-during-the-addis-foto-fest-2-11453/.

Goody, Jack. *The Interface between the Written and the Oral.* Cambridge: Cambridge University Press, 1987.

Gosselin, Claudie. "Campaigning against Excision in Mali: Global and Local Hierarchies, Hegemony and Knowledge." PhD diss., University of Toronto, 2001.

Grabski, Joanna. *Art World City: The Creative Economy of Artists and Urban Life in Dakar.* Bloomington: Indiana University Press, 2017.

Graburn, Nelson. "Epilogue: Ethnic and Tourist Arts Revisited." In *Unpacking Culture: Art and Commodity in Colonial and Postcolonial Worlds*, edited by Ruth B. Phillips and Christopher B. Steiner, 335–354. Berkeley: University of California Press, 1999.

Graburn, Nelson, ed. *Ethnic and Tourist Arts: Cultural Expressions from the Fourth World.* Berkeley: University of California Press, 1976.

Grundlingh, Geoffrey, ed. *Cape Town Month of Photography Festival (2002).* Cape Town: South African Centre for Photography, University of Cape Town, 2002.

Grundlingh, Kathleen, ed. *Lines of Sight: Perspectives on South African Photography.* Cape Town: South African National Gallery, 2001.

Grundlingh, Kathleen, ed. *Photosynthesis: Contemporary South African Photography.* Cape Town: South African National Gallery, 1997.

Hall, Bruce S. "Bellah Histories of Decolonization, Iklan Paths to Freedom: The Meanings of Race and Slavery in the Late-Colonial Niger Bend (Mali), 1944–1960." *International Journal of African Historical Studies* 44, no. 1 (January 2011): 61–87.

Halpern, David. *Social Capital.* Cambridge, UK: Polity, 2005.

Haney, Erin. *Photography and Africa.* London: Reaktion, 2010.

Haney, Erin, and Jennifer Bajorek. "Eye on Bamako: Conversations on the African Photography Biennial." *Theory, Culture and Society* 27, nos. 7–8 (2010): 263–284.

Hantel, Max. "Toward a Sexual Difference Theory of Creolization." In *Theorizing Glissant: Sites and Citations*, edited by John Drabinski and Marisa Parham, 85–102. London: Rowman and Littlefield International, 2015.

Harding, Sandra. "Women as Creators of Knowledge." *New Environments* 32, no. 6 (1989): 700–707.
Harney, Elizabeth. *In Senghor's Shadow: Art, Politics, and the Avant-Garde in Senegal, 1960–1995*. Durham, NC: Duke University Press, 2004.
Hassan, Salah M., and Olu Oguibe. "Authentic/Ex-centric: Conceptualism in Contemporary African Art." In *Authentic/Ex-centric: Conceptualism in Contemporary African Art*, edited by Salah M. Hassan, Olu Oguibe, and Siemon Allen, 10–25. Ithaca, NY: Forum for African Arts/Prince Claus Fund Library, 2001.
Hassan, Salah M., Olu Oguibe, and Siemon Allen, eds. *Authentic/Ex-centric: Conceptualism in Contemporary African Art*. Ithaca, NY: Forum for African Arts/Prince Claus Fund Library, 2001.
Hight, Eleanor M., and Gary D. Sampson. "Introduction: Photography, 'Race,' and Post-colonial Theory." In *Colonialist Photography: Imag(in)ing Race and Place*, edited by Eleanor M. Hight and Gary D. Sampson, 1–19. New York: Routledge, 2002.
Hoffman, Barbara G. "Secrets and Lies: Context, Meaning, and Agency in Mande." *Cahiers d'Études Africaines* 38, no. 149 (1998): 85–102.
Houlberg, Marilyn Hammersley. "Feed Your Eyes: Nigerian and Haitian Studio Photography." *Photographic Insight*, no. 1 (Winter–Spring 1988): 3–8.
Houlberg, Marilyn Hammersley. "Haitian Studio Photography: A Hidden World of Images." *Aperture* 126 (1992): 58–65.
Huguier, Françoise. Interview by Balkissa Maïga [Rencontre avec Françoise Huguier]. *BKO Photo*, no. 6, November 16, 2005, 8.
Huguier, Françoise. *Sur les traces de l'Afrique Fantôme*. Paris: Maeght Éditeur, 1990.
Imperato, Pascal. *Mali: A Search for Direction*. Boulder, CO: Westview, 1989.
Jameson, Fredric. *Postmodernism, or, The Cultural Logic of Late Capitalism*. Durham, NC: Duke University Press, 1991.
Jay, Martin. *Downcast Eyes: The Denigration of Vision in Twentieth-Century French Thought*. Berkeley: University of California Press, 1993.
Johnson, Anna. "Art Interview: Coco Fusco and Guillermo Gómez-Peña." *Bomb* 42 (Winter 1993). https://bombmagazine.org/articles/coco-fusco-and-guillermo-g%C3%B3mez-pe%C3%B1a/.
Jones, Caroline A. "Biennial Culture: A Longer History." In *The Biennial Reader: An Anthology on Large-Scale Perennial Exhibitions of Contemporary Art*, edited by Elena Filipovic, Marieke Van Hal, and Solveig Øvstebø, 66–87. Bergen: Bergen Kunsthall, 2010.
Jones, Jonathan. "Boy Done Good." *Guardian*, October 6, 2004. http://www.guardian.co.uk/culture/2004/oct/06/1.
Jones, Kellie. *Eyeminded: Living and Writing Contemporary Art*. Durham, NC: Duke University Press, 2011.
Jones, Rachel A. "'You Eat Beans': Kin-Based Joking Relationships, Obligations, and Identity in Urban Mali." Honors thesis in Anthropology, Macalester College, 2007.
Jules-Rosette, Bennetta. "Airport Art." In *An Anthology of African Art: The Twentieth Century*, edited by N'Goné Fall and Jean Loup Pivin, 118–119. New York: Distributed Art Publishers, 2002.

Jules-Rosette, Bennetta. *The Messages of Tourist Art: An African Semiotic System in Comparative Perspective.* New York: Plenum, 1984.

Jules-Rosette, Bennetta. "Simulations of Postmodernity: Images of Technology in African Tourist and Popular Art." In *Visualizing Theory: Selected Essays from V.A.R. 1990–1994*, edited by Lucien Taylor, 345–362. New York: Routledge, 1994.

Kasfir, Sidney Littlefield. "African Art and Authenticity: A Text with a Shadow." *African Arts* 25, no. 2 (April 1992): 41–97.

Kasfir, Sidney Littlefield. *Contemporary African Art.* New York: Thames & Hudson, 1999.

Keita, Cheikh M. Cheríf. *Outcast to Ambassador: The Musical Odyssey of Salif Keïta.* N.p.: CreateSpace, 2011.

Keita, Kalifa. "Conflict and Conflict Resolution in the Sahel: The Tuareg Insurgency in Mali." Report for Strategic Studies Institute, US Army War College, 1998.

Keller, Candace. "Framed and Hidden Histories: West African Photography from Local to Global Contexts." *African Arts* 47, no. 4 (Winter 2014): 36–47.

Keller, Candace. "Visual Griots: Identity, Aesthetics, and the Social Roles of Portrait Photographers in Mali." In *Portraiture and Photography in Africa*, edited by John M. Peffer and Elisabeth Lynn Cameron, 363–406. Bloomington: Indiana University Press, 2013.

Keller, Candace. "'Visual Griots': Identity, Invention and Style, One Aspect of the Social Role of Portrait Photographers in Mali." Paper presented at University of California, Santa Cruz, February 3–4, 2006.

Keller, Candace. "Visual Griots: Social, Political, and Cultural Histories in Mali through the Photographer's Lens." PhD diss., Indiana University, 2008.

Klein, Martin A. *Slavery and Colonial Rule in French West Africa.* Cambridge: Cambridge University Press, 1998.

Konaté, Yacouba, ed. *Dak'Art 2006, 7ème biennale de l'art africain contemporain: Afrique Entendus, Sous-entendus et Malentendus / Seventh Biennial of African Contemporary Art: African Agreements, Allusions and Misunderstandings.* Dakar: Secrétariat Général de la Biennale de l'Art africain contemporain de Dakar, 2006.

Koné, Awa. "La photographie en tant que moyen de lutte contre le chômage." Rapport de Fin des Cycles, Institut National des Arts, Mali, 2006.

Koné, Barthélémy, and Mamadou Koné. *Coiffures traditionnelles et modernes au Mali/ Traditional and Modern Hairstyles of Mali.* Bamako: Éditions Populaires du Mali, n.d.

Kouroupas, Maria Papageorge. "U.S. Efforts to Protect Cultural Property: Implementation of the 1970 UNESCO Convention." *African Arts* 28, no. 4 (Autumn 1995): 32–37.

Krauss, Rosalind. "Photography's Discursive Spaces: Landscape/View." *Art Journal* 42, no. 4 (Winter 1982): 311–319.

Krifa, Michket, and Laura Serani, eds. *For a Sustainable World: Rencontres de Bamako African Photography Biennale.* 9th ed. Arles: Actes Sud; Paris: Institut Français, 2011.

Krifa, Michket, and Laura Serani, eds. *Rencontres de Bamako 2009: Biennale Africaine de la Photographie: Frontières*. Nantes: Actes Sud; Paris: CulturesFrance, 2009.

Laclau, Ernesto, and Chantal Mouffe. *Hegemony and Socialist Strategy: Towards a Radical Democratic Politics*. London: Verso, 2001.

La Meslée, Valérie Marin, and Christine Fleurent. *Novembre à Bamako*. Marseille: Le Bec en l'Air Éditions, 2010.

Lamunière, Michelle. *You Look Beautiful Like That: The Portrait Photographs of Seydou Keïta and Malick Sidibé*. Cambridge, MA: Harvard University Art Museums; New Haven, CT: Yale University Press, 2001.

Landau, Paul S., and Deborah D. Kaspin, eds. *Images and Empires: Visuality in Colonial and Postcolonial Africa*. Berkeley: University of California Press, 2002.

Larson, Ruth. "Ethnography, Thievery, and Cultural Identity: A Rereading of Michel Leiris's *L'Afrique fantôme*." PMLA 112, no. 2 (1997): 229–242.

Leiris, Michel. *L'Afrique fantôme: De Dakar à Djibouti (1931–1933)*. Paris: Gallimard, 1988.

"L'hôpital Sominé Dolo de Mopti / The Sominé Dolo Hospital of Mopti." In *Bamako 2007 VIIIes Rencontres Africaines de la Photographie: Dans la ville et au-dela*, edited by Simon Njami, 188–189. Paris: Marval, 2007.

Llobera, J. R. "The Role of Historical Memory in Catalan National Identity." *Social Anthropology* 6, no. 3 (1998): 331–342.

Loichot, Valérie. "Le tout-art d'Édouard Glissant." *Contemporary French and Francophone Studies* 20, nos. 4–5 (2016): 558–568.

Loock, Ulrich. "Opacity." *Frieze*, November 7, 2012. https://frieze.com/article/opacity.

Lortie, Marie. "Colonial History, Curatorial Practice and Cross-cultural Conflict at the Bamako Biennial of African Photography (1994–2007)." MA thesis, Carleton University, Ottowa, Canada, 2008.

MacSweeney, Eve. "Sunday Best." *Harper's Bazaar*, May 1998, 172–179.

Magnani, Gregorio. "Ordering Procedures: Photography in Recent German Art." *Arts Magazine* 64 (March 1990): 81–82.

Magnin, André, ed. *J. D. 'Okhai Ojeikere*. Arles, France: Actes Sud, 2000.

Magnin, André, ed. *Malick Sidibé*. Translated by Simon Pleasance and Fronza Woods. Zurich: Scalo, 1998.

Magnin, André, ed. *Seydou Keïta*. Zurich: Scalo, 1997.

Maison Africaine de la Photographie (African House of Photography) website. Accessed July 29, 2008. http://www.pro2m.net/fotoafrica/index.php3. https://www.facebook.com/maisonafricainedelaphotographie/.

Malick Sidibé—Photographs. Gothenburg, Sweden: Hasselblad; Göttingen, Germany: Steidl, 2003.

Mamdani, Mahmood. *Citizen and Subject: Contemporary Africa and the Legacy of Late Colonialism*. Princeton, NJ: Princeton University Press, 1996.

Marion, Sara L. "Syncretic Topographies: The Portraits of Seydou Keïta." MA thesis, University of New Mexico, 2002.

Matt, Gerald, and Thomas Mießgang, eds. *¡Flash Afrique! Photography from West Africa*. Vienna: Kunsthalle Wien, 2001.

Mbembe, Achille. *On the Postcolony*. Translated by A. M. Berrett, Janet Roitman,

Murray Last, and Steven Rendall. Berkeley: University of California Press, 2001.

Mbembe, Achille. "The Seed and the Silt." In *For a Sustainable World: Rencontres de Bamako African Photography Biennale*, 9th ed., edited by Michket Krifa and Laura Serani, 27–29. Arles: Actes Sud; Paris: Institut Français, 2011.

McNaughton, Patrick R. *A Bird Dance near Saturday City: Sidi Ballo and the Art of West African Masquerade*. Bloomington: Indiana University Press, 2008.

McNaughton, Patrick R. *The Mande Blacksmiths: Knowledge, Power, and Art in West Africa*. Bloomington: Indiana University Press, 1988.

Melis, Wim. *Africa Inside: Noorderlicht Photo Festival*. Groningen, the Netherlands: Aurora Borealis, 2000.

Mercier, Jeanne. "Les Rencontres Africaines de la Photographie, Bamako 2005." MA thesis, École des Hautes Études en Sciences Sociales, 2006.

Merewether, Charles, ed. *The Archive: Documents of Contemporary Art*. Cambridge, MA: MIT Press, 2006.

Mesplé, Louis. "Bamako, the Capital of African Photography." *Cimaise* 42, no. 244 (November–December 1996): 5–28.

Mesplé, Louis, ed. *2èmes Rencontres de la Photographie Africaine*. Translated by Jed English. Paris: Extrait de Cimaise no. 244, 1996.

Mesplé, Louis, ed. *Ja Taa: Prendre l'Image: 3e Rencontres de la Photographie Africaine, Bamako, 1998*. Nantes: Actes Sud, 1998.

Michel, Nicolas. "Honneur aux artists de l'image." *Jeune Afrique—L'Intelligent*, October 12/18, 2003.

Mikell, Gwendolyn. "African Feminism: Toward a New Politics of Representation." *Feminist Studies* 21, no. 2 (Summer 1995): 405–424.

Mills, Charles. *Blackness Visible: Essays on Philosophy and Race*. Ithaca, NY: Cornell University Press, 1998.

Momodu-Gordon, Hansi, and Guilhem Monceaux. "Les Rencontres de Bamako, 1994–2015." In *Telling Time: Rencontres de Bamako Biennale Africaine de la Photographie (Tenth Biennale)*, English and French ed., edited by Antawan Byrd, Yves Chatap, and Bisi Silva, 410–424. Heidelberg: Kehrer, 2015.

Monti, Nicolas. *Africa Then: Photographs 1840–1918*. New York: Alfred A. Knopf, 1987.

Moore, Allison. "A Lightness of Vision: The Poetics of *Relation* in Malian Art Photography." *Social Dynamics* 40, no. 3 (2014): 538–555. https://doi.org/10.1080/02533952.2014.991181.

Moore, Allison. *Photographing the Social Body: Malian Portraiture from the Studio to the Street*. Northfield, MN: Pearlman Teaching Museum, Carleton College, 2012.

Moore, Allison. "Promo-femme: Promoting Women Photographers in Bamako, Mali." *History of Photography* 34, no. 2 (2010): 170–180. https://doi.org/10.1080/03087290903361530.

Moore, David Chioni. "Is the Post- in Postcolonial the Post- in Post-Soviet? Toward a Global Postcolonial Technique." *PMLA* 116, no. 1 (January 2001): 111–128.

Morrison, Donald, and Antoine Compagnon. *The Death of French Culture*. Cambridge, UK: Polity, 2010.

Mouffe, Chantal. "Democratic Politics in the Age of Post-Fordism." In "The Art

Biennial as a Global Phenomenon: Strategies in Neo-political Times," special issue, *Open* 16 (2009): 32–40.
Mudimbe, V. Y. "African Art as a Question Mark." *African Studies Review* 29, no. 1 (1986): 3–4.
Mudimbe, V. Y. "*Reprendre*: Enunciations and Strategies in Contemporary African Arts." In *Africa Explores: 20th Century African Art*, edited by Susan Vogel, 276–287. New York: Center for African Art, 1991.
Mulhearn, Kevin. "Photography in Africa: Central and West." In *Encyclopedia of Twentieth-Century Photography*, vol. 1, edited by Lynne Warren, 27–30. New York: Routledge, 2006.
Mulhearn, Kevin. "Photography in Africa: East and Indian Ocean Islands." In *Encyclopedia of Twentieth-Century Photography*, vol. 1, edited by Lynne Warren, 30–32. New York: Routledge, 2006.
Mulhearn, Kevin. "Photography in Africa: North." In *Encyclopedia of Twentieth-Century Photography*, vol. 1, edited by Lynne Warren, 32–34. New York: Routledge, 2006.
Murdoch, H. Adlai. "Édouard Glissant's Creolized World Vision: From Resistance and *Relation* to *Opacité*." *Callaloo* 36, no. 4 (Fall 2013): 875–889.
Murdoch, H. Adlai. "Glissant's *Opacité* and the Re-conceptualization of Identity." In *Theorizing Glissant: Sites and Citations*, edited by John Drabinski and Marisa Parham, 7–27. New York: Rowman and Littlefield International, 2015.
Musée National du Mali (National Museum of Mali) website. Accessed July 29, 2008. http://www.museenationaldumali.org.ml/historique.html.
Mustafa, Hudita Nura. "Portraits of Modernity: Fashioning Selves in Dakarois Popular Photography." In *Images and Empires: Visuality in Colonial and Postcolonial Africa*, edited by Paul Landau and Deborah Kaspin, 172–192. Berkeley: University of California Press, 2002.
Nimis, Érika. "The Golden Age of Black-and-White in Mali." In *Anthology of African and Indian Ocean Photography*, edited by Ngoné Fall and Pascal Martin Saint Léon, 104–117. Paris: Éditions Revue Noire, 1998.
Nimis, Érika. "Mali's Photographic Memory: From Outsider Readings to National Reclaiming." *Visual Anthropology* 27 (2014): 394–409.
Nimis, Érika. "Nigeria: The Photographic Giant." *Africultures*, May 31, 2001. http://africultures.com/nigeria-the-photographic-giant-5534/.
Nimis, Érika. *Photographes de Bamako de 1935 à nos jours / Photographers in Bamako from 1935 to the Present*. Paris: Éditions Revue Noire, 1998.
Nimis, Érika. "Yoruba Studio Photographers in Francophone West Africa." In *Portraiture and Photography in Africa*, edited by John Peffer and Elisabeth L. Cameron, 102–140. Bloomington: Indiana University Press, 2013.
Njami, Simon, ed. *Africa Remix: L'art contemporain d'un continent*. Paris: Centre Georges Pompidou, 2005.
Njami, Simon, ed. *Bamako 2007 VIIIes Rencontres Africaines de la Photographie: Dans la ville et au-dela*. Paris: Marval, 2007.
Njami, Simon, ed. *Mémoires intimes d'un nouveau millénaire: IVes Rencontres de la Photographie Africaine, Bamako, 2001*. Paris: Éditions Eric Koehler, 2001.

Njami, Simon, ed. *Ves Rencontres de la Photographie Africaine, Bamako 2003: Rites sacrés / Rites profanes*. Paris: Éditions Eric Koehler, 2003.
Njami, Simon, ed. *VIes Rencontres Africaines de la Photographie, Bamako 2005: Un autre monde / Another World*. Paris: Éditions Eric Koehler, 2005.
El Nour website. Accessed July 29, 2008. http://www.elnour.org/images/photographes/index_photogra.htm.
Nzegwu, Nkiru. *Family Matters: Feminist Concepts in African Philosophy of Culture*. Albany: SUNY Press, 2006.
Obrist, Hans Ulrich, and Asad Raza, eds. *Mondialité: The Archipelagos of Édouard Glissant*. Paris: Éditions Skira, 2017.
O'Connor, Anthony. *The African City*. New York: Africana, 1983.
Oguibe, Olu. Interview by Saul Ostrow. *Bomb* 87 (Spring 2004): 30–37.
Oguibe, Olu. "Photography and the Substance of the Image." In *In/Sight: African Photographers, 1940 to the Present*, edited by Clare Bell, Okwui Enwezor, Danielle Tilkin, Octavio Zaya, and Olu Oguibe, 231–249. New York: Guggenheim Museum, 1996.
Oguibe, Olu, and Okwui Enwezor, eds. *Reading the Contemporary: African Art from Theory to the Marketplace*. Cambridge, MA: MIT Press, 1999.
Okeke-Agulu, Chika. *Postcolonial Modernism: Art and Decolonization in Twentieth-Century Nigeria*. Durham, NC: Duke University Press, 2015.
O'Neill, Paul. *The Culture of Curating and the Curating of Culture(s)*. Cambridge, MA: MIT Press, 2012.
Ong, Walter J. *Orality and Literacy: The Technologizing of the Word*. London: Methuen, 1982.
Owens, Craig. "The Discourse of Others: Feminists and Postmodernism." In *The Anti-aesthetic: Essays on Postmodern Culture*, edited by Hal Foster, 57–82. Seattle: Bay Press, 1983.
Panzieri, Cecile. "Contested Images." *Artforum* 44, no. 10 (Summer 2006): 24.
Papastergiadis, Nikos, and Meredith Martin. "Art Biennales and Cities as Platforms for a Global Dialogue." In *Festivals and the Cultural Public Sphere*, edited by Liana Giorgi, Monica Sassatelli, and Gerard Delanty, 45–62. New York: Routledge, 2011.
Parry, Benita. *Postcolonial Studies: A Materialist Critique*. London: Routledge, 2004.
Peffer, John. "Photography in Africa: South and Southern." In *Encyclopedia of Twentieth-Century Photography*, vol. 1, edited by Lynne Warren, 35–37. New York: Routledge, 2006.
Peffer, John, and Elisabeth L. Cameron, eds. *Portraiture and Photography in Africa*. Bloomington: Indiana University Press, 2013.
Phillips, Ruth B. "Why Not Tourist Art? Significant Silences in Native American Museum Representations." In *After Colonialism: Imperial Histories and Postcolonial Displacements*, edited by Gyan Prakash, 98–125. Princeton, NJ: Princeton University Press, 1995.
Phillips, Ruth B., and Christopher B. Steiner, eds. *Unpacking Culture: Art and Commodity in Colonial and Postcolonial Worlds*. Berkeley: University of California Press, 1999.

Picton, John. "Colonial Pretense and African Resistance: Commemorative Textiles in Sub-Saharan Africa." In *The Short Century: Independence and Liberation Movements in Africa 1945–1994*, edited by Okwui Enwezor, 159–162. Munich: Prestel, 2001.

Picton, John. "Desperately Seeking Africa." Review of *Africa Explores*, New York, 1991. *Oxford Art Journal* 15, no. 2 (1992): 104–112.

Picton, John. "In Vogue, or, The Flavour of the Month: The New Way to Wear Black." In *Reading the Contemporary: African Art from Theory to the Marketplace*, edited by Okwui Enwezor and Olu Oguibe, 114–126. Cambridge, MA: MIT Press, 1999.

Pinder, Kymberly N., ed. *Race-ing Art History: Critical Readings in Race and Art History.* New York: Routledge, 2002.

Pinney, Christopher. "Introduction: 'How the Other Half . . .'" In *Photography's Other Histories*, edited by Christopher Pinney and Nicolas Peterson, 1–14. Durham, NC: Duke University Press, 2003.

Pinney, Christopher. "Notes from the Surface of the Image: Photography, Postcolonialism, and Vernacular Modernism." In *Photography's Other Histories*, edited by Christopher Pinney and Nicolas Peterson, 202–220 (Durham, NC: Duke University Press, 2003).

Pinther, Kerstin, and Julia Ng. "Textiles and Photography in West Africa." *Critical Interventions* 1, no. 1 (2007): 113–123.

Pluhacek, Stephen, and Heidi Bostic. "Thinking Life as Relation: An Interview with Luce Irigaray." *Man and World* 29, no. 4 (October 1996): 343–360.

Poe, Danielle. "Can Luce Irigaray's Notion of Sexual Difference Be Applied to Transsexual and Transgender Narratives?" In *Thinking with Irigaray*, edited by Mary C. Rawlinson, Sabrina L. Hom, and Serene J. Khader, 111–128. Albany: SUNY Press, 2011.

Poole, Deborah. *Vision, Race, and Modernity: A Visual Economy of the Andean Image World.* Princeton, NJ: Princeton University Press, 1997.

Potoski, Antonin. *Les Dogons par les Dogons*. Montreuil: Éditions de l'Œil, 2001.

Potoski, Antonin, ed. *BKO-RAK: Photographes de Bamako et de Marrakech*. Paris: Éditions Revue Noire, 1998.

Potoski, Antonin, ed. *Youssouf Sogodogo: Photographies*. Montreuil: Éditions de l'Œil, 2000.

Prakash, Gyan. *After Colonialism: Imperial Histories and Postcolonial Displacements.* Princeton, NJ: Princeton University Press, 1995.

Prakash, Gyan. "Postcolonial Criticism and Indian Historiography." *Social Text*, nos. 31/32 (1992): 8–19.

Pringle, Robert Maxwell. *Democratization in Mali: Putting History to Work.* Peaceworks, no. 58. Washington, DC: United States Institute of Peace, 2006.

Prochaska, David. "Fantasia of the *Photothèque*: French Postcard Views of Senegal." *African Arts* 24, no. 4 (October 1991): 40–47, 98.

Programme d'appui et de valorisation des initiatives artistiques et culturelles (PSIC) website. Accessed July 29, 2008. http://www.psic-mali.org/.

Promo-femme: Centre de Formation en Audiovisuel pour Jeunes Filles (Promo-

femme: Center of Audiovisual Education for Young Women) website. Accessed September 8, 2008. http://promofemme.courantsdefemmes.org/index.html.
Rasmussen, Susan J. "Urban and Rural Performances of Tuareg Smith Women." *Journal of Anthropological Research* 59, no. 4 (Winter 2003): 487–509.
Ravenhill, Philip L. *Dreams and Reverie: Images of Otherworld Mates among the Baule, West Africa.* Washington DC: Smithsonian Institution Press, 1996.
Relyea, Lane. *Your Everyday Art World.* Cambridge, MA: MIT Press, 2013.
Reuters. "Mali's Tuareg Rebels Agree Timetable to Disarm." February 20, 2007. http://www.alertnet.org/thenews/newsdesk/L20638876.htm.
Richard, Frances. "Seydou Keïta, Sean Kelly Gallery" (review). *Artforum* 44, no. 8 (April 2006): 242–243.
Richards, Thomas. *The Imperial Archive: Knowledge and the Fantasy of Empire.* London: Verso, 1993.
Rovine, Victoria. *Bogolan: Shaping Culture through Cloth in Contemporary Mali.* Washington, DC: Smithsonian Institution Press, 2001.
Sagay, Esi. *African Hairstyles: Styles of Yesterday and Today.* London: Heinemann, 1983.
Said, Edward W. *Orientalism.* New York: Vintage Books, 1979.
Saint-Cyr, Agnès de Gouvion. "Antoine Freitas." In *Anthology of African and Indian Ocean Photography,* edited by N'goné Fall and Pascal Martin Saint Léon, 18–19. Paris: Éditions Revue Noire, 1998.
Saint Léon, Pascal Martin, and Jean-Loup Pivin. "The Official Agencies." In *Anthology of African and Indian Ocean Photography,* edited by Ngoné Fall and Pascal Martin Saint Léon, 195–201. Paris: Éditions Revue Noire, 1998.
Saltz, Jerry. "Jerry Saltz on '93 in Art." *New York Magazine,* February 1, 2013. https://nymag.com/arts/art/features/jerry-saltz-1993-art/.
Samake, Nana Flama. "La photographie documentaire en tant que moyen d'identification et de classification des objets au Musée National." Rapport de Fin des Cycles, Institut National des Arts, Mali, 2006.
Sandbye, Mette. "It Has Not Been—It Is: The Signaletic Transformation of Photography." *Journal of Aesthetics and Culture* 4, no. 1 (2012). https://doi.org/10.3402/jac.v4i0.18159.
Sanogo, Siaka. "Rôle de la photographe dans la sauvegarde des masques et statuettes Senoufo au Musée National." Rapport de Fin des Cycles, Institut National des Arts, Mali, 2006.
Schildkrout, Enid. "The Spectacle of Africa through the Lens of Herbert Lang: Belgian Congo Photographs 1909–1915." *African Arts* 24, no. 4 (October 1991): 70–85, 100.
Schildkrout, Enid, and Curtis A. Keim. *The Scramble for Art in Central Africa.* Cambridge: Cambridge University Press, 1998.
Schneider, Jürg. "Portrait Photography: A Visual Currency in the Atlantic Visualscape." In *Portraiture and Photography in Africa,* edited by John M. Peffer and Elisabeth Lynn Cameron, 35–66. Bloomington: Indiana University Press, 2013.
Schulz, Dorothea E. "Competing Sartorial Assertions of Femininity and Muslim Identity in Mali." *Fashion Theory* 11, nos. 2/3 (2007): 253–280.

Schulz, Dorothea E. "Drama, Desire, and Debate: Mass-Mediated Subjectivities in Urban Mali." *Visual Anthropology* 20 (2007): 19–39.

Schulz, Dorothea E. "Music Videos and the Effeminate Vices of Urban Culture in Mali." *Africa* 71, no. 3 (2001): 345–372.

Schulz, Dorothea E. *Perpetuating the Politics of Praise: Jeli Singers, Radios, and Political Mediation in Mali.* Cologne: Ruediger Koeppe, 2001.

Sean Kelly Gallery. *Seydou Keïta: The Image King of Africa.* Exhibition pamphlet, January 8–March 4, 2006.

Sekula, Allan. "The Body and the Archive." *October* 39 (Winter 1986): 3–64.

Senghor, Léopold Sédar. "Negritude." In *Senghor: Prose and Poetry,* edited and translated by John Reed and Clive Wake, 97–105. London: Oxford University Press, 1965.

Sheikh, Simon. "Marks of Distinction, Vectors of Possibility: Questions for the Biennial." In "The Art Biennial as a Global Phenomenon," special issue, *Open* 16 (2009): 68–79.

Shohat, Ella, Anne McClintock, and Aamir Mufti, eds. *Dangerous Liaisons: Gender, Nation, and Postcolonial Perspectives.* Minneapolis: University of Minnesota Press, 1997.

Shryock, Andrew. *Nationalism and the Genealogical Imagination: Oral History and Textual Authority in Tribal Jordan.* Berkeley: University of California Press, 1997.

Shumard, Ann M. *A Durable Memento: Portraits by Augustus Washington, African American Daguerreotypist.* Washington, DC: National Portrait Gallery, 1999.

Sidibé, Malick. "The Movement of Life." Interview with Simon Njami. In *¡Flash Afrique! Photography from West Africa,* edited by Gerald Matt and Thomas Mießgang, 94–96. Vienna: Kunsthalle Wien, 2001.

Sidibé, Malick. "Ready to Wear: A Conversation with Malick Sidibé." Interview by Michelle Lamunière, assisted by Baba Magia and translated by Lia Brozgal. *Transition* 10, no. 4, issue 88 (2001): 132–159.

Sidibé, Samuel. "contours/outlines." In *Bamako 2007 VIIIes Rencontres Africaines de la Photographie: Dans la ville et au-dela,* edited by Simon Njami, 164–165. Paris: Marval, 2007.

Sidibé, Samuel. "For a Sustainable Biennale." In *For a Sustainable World: Rencontres de Bamako African Photography Biennale,* 9th ed., edited by Michket Krifa and Laura Serani, 13–15. Arles: Actes Sud; Paris: Institut Français, 2011.

Sidibé, Samuel. Untitled note. In *Rencontres de Bamako 2009: Biennale Africaine de la Photographie: Frontières,* edited by Michket Krifa and Laura Serani, 9. Nantes: Actes Sud; Paris: CulturesFrance, 2009.

Sidikou, Aïssata G. *Recreating Words, Reshaping Worlds: The Verbal Art of Women from Niger, Mali, and Senegal.* Trenton, NJ, and Asmara, Eritrea: Africa World Press, 2001.

Sieber, Roy, and Frank Herreman, eds. *Hair in African Art and Culture.* New York: Museum for African Art, 2000.

Silla, Eric. *People Are Not the Same: Leprosy and Identity in Twentieth-Century Mali.* Portsmouth, NH: Heinemann, 1998.

Silva, Bisi. "8th Encounters of Bamako, African Photography Biennale." *Artforum* 48, no. 6 (February 2010): 221–222.

Silva, Bisi. "100 Écoles / 10 000 Étudiants." In *Telling Time: Rencontres de Bamako Biennale Africaine de la Photographie (Tenth Biennale)*, English and French ed., edited by Antawan Byrd, Yves Chatap, and Bisi Silva, 328–329. Heidelberg: Kehrer, 2015.

Silva, Bisi, and Yves Chatap. "Mali Jaw." In *Telling Time: Rencontres de Bamako Biennale Africaine de la Photographie (Tenth Biennale)*, English and French ed., edited by Antawan Byrd, Yves Chatap, and Bisi Silva, 320–321. Heidelberg: Kehrer, 2015.

Smith, Terry. "Contemporary Art and Contemporaneity." *Critical Inquiry* 32, no. 4 (Summer 2006): 681–707.

Sokkelund, Svend E., and Tanya Elder. *Hamadou Bocoum*. Copenhagen: Fotografisk Center and Copenhagen Capital of Culture, 1996.

"Sokkelund African Collection" website. Accessed July 29, 2008. http://www.african-collection.dk/english/kontakt.htm.

Solomon-Godeau, Abigail. "Playing in the Fields of the Image." In *Photography at the Dock: Essays on Photographic History, Institutions, and Practices*, 86–102. Minneapolis: University of Minnesota Press, 2003.

Sontag, Susan. *On Photography*. New York: Farrar, Straus and Giroux, 2001.

South African National Gallery. *Through a Lens Darkly: 6 Portfolios of South African Photographers*. Cape Town: South African National Gallery, 1993.

Spiegler, Marc. "Negative Charges." *Art + Auction* (February 2005): 95–101.

Spivak, Gayatri. "Can the Subaltern Speak?" In *Marxism and the Interpretation of Culture*, edited by Cary Nelson and Lawrence Grossberg, 271–313. Chicago: University of Illinois Press, 1988.

Spivak, Gayatri. *A Critique of Postcolonial Reason: Toward a History of the Vanishing Present*. Cambridge, MA: Harvard University Press, 1999.

Sprague, Stephen F. "How I See the Yoruba See Themselves." *Studies in the Anthropology of Visual Communication* 5, no. 1 (1979): 9–28.

Sprague, Stephen F. "Yoruba Photography: How the Yoruba See Themselves." In *Photography's Other Histories*, edited by Christopher Pinney and Nicolas Peterson, 240–260. Durham, NC: Duke University Press, 2003.

Steiner, Christopher. *African Art in Transit*. Cambridge: Cambridge University Press, 1994.

Steiner, Christopher B. "Authenticity, Repetition, and the Aesthetics of Seriality: The Work of Tourist Art in the Age of Mechanical Reproduction." In *Unpacking Culture: Art and Commodity in Colonial and Postcolonial Worlds*, edited by Ruth B. Phillips and Christopher B. Steiner, 87–103. Berkeley: University of California Press, 1999.

Storr, Robert. "Bamako: Full Dress Parade." *Parkett* 49 (1997): 24–34.

Tagg, John. *The Burden of Representation: Essays on Photographies and Histories*. Minneapolis: University of Minnesota Press, 1988.

Tamari, Tal. "The Development of Caste Systems in West Africa." *Journal of African History* 32 (1991): 221–250.

Tamari, Tal. "'Hady': A Traditional Bard's Praise Song for an Urban Teenager." *Research in African Literatures* 38, no. 3 (Fall 2007): 77–111.
Thompson, Robert Farris. "Afro-Modernism." *Artforum* 30 (September 1991): 91–94.
Togola, Téréba. "The Rape of Mali's Only Resource." In *Illicit Antiquities: The Theft of Cultures and the Extinction of Archaeology*, edited by Neil Brodie and Kathryn Walker Tubb, 250–256. London: Routledge, 2002.
Torgovnick, Marianna. *Gone Primitive: Savage Intellects, Modern Lives*. Chicago: University of Chicago Press, 1990.
Touré, Amadou Chab. *Hamidou Maïga, photographie les "Tomboctiens."* Bamako: Galerie Chab, 2000.
Touré, Amadou Chab. *Malick Sidibé: Photographe*. Montreuil: Éditions de l'Œil, 2001.
Touré, Amadou Chab. "Les têtes des femmes tournent." In *Youssouf Sogodogo: Photographies*, edited by Antonin Potoski, n.p. Montreuil: Éditions de l'Œil, 2000.
Traoré, Alimata dite Diop. "Regard de Femmes" (interview). *Afriphoto*, November 23, 2003. http://www.afriphoto.com/index.asp.
Turner, Terence S. "The Social Skin." In *Not Work Alone: A Cross-cultural View of Activities Superfluous to Survival*, edited by Jeremy Cherfas and Roger Lewin, 112–140. London: Temple Smith, 1980.
Turrittin, Jane. "Aoua Kéita and the Nascent Women's Movement in the French Soudan." *African Studies Review* 36, no. 1 (April 1993): 59–89.
University of Cape Town. *Encounters with Photography: Photographing People in Southern Africa, 1860–1999*. Rondebosch, South Africa: University of Cape Town, 2000.
US Department of State. "U.S. Relations With Mali," September 6, 2018. Accessed December 3, 2008. http://www.state.gov/r/pa/ei/bgn/2828.htm.
Van der Belen, Martin, ed. *L'Afrique en regards: Une brève histoire de la photographie*. Trézélan, France: Filigranes Éditions, 2005.
Van Dyke, Kristina. "The Oral-Visual Nexus: Re-thinking Visuality in Mali." PhD diss., Harvard University, 2005.
Vine, Richard. "Report from Mali: The Luminous Continent." *Art in America* 92, no. 9 (October 2004): 68–73.
Vine, Richard. "Seydou Keïta Legacy Disrupted." *Art in America* 91, no. 12 (December 2003): 29–31.
Vogel, Susan. "Art History and Bad Housekeeping." Paper presented at the conference Portrait Photography in African Worlds, University of California, Santa Cruz, February 3–4, 2006.
Vogel, Susan, ed. *Africa Explores: 20th Century African Art*. New York: Center for African Art, 1991.
Waïgalo, Amadou. "15e anniversaire du décès d'Abdoulaye Barry: Les langues nationales pour affermir la decentralization." *Afribone.com*, October 2, 2006. www.afribone.com/article.php3?id_article=4546.
Wall, Jeff. "Marks of Indifference: Aspects of Photography in, or as, Contemporary Art." In *Reconsidering the Object of Art: 1965–1975* (exhibition catalog), edited by

Ann Goldstein and Anne Rorimer, 247–267. Los Angeles: Museum of Contemporary Art, 1995.
Wallerstein, Immanuel. *The Modern World-System, I: Capitalist Agriculture and the Origins of European World-Economy in the Sixteenth Century.* New York: Academic Press, 1974.
Wendl, Tobias. "Entangled Traditions: Photography and the History of Media in Southern Ghana." *RES: Journal of Anthropology and Aesthetics* 39 (Spring 2001): 78–100.
Wendl, Tobias. "Photographic Portraiture in Ghana." Paper presented at the conference Portrait Photography in African Worlds, University of California, Santa Cruz, February 3–4, 2006.
Wendl, Tobias, and Heike Behrend, eds. *Snap Me One! Studiofotografen in Afrika.* Munich: Münchner Stadtmuseum and Prestel, 1998.
Werner, Jean-François. "Les tribulations d'un photographe de rue africain." *Autrepart* 1 (1997): 129–150.
Wesseling, H. L. *Divide and Rule: The Partition of Africa, 1880–1914.* Translated by Arnold J. Pomerans. Westport, CT: Praeger, 1996.
West, Harry G., and Stacy Sharpes. "Dealing with the Devil: Meaning and the Marketplace in Makonde Sculpture." *African Arts* 35, no. 3 (2002): 32–39, 90.
Wiedorn, Michael. "Glissant's *Philosophie de la Relation*: 'I have spoken the chaos of writing in the ardor of the poem.'" *Callaloo* 36, no. 4 (Fall 2013): 902–905.
Wiedorn, Michael. "Go Slow Now: Saying the Unsayable in Édouard Glissant's Reading of Faulkner." In *American Creoles: The Francophone Carribbean and the American South*, edited by Martin Munro and Celia Britton, 183–196. Liverpool: Liverpool University Press, 2012.
Wiedorn, Michael. *Think Like an Archipelago: Paradox in the Work of Édouard Glissant.* Albany: SUNY Press, 2018.
Williams, Patrick, and Laura Chrisman, ed. *Colonial Discourse and Post-colonial Theory: A Reader.* New York: Columbia University Press, 1994.
Wilson, Erika. "Navigating Competing Discourses: Narratives of Womanhood in Bamako." MA thesis, Simon Fraser University, 2000.
Wing, Susanna Denholm. "Constitutional Dialogues: Participation and Citizenship in the Transition towards Democracy in Mali, 1991–1999." PhD diss., University of California Los Angeles, 2000.
Wing, Susanna Denholm. "Women's Rights in West Africa: Legal Pluralism and Constitutional Law." Abstract for paper presented at American Political Science Association Annual Meeting, Boston, MA, 2002.
Wooten, Stephen. *The Art of Livelihood: Creating Expressive Agri-Culture in Mali.* Durham, NC: Carolina Academic Press, 2009.
Xpo September. *Samuel Fosso. Seydou Keïta. Malick Sidibé. Portraits of Pride.* Stockholm Fotofestival and Rencontres de la Photographie Africaine, 2002.
Yarak, Larry W. "Early Photography in Elmina." *Ghana Studies Council Newsletter*, no. 8 (Spring/Summer 1995): 9–11. http://www.ghanastudies.com/gsa/gsc_newsletter_8.pdf.

Index

CPSIA information can be obtained
at www.ICGtesting.com
Printed in the USA
BVHW020753010720
582577BV00010B/217

* 9 7 8 1 4 7 8 0 0 6 6 2 6 *